Sermons On The Gospel Readings

Series II

Cycle A

Charles L. Aaron Jr.
Lee Griess
Mark Ellingsen
Wayne Brouwer
Chris Ewing

CSS Publishing Company, Inc., Lima, Ohio

Most scripture quotations are from the *New Revised Standard Version of the Bible*, copyright 1989 by the Division of Christian Education of the National Council of the Churches of Christ in the USA. Used by permission.

Some scripture quotations are from the Holy Bible, New International Version. Copyright © 1973, 1978, 1984 International Bible Society. Used by permission of Zondervan Bible Publishers. All rights reserved.

Some scripture quotations are from the Holy Bible, New Living Translation, copyright © 1996. Used by permission of Tyndale House Publishers, Inc., Wheaton, Illinois 60189. All rights reserved.

For more information about CSS Publishing Company resources, visit our website at www.csspub.com or email us at custserv@csspub.com or call (800) 241-4056.

Cover design by Barbara Spencer

ISSN: 1937-1330

ISBN-13: 978-0-7880-2453-5
ISBN-10: 0-7880-2453-1

PRINTED IN USA

Table Of Contents

**Sermons For Sundays
In Advent, Christmas, And Epiphany**
Becoming The Salt And The Light
by Charles L. Aaron Jr

Sermons For Sundays
In Lent And Easter
Return To The Lord, Your God
by Lee Griess

**Sermons For Sundays
After Pentecost (First Third)
*Jesus' Vision Of A Fun, Free Life,
Not Driven By Purpose*
by Mark Ellingsen**

Sermons For Sundays
After Pentecost (Middle Third)
Political Religion
by Wayne Brouwer

Sermons On The Gospel Readings

For Sundays In
Advent, Christmas,
And Epiphany

Becoming The Salt
And The Light

Charles L. Aaron Jr.

Ruining The Christmas Spirit

This morning is the first Sunday of Advent, and therefore the first Sunday of the church year. We begin Year A of the cycle, which is Matthew's year. When I read the scripture lesson, you may have noticed a couple of things. You may have noticed that we read a passage from near the end of Matthew. It may seem strange to read from near the end of the book that will guide us during the next year. Shouldn't we start at the beginning? We don't actually read from near the beginning of the book until the fourth Sunday of Advent. The other thing you may have noticed about this passage is that it doesn't sound very much like Christmas. It certainly isn't jolly. Nothing about it helps us enter into the Christmas spirit. Certainly when we preachers use the lectionary, we run into passages of scripture that we might never think to preach from, especially on certain Sundays. None of us might associate this passage with the first Sunday of Advent. Yet, the church encourages us to read this passage for today. Let us follow the church's wisdom, trusting that we will not lose our Christmas spirit, but see it transformed.

Matthew presents us with four vignettes, each told with a minimum of detail. To be honest, each vignette seems intended to get our attention, if not to scare us. The four vignettes teach us something about what verse 36 calls "that day and hour." This imposing phrase alludes back to the events described in verses 30 and 31. Verses 30 and 31 tell us about an event, or a promise, or an assurance that permeates the whole New Testament. The way Matthew depicts this event is to say that "the Son of Man [will come] on the clouds of heaven with power and great glory." By saying it that way, Matthew gives us spectacular imagery of the risen Christ riding a cloud to enter again into our world. The imagery points to the reality that the future is in God's hands. This word picture of Christ riding on the clouds assures us that God will intervene in the creation. Some other biblical writers talk about God's future for the creation in joyous terms. Paul talks about the "glory about to be revealed to us" (Romans 8:18). The author of 1 Peter writes of "an inheritance that is imperishable, undefiled, and unfading, kept in heaven for you" (1 Peter 1:4). These four vignettes remind us that God's decisive action in history will be a time of judgment as well.

These four scenes that Matthew paints for us jump start our imaginations. Because they are concrete scenes with people and action, they draw us in. We need to be careful, however, because these four vignettes intend to make us sweat and squirm in our seats. Getting ready for Christmas can make us feel that way anyhow. Now Matthew makes us feel that way, too!

The first vignette is an allusion to Noah and the flood story in Genesis. We know that story, but we often miss how terrible it really is. God was sorry for making human beings. God decided to drown the whole lot of us. One family would be left. God told Noah to build an ark. You know the rest. Except for those on the ark, all the animals and people on earth drown in the flood. As I said, this is a terrible story. Someone who read this story without considering the whole context of the Bible might think that the image of God here comes disturbingly close to the real life case of Andrea Yates, the Texas woman who drowned her children in the bathtub [eventually found not guilty by reason of insanity]. Matthew has Jesus say that this terrifying story helps us understand the coming of the Son of Man. In just a few sentences, Jesus paints a scene of real terror. Jesus focuses on the part of the story that Genesis ignores: what it was like for the people caught in the flood. People were simply going about their business: eating lunch, drinking a soda, planning a wedding. All of those things sound innocent. We would expect scenes of merchants cheating their customers, or someone abusing the poor. What we get is the judgment hitting right as the bride and groom are feeding each other cake.

16

With no warning, the floods come down and sweep them all away. If you saw the movie *Titanic*, some of the scenes in that movie — with water crashing all around and dead bodies floating in the water — may give us a mental picture of the scene Jesus describes here.

The next two vignettes are very similar. With one sentence each, Jesus presents two pairs of people. In both scenes, the two people depicted are working hard at tedious jobs. Two workers are in a field; two women are grinding meal. From each pair one is received into God's new action and one is left outside of it. These vignettes are not quite as harsh as the first one. They do not threaten destruction, and they offer more hope, at least for the one person in each pair who is received. Still, the vignette is heartbreaking. When God acts, when God reaches into the creation in grace and power, some will not be included. How lonely that sounds. Even a quick drowning might be more merciful than being turned away by God.

The last vignette does not make us feel any better than the first three. The only way we can understand God is to compare God to things we know. Here, Jesus describes God breaking into our world with the image of a thief breaking into a house. Every pastor counsels people who have been victims of crime, including burglary. With burglary, the value of what we lose is only part of the problem. If someone breaks into our house, we feel violated. It takes time to feel comfortable in our own house again. Even if Jesus is trying to make a point with this scene, the image he uses leaves us with an uneasy feeling in the pit of our stomach.

These stories seem like the last thing we need to hear right as we are coming into the Christmas season. Why do we need stories about flood-waters drowning people with no warning that the flood is coming, or people being shut out by God, or thieves intruding into the place where we most want to feel safe? Let's just be honest: Christmas is a difficult time. We've turned a blessing into a burden. Most of us find this time of year stressing us to the snapping point. We rush around trying to buy presents, cook food, make travel arrangements, or send out cards and letters. The choir at church has extra practice sessions. For some people the holidays

17

are the saddest time of the year. Lonely people are lonelier at Christmas. If we have had a death in the family, Christmas makes the loss stand out. All of that leaves little time for Christmas cheer.

What we often try to do at Christmas is to hang on as best we can. We fill the holiday with reindeer, snowmen, eggnog, and cookies. We try to fake a little Christmas spirit, but trying to paste on Christmas cheer can just mask the emptiness inside. We try to fill the emptiness with sentimentality.

Maybe the lectionary committee knew what it was doing by assigning this text for the first Sunday of Advent. If these unsettling stories from Matthew do nothing else, they tear away our attempts at sentimentality. Nothing about the Noah story is sentimental. Can we even think about God being as angry as that story sounds? There is nothing sentimental about being excluded by God. Certainly, there is nothing sentimental about a thief breaking into our house. When we hear one more rendition of "Frosty The Snowman" coming from our dashboards this season, we need Matthew to remind us that Christmas is about serious business. Christmas is about a God who aches over the sin of the world. We don't like to hear stories about judgment, but God's judgment means that God cares when people are hurt.

These unsettling stories proclaim to us at the start of Advent that God hears the cries of the oppressed, of the abused, of the world's victims. Those are the things God judges. If God could come in a flood or like a thief in the night, then God is free to act and powerful enough to make us take notice. Matthew shows us that preparation for the season means more than making sure the presents are wrapped. We are called to discipleship and witness. We are called to obedience. We are called to resist the world's evil.

Matthew is about more than judgment, of course. The fact that the floodwaters didn't come yesterday means that God gives us time. Just a little bit after this passage is the familiar parable of the bridesmaids. Everybody falls asleep because the bridegroom is taking his time. After the word of judgment comes the word of hope, the word of forbearance, the word of grace. God holds the rushing waters back. The thief takes the night off. We have time to hear, to repent, to obey.

18

We may not like it that God speaks right before Christmas through Jesus and Matthew with these frightening stories, but God needs to get our attention. We are the church, called to show and teach the world what it means that this baby was born. We have more to do this Christmas season than we thought. Amen.

Hard Words To Hear
At Christmas

We've gathered here today on the second Sunday of Advent to continue to prepare ourselves for the coming of our Lord. This task of preparing for the arrival of the Lord is not as easy as we might think it is. As in other areas of life, we find ourselves having to unlearn some things in order to see what the scriptures teach us about God's act in Jesus. We've let the culture around us snatch away much of the meaning of the birth of the Savior. We have to reclaim that meaning if we really want to be ready for what God is still doing in the miracle of Christmas. This morning we will hear about the meaning of the arrival of Christ from someone who may actually have gotten ahead of himself.

No one would be better for helping us get back to basics than John the Baptist. John was about as outrageous as they come. He certainly was never boring. No one ever slept through his sermons. His contemporaries considered him a prophet, one who interpreted God's ways to the people. Prophets had been in short supply for a long time. Without prophets, the faith of the people might shrivel up. Maybe that is why John drew such large crowds. Let's not miss the significance of what Matthew tells us about the crowds that came to hear John preach. People came from Jerusalem and Judea to hear John preach in the wilderness near the Jordan River. Urban dwellers and country folk don't usually like the same kind of preaching, but John drew them both in. This wasn't a case of people being in the neighborhood and stopping by to hear John. John's congregation went a long way to hear him. His sermons must have been so genuine, so compelling, and so prophet-like that people made the effort to get there before the pews filled up.

Would we even tolerate John's preaching today? John certainly had an interesting preaching style. Most preachers warm up the crowd with a joke. Most preaching professors tell their students to say "we" instead of "you," as in "*we* need to repent," not "*you* need to repent." John ignored such niceties. He looked right at the religious leaders of the day, snarling out the words, "You brood of vipers! Who warned you to flee from the wrath to come?" According to one New Testament scholar, the image here is of snakes slithering as fast as they can out of a burning field. If the bishop [or other denominational official or religious leader] were to show up to worship with us, is that the way you would expect me to speak to him/her? People often say that they want sermons to be biblical, so here's a biblical sermon. Is this what we want?

When John really got cranked up, his words must have blistered the ears of all those people who came such a long way to hear him. When John begins the heart of his sermon in verse 10, the judgment roars out. Fire seems to be John's favorite threat. John presents two images of judgment. The first is an axe chopping down a tree that bears no fruit. The dead wood will be tossed into the fire. The second image is familiar to every farmer. The farmer sifts the grain with a winnowing fork. The heavier wheat falls to the ground. Usually the chaff just blows away. John tosses the chaff into the fire along with the dead wood.

These two images are the part of John's message with which we wrestle this morning. John sees the arrival of the Messiah with heavy emphasis on wrath. John may well have been furious about the corruption of the people of God. If scholars are correct that John was an Essene, he had gone out into the wilderness as a protest against all of the Jewish leadership of his day. The Essenes thought that everyone had it wrong. They went out into the wilderness to get away from the Romans and the Jewish leadership. They wanted to worship God in their own way. We don't know exactly who John had in mind when he predicted that the trees would be chopped down and thrown in the fire along with the chaff from the wheat. We might be safe in assuming that he thought the corrupt religious leaders would at least be set straight when the Messiah arrived. The writings of the Essenes support the idea that the coming of the Messiah would prove a comeuppance for those who oppose God. One of their prayers implored God to "Lay Thy hand upon the neck of Thine enemies."[1]

How does this work for us as preparation for Advent? We usually think of the Christmas season as a time for peace. During a war, both sides often honor a cease-fire around Christmas. We hope Christmas will be a kind of cease-fire in the stress and strain of life. We are used to quotes from the Bible in our Christmas cards. How often do we find Christmas cards that talk of the chaff being burned in unquenchable fire?

Not only do John's words grate on our ears during Advent, they seem not to be an accurate depiction of Jesus' actual ministry. If John expected the arrival of Jesus the Messiah to be the time when corrupt leaders — both religious and secular — would be put in their place, that is not what happened. Jesus healed and taught, both signs of the coming near of the dominion of heaven. Jesus' ministry was not a time when the trees were cut down or the chaff separated out, with all of it burned up. The religious and secular leaders did not change because of Jesus' ministry. They did not face punishment for their sins or God's wrath for their corruption. Even the Essenes understood that the coming of the Messiah would be a time of healing. As one of their prophecies puts it, "For He will heal the wounded, and revive the dead and bring good news to the poor."[2]

Ironically, John understood his own ministry in connection with Isaiah's words about preparing a way in the wilderness. Isaiah's words originally were a message of comfort and hope to people whose souls were dragging the ground. Isaiah's words offered forgiveness and encouragement to those who thought God had turned the divine back on them. Jesus' earthly ministry was closer to Isaiah's original intent than to what John had in mind. In the Sermon on the Mount, Jesus offers blessings to those who are downtrodden and at the end of their spiritual ropes.

Matthew records John's words, even if they did not quite fit with what the first coming of the Messiah meant for the world.

23

The church assigned this passage for this morning. If we hang in there with this passage it still might help us understand Christmas.

Do we not share some of John's apparent anger at the corruption of the world? Do we not grieve over war, crime, hatred, abuse, and a host of other ills? Isn't it true that we read every year at Christmas time of someone who steals from a charity that is trying to help needy children? One of the questions John's sermon raises is why the evil of the world is still as strong as it is if the Messiah has already come. If we are honest with ourselves we know that we are not what we ought to be.

Maybe the persistence and intractability of sin is a good background for reading John's words here. John gives us powerful, almost frightening images: trees chopped down and chaff thrown into unquenchable fire. What exactly does he mean? He doesn't specify who the trees and chaff are. We often think he means the Sadducees and the Pharisees. We can sometimes be too self-righteous looking at the Jewish leaders in the New Testament. We want to make them the bad guys. We forget that we can be just as legalistic, unseeing, stubborn, and arrogant as we think they were. Even if the New Testament seems to condense all human foibles into the Jewish leaders, we should remember that they are a mirror for us. If all of the evil people are chopped down, where would the chopping stop? What if the chopped down trees and burned up chaff refers not to specific people, but to evil itself, even the evil inside of us? Some of the writings of the Essenes seems to support that idea. One of their documents talks about what God will do with evil and injustice. The document says that at the appointed time of judgment, "God will then purify every deed of man with His truth"[3] Might John be promising us not the destruction of evil people, but the destruction of evil and injustice themselves?

John's timing may have been off. The first coming of the Messiah did not accomplish the destruction of evil. Still, John holds out this hope for God's continuing work in creation. We may not quite be ready to put John's sermon on a Christmas card, but a promise of the complete destruction of evil is cause for joy and celebration. Let us be thankful to John for helping us understand

what we celebrate this season. Let us hold on to the promise of a
time when the evil of the world has been chopped down and burned
up. Amen.

---

1. Geza Vermes, ed., *The Complete Dead Sea Scrolls in English,* IQM XIX, 2-8
   (New York: The Penguin Press, 1997), p. 85.

2. *Ibid*, 4Q521, p. 391.

3. *Ibid*, 1QS IV, 20-21, p. 103.

Advent 3
Matthew 11:2-11

Looking At Jesus
From Behind Prison Bars

How different things must have looked for John behind prison walls. If ever the word "free spirit" applied to anyone, it applied to John. He said what he wanted to say, without holding back. If the scholars are correct that he was an Essene, then he had gone into the wilderness specifically to get away from everyone. The Essenes wanted to worship their way, with no interference from anyone. Now, those prison walls confined John.

We can't know what it was like for John to be the superstar preacher. We don't really know much about him, so we don't know if he was able to keep his ego in check when crowds of people from all over came to hear him preach. Perhaps it is safe to say that John at least felt a kind of excitement with so much religious energy in the air. All of that religious energy was part of the expectation in the beginning of John's ministry that something was about to happen. Matthew records John's first words as the proclamation that "the kingdom of heaven has come near" (Matthew 3:2). John's mission was to prepare people because someone was coming who was "more powerful" than he was (Matthew 3:11). John was sure that when this powerful person arrived, things would change. John expected that evil and corrupt people would be confronted. John's words sound as if he thought evil itself would be destroyed, burned up like chaff in a fire (Matthew 3:12).

From where John sat behind those prison walls, the chaff was still very much around. Things hadn't worked out the way John expected. As an Essene, he thought his community worshiped God the right way, preserving the pure faith. He must have expected that when the powerful one came, he and his group would be vindicated. The corrupt leaders, like Herod, would be judged. Now he was the one subject to judgment. He was the one in prison. God hadn't released him. The powerful one hadn't released him. He woke up each day to the same four walls. He had been thrown in that prison for speaking the truth. Was he frustrated? Was he angry? Was he bitter? With our lack of information, should we choose the safest adjective and say he was disappointed?

John had once made the crowds tremble with his words. Now he had to pass messages by way of his disciples. He couldn't even ask Jesus the question himself. He couldn't look Jesus in the eye and give the question the exact inflection he wanted to give it. He had to ask the question second hand and receive the answer second hand, through his disciples.

The question was, "Are you the one who is to come or are we to wait for another?" John knew that someone was coming. Whatever else had happened within him, he hadn't lost his faith in God. He wondered whether Jesus was really the one, or just another flash in the pan who raised everyone's hopes just to have them dashed all over again. Jesus tells us that John was a good man, even among the best of humanity (Matthew 11:11). These were not the doubts of a scoffer. John had been willing to accept Jesus as the one who was coming, but he had had some questions all along.[1] John didn't understand why the one who would judge the whole world needed to be baptized for the cleansing of sin (Matthew 3:14). After John was put in prison, John's disciples questioned why Jesus' disciples didn't fast, especially if even the Pharisees fasted (Matthew 9:14). Was Jesus really the one? Even worse, was Jesus supposed to be the one, but lacked the discipline to follow through?

Now, while John languished in prison, those doubts really began to matter. Could John have known that he never would walk out of that prison? Could he have at least suspected that he never would breathe air as a free man again? Could we blame John if, under these circumstances, he began to wonder if he had invested himself in the wrong cause? Could we blame him if he thought his life had been based on a mistake? The answer to his question really mattered to John.

Where do we find ourselves in this Advent season? As we approach Christmas, how is our mood? Do any questions or doubts plague us in the midst of holiday cheer? Does some grief or worry have us down? Even if we are able to enter into the spirit of the season, does some of the singing and merry-making just hide our anxiety for a time? Do we use the Christmas spirit to cover up deeper problems?

John's question about whether Jesus was really the one who was to come may lead us to ask some of our own questions at this time of the year. How has it made a difference to the world that Jesus was born? If the Messiah has come, why do so many of us find ourselves in one kind of prison or another?

We could all name some of those prisons. For John the Baptist, the prison was literal. For too many people that is still true. The prisons in this country are practically standing room only. We know what lies behind that overcrowding: drug addiction, poor education, childhood abuse, a loss of values, and poverty. Those in prison have committed a crime, but they also reflect some of our society's ills. We can't know true Christmas joy until we've owned up to those problems.

John's incarceration was political. Certainly, we can see some joy-killers in politics. Our two parties seem almost unable to work together for the good of the country. Each party seems to spend all of its time attacking and discrediting the other party. Meanwhile the national debt soars to the stratosphere. Social Security is heading for a train wreck. The war on terror is based more on ideology than research.

Our problems this Christmas do not have to be as big as the whole country. Maybe we have lost our job and the frustration eats away at us. At Christmas time, not having a job really stings. Maybe an addiction to gambling, substances, or pornography has us in its grip and, no matter how much we strain, we can't break free. Maybe the memory of some mistake we have made hangs over us. We can't find any oasis from the guilt. Our prison may be something else, and we feel isolated because we think no one would understand. We hold on tight to our secret.

If we look at some prisons that hold us in, we may ask a question that sounds a lot like John's question. If Jesus is the one, if Jesus came in power, if God has reached into our world through Jesus, why aren't things different? Why hasn't God chopped down the trees of evil? Why hasn't God burned up the chaff, even the chaff inside our own souls?

Not only do we struggle to understand the continued existence of evil, we wonder about the persistence of evil. We don't even seem to be making progress against evil. When Coretta King died, the media revealed that the percentage of African-American children living in poverty remained about the same as it was when her husband had died. All the years of the civil rights movement had not made much of a dent in childhood poverty. The more we have invested in these issues, the more we share John's apparent frustration.

Jesus sent an answer back to John. It wasn't the answer John wanted or expected. "Go and tell John what you hear and see: the blind receive their sight, the lame walk, the lepers are cleansed, the deaf hear, the dead are raised, and the poor have good news brought to them" (Matthew 11:4-5). Jesus came in power, but not the kind of power John anticipated. Jesus' power was the power of healing and grace. Jesus' power was in his message of the reign of God. Jesus' power was in his deeds and his teaching. In spite of the evil of the world, we see that power now. The arrival of the Messiah didn't instantly fix all of our problems. It didn't free John from prison. Nevertheless, Jesus came bringing power. When we see the church working in the inner city teaching job, parenting, and life skills, that is Jesus' kind of power. When we see people break the power of addiction and live free, that is Jesus' kind of power. When we see the walls of prejudice shattered brick by brick, that is Jesus' kind of power. When we see families healed and love restored, that is Jesus' kind of power. When people find the courage to live with things that won't change, that is Jesus' kind of power. When people hear of the coming reality of God's reign and learn to trust it, that is Jesus' kind of power.

Not only did Jesus answer John's question, he answered it just when John needed to hear it. John recognized Jesus at his baptism, but still had questions. Those questions grew into doubts when Jesus' disciples did not fast. Now, with John in prison, the doubts had intensified so that John had to know the answer. Was Jesus the one or not? As New Testament scholars point out, when John's uneasiness was at its most intense, Jesus gave the clearest answer about his identity as the Messiah.[2]

Where are we this Christmas season? Are we as convinced as ever that Jesus is the Messiah and that the future is in God's hands? Are we covering up doubt with Christmas cheer? Are any doubts or uneasiness right before us, making us wonder what difference Christmas really makes? John has been there before us. Jesus' answer to John is our answer. Where we see the power of healing and the wisdom of true teaching, we see the difference the coming of the Savior has made, and we anticipate the full realization of that difference. Amen.

---

1. Throughout this sermon, I am indebted to the insights of Canadian New Testament scholar, Gary Yamasaki, whose discourse analysis of the passages about John in Matthew are contained in the book, *John the Baptist in Life and Death: Audience-Oriented Criticism of Matthew's Narrative* (Sheffield, England: Sheffield Academic Press, 1998).

2. *Ibid*, p. 109.

Center Stage

Now that Matthew has finished his genealogy, he starts his narrative. We would not have much of a Bible without the narratives, but sometimes the biblical authors frustrate us. We always want more details. We want to know where the characters come from, what happens to them as they walk off stage. Just as we are starting to identify with a character, she will disappear, never to return. Matthew is no different. Right in his second sentence, he does the thing that frustrates us. He presents a scene that could be full of drama and emotion, but glosses over it in a few words. Speaking of Mary, he says, "she was found to be with child from the Holy Spirit" (Matthew 1:18). When we read that sentence, we don't want to skip over it so quickly. To us, this looks like a drama that *Days of Our Lives* couldn't hope to match! What might have been behind Matthew's short phrase, "she was found to be with child"? What did Mary think when she discovered she was pregnant? We might think she was in anguish, worried sick about how to tell Joseph. Can't we just see her, teary-eyed, shoulders heaving, handkerchief in a bunch, wondering what to do? What was the scene like when she told him? Surely his first impulse was that she had betrayed him. Can't we just see his jaw drop? Only the readers know by verse 18 that the child is of the Holy Spirit. Neither Joseph nor Mary knows of this until Joseph has his dream. Wouldn't Mary be beside herself, not knowing how her pregnancy had happened? Even though Matthew tells us that Joseph was a good man, surely he was confused by the story Mary told him.

33

Because Joseph is a good man, he doesn't punish Mary as he might have. He could have humiliated her. Deuteronomy 22 even talked of adulterous women deserving death. Joseph wanted to spare Mary's reputation and feelings. He arranged to divorce her quietly or secretly. No one needed to know the couple's sense of shame and confusion. We admire Joseph that he did not try to punish Mary, or hold her guilt over her in a kind of power play. Joseph is like the wise husband or understanding wife who doesn't bring up stuff from years ago in the middle of an argument. He is like the compassionate parent who allows a child to grow out from under past mistakes. Wise parents avoid labeling a child based on a few early goof-ups. Even as much as we admire Joseph's character, we wish we had some insight into his inner struggle when he tried to decide what to do about Mary's pregnancy. Did he fight within himself over a course of action?

However juicy these details might have been, however much they might have drawn us more deeply into the narrative, they only hover briefly in the background for Matthew. He touches on them only enough to set the stage. What takes center stage for Matthew is how God is working in this messy love affair between Joseph and Mary. Mary's pregnancy is of the Holy Spirit. That is far too mysterious a matter for us to speak of it in much detail. We cannot probe too deeply into the biology of this pregnancy. We cannot even discover what Mary thought about bearing this child. God takes the initiative in this narrative. God takes so much initiative that we even wonder whether Mary felt overwhelmed. We would never say that God did not care about Mary's needs. Yet, here might be a case where God's purposes were larger than the needs of one couple. However difficult and awkward the pregnancy may have been for Mary and Joseph, God was acting for the salvation of creation.

If we cannot say much about the biology or psychology of this narrative, we can speak of what God is doing. God is working through this pregnancy and birth. The baby growing, thrashing, kicking in Mary's womb is God's act of salvation. This baby — beyond any ability we have to explain — is God in human flesh. Matthew quotes Isaiah as a way of saying what can't be said. "Look, the virgin shall conceive and bear a son and they shall name him

Emmanuel," which means, "God is with us." The words from Isaiah seem almost not to fit. The quote from Isaiah says that the baby's name is to be Emmanuel, which, of course, was not Jesus' name. Nevertheless, Jesus embodies God with us. The quote, almost shoehorned in by Matthew, helps us to see who Jesus is. The proclamation that Jesus is God with us — God in human flesh — may seem strange to us. We may struggle to think of any words to express it so that it makes sense. Nevertheless, that affirmation is at the heart of our faith. Jesus is God with us and for us. As one theologian puts it, "According to the witness of the New Testament, the very basis of our salvation, the very ground of our hope consists in the fact that we are permitted to believe, know, and confess the authoritative presence of God in the human life and destiny of Jesus."[1]

The angel tells Joseph to name the baby Jesus. Jesus is the Greek form of Joshua, which in Hebrew means "Yahweh saves." God acts in Jesus to save us from our sins. God saves us from the effects of our sins. Those effects include the hurts other people have caused us. For all the ways we have been neglected, for all the times someone took their problems out on us, for all the ways people have held us back, God saves us. God soothes our hurts and gives us the strength to move on. God saves us from the things we've done that we can't undo. For the regrets that seem to hold us hostage, God offers us release. God saves us from the big sins for which we all chip in our two cents' worth. For pollution, and racism, for poverty, and the ways we just let things keep going, God saves us. God doesn't want us just to keep letting these things be, but God saves us. God saves us from the guilt of our sins. On our own we cannot reestablish the relationship we might have had with God. That relationship has been shattered. Only God can pick up the crushed pieces of that relationship and reform them. In Jesus — in this birth we cannot explain — God saves us.

We always need to hear that God took the first step to save us. Especially at this time of year, though, we need to hear that God acted to save us in the midst of what looks to us like a better soap opera than we could ever see on a weekday afternoon. If our lives are messy, full of tough decisions and awkward moments, we take heart knowing that God has been there before. God's act

35

of salvation didn't take place in a sweet, serene little family. Mary may have cried her eyes out while telling Joseph about her pregnancy. Joseph's heart may have nearly popped out of his chest when he decided that he had to let Mary go. Matthew doesn't let us know those details, but certainly this story has its share of loose ends. God brings salvation out of those loose ends. Theologians tell us that Jesus was both human and divine. Matthew, a theologian who tells stories, tells us that Jesus' humanity arose from the same pain and family conflict that marks our lives. Christmas time can bring out the tensions that often lie just under the surface. We need to hear that God is working for salvation in those tensions.

Look at how this gospel starts and how it ends. Joseph was going to dismiss Mary quietly, in secret. No one would have known. Mary would have saved face, but it wouldn't have mattered to anyone. Look, though, at how Matthew's gospel ends! Jesus commissions the disciples to go make disciples of all nations (Matthew 28:19). What almost was snuffed out in secret ends up changing the whole world, all the nations. However things look to us now, God is working. God is healing. God is saving. When God takes initiative, we never know how it will turn out.

What do we think is important in these last few days before Christmas? Are we scurrying around, enslaved to our to-do list? Are our travel plans finished? Can we make the end-of-year deadlines on all things personal and professional? We may have no choice in the flurry of this season. In all of those details let us not forget that they are really behind the scenes stuff. What we think really matters might rate only half a line from Matthew. Matthew wants us to see what God is doing in the craziness of Christmas. Let us see how God is acting, even in situations that seem to us to be pure pain. Let us see how, no matter how lost and broken we may feel, God is saving us. Let us see that, no matter how divided up we are, or how hostile our world seems, God is with us. Amen.

---

1. Jan Milic Lochman, *The Faith We Confess*, translated by David Lewis (Philadelphia: Fortress Press, 1984), p. 104.

A Shepherd's Story

It's not an easy life, I'll tell you that. I work my small farm during the day, but that doesn't bring in enough money. I have a family to support, taxes to pay — oy, don't get me started on taxes — so I need more than my farm brings in. I do the only other thing I know how to do. I hire myself out for the night shift watching other people's sheep. Tending sheep would not be my first choice, you understand. First, I have to stay awake all night. Then, there's counting the sheep to make sure one or two haven't wandered off. Thieves are always a problem. Wild animals, now that's what really scares me. I don't want them to get the sheep, but I sure don't want them to get me.

None of us could get by without sheep. Where else would we get the wool, the meat, the skins, even the horns? If sheep are that important, surely we shepherds are important, too, right? I guess that as long as people have been around, shepherds have been around. It's not like some great people haven't worked as shepherds. Moses was watching flocks at Midian when God spoke to him from a burning bush. He didn't turn out too badly. The great king, David, was a shepherd when he was a boy. You'd think we'd get a little more respect than we do. As important as we are, and as many great leaders who started out in the business, we still are treated like dirt. We're poor and we are pretty far down on the social ladder.

One of the ways I pass the time is to daydream — yeah, I know it's at night, but what else are you going to call it? If nothing much is going on with the sheep, I wonder what it would be like to

37

be somebody important. I wonder want it would be like not to have to work so hard to eke out a living. What would it be like to be Emperor Augustus? He's a big shot who can do what he wants. I guess you could order everyone around if your uncle was Julius Caesar, and you were handpicked to be emperor. Not so awful long ago, he decided to call for a census. He wanted to know how many subjects he had, and how big his tax base was. Everybody had to go back to the hometown to be counted. You wouldn't believe the grumbling that caused. A few hot heads even tried to start a revolt. You can guess how far they got with that! What a mess this census was. I heard that nearby, in Bethlehem, it was so packed there wasn't room for everyone. All because Emperor Augustus wanted a census. What Augustus wants, he gets.

Anyway, the thing I wanted to tell you about happened around the time of this census. My buddies and I were passing the time on what looked like an ordinary night. We were watching the sheep and trying to keep awake. All of a sudden, the most amazing thing happened. An angel showed up — no kidding. I know what you're thinking: late at night, a little wine to keep warm, we only thought we saw an angel. Let me tell you, it was a real angel! We all saw him. None of us had ever seen an angel before, trust me. We were terrified. I don't know what you think seeing an angel is supposed to be like, but it scared us to death. The angel must have seen the looks on our faces, because the first thing he said was, "Do not be afraid." That's easy for him to say!

After we calmed down a bit, the angel said to us, "I am bringing you good news of great joy for all the people." That's the kind of thing they say when a member of the royal family is born, only the joy is mostly for the royals and the big shots. This was great joy for *all* the people, even working stiffs like us. The angel went on, "to you is born this day in the city of David a Savior, who is the Messiah, the Lord." Did you catch that? "To *you* is born...." This baby mattered for us. I had heard about a messiah, an anointed one, since I was a kid. Everybody expected a messiah. Every now and then, some hot shot would come along. People would get all excited, calling him the messiah. Then the Romans would put a stop to that. This was an angel saying that this baby was the Messiah. Then — and I swear I'm not making this up — it was more than just one angel. The whole pasture was filled with heavenly beings. They were praising God and offering us peace. Peace, real peace, has been in short supply. Military occupation doesn't make for peace. Staying up at night until you're bleary-eyed to make a living doesn't seem too much like peace. Being treated like dirt isn't peace. There they were anyway, talking about peace for all people.

Do you understand what this thing was like? Here we were out in the middle of a sheep pasture, fighting off the weariness — all kinds of weariness — expecting the same old thing. First one angel, then more angels than anyone could count, show up. Now, heaven is up there, and we're down here, but for that one moment, heaven was down here, in our sheep pasture!

They told us to go on into Bethlehem to see this baby. Just as they said, we found the baby in a manger. Can you imagine what all of this must have been like for the parents, especially the mother? Nazareth to Bethlehem is — oh, I'd say about 100 miles. They have to travel that path while momma is pregnant! Ain't no good way to travel 100 miles when you're eight months and 29 days pregnant. How would you get there? If you ride a donkey, a Roman soldier might steal your donkey. What else would you do but walk — 100 miles with a stomach out to here.

Once they arrived in Bethlehem, nobody could find room for them. They finally found a house where someone would take them in, but it wasn't much. The more important guests had the best rooms. They had to stay out with the animals. They put that baby in a feeding trough, for heaven's sakes! This baby was the one the angels said was the Messiah! You should have seen the look on the mother's face when we told her about the angels. You could tell she knew something was up, but you could tell she thought long and hard about what we told her.

It's been a few days since this happened, so it's still sinking in. It doesn't necessarily surprise me that God would send a Messiah. We sure need God's grace around here. The part that really gets me is that the angels appeared to us, a bunch of guys moonlighting to make a few extra bucks. The angels didn't appear to the priests, or even to Emperor Augustus. They came to us. We know what it's like to be pushed around, and for sure that family knows what it's like to be pushed around. Another thing I don't quite understand is that the angel said this baby was the Lord. That's what he said, "the Messiah, the Lord." There's only one Lord. What could that have meant?

So far, I haven't noticed much difference in the details of my life. I still have to work day and night to make ends meet. I'm still at the bottom of the social ladder. Still, somehow that experience helps me know that I matter to God. That keeps me going. Besides that, I wonder what this experience means for you. That angel talked about peace for all people. That means you, too. One more thing, though, before I head out. I'm just a shepherd, but the angels came to me. Maybe you could show people like me a little more respect. The guy who works the graveyard shift at the convenience store is a lot like me. The people who pick your fruit and take away your garbage are a lot like me. What they do for the economy is important like what I do for the economy. The people who have no place to live are a lot like that family with the baby. Maybe you could notice them a little more, maybe even a lot more. What are their needs? How can you help them? What can your church do for them? How much attention from the government do they deserve? It was someone like that who gave birth to your Savior. Just think about that; it's all I ask. Amen.

The Horror Before The Blessing

A few years ago, a woman wrote in exasperation to the editor of her newspaper. She demanded to know why the media always publish negative and sad stories during the holiday season. As she pointed out, "Christmas is supposed to be a happy, joyous time."[1] Her letter sounds almost as if she thinks that, even if bad news happens during the holiday season, the newspapers and television should simply ignore those things. Maybe we all wish Christmas time had a kind of protective bubble around it. Christmas could be the oasis we experience instead of the sorrow and tragedy of the rest of the year.

The events behind the bad news just won't have it that way. Rather than a break from bad news, the Christmas season almost seems to create its own kind of bad news. Perhaps we simply notice it more. Three years ago, just before Christmas, the nation read in horror about a woman who allegedly strangled a pregnant mother, then cut her fetus out of her lifeless body. The police used email to locate the suspect; they recovered the baby in time to save him. Besides the gruesome nature of the crime itself is the long-term effect. The child will someday have to learn the circumstances of his mother's death. Father and child will have to find some way to cope with what has happened. The picture of the suspect looked nothing like the monster we would suspect of committing a crime that turns our stomachs. She looked somewhat shy, holding a dog in her arms, smiling at the camera. What would we want the media to do, wait until the glow of Christmas has faded and then dump these kinds of stories on us? A couple of years ago, the tsunami hit

41

right after Christmas. Whatever the Christmas season means to us, it doesn't mean that we can switch off the bad news. The forces of evil do not lay down their arms for a cease fire just because we've turned the calendar to December.

Not even the lectionary committee will give us a break. For the Sunday after Christmas, they assign us one of the most brutal stories in scripture. The birth of Jesus has been heralded in Joseph's dream. The baby "will save his people from their sins" (Matthew 1:21). The birth of Jesus is a time of hope, of rejoicing. Maybe a year, but certainly not more than two of relative tranquility follow. The visit from the Magi reveal Jesus to the wider world. The tranquility comes to a bitter end. Herod learns of the significance of Jesus' birth. With cold deception he discovers that Jesus is in Bethlehem. What Herod does next seems almost unthinkable. Herod considers Jesus a threat. He wants to eliminate the threat as quickly as possible, so he sends soldiers to Bethlehem to kill Jesus before he has a chance to grow up. With diabolical efficiency, Herod has the soldiers kill all of the children under two years of age in Bethlehem. Terrorism is nothing new. Matthew tells the story with dignified understatement. The scene itself and the immeasurable grief afterward might be almost more than we can bear to imagine.

Christians in our world today know of grief this heavy. In Latin America, people know what it is like for a family member who has challenged the government simply to disappear. In some cases, the family never knows what became of the "disappeared one." A Catholic priest, Ernesto Cardinal, went to the Archipelago of Solintename in Central America to teach the natives there about the Bible. When they heard this story, one local artist painted a picture of this scene, as though it had happened on his island. His rendering of the this scene showed green-uniformed soldiers with AK-47s, shooting babies, and tying up the men. The background to the scene is the lush vegetation of the island. In the foreground are dead babies, cackling soldiers, and sobbing women. The beauty of the island contrasts sharply with the horror of the crime. We must not forget that at the height of the Civil Rights Movement, part of the backlash was the bombing of a black church in Birmingham, Alabama. Four little girls on their way to Sunday school died in that blast.

How would we portray the grief of the women who watch the soldiers murder their children? Steven Spielberg portrays the grief of a woman who has lost her sons in World War II. In the movie, *Saving Private Ryan*, Spielberg directs a scene in which Ryan's mother watches the car carrying military officials to her house. Before the men even come in, she knows what they have come to say. She collapses in grief on her porch, sinking to her knees in sorrow. Matthew does not describe directly the grief in Bethlehem. He simply quotes Jeremiah, but those words tell us all we need to know. "A voice was heard in Ramah, wailing and loud lamentation, Rachel weeping for her children; she refused to be consoled, because they are no more."

Herod joins a long line of brutal political leaders in scripture. Part of what Matthew wants us to know in his gospel is that Jesus is a new Moses. Pharaoh threatens Moses just after his birth. With a cold-hearted paranoia similar to Herod's, Pharaoh sets out to kill all of the male Hebrew children. The book of Exodus spares us any scenes in which children actually die, but Pharaoh's brutality is real. Pharaoh feels threatened by all of the Hebrews in his land.

Moses' mother saves him in a bold act. You know the story. She places him in a basket on the river and hopes for the best. In sweet irony, Pharaoh's own daughter finds Moses and defies her father's order, much like the Magi defy Herod's orders. Jesus' parents saved him when Joseph encountered an angel in a dream. Off they go to Egypt, where the people of Israel had once found salvation from a famine. Here is a sticking point in the story. Why does God send only one dream? Why not a dream for every parent? Why not a dream for the soldiers, so that they could sneak away like the Magi?

That sticking point in the story brings us back to today, to our own present day horrors, like the genocide in Sudan, or inner-city violence where too many stray bullets find a young target. Matthew does not answer the question of why God did not stop the slaughter in Bethlehem. Matthew does not help us understand why

God does not stop the slaughter today. Even though Jesus was spared while he was an infant, he died later on the cross for us. If it seems as though Jesus gets away, leaving the other children to take the brutality, Jesus' escape is only temporary. As a man, Jesus faces the brutality, the senseless violence, the repression born of insecurity that marks this story and too many other stories.

We may long for a respite from the news reports that break our hearts, even if only for a few days this time of year. Matthew reminds us that we will not get such a break. The evil of the world keeps right on going. Christmas time even seems to make some of it worse, as we read of thieves making off with toys or money intended for charity. Some years, even Salvation Army bell ringers are not safe. For the families of the children who were killed in Bethlehem, the birth of the Savior made life worse in the short run. They experienced a grief that never would have happened if Jesus had been born in another time or place. Our faith does not always make life easier in the short run.

We are not promised an end to suffering, or an answer to the why of suffering. Matthew offers us something else. Jesus' title, according to the angel in one of Joseph's dreams is to be Emmanuel, God with us. When we hear of terrible violence, of unspeakable suffering, of tragic deaths, we should put away the idea that these things mean God is not at work. Even in the deepest of tragedies, even when evil is at its most mystifying, God's plan for salvation for the whole creation has not been diverted. God's ultimate joy and victory cannot be derailed. God is in the midst of the suffering, bringing strength, healing, and comfort. Whatever happens, God is with us. Now that Christmas is over some people really need to hear that. Whatever glow they received from Christmas, if any, has faded by now. The media will not report God's presence in the midst of suffering. Only people of faith know about this good news. That is why we must share it. Amen.

---

1. Jean Roberts, "Isn't There Good News?" *Dallas Morning News*, December 29, 2004, 22A.

Light And Hope
For The New Year

Early January always feels like a fresh start. The Christmas whirlwind has settled down. We still have a fighting chance to keep our resolutions for the new year. Cartoons always depict the New Year as a baby, full of possibilities and innocence. We hope that with a new year we can leave the baggage behind us, stretching toward a brighter future.

The gospel of John begins when everything was new, before the creation itself had any baggage. John begins when the only thing that existed was the Word. We cannot do full justice to the complexity of John's thought just in this opening sentence. We could spend all of our sermon time for this year trying to bring out all of the nuances of this opening phrase from John, "In the beginning was the Word." John drew here on Greek philosophy, in which the Word (*Logos*) was the ordering principle of the universe. He drew from the book of Proverbs as well, where personified Wisdom said, "The Lord created me at the beginning of his work, the first of his acts of long ago. Ages ago I was set up, at the first, before the beginning of the earth" (Proverbs 8:22-23). We can say that, in John's mind, at the very beginning of everything, there was order, purity, goodness, and wisdom.

This Word, this manifestation of goodness and order ,was not static and unchanging. The Word was creative and dynamic. This Word brought into being the world and all that exists. As abstract as this language sounds, it helps us to hear that our world has meaning and purpose. God created the world; it didn't just happen.

Something happened to God's creation. Darkness crept into God's world, polluting the goodness, the order, and the purpose. Darkness is John's word here for the evil in God's creation. Those of us who love dark chocolate know that dark is not always evil. John uses it to contrast with the light that Christ brings into the world. This darkness is a mystery in God's creation. John doesn't explain it or tell us where it came from. The darkness just seems to pop up in verse 5. It sounds almost like a virus that somehow gets past the best filter. John's silence about the origin of the darkness seems appropriate. Despite the best efforts of the best minds, we don't know why evil exists or where it comes from. It is just there. That's the way John says it. The darkness is just there in verse 5.

If we don't understand this darkness, we still recognize it. We have seen it in the rest of the gospel of John. Nicodemus comes to Jesus at night, the darkness that represents doubt struggling to find faith. Jesus' encounter with Nicodemus leads to John's declaration that "the light has come into the world, and the people loved darkness rather than light" (John 3:19).The blind man in chapter 9 becomes the symbol for the spiritual blindness of Jesus' opponents. Even though they could see physically, they still walked in darkness. When Judas goes out to betray Jesus, John summarizes the evil about to be unleashed with the simple statement, "And it was night" (John 13:30).

We recognize this darkness today in our world. John understands the darkness as that which has invaded God's good creation. We know of the ways evil corrupts what should be good. Evil always plays the role of spoiler. A friend once returned home from a vacation to find that his refrigerator had broken down sometime during the trip. The freezer part of the appliance was full of bugs. The eggs embedded in the meat had hatched. That's the evil of the world: waiting for the right conditions to bring it out to do its damage.

We see the evil of creation in things that happen naturally. Tsunamis kill thousands. Millions die from drought and famine. Tiny babies battle cruel cancer. Alzheimer's eats away at a person's mind until only a shell is left. Surely, these things are part of the

46

darkness of creation. They are not part of the order and goodness God intended.

We cannot help but see the darkness in society and politics. If we start small, we could mention the bickering between the parties that leads to cynicism. Surely, there is more common ground and ways to work together than the politicians seem to be able to find. If we move up the scale, we encounter the drug war, fueled by human weakness and spread by the callous indifference to human life. The darkness becomes nearly pitch black when we talk about terrorism and the genocides of Rwanda and Darfur. How can people, created by God, loved by God, become so full of hatred and violence?

As if the problems in nature and human interaction were not enough, too often the two manifestations of evil work together. AIDS, caused by a virus but spread with the help of human irresponsibility on multiple levels, threatens to wreak havoc on the entire continent of Africa. The desire for sexual gratification teams up with government arrogance and passivity to block the light from reaching the darkness. AIDS affects more than those who die directly from it. Innocent children by the millions have been left orphaned. So many of the adults are dead or sick, that no one is available to grow crops, adding to the misery.

We see the darkness in ourselves. We have tempers we exploit, prejudices we indulge, and weaknesses we ignore. We hurt the ones we love. We undermine our own growth and progress. We become our own worst enemies.

Most tragically, we see the darkness in the church. The media blare out our stories of corruption and arrogance. On a smaller scale, we hurt each other in the church by our insensitivity and pettiness. With diminishing influence, we seem to stand on the sidelines wringing our hands at the pain, violence, and hopelessness of the world.

I know it is beginning to sound as though I wrote this sermon intending to crush any optimism for the new year. It is important that, however gloomy I have made things sound, we look squarely at the darkness. We cannot turn away from it if we are to grasp the full significance of what John says. John knew the evil of the human heart, the corruption of politics, the cruelty of disease. Nevertheless, he declares, "the light shines in the darkness, and the darkness did not overcome it" (John 1:5). The grammar of the sentence is important. The light *shines* — present tense. The darkness did not overcome it. The darkness tried but failed. As is typical of John, who uses words with multiple meanings, the Greek word for "overcome" can also mean, "understand." The darkness has intelligence; it plots strategy, it actively opposes God but it failed in its attempt to put out the light.

The light, of course, is God's goodness, God's intentions for creation, God's grace. John's affirmation is that the light shines on in spite of the darkness. The light is stronger than the darkness, smarter than the darkness. If we are not realistic about the darkness, we cannot see how powerful John's affirmation is. If we are naïve about the darkness, we don't see the audacity of John's claim. However intractable, however persistent, however treacherous the darkness seems to be, it cannot win. God's light continues to shine. That statement is not just wishful thinking, not just looking on the bright side. That statement is faith. It is a faith that refuses to give up, refuses to surrender to the darkness of the world. It is a faith that claims the promise of the victory of the light. It is a faith that seeks to bring light to the darkened parts of our world, sharing grace and healing with those plunged into the deepest part of the darkness.

Jesus reveals this light to us. He is the one who comes down to this darkened world. John does not give us an intriguing birth story as Matthew and Luke do. John uses the language of abstraction, but his version is just as thrilling in its own way. John says, "The Word became flesh and lived among us" (John 1:14). God's creativity, God's sense of order, God's direction of the universe, God's wisdom became weak, human flesh. If we think oil and water do not mix, Word and flesh really don't mix. Yet, that is what John says. The Word came into this corrupt, painful, dangerous world and lived among us. God shared the danger, the sadness, the pain of our world.

Even if we don't see how the light shines on, or how the light will ultimately get the best of the darkness, we trust John's words by our faith. We remember Jesus' words later in John, "... all who see the Son and believe in him may have eternal life, and I will raise them up on the last day" (John 6:40). We may not see the triumph of the light now, but we trust John's promise that in the resurrection the light will shine brightly.

What will this coming year hold for us? Will it be the year that we get our act together? Will it be the year that the politicians clean up the corruption? Will it be the year that science finds a breakthrough for AIDS or any of the other diseases that threaten us? Will it be the year that the church boldly proclaims its message and lives out its faith? Will things simply turn out the way they always have? Will our old problems barge back into our sunny January optimism? We don't know what this year holds for us. Likely, we will experience grace and love along with the pain and frustration. We will see the darkness in its full fury. We will also see shafts of light that burst through the darkness. Let us hold on to those shafts of light this year. We can face this year courageously, come what may, because we know that the light shines in the darkness, and the darkness has not overcome it. Amen.

The Epiphany Of Our Lord
Matthew 2:1-12

A Strange Way In
And A New Way Out

The heroes of this little narrative certainly seem familiar to us. Each year we all receive at least one Christmas card with their picture on the cover. Every card depicts them exactly the same way: long flowing robes, beards, and big turbans. They are always in one of two poses: either kneeling at Jesus' crib or sojourning across the desert on camels. In our carefully carved nativity sets, they rub elbows with the shepherds from Luke. We don't really know them very well, though. Most of us have probably heard by now that what we think we know about them is not accurate. They weren't kings; there weren't necessarily three of them; they didn't come on the night of Jesus' birth. After the service, someone will come up and tell me that "We Three Kings" is a favorite hymn and I just ruined it! Whether there were two, three, or twenty of them, and even if they didn't quite make it in time to help boil water for the birth, they have some things to teach us about what it means to encounter Jesus.

We rejoice that, early in his gospel, Matthew has Gentiles come to celebrate Jesus' birth and to offer him worship. The church has long understood this passage as a message about opening the gospel to the world, represented by the three outsiders who come to Jesus. We find curious not that Matthew has Gentiles come to worship Jesus, but that they find Jesus the way they do. These Gentile visitors are not kings, but Magi. We often call them "wise men." That title bears some explanation.

In biblical times, especially in the Old Testament, "wisdom" meant many things. A wise person could be someone who had a

51

particular skill, such as an artisan. A wise person could be someone who observed life, arriving at mature conclusions about how we should live our lives. This kind of wisdom is the basis for the book of Proverbs. Proverbial wisdom warns us away from such things as pride, sloth, and foolishness. One form of this wisdom was to draw analogies about life. "The crucible is for silver, and the furnace is for gold, but the Lord tests the heart" (Proverbs 17:3). This wisdom saying compares the processing of metal to the testing of human hearts. We value this kind of wisdom.

Yet another kind of wisdom is mantic wisdom. A person who had the skill, or maybe the gift, of mantic wisdom could discern things that could not be learned just by observation. Mantic wisdom had a touch of the supernatural. A person with the gift of mantic wisdom could interpret dreams and visions. A person with the gift of mantic wisdom could explain signs and omens. The Magi in this passage fall more into this category. They studied the stars to interpret life. In that practice lies the strangeness of this passage.

The Old Testament authors ridiculed the idea that the stars had any influence on life. The future unfolded with God's providence and our own choices. The belief that the stars exerted power over people originated with the Babylonians, the staunch enemies of the people of Judah. Astrology, then, was a foreign belief system, one that the Old Testament writers tried to steer the people of Israel and Judah away from. In the first chapter of the Bible, Genesis 1, the author describes God creating the heavenly bodies, including the stars. For the biblical authors, the stars were nothing but lights in heaven placed there by God. They held no power; they could not predict the future. They provided no signs or omens.

For that reason, we consider it strange that Matthew would tell us of astrologers who use their mantic wisdom to find Jesus. Certainly, Matthew is not endorsing astrology. We need to be clear on that. Even in the church today, some folks are confused about astrology. They are Christians, but they want to make decisions based on their horoscope readings. Matthew is not giving his okay for that. We face the future trusting in God, not knowing what will happen on any given day.

Where Matthew may be leading us, though, is to affirm that God meets us where we are. We can make our initial steps toward Jesus in any number of ways. We hear every now and then that our experience of coming to Jesus has to match someone else's experience. Matthew knows better. God can draw us to Jesus from wherever we are and by whatever path we follow. One of the delights of our faith is to hear how God has brought people to faith. Some people inch their way to Jesus, starting in early childhood. Others undergo a dramatic experience later in life, so that all of who they are is transformed. Some pastors even went to seminary in the late sixties to avoid the draft. Despite such a start, they became faithful Christians and helpful pastors, almost in spite of themselves. Many people come to Jesus in ways that don't match our expectations. Whoever these wise men were, they show us that we can never predict how God will bring us to Jesus.

These wise men teach us not only in the strange way they come to Jesus, they also teach us in the way they leave. King Herod lurks behind this story of the Magi. Herod cannot see the good news behind the birth of Jesus. Herod seethes with jealousy over Jesus as a threat to his power and his family line. He makes the foolish decision to try to hold back what God intends. He wants to stand in God's way. With a fake smile on his face and treachery in his heart, he invites the Magi in for a talk. Claiming that he wants to pay homage to Jesus, he asks the Magi to let him know the whereabouts of the child.

Herod represents all those in power who claim a noble purpose, but who act out of self-interest and greed. He stands in for all who clutch at power without regard for who might be hurt. When he claims a desire to pay homage to Jesus, he becomes the ancestor of all politicians and leaders who have used religion to gain votes and exert control over others.

Herod's plan would have worked, except for God. Speaking to the Magi in a way they could understand — through a dream — God points them to a different path, away from Herod. The wise men have taught us by the way they arrived, and now they teach us by the way they leave. "They left for their own country by another road" (Matthew 2:12). When we stand up after kneeling before

Jesus (even if we can kneel only in our hearts), we stand up to resist the evil of the world. Worshiping Jesus gives us the motivation and the strength to fight back against greed, oppression, and injustice. The Magi practice a form of "civil disobedience." They refuse to do what the government tells them to do.

We may have an easier time seeing Herod as an example of evil government than we do our own government. We should not deceive ourselves. Are our minimum wage laws and tax policies fair to the poor? Does our government turn a blind eye to pollution and its effects? Do our leaders condone torture of prisoners? Do our leaders seek to ensure access to health care for all people? Many in the church do not want to hear criticism of our government. A pastor in Minnesota preached a series of sermons in which he challenged the notion that the United States is a Christian nation. Gregory Boyd, pastor of Woodland Hills Church in St. Paul, Minnesota, refused to endorse candidates for office and to promote political rallies. Reverend Boyd wanted to go on another road. He did not want the church to be too beholden to political candidates. At the end of the sermon series, 20% of the congregation left Woodland Hills.[1] We may not want to hear it, but we are not called to cozy up to politicians and leaders.

We are called to go on another road. We are called to resist such evil. If we kneel before Jesus, we rise ready to go another road from the evil of the world. Matthew Herbst, a pastor in San Diego, saw an evil that the church needed to resist. He leads the church community in its fight against domestic violence. Domestic violence may be the closest thing we have here and now to Herod's actions. Domestic violence is usually based on irrational fear and a sense of threat. It harms and kills children, leaving grief and agony behind. The problem is much more widespread than most people think. Its influence is more pervasive. In response, Herbst started the *Peaceful and Healthy Relationships Project* in San Diego. The program teaches teens about healthy relationships, concentrating on groups with the highest rates of potential abuse.[2]

We have some new things to think about when we see the Magi in the nativity scenes and Christmas cards each year. They teach us that God welcomes us wherever we might have started out. They show us the call of those who worship Jesus to resist the evil of the world. As we begin a new year, let us pledge ourselves to going on another road. Amen.

---

1. Laurie Goodstein, "Disowning Conservative Politics Is Costly for Pastor," *The New York Times Online*, July 29, 2006.

2. "Domestic Terror," *Christian Social Action* 17.1 (January/February 2004), pp. 9-11.

John The (Reluctant) Baptizer

Many pastors and church boards have a policy against flash photography during any worship service, especially while the pastor is administering the sacrament of baptism. That is an appropriate restriction. A baptism is a holy moment, not a Kodak moment. Also, as any pastor can tell you, when twenty flash bulbs go off in your face, the resulting temporary blindness can be pretty unnerving. It also distracts from the ceremony. Most importantly, a camera cannot capture what really matters about a baptism.

If the technology had existed, and someone had taken a picture of Jesus' baptism, what would have turned up on the film? Certainly, as Matthew describes it, this scene is about as dramatic as any in the Bible. When you think about it, that's saying a lot. If we conducted a poll to determine the most dramatic scene in the Bible, we would have a number of candidates. We could choose the exodus event: the desperate band of freed slaves glancing furtively back at the oncoming Egyptian army as the waters of the Sea of Reeds billow up on both sides. We might pick the Transfiguration, where Jesus' body turns white all over, with Elijah and Moses as eyewitnesses. Certainly, Jesus' resurrection might be a candidate, except that none of the gospel writers actually describes the resurrection, only the aftermath. For today, let us consider Jesus' baptism as a candidate for the most dramatic scene in the Bible, the one we most would like to have captured on film.

We see Jesus for the first time in Matthew at his baptism. Until now, Jesus has appeared in Matthew only as a baby. He has been in the background while the focus has been on Herod, who

57

wanted to kill him and the Magi who visited him and his parents who protected him. Jesus' very first initiative in the gospel of Matthew is to present himself for baptism.

The official at the baptism is John, the rough-hewn preacher who has stirred up a spiritual fervor. John has stirred up a spiritual fervor by announcing the impending arrival of an (almost literally) fire-breathing Messiah-figure who will execute end-time judgment. John's preaching actually sets up a tension in the passage between what John expects and what Jesus requests. John seems to expect that Jesus will step onto the scene to take charge. Instead, Jesus presents himself for baptism. By submitting himself to John for baptism, Jesus acts in humility, placing himself for that act under the authority of John. John protests. Jesus is the authority figure. Jesus does not need a baptism of repentance for sins. Jesus insists on the baptism, despite John's protests. Jesus submits to baptism as an act of faith in the way God works through baptism.

Up to this point, the images on our film of this scene would not be especially dramatic. Jesus steps into the murky waters of the Jordan. John's muscular arm thrusts him below the surface. Jesus' head splashes up from the river with water flying everywhere. All of a sudden, though, something totally unexpected happens, according to Matthew's narrative. Just as Jesus comes up from the water, the heavens open up. Now a fairly ordinary event becomes a candidate for the most dramatic scene in the Bible. If we could capture on film the scene as Matthew describes it, what a picture it would make. Matthew, of course, is not using the language of science. The heavens cannot be torn open in a literal sense. What we call the heavens above us are nothing but empty space. Matthew is using the language of faith.

When Matthew tells us that "the heavens were opened" he alludes to Isaiah 64. There the prophet pleads with God, "O that you would tear open the heavens and come down." Could anyone pray a bolder prayer? The prophet seems to want the same kind of thing that John expects. He writes during a time of deep distress within the community that has returned from exile. He implores God to act in power. The prophet wants fire to kindle brushwood.

He wants nations to tremble. He wants awesome deeds and the quaking of mountains. He expects those kinds of things to happen when God tears open the heavens. When the heavens open up, the prophet expects judgment for sin and wrongdoing. John expected much the same thing when the Messiah arrived. When Matthew tells us that the heavens opened, he transforms the event from the prophet's call for judgment into an act of grace.

In this scene of Jesus' baptism, Matthew arranges a faith encounter for each of us. Canadian New Testament scholar, Gary Yamasaki, leads us carefully through this passage to show how Matthew enables us to experience this encounter.[1] Imagine that this scene of Jesus' baptism was conducted on a stage. The characters have spotlights shining on them. By careful use of language, Matthew empties the stage, so to speak, so that the stage is set for our faith encounter.

We presume that when Jesus comes to John for baptism, he is only one such candidate. The crowds who regularly came to John would have surrounded John and Jesus. Matthew does not mention them in the scene, so they are in the background. Matthew turns their spotlight off, so that by verse 13 they are in the dark. The audience can see only Jesus and John. In describing Jesus' actual baptism, Matthew uses the passive voice, "when Jesus had been baptized." That takes the spotlight off of John. Only Jesus appears on stage after verse 16. Matthew then uses a singular pronoun to indicate that only Jesus saw the Spirit of God descending. Finally a voice from heaven speaks in third person, "This is my Son, the Beloved, with whom I am well pleased." Only Jesus had been on stage until this verse. If the voice had been speaking to Jesus, the voice would have said "You are my Son." By now, though, the stage is dark. We, the readers of the gospel, are alone with God's voice. Matthew allows us to experience what cannot be seen: the opening of the heavens. He allows us to hear what cannot be heard: the voice of God.

A camera snapping away at Jesus' baptism would not have picked up a giant tear in the sky. A microphone would not have recorded the booming voice of God declaring Jesus to be God's Son. No one could have picked up a dove's feather to keep as a souvenir. God acts even if we don't see or hear anything flashy around us. Even though everything may have looked ordinary to bystanders at Jesus' baptism, Matthew tells us that heaven and earth came together that day. The divine realm touched the earth. God answered the prophet's prayer, reaching down into our world to bring hope, comfort, and power. Our faith encounter in this text is trusting that God acted in Jesus' baptism, that God brought heaven near.

What was true for Jesus' baptism is true for every baptism. Even if a baptism looks ordinary, God comes near. In the water and the words of baptism, the heavens open up and the Holy Spirit descends. We can't capture that on our cameras, no matter how sophisticated they might be. A camcorder can catch the details of the baptism, but not what really happens. Our world and God's world come together.

Jesus needed the touch of God in his baptism. Right after his baptism, the Spirit led Jesus into the wilderness to be tempted. Before the temptation, God claimed Jesus, affirming their relationship. Matthew doesn't tell us this in so many words, but maybe his baptism and the opening of heaven sustained Jesus in the wilderness.

Maybe we are now in some wilderness. The wilderness is a lonely and frustrating place. The wilderness can dry up our spiritual resources. We feel as though our faith is not being nourished in the wilderness. If we are not personally in a wilderness, much of our world is in the wilderness. We know the names these wilderness experiences can take: war, violence, hunger, poverty, hatred, grief. The wilderness has many names. As we look at our own wilderness experience, or the experiences of the world, we may ask where God is. We may ask why God doesn't act. We may even ask with the prophet why God doesn't tear open the heavens and fix this world.

God does tear open the heavens. God reaches into our world in grace and healing. God tore open the heavens at our baptism. No camera caught it, but happened just the same. Only the eyes of faith can see the heavens open up. Wherever we are, whatever we see in our world, let us never give up in despair. Let us never assume God has left us alone. Again and again, God tears open the heavens and reaches down to touch us. Amen.

---

1. Gary Yamasaki, *John the Baptist in Life and Death: Audience-Oriented Criticism of Matthew's Narrative* (Sheffield, England: Sheffield Academic Press, 1998), pp. 95-100.

Epiphany 2
Ordinary Time 2
John 1:29-42

Who's Who?

The first chapter of John bears some similarity to the pilot episode of a television series. In that first episode, the writers and director want to introduce all of the main characters. In a television series, what we learn about the main characters in the first episode helps us understand them for the rest of the time the show is on the air and to see how they develop over the course of the series. John's narrative begins after the prologue, a hymn or poem that sets John's theological agenda. Once the narrative begins in verse 19, John focuses on identifying the characters of his gospel.

All of the gospels introduce John the Baptist early in their narratives. John introduces him differently than the other gospels. The other gospels tell us something about John's preaching and ministry of baptism at the Jordan River. John skips over that part of the Baptist's ministry. We don't hear about the Baptist denouncing the religious leaders as "broods of vipers." John skips over the Baptist's thunderous preaching and the enraptured crowds flocking to hear him. John's beginning presupposes that we know the baptist created a buzz. John begins by having a delegation of religious leaders ask him point blank, "Who are you?" They must know what the Baptist has said and done, but they want to know who is saying and doing these things. The Baptist answers their questions by declaring intently who he is not. He is not the Messiah. Many Jews were waiting for a messiah to bring them back to political prominence. He is not Elijah. Elijah had been taken up into heaven without actually dying. Some people expected him to come back. He is not the prophet. Some people expected a prophet like Moses. The baptist identifies himself only as a voice, calling out in the wilderness. The baptist embodies the words of Isaiah. He prepares the way for Jesus. The baptist wants the religious leaders to know that he is not the main character.

In the next scene, the Baptist does what he has come to do. He identifies Jesus. The scene itself is confusing. John divides this first chapter into a series of days, perhaps reflecting the days of Passover. This day is devoted to one dramatic and important speech by John the Baptist. Other than Jesus himself, we don't even know who else is on the set with the Baptist. John doesn't tell us who hears the Baptist's speech. No one responds to the Baptist; no one else speaks. All the focus is on the speech itself.

This speech by the Baptist gives Jesus his first title in the narrative part of John — a favorite of John's gospel. Directing his gaze at Jesus, John the Baptist announces, "Here is the Lamb of God who takes away the sin of the world!" As we see in the rest of the chapter, no one phrase can identify Jesus fully. This title from the Baptist's lips, "Lamb of God," is only one way to identify Jesus. We will leave for other sermons the various titles for Jesus. Calling Jesus "The Lamb of God" connects Jesus with the Passover in Exodus. This phrase stirred up memories. At the Passover, the people of Israel were spared from the angel of death, just before they escaped from slavery in Egypt. The Passover is a time of salvation, of forming the community, of celebrating God's power. At the Passover feast, each family in Israel was to prepare a lamb (Exodus 12). Jesus is God's lamb. God acts again in Jesus for salvation.

John's speech tells us not only who Jesus is — the Lamb of God — but also what Jesus does, takes away the sin of the world. When the fourth gospel talks about "the world," it refers to all of creation. Jesus has come to take the sin and the darkness from God's creation. Jesus does more than just forgive sin; Jesus conquers sin. We live in a world full of sin and darkness. Sin surrounds us all the time, but sometimes it seems to erupt in overflows of hatred and violence. When we see pictures on our television screens of babies burned by bombs, we need to hear that Jesus takes away the sin of the world. John makes sure we know who Jesus is and what he does.

The next group of characters to appear on the set are the disciples. Only the gospel of John tells us that at least some of Jesus' disciples originally were disciples of John the Baptist. Matthew, Mark, and Luke write as if Jesus chose his disciples at random. In John, Jesus' first disciples make a shift in loyalty. The Baptist himself encourages this shift in loyalty, by pointing away from himself and toward Jesus. The Baptist again calls Jesus, "The Lamb of God" in front of his disciples. Sometimes, claiming to be disciples of Jesus means that we place our loyalty to Jesus above some of our other ways of defining ourselves. If we define ourselves as an athlete, our loyalty to Jesus has to come first, over the Sunday golf game. If we define ourselves by our political party, our loyalty to Jesus comes first. We have to remember what the bumper sticker says, "God is neither a Republican nor a Democrat." Both parties distort the facts to receive votes. Both parties are stained with corruption. The church must speak out prophetically to name the sins of both parties. Our loyalty to Jesus sometimes interferes even with our loyalty to our country. We are Christians first, Americans second. As Christians we cannot be so patriotic that we refuse to admit that our government commits sins in our name. Our first loyalty is to Jesus and to the truth.

John's picture of how the disciples make their change in loyalty is important. Here John differs from the other gospels. Matthew especially presents a scene in which the disciples immediately drop everything to follow Jesus. Some of us are just not that way. Some of us need for one reason or another to take our time. John allows for that. In John, the disciples begin with a conversation. As always seems to happen in John, the conversation doesn't quite follow. Jesus asks the potential disciples, "What are you looking for?" We can think of a number of answers that would make sense. "We're looking for spiritual fulfillment." "We're looking for a deeper connection to God." "We're looking for a way to make sense of our lives." Instead, they answer Jesus' question with another question, "Rabbi, where are you staying?" What in the world do they mean by that response? Are they trying to avoid Jesus' penetrating question by changing the subject? How many opportunities for a real encounter do we lose by cracking a joke, or keeping things only on the surface, or switching to a safe topic? Are they trying to check Jesus out by seeing if his quarters are worthy of a great prophet? Are they opening themselves up a little, asking to go to Jesus' dwelling place for quality time? The important thing for us is that the discipleship moves slowly. Now, we can move so slowly that we never get around to it, but John gives an okay to developing the relationship with Jesus slowly. If we keep reading in John, we discover that the disciples did not come fully to believe in Jesus until they had seen the water turned to wine at the wedding in Cana. Coming to believe can be a process.

As do all of the gospels, John singles out Simon. In John, Simon's brother, Andrew, brings him to Jesus. We do not often meet someone who immediately changes our name, but that's what Jesus did with Simon. Jesus nicknames Simon, *Cephas*, Aramaic for the "Rock." The Aramaic comes out in Greek as *Petros*, and in English as Peter. In whatever language you say it, Jesus' words sound strange. What does Jesus see in Simon that deserves this nickname, the Rock? We know that Simon does not always act like the Rock. The Rock quivered in his sandals standing by the fire as Jesus was led away by the soldiers. The Rock denied being a disciple of Jesus when the going got tough. Jesus looked at Simon and saw the Rock. "What are you looking for?" Jesus asked. Whatever Simon was looking for when his brother told him they had found the Messiah, what Simon found was himself. He found himself as Jesus saw him.

John wanted us to know who the Baptist was, who Jesus was, and who the disciples, especially Simon, were. We might have come here looking for who we are. Simon found himself by trying to find the Messiah. What Jesus says to Simon is good for us to hear. We often hear in church not to be too full of pride, not to think too much of ourselves. We need to hear that from time to time. Jesus saw more in Simon than Simon knew was in him. We need to hear that, too. Do we see ourselves as spiritually weak? Have we let the putdowns of others sink in? Maybe the risen Christ sees in us abilities, strength, potential that no one else, including ourselves, can see. Maybe the risen Christ sees our inner Rock. Amen.

Letting Go Of Our Nets

Did they have any idea what they were getting themselves into? Peter, Andrew, James, and John had no crystal ball that day when Jesus called them. When the call came, they were going about business as usual: casting nets, pulling them back in, sorting and salting the fish, taking them to market, and maintaining their equipment. However it was that they became fishermen, they had not chosen an easy profession. Yes, I've seen the bumper sticker: "A Bad Day Fishing is Better than a Good Day at Work." These four men were not fishing for fun and recreation. They were not nestled into a drifting boat on a smooth pond. They didn't have their caps pulled down over their eyes with a pole resting in the crook of their arms. Their call did not occur on a lazy day with plenty of refreshments in the cooler. These men did hard work. Their muscles ached from throwing and hauling the nets. Their hands were cut from the sharp knives and fish spines. Of course, there was always the smell. Fishing was a stable and profitable occupation. They were not rich, but they were not dirt poor, either. They made a good living, but it certainly wasn't glamorous.

Jesus called them from that life. They knew what they were leaving, both the pros and the cons. They didn't know what Jesus was calling them to. We have the advantage of knowing how things turned out. We know the joys and wonders in store for them. We know they will see and experience things they could not imagine on the first day. They saw miraculous healings. Would it be worth leaving everything behind in order to see a paralyzed man walk away? (Matthew 9:2-8). To see a little girl raised from the dead?

(Matthew 9:25). We know that they heard intriguing parables. What would we give up to hear Jesus say to us, "to you it has been given to know the secrets of the kingdom of heaven"? (Matthew 13:11). What would that kind of spiritual insight be worth? How much of a pay cut would we endure in order to see the power, intensity, and energy of the Transfiguration, as Peter, James, and John saw? (Matthew 17:1-8). Responding to Jesus' call opened up for these four men a spiritual adventure they never could have found on their own.

What decision would the men have made if they had known everything? Would they have considered the miracles, the parables, and the presence of Jesus worth the cost? Accepting Jesus' call put them at risk. John has been arrested. Danger lurks behind the scenes in Jesus' call. Would they have responded so readily if they had known about the Garden of Gethsemane or the crucifixion? What would James have done if he had known that Herod would have him beheaded? (Acts 12).

The way Matthew presents this call scene, not one of them hesitated for a second. In the gospel of John, the first disciples take some time to respond to Jesus. John the Baptist announces boldly to them who Jesus is. The would-be disciples check out Jesus' living quarters. They have a chance to think it over (John 1:29-42). The way Matthew presents the call, we aren't even sure these four know who Jesus is. The emphasis in Matthew's gospel is on how much we don't know when we respond. Matthew seems to want us to know that we really are taking a leap into the dark when we respond. Some of us may like John's gospel a little better. We receive some assurance of who Jesus is and we can take a little time to decide. The emphasis in John's gospel is important. We don't want to follow blindly some cult leader or charlatan. We need John's emphasis on getting some things straight and taking some time. Matthew is right, though. No matter how much we study up, or how carefully we make our decision to follow Jesus, we won't know what lies ahead of us when we respond.

Not only do the four men leave quickly when Jesus calls them, but they leave everything behind. Even though fishing was hard work, it was their livelihood. They had invested time in learning the trade, acquiring fishing rights, procuring boats and equipment.

A person didn't become a successful commercial fisherman overnight. In both cases, Jesus calls the new disciples in the middle of an important activity. Simon and Andrew had just cast their net. Apparently, they did not even wait to pull the net back in one last time. Matthew says they responded immediately. They don't even cash in that day's profits! James and John are mending their nets as they hear the call. They are preparing for their next expedition. They are looking to the future. The way the scene reads, if Jesus had called golfers, he would have called them when they were at the top of their backswing. We don't know what went through their minds, but they let go of their nets.

We don't know what the four disciples thought, but we know some things about what Matthew thought of Jesus' mission. Jesus came to bring light to those who had sat in darkness. Part of that darkness was political oppression. Isaiah had talked about the darkness caused by the Assyrian domination of the new disciples' ancestors. Now, it was the Romans doing the oppressing. Part of that darkness was hopelessness. Part of that darkness was illness. Part of that darkness was spiritual depression and anguish. Jesus came to bring light into the darkness. Jesus came to bring the dominion of heaven near. Jesus brought a sample of what it will be like to be in God's full presence, to experience true justice and fairness where everyone has enough, to live in joy. In Jesus, God has reached into our world to bring hope. For Matthew, being part of that ministry was worth letting go of our fishing nets and leaving our old life behind.

Jesus continues to call disciples. We are not always called to leave our jobs or our security to follow. Many people leave high-paying jobs to do a ministry that pays a fraction of what their old job paid. A middle-aged couple in Florida left their comfortable jobs and neighborhood to become house parents at a boys' ranch in Alabama. The four disciples responded immediately; this couple took three years to decide. The couple had compassion for boys who had never had a birthday party or been tucked into bed. Perhaps alluding to the passage, the founder of the boys' ranch said that the couple would "bring light to children long accustomed to darkness."[1] We are not all called to that, but we are called to let go of our nets and follow Jesus.

Sometimes the nets we let go of are our jobs and careers, but we hold on tightly to other nets. I'm not sure what to say about James and John leaving their father in the boat. They left him to carry on the family business while they followed Jesus. I have known people who neglected their families for church work. It was not always the best decision. I have known other people who found a way to do church work and spend time with their families. Taking care of our families can be our ministry. If family is your net, search your heart about what it means to follow Jesus. One other net we hold on to is a feeling of inadequacy. "I can't do that; I can't chair a committee; I wouldn't know where to begin." It's true that we should seek out where we can serve most effectively, but God's call can stretch us in ways we hadn't expected. Another net we hold on to is a bad experience from the past. We tried a ministry and it didn't go well. We experienced deep frustration. We vowed never to try that again. Sometimes the mistakes of the past are the building blocks of our later successes. Maybe God can work through the pain of past experience to bring real fruit from our next attempt.

When we let go of our nets, we carry on the ministry of Jesus. Verse 23 of this passage describes Jesus' ministry as teaching, proclaiming, and healing. We teach in Sunday school, in VBS, and in quiet conversations. We proclaim when we announce our faith to the world. We proclaim when we declare our values are not the same as the world's values. We are not ruled by money, success, or prestige. We resist violence, greed, and exploitation. We heal when we take care of one another in times of sickness, grief, or trouble. We heal when we pray for one another.

We don't always know what will happen when we respond to God's call. We know that God is with us and that he will work through our ministries, even our shortcomings and incomplete successes. If God calls us, let us drop our nets and respond. Let us shine the light of God's dominion into the darkness of the world. Amen.

---

1. Troy Moon, "Couple Takes Pay Cut to Help Children," *United Methodist Reporter* July 7, 2006, p. 8B.

Those Who Most Need A Blessing

Can a child pass up a tasty marshmallow? A researcher who wanted to know set up an experiment. He left a succession of four-year-olds alone in a room, seated at a table. On the table was a single marshmallow. The researcher told the children that they could eat the marshmallow when he left the room, or they could wait until he returned. If they waited, they would receive a second marshmallow. The children had a choice: one marshmallow now or two marshmallows if they were patient. The researcher then left the room. As you would guess, the researcher watched and recorded the responses of the children through a hidden window. You can probably guess the results. Some of the children snarfed down the marshmallow as soon as the door shut. Some squirmed and fidgeted for a while, but, in the end, couldn't hold out long. They gave in and ate the marshmallow after a couple of minutes. A few of the children — in a show of steely self-discipline — picked the marshmallow up, licked it, and nibbled just a bit to get the taste, but didn't eat the whole thing. The heroes of the experiment endured the agony, waiting for the experimenter to return, so that they could savor the second marshmallow.[1]

What's true of children is true for all of us. We don't like to wait for something good. Even if we know we will get something better in the long run, we don't like waiting. We don't even like to wait for our blessings from God. We want them now.

Jesus offers blessings in the opening lines of the Sermon on the Mount. Jesus has been traveling throughout Galilee preaching, teaching, and healing. Jesus' ministry manifests the realization of

71

his proclamation that the dominion of heaven has come near (Matthew 4:17). Matthew refers to the dominion of heaven, rather than the dominion of God — as the other gospels do — because strict members of the Jewish faith avoid saying the word "God" whenever they can. The New Revised Standard Version reads the "kingdom of heaven" as a translation of the Greek. Kingdom is not a wrong translation, but it makes what Jesus is talking about sound like a place. The dominion of heaven is as much a time as it is a place. The dominion of heaven is the time and place where God will restore the creation, making the creation what God wants it to be. In the restored creation, sin, death, and evil will be vanquished, so that God's creatures can thrive in harmony and peace. Jesus' ministry brought the dominion of heaven near. We cannot follow Jesus' teachings in the Sermon on the Mount unless we are willing to wait for the fullness of the dominion of heaven.

After manifesting the dominion of heaven through his ministry, Jesus ascends a mountain. A common assumption in biblical times was that mountains were a kind of bridge between earth and heaven. Important things happened on mountains. Moses received the commandments, the law of God, on Mount Sinai. Now, as a kind of new Moses, Jesus ascends the mountain to offer new teachings.

Jesus begins his teaching with a series of blessings, the well-known beatitudes. When Jesus speaks these blessings, he does not describe the people we most think of as blessed. Jesus' words have power. Jesus' words promise blessing for the future, but that future stretches back to the present. Jesus' blessings will not be fully realized until the dominion of heaven, but they transform our understanding of the present. They sustain and comfort us. Jesus' blessings are often misunderstood. They are not attitudes that will make us happy. Jesus pronounces God's favor on people, sometimes for situations beyond their control. Let us open our ears to Jesus' unexpected blessings.

Jesus speaks his first blessing to the "poor in spirit." If we are poor in spirit, we are at the end of our spiritual ropes. If we are poor in spirit, we are spiritually exhausted. Life may have sapped our spiritual energy. Poverty can sap our spirits. Loneliness can sap our spirits. Being abused can sap our spirits. All of us are poor in spirit sometimes, but some people spend their whole lives poor in spirit. Besides simply being the first in line, this beatitude seems to set the tone for the next few verses.

Jesus then pronounces a blessing on those who mourn. Surely, we feel least blessed when we mourn. Grief can be a long, arduous process. In our deepest grief, we don't feel like doing anything. The pain seems to clutch at our souls, unwilling to let go of us. No matter how much we cry, it is never enough. When we grieve, we surely are poor in spirit.

Many of us might decline Jesus' next blessing. We do not much admire the meek in North American society. We want others to respect us. We want leaders who are tough, who stand up to our enemies. We do not want to be victims. Yet, here is Jesus, offering a blessing to the meek. Sometimes the meek are those who choose not to retaliate. Sometimes the meek are those who simply cannot fight back. The meek can be those who lack the resources, the power, money, and organization to take care of themselves.

When we see how far the world is from where it should be, we hunger and thirst for righteousness. When we see children starving, when we see violence shatter bodies and souls, when we see poverty squeeze the joy out of people's lives, we hunger and thirst for righteousness. We hunger for things to be right in the world. We thirst for people to recognize God's sovereignty and our common humanity. Some people hunger and thirst for righteousness because *they* are the ones deprived of justice, fairness, and the chance to flourish.

With this beatitude, Jesus' blessings begin to make a subtle shift. Jesus blesses some people for the choices they make in life. Jesus blesses others simply for the way they find their lives to be. We cannot always make a sharp distinction between these two blessings. Sometimes we mourn because grief has intruded uninvited into our lives. We find ourselves mourning. Other times we mourn because we see the way the world is, and we mourn because we know it can be better. That kind of mourning can be a choice. By blessing those who hunger and thirst for righteousness, Jesus speaks both to our choices and the things we have no choice over.

73

When Jesus blesses the merciful, he moves fully toward those who make a choice. We do not choose to be wronged, to be violated, to be hurt. We can choose how we will respond. We can strike back, or we can be merciful. If we strike back, we keep the cycle of hurt going. We may feel better over the short term, but we will never fully heal. If we choose to show mercy, we take risks. Someone may sneer at our mercy. Someone may call us weak. Mercy may take more strength than we think we have. Yet, only mercy can bring healing.

If we find showing mercy difficult, purity of heart may be the trickiest beatitude of them all. Surely, we miss Jesus' blessing when we make no effort to focus our devotion on God and seek only our own needs, our own power. Even our most sincere efforts to give full devotion to God can be sidetracked. Temptation to idolatry sneaks up on us. We need money to live, so we don't notice when we begin to worship money. We want to succeed, not fail, so we don't notice when we begin to worship success. We want our families to be safe from threat, so we don't notice when we begin to worship our military might. We think we are most blessed when we are most comfortable, successful, and secure. Jesus blesses us when we are most devoted to God alone.

Peacemakers are those who take the initiative. Peace is more than the absence of violence and war. Peace is harmony and a sense of rightness about things. Peace is flourishing. Just as the merciful, peacemakers take risks. Peacemakers become vulnerable. Peacemakers fight conflict with love. Peacemakers seek healing.

Jesus saves his last blessing for those who are persecuted and reviled. Many of us in the mainline churches in North America don't know what to do with this blessing. We assume it applies only to Christians in countries openly hostile to Christianity. We may find, though, that if we really live out our faith, if we really challenge comfort and complacency, we may be more "blessed" than we ever imagined.

The blessing Jesus offers may not be obvious now. We may not see a blessing for the meek, or those who mourn, or those who take the risk to make peace. Jesus' blessings here are in the future

74

tense. Those who mourn *will be* comforted. The pure in heart *will* see God. Those who hunger and thirst for righteousness will be filled. Jesus begins the beatitudes by saying that the poor in spirit are blessed because theirs is the dominion of heaven. The dominion of heaven is the second marshmallow. We in the church wait now for the dominion of heave to come in its fullness. Every now and then, we get to nibble at the first marshmallow. The sacrament of the Lord's Supper is a nibble at the first marshmallow. Experiencing God's presence in a crisis is a nibble at the first marshmallow. Feeling the love of other Christians is a nibble at the first marshmallow. Vibrant prayer is a nibble at the first marshmallow. Yet, we wait for the second marshmallow. We trust that God will fully bring in the dominion of heaven. The dominion of heaven is for all of us. Yet, when Jesus says that the poor in spirit will find that theirs is the dominion of heaven, maybe he means that, for them, the second marshmallow will be that much sweeter. The second marshmallow will be sweeter if we have hungered and thirsted for it. It will be just as sweet if we have chosen to hunger and thirst for righteousness, or if life has placed us in a position where we hunger and thirst.

Glen Mitchell, of Jacksonville, Florida, qualifies for Jesus' blessings many times over. More than a decade ago, his son was murdered in a senseless crime. That crime placed him among those who mourn. Rather than giving in to bitterness or seeking retribution, he began a relationship with one of the young men involved in his son's slaying. Of those who participated in the murder, Ellis Curry showed genuine remorse. He served twelve years in prison for his part in the crime. After Curry's release, Mitchell invited him to a meeting of those trying to address Jacksonville's crime rate. Now Curry and Mitchell speak at schools, reaching out to at risk youth. Curry praises Mitchell's spirituality. Mitchell is among the merciful. He hungers and thirst for righteousness; he is a peacemaker. The sense of meaning he derives now from his work is a taste of the first marshmallow. In the dominion of God, he will be among those who inherit the earth.[2]

Let us choose the values of the dominion of God. Let us keep our faith if we do not experience our blessings now. Let us sustain those who are poor in spirit. Let us show mercy and make peace. Let us live out our faith, even if that leads to persecution. Let us enable each other to wait for the second marshmallow. Amen.

---

1. David Brooks, "Marshmallows and Public Policy," *The New York Times*, May 7, 2008 (Online). The name of the researcher was Walter Mischel.

2. Ron Word, "Man, Son's Killer Work to Stop Violence," AOL News, September 12, 2006.

Scaring The Church,
So It Will Be The Church

Sometimes when we read a passage of scripture, we may need to pay careful attention to who in the text is speaking. Our understanding of the words themselves may change, depending on whose mouth they come from. If we are reading Job, we need to know which character is speaking in the passage. If Job's friends are talking, we know their words cannot be trusted. They are too self-righteous. Sometimes, we are not sure who is speaking. Job 28 is a beautiful poem extolling the virtue of wisdom, but we can't be sure who delivers this elegant piece. The poem comes at the end of one of Job's speeches, but it isn't attributed to anyone. Whose viewpoint does it represent? Sometimes, it isn't clear where one character's words end and someone else's words begin. The third chapter of John begins with Jesus talking to Nicodemus. Do Jesus' words end at verse 15 or verse 21? When we come to John 3:16, the famous passage that reads, "For God so loved the world that he gave his only Son, so that everyone who believes in him may not perish but may have eternal life," is Jesus saying that to Nicodemus, or is the narrator saying that to us? Deciding who is speaking is important in reading scripture.

The question in the Sermon on the Mount is not who is speaking. Every now and then, we hear of a survey that tells us that a surprising percentage of people in the church do not know who preached the Sermon on the Mount. In case a surveyor ever asks you, the answer is Jesus. Jesus is speaking in this passage. The question is, who is listening? In Matthew's mind, to whom does Jesus preach the Sermon on the Mount? Matthew is not quite clear

77

about who the audience is. Matthew 5:1 says that Jesus saw the crowds, went up the mountain and sat down. Then Matthew tells us that the disciples came to him. What picture does Matthew want us to see in our minds? Do Jesus and the disciples go up the mountain to get away from the crowds? Are Jesus' words here intended only for the disciples? That's what the beginning of the sermon sounds like. What's confusing is that at the end of the Sermon on the Mount, Matthew tells us that the crowds were astounded at his teaching, for he taught them as one having authority, and not as their scribes. So, who was listening to the Sermon on the Mount? The answer to that question makes a difference in how we understand some of what Jesus teaches here.

When Jesus pronounces the beatitudes, he seems either to be speaking directly to the crowds, or at least with the crowds in mind. Before preaching the sermon, Jesus had been healing the crowds and casting out demons. When he blesses the poor in spirit, he has just been among the poor in spirit. When he blesses those who mourn, he has just finished wiping their tears. When he blesses the meek, he has just helped them rise to their feet, hold their heads up, and stick their chests out. Jesus' blessings are either to or for the crowds.

The whole sermon does not seem to be for the crowds. Jesus seems to direct much of the rest of the sermon to those who have made the decision to follow him. I wonder if Matthew presents Jesus as the kind of preacher we all have seen from time to time. Some preachers will turn to a particular group within the congregation, preaching part of the sermon to that group. If you ever have seen Dr. James Forbes, pastor of Riverside Church in New York City, preach, you know that he does that in his sermons. He will turn toward one group, or even one individual, and preach for a while. Then he will turn back and address the whole congregation. I wonder if Jesus changes the focus during different parts of the sermon. At first, he speaks with the crowds in mind. Then, maybe he changes focus and directs his words to the disciples. When he blesses those who are persecuted for following him, surely he has the disciples in mind. One might say that Jesus changes focus about halfway through the beatitudes. Certainly, by the time he begins verse 13, he speaks directly to the disciples. "You are the salt of the earth. You are the light of the world." He directs those words to the disciples, not to the crowds. The crowds at the foot of the mountain are part of the world. They are the ones who need salt and light. They are not the only ones. The Roman soldiers who bully the people need salt and light as well. Jesus narrows his focus. These words are not for the world, but for the church in the world. Jesus sets the tone for much of what follows. If the church is the salt and the light, then this is how you live. If the church is the salt and the light, then this is how to pray, how to give, how to act toward others, even how to think.

Matthew is the only gospel writer who puts these two metaphors — the church as both salt and light — side by side like this. These two images define what Matthew thinks the church should be in the world. As we try to understand what that means, maybe the best place to begin is not with what salt and light mean, but with what the world is like, with why the world needs salt and light to begin with. Scripture teaches us that the world is God's creation, and is inherently good (Genesis 1:31). Nevertheless, the creation is not what God intended for it to be. Sin has corrupted God's good creation. Matthew shows us some of that corruption in the narrative about Herod ordering the slaughter of the innocent babies in Bethlehem. Herod, operating out of fear, unleashes a cruel and brutal force that ends in grief and anguish. The world needs salt and light because the world is callous, fearful, and violent. It needs salt and light because it is full of grief, frustration, and powerlessness.

Jesus calls disciples out of the world to be the salt and the light. Jesus gives us these evocative images of salt and light, but never quite explains them. How is the church the salt of the earth? What does salt do for the earth? We can start with the most obvious thing: salt adds flavor. Towards the end of his long life, George Burns had to go on a salt-free diet because of his heart. He said that when he ate eggs without salt, the eggs were tasteless. He thought the chicken was overpaid! Many people find life to be without flavor, bland and uninteresting. The church as the salt shows them the joy and purpose of God's creation. We are the salt of the earth if we visit folks in nursing homes who are lonely and bored.

Salt is also a preservative. In Jesus' day, it was almost the only preservative available. The church keeps the world from destroying itself. If we are true to our task, we preserve the word of God's grace in a world that, like Herod, would try to stamp it out. We are the salt of the earth when we continue ministry in countries that try to prevent Christian preaching. Salt can also be an irritant. We have all heard the expression about pouring salt in a wound. When we speak prophetically, we are the salt of the earth that irritates the world's power. Peter Storey was a Methodist bishop in South Africa during apartheid. Before he was elected bishop, he was pastor of a large church in Johannesburg. He wanted to integrate his church, with all races welcome. Two hundred people left his church when he sought to integrate. By seeking to be the salt of the earth, Storey irritated those who wanted to maintain segregation in South Africa. Storey summarized the role of the church well. He said, "The richest gift the church can give the world is to be different from it."[1] We are the salt of the earth when we name oppression and injustice, even if it irritates the powerful.

The church as the light of the world is a more familiar image to us. God's first act of creation was to bring light into the darkness. The prophet Isaiah said that those who have walked in darkness have seen a great light (Isaiah 9:2). John said that the light has shined in the darkness and the darkness has not overcome it (John 1:5). Light in darkness enables us to see and we are grateful for that. The church shines the light in the darkness so that the world can see. The world needs to see God and to see grace and hope. Light also shows us our sinfulness. No evildoer wants the glare of light. The church shines the light in the midst of fear, hatred, and violence so that the world can see the way out.

What will motivate the church to be the salt and the light? Will we fulfill our task only if we are frightened? Matthew adds a twist to this saying of Jesus. In Mark, Jesus asks essentially the same rhetorical question as in Matthew, "If salt has lost its saltiness, how can you season it?" (Mark 9:50). Matthew adds the phrase about throwing the salt out and trampling it underfoot. Matthew adds a little bit of a fear factor. If we don't fulfill our calling, we'll be thrown out and trampled underfoot. The image that comes to my mind is popcorn in a movie theatre. We walk over it to get to our seats. We crunch it under our shoes. If we don't fulfill our mission, we're like the salt on that popcorn.

We don't need to be frightened into being the salt and the light, do we? We can be the salt and the light out of joy and gratitude, can't we? We can live out our faith in the world. Our youth can set examples in their schools. Let us adults not forget how hard it is to live obediently in school today. I think sometimes that Jesus had an easier time with his temptations than today's teenagers do. Let's pray for and support our youth as they seek to be the salt and the light in their part of the world.

Bible scholar Gene Davenport reminds us that these word of Jesus about being the salt and the light are not exhortations or commands, they are declarations.[2] God has chosen us as the salt and the light. God works through us, maybe even in spite of ourselves. Let's show Jesus that we can be the salt and the light without the threat of being trampled on. Let us share the good news with the world. Let us offer grace to those who are down and out, the poor in spirit. Let us offer comfort to those who mourn. Let us stand up against injustice and oppression. Let us offer the word of grace to the poor as well as the rich.

Jesus tells us we are the salt and the light. The world needs us. Let us fulfill our calling. May Jesus know that when he preaches, we are listening. Amen.

---

1. Peter Storey, *With God in the Crucible: Preaching Costly Discipleship* (Nashville: Abingdon Press, 2002), p. 151.

2. Gene Davenport, *Into the Darkness: Discipleship in the Sermon on the Mount* (Nashville: Abingdon Press, 1988), p. 121.

Becoming Good Trees

Most pastors have seen the damage caused when a purple-faced preacher has sought to scare a person into faith. Pastors counsel with people even into their eighties and nineties who still have trouble feeling love from God because when they were children, someone had frightened them with images of an angry God, ready to smack them down if they didn't behave and believe. Parents will tell us of children coming home in tears from other churches. An adult had gotten in the face of a child demanding an answer to the questions, "What would happen to you if you died tonight?" That is not the most pastoral question to ask a six-year-old.

Fear alone is not a good basis for our faith. An irrational or excessive fear is especially destructive to genuine faith. We have to hold that thought in mind because in chapter 5 of Matthew, Jesus says some scary things. "For I tell you, unless your righteousness exceeds that of the scribes and Pharisees, you will never enter the kingdom of heaven" (Matthew 5:20). "But I say to you that if you are angry with a brother or sister, you will be liable to judgment" (Matthew 5:22). Throughout this chapter we encounter the language of judgment and exclusion. Jesus even holds out the threat of our whole body being thrown into hell (Matthew 5:30).

We must handle these words about judgment carefully. Because Matthew has given us these words, they are for our edification. Yet, they can be dangerous. When we read passages about harsh judgment, we want to avoid two pitfalls. On the one hand, we don't want to turn our faith into a guilt trip, heavy on the fear. A pastor friend of mine once met a man who actually did exactly

83

what verses 29 and 30 call us to do. Throughout his life he had struggled with mental illness. One night in a fit of depression he plucked out one eye and chopped off his right hand. His tragedy is an extreme example of taking these words of judgment too much to heart, of not hearing them in the context of the whole gospel message. We can misunderstand these words of judgment in other, less extreme ways. Many people cannot forgive themselves for their sins. They carry around a burden of unrelieved guilt. Some people cannot be honest with their anger. They paste a smile on their faces, but inside their emotions are churning away. They have read that the Bible forbids anger, so they convince themselves they are not angry. Guilt and fear over judgment can paralyze us. The other pitfall is to dismiss too easily the Bible's talk of judgment. We can assume that God is too indulgent to call us to account. That pitfall leaves our faith too shallow. It cannot lead us to repentance.

Not only does Matthew present us with frightening words of judgment, but the things this passage calls for seem impossible to fulfill. Our righteousness must exceed that of the scribes and Pharisees. We probably have such an image of the scribes and Pharisees as nit-picking legalists who always missed the forest for the trees that we don't hear what a tall order exceeding their righteousness is. The scribes and Pharisees were scrupulous in their religious life. They were thoroughly dedicated to living obedient lives, seeking to remain distinct from the world so that they could be God's chosen people. We should not dismiss their diligence lightly. When Jesus calls us to a righteousness exceeding theirs, he calls us to deep obedience. This passage calls us to go beyond merely checking off the performance of the written rules. We in the church must control even our thoughts and impulses. We must follow the law from the inside out. For the people of Israel and for us, the law was God's gift. The law teaches the people of God how to live, how to become the community of faith. Jesus says that he did not come to abolish the law, but to fulfill it (Matthew 5:17).

Let us look specifically at two of the things this passage calls us to do. Jesus reinterprets two of the Ten Commandments: You shall not murder and you shall not commit adultery. Both of these commandments prohibit actions. We can debate the meaning of these commandments, especially what the commandment for murder means about war and capital punishment. Once we decide on a meaning, however, we can determine clearly whether we have committed the act or not. We either obey the commandments as we understand them, or we don't. What Jesus calls for in this passage makes obedience that much more difficult. We must guard even our thoughts. How can we do that? How can we go through life without becoming angry? It seems a little unfair for Jesus to command us to guard our anger when he never had to drive on the expressway! Jesus can command us not to lust, but he never had to go the grocery store and see eight models on the cover of the *Sports Illustrated* swimsuit edition! The passage speaks specifically of male lust, but women are not exempt. One of the characters on *Grey's Anatomy* is nicknamed Dr. McDreamy! Jesus seems to have reinterpreted these commandments so that we need superhuman strength to fulfill them. We fight all the time for control of our emotions, especially anger and lust. After Jesus makes what seems like impossible demands, then he threatens us with punishment if we don't carry out his commands. If we aren't careful, we can end up in despair over this passage.

Even with all of this talk of obedience and judgment, Matthew knows that we are saved by grace not works. In chapter 20 he recounts the parable of the laborers in the vineyard. Some of the workers toil away in the heat for hours. Others work half a day. Some barely break a sweat in a short hour of work. At the end of the day, they all receive the same wage from the owner of the vineyard. That is grace. We do not earn the dominion of God by our obedience. We enter into it by God's gracious act in Jesus.

Matthew is not contradicting himself here with these calls to obedience and these words about judgment. Matthew is teaching us. Matthew is teaching us how to be the church, how to be the salt and the light (Matthew 5:13-16).

Perhaps these harsh words here are something like teaching music to children. Parents who encourage their children to learn music often have to be strict. It is stressful, but it can produce great rewards. One must nag, scold, cajole, and maybe even threaten in order to motivate a child to practice. Eventually, however, if all goes well (and it doesn't always) the child begins to develop some skill at music. Maybe the child hears a song on the radio and learns to play that song. A turning point occurs. After years of strong-arm tactics, the child begins to practice without scolding. The day finally arrives when the child sits down to play because making music brings joy.

If we are able to see Jesus' word here about judgment, prison, and the hell of fire in the context of grace, maybe we can see Jesus motivating us to a life of obedience. Impulses such as anger and lust can be so powerful that we may need something to get our attention. Jesus' long-term goal is our joy.

In an early scene of Plato's *Republic*, Socrates is at the home of Cephalus having a nice conversation. Cephalus is an old and wealthy man who lives in a suburb of Athens. Socrates asks him what he has learned after growing old. Socrates wants to know what awaits him. One of the things the man talks about is a quote from Sophocles, the author of Oedipus Rex. Sophocles said that when he became old he no longer felt the lusts of his youth. Being freed from his lust was like escaping from bondage to a raging madman![1]

Isn't it true? Don't our anger and lust control us and make us into people we don't really want to be? We know the psychological and medical reasons to control our anger. Anger clouds our judgment. Anger raises our blood pressure and constricts our blood vessels. We run the risk of heart attack and stroke if we don't control our anger. Anger and lust constrict our souls as well. Our anger keeps us from seeing other people as God's children. We do things we wouldn't do if we weren't angry. How much violence has been perpetrated, how many hate crimes have been committed because people couldn't control their anger? Our anger blocks our spiritual growth and our reception of God's grace. Our lust keeps us from seeing people as people. We reduce other people to body parts, assuming they exist for our pleasure. Lust makes us act in ways we never would if our minds were clear. Jesus really is offering us freedom. Freedom from the things that control us really is a joy.

If we look at this passage in light of the whole of Matthew's gospel we can see what Jesus really wants for us. In chapter 7 and in chapter 12 Jesus talks about good trees bearing good fruit (Matthew 7:17-20; 12:33-35). Only we know our thoughts, but our thoughts produce fruit. Jesus wants us to grow in grace so that we control our thoughts and impulses out of the goodness that has taken root in us. Then obedience becomes a joy, like playing music after years of practice becomes a joy.

We in the church support one another, pray for one another, and help each other to live out this new law that Jesus gives us. God's sanctifying grace and the Holy Spirit empowers us. We show the world that our emotions and our impulses do not control us. God's righteousness can go to the deepest part of our souls, transforming even our most basic emotions. Then we can bear good fruit. Then we can become the salt and the light. Then we can build our faith on love, not fear. Amen.

---

1. Plato, *The Republic of Plato*, translated with Introduction and Notes by Francis MacDonald Cornford (New York: Oxford University Press, 1960), pp. 4-5.

God's Weather Report

In the 1985 movie, *Witness*, Harrison Ford plays a tough Philadelphia detective who uncovers corruption within his department. To protect himself and a young boy who has witnessed a murder, Ford's character, John Book, hides out among the Pennsylvania Amish, the community from which the little boy comes. In one scene of the movie, Book and several of the Amish go into town for a day of shopping. While they are in town, the buggies driven by the Amish are involved in a traffic jam with a car. The occupants of the car emerge to confront the Amish in the buggies. With unwarranted hostility, they taunt one young Amish man. One of the men from the car, a young tough, smears ice cream in the Amish man's face. Ignoring the protests of an older Amish man, Book goes over to beat up the ruffians who have bullied the young Amish man. The older Amish man insists to Book that, "it's not our way." To which Book responds, "Yeah, but it's *my* way."

The scene from the movie helps us focus on the content of our passage of scripture for this morning. The Amish, a community in the Anabaptist tradition, sees the Sermon on the Mount as part of their core scripture. The reason the young man in the scene doesn't fight back against the bullies is that he is turning the other cheek, as Jesus said to do. In order to avoid violence, in order to avoid anyone getting hurt, he willingly accepts humiliation. When Jesus tells us to turn the other cheek in this passage, he almost certainly refers to how to respond to an insult, not to a situation of self-defense. The image is of someone giving the backhand to another

89

person on the right cheek, as a putdown. The bullies insult the Amish man, but didn't threaten to physically hurt him.

The progression of the scene in the movie, from the taunting to the ice cream in the face to Book punching out two of the bullies was designed to create in the viewers a sense of catharsis, a release of emotions. Watching the bullies pick on the Amish man creates a building anger inside of us. Something inside of us doesn't want them to get away with what they did. Something inside of us resists hearing and acting out what Jesus calls us to do in this passage. Something in us wants to be John Book, not the young Amish man. We don't want to turn the other cheek. We don't want to love our enemies.

In May of 2006, the whole country had to confront an enemy. His cold angry eyes stared at us from our newspapers and television sets. Zacarias Moussaoui was sentenced to life in prison. He was the only person tried in American courts for the terrorist attack on 9/11. Many people in our country, including many family members of the victims of 9/11, had hoped that the courts would sentence Moussaoui to death. Some people see a life sentence as an act of mercy. One juror kept Moussaoui from a death sentence. Technically, one of the issues was just how involved Moussaoui was in the 9/11 plot. Nevertheless, many people interpreted the jury's decision as a declaration that we in the United States are not ruled by vengeance. We can step back from our rage at 9/11 and make careful distinctions. We are angry over 9/11, but our anger doesn't control us.

We should be gratified that our system of justice is able to understand that Moussaoui is still a human being. Nevertheless, even though we in the church can affirm the mercy that our courts showed to Moussaoui, a situation like this always feels unfinished. Often when we show mercy, the person we show mercy to doesn't respond the way we hope they will. We like situations in which, when we show mercy, the other person has pangs of conscience, feels sorry, and becomes changed by our mercy. That doesn't always happen. Moussaoui is a good example. After the verdict, in which his life was spared, he gloated. He shouted out that he had won and America had lost. Not only does such an outburst increase our anger, but we may feel as though our mercy has been wasted. He didn't learn anything from our mercy. We might begin to wonder whether we can follow Jesus' teachings here. How can we let the bad guys gloat? How can we allow ourselves to appear weak?

We may need to go back to the beginning of the Sermon on the Mount. As you recall the Sermon begins with a series of blessings. These blessings sound strange to our ears. Blessed are the poor in spirit, blessed are those who mourn. The blessings are for those we do not at all see as blessed. They are blessed because of the dominion of God. When the dominion of God comes in it fullness, that's when the blessing will be fully realized. We have to wait for it. We have to resist our impulses, our emotions, and our urges for the sake of the dominion of God.

The church has two legitimate stances toward war: pacifism and just war theory. We cannot give a full account of both positions today. In the simplest terms, a pacifist believes that no situation justifies violence or war. A just war theorist believes that some use of violence and some acts of war are justified. The violence must be defensive, proportional, and a last resort, among other qualifications. A believer in just war thinks that sometimes countries need to use their military. Sometimes we have to defend ourselves, or our loved ones. We do need to resist the urge for vengeance. It is difficult to determine what exactly we should do in each situation. As best we can, we should resist violence. In the movie, *Witness*, many in the audience felt a catharsis when Harrison's Ford's character beat up the two bullies. Maybe, because of Christ, sometimes we must wait for that sense of catharsis, that release of emotions. At times, we must resist what we feel. Maybe all of our desire for justice, for people to learn their lesson, for things to be set right may have to wait for the dominion of God. We can work for change now, but peacefully.

Throughout the Sermon on the Mount, Jesus has taught us to resist what we feel. Jesus has taught us to resist our lust, our greed, our anger, our desire for security. We resist these things because we wait for God's blessings to come, for the dominion of God.

Now Jesus teaches us maybe the hardest thing of all: to love our enemies, to turn the other cheek. Jesus calls us to this teaching because of who God is. God makes the sun to rise on the evil and the good. God sends rain on the righteous and the unrighteous. Sun and rain are concrete. They bring life to our world. They provide our food. Sun and rain are also reminders of God's grace. God's grace is available to all. God's grace is available to bullies, to Zacarias Moussaoui, to the people who have hurt us. God offering grace to people who have hurt us does not mean God doesn't care about our pain. God offers us healing. Part of that healing is forgiveness.

Immaculee Ilibagiza was a 22-year-old university student in the 1990s when terrible violence broke out in her home country of Rwanda. Hutus killed her parents, her brothers, and hundreds of her Tutsi friends. A Hutu pastor, who risked his life to save her, hid her and six other women. They lived in a small bathroom, a wooden wardrobe covering the door. For three months, they endured hunger, fear, and the sounds of soldiers in the house unsuccessfully searching for Tutsis. In those cramped quarters, she began to pray the Rosary. Always she stumbled over the Lord's Prayer: "Forgive us our trespasses as we forgive those who trespass against us." She knew that the prayer called her to forgive those who had killed her family and endangered her. She didn't think she could do it, but she realized she was consumed by hate. She was afraid she would become like the people who had killed her family. Nevertheless, in her mind, forgiving her family's killers was like forgiving the devil. Finally, afraid that her hate would crush her heart, she asked God to forgive those who had done her so much harm. Slowly, with God's help, she was able to let go and forgive her family's killers. Eventually, she even visited one of her brother's killers in prison, taking his hand and offering forgiveness. She says that forgiveness saved her life. "It's a new life, almost like a resurrection."

Our passage ends with Jesus calling us to be prefect as God is perfect. That is not perfection as in not making mistakes. It is perfect as in being whole. We live in a broken, imperfect world. We will not all face the situation that Immaculee Ilibagiza faced. We will face challenges in showing love and offering forgiveness. We bear witness to the character of God, who causes the sun to shine on the good and the bad. We are the salt of the earth and the light of the world. We in the church show the world what it means to love, to forgive, to resist our feelings and our anger. We show the world that even with all of the brokenness, because of God, we can be whole. Amen.

---

1. Bob Smietana, "Woman Challenged to Forgive Massacre of Family in Rwanda," *United Methodist Reporter*, 152.51, April 28, 2006, p. 3A.

Choosing A Master

It was supposed to have been fun. No one was supposed to have gotten hurt. Little children haven't become greedy yet have they? A minor league baseball team in Michigan held a promotion after a game, dropping $1,000 in cash from a helicopter over the outfield. Then they let the children run after it. The air should have been filled with giggles as the children plucked dollar bills from the air and scooped them off the ground. No one expected cries of pain. No one expected the older, bigger children to trample over the smaller children just to snatch up a few extra greenbacks. No one expected a seven-year-old girl with a bloody lip, or a seven-year-old boy riding in an ambulance after being trampled by the other children.[1]

Greed can seep into the souls even of children. Larger children ran right over smaller ones, and didn't stop to help if they even noticed that the younger children were in trouble. We would assume that the older children would not have hurt the younger children under ordinary circumstances. Greed hurts people. Greed changes us into something we don't want to be.

Jesus had a lot to say about money, more than we usually think. How we handle our money is an important indicator of our faith and trust in God. What Jesus says here about money is as strong as anything he had to say. Jesus uses the language of slavery. Jesus' words suggest that we do not have a choice about being slaves. We are slaves one way or another. Our only choice is which master we will serve. The option we would most likely choose is the one Jesus is careful to eliminate. We cannot choose to have both God and money as our masters. We cannot truly serve God if we allow money to rule over us.

Jesus illustrates his point by talking not about money itself, but about two things money helps us attain: food and clothes. Both of these commodities are good in themselves. We need both of them, but our sinfulness, our pride, and our lack of self-control have corrupted our use of them.

I know I am inching out onto a limb to talk about food in a sermon. I risk offending people. I risk the charge of hypocrisy. I risk every eye following me at the next potluck supper! As a pastor, I have the responsibility of interpreting scripture, and of speaking the truth. The truth is that most of us do not have a good relationship with food, even if we think we do. I know that some of us would say that we get along just great with food. Some of us seem to have a great love affair with pizza. Still, it is a well-documented fact that we in this country do not handle food responsibly. Seven out of ten Americans are overweight. A growing number of children are overweight. I must preach about food because the statistics are dangerous. We have turned food, which should be nourishing and good for us, into a danger.

Now that I am at the end of that limb, I'm going to saw it off! We are not much better about food in the church. Seventy-six percent of clergy are overweight, a higher percentage than the general population. In one United Methodist Annual Conference, the bishop challenged the clergy to lose weight during Lent. She promised to donate $2 to the conference mission project for every pound the pastors lost. Four months later she wrote a check for $1,000. Sometimes we in the church enable one another in unhealthy eating, don't we? One pastor found help in his congregation. His physician ordered him to lose weight to bring down his blood pressure. He preached about his situation in a sermon. At the next church supper, four of the women in the church stood between him and the dessert table, arms folded. Now that's tough love![2]

I have no wish to be judgmental. I hope that what I am saying comes across as preaching for you, not at you. I know that losing weight is more difficult for some than for others. I know some people have a real problem with weight, enduring much teasing.

Nevertheless, our relationship with food affects our health and our self-image. Jesus raises the spiritual questions about food. Jesus tells us not to worry about food. Worrying about food affects our concentration on God. To be concerned about food means we are less concerned about God. If we always indulge ourselves, we forget about those who do not have enough food.

One Christian discipline that speaks to our relationship to food is fasting, denying ourselves food. Amy Johnson Frykholm has written about the spiritual rewards of fasting. She says, "Fasting as a spiritual practice is not about improving your health. It is not about becoming thinner, stronger, or more supple."[3] Her experience has led her to discover that fasting enables her to pay attention to her place in the larger world and to build compassion for people who have genuine problems with food. Her most important insight was that fasting freed her from compulsions about food. Fasting created room "where grace might flow." She begins to help us see what Jesus meant by slavery.[4]

If food can enslave us, Jesus tells us that our concern for clothing can enslave us as well. As with food, we have taken a necessity and turned it into a burden. Clothes are supposed to protect us from the elements. Clothes also protect our emotional vulnerability. As Adam and Even in the garden, we are ashamed if we don't wear them. Clothes are a necessity, but look at how they end up controlling us. Not only do we crave the latest fashions, but we even wear clothes that are uncomfortable just to be popular. We wear shoes that pinch or limit our mobility if that's what's in style. Men complain about having to wear neckties. Ties add color and beauty to a man's ensemble, but have you even noticed how much a tie looks like a leash?

More seriously, we judge people by the clothes they wear. We do this even in church. People often refuse to go back to a church if they feel their clothes do not fit in with the unofficial dress code of a congregation. Older members often complain about the way youth dress. No scripture verse tells us we must dress up for church. This passage points us away from worrying about how to dress for church.

Our youth may feel the burden of dress most acutely. Clothes are so serious for young people that we even hear of children having been shot for their athletic shoes. Our teenage girls feel the pressure to dress like pop stars, where the rule seems to be that the lower the jeans go the better. One youth minister holds retreats where the girls wear sweatshirts and sweatpants. Here's what she says about the retreats, "The girls breathe more easily, the burden of being cool and sexy having been lifted from their shoulders."[5] Did you hear how she talked about clothes: a *burden* lifted from their shoulders? I do not intend for this sermon to become a harangue about current teen fashion. Yet, is it not true that having to wear the right thing can make us feel trapped?

The youth group at a church in Virginia found a way to break the chains that clothes put on them. If any event in youth can become a burden, it is prom night. Every year the bar seems to be raised: the right dress, the right tux, the right limo. Everything becomes a contest. The youth at this church gathered up clothes, purses, shoes, and all of the other necessities for prom night. They shipped all of the gear to a community in Mississippi ravaged by the hurricanes. Prom became a joy rather than a burden.

Those youth understood the spirit of what Jesus teaches us in this passage. Jesus is not scolding; Jesus is offering us freedom. Jesus calls us to throw off the chains forged by money, clothes, and food. The youth in Virginia broke free by giving away instead of reaching for more. Jesus may have startled us by using the language of slavery, but he was right. Clothes, food, and money can trap us. Maybe we should say that our insecurity about these things trap us. Our trust in God enables us to break free.

A math professor in northern Virginia, Richard Semmler, has broken free from the hold money might have had on his life. Every year he gives away over half of his income. He makes decisions about where to live and what car to drive based on his commitment to give. His goal is to donate one million dollars before he retires. At 59, he has already given away almost $800,000. Not only does he give money, he gives his time, working on houses for Habitat for Humanity. He's a bachelor, and he makes a six-figure salary, so maybe he has an easier time than those with family obligations. Nevertheless, he shows us how to break free. His money doesn't control him. His friends and colleagues say he is always smiling. He has turned a burden back into a joy.[6]

Jesus tells us to seek first the dominion of God. The values of God's dominion include generosity, self-discipline, and love for others. In pursuing those values we find freedom from the things that enslave us. As an affirmation of the goodness of life, of stewardship for our bodies and as an expression of love to others, let us break free from our slavery to food, clothes, and money. Let us serve God. Amen.

---

1. "Two Kids Hurt in Money Drop at Minor League Game," AOL Sports News, April 16, 2006.

2. Both illustrations in this paragraph come from the article, "Clergy Choose Path to Fitness," by Bill Fentum in *The United Methodist Reporter*, July 14, 2006, pp. 1B-2B.

3. Amy Johnson Frykholm, "Soul Food: Why Fasting Makes Sense," *Christian Century* 122.5, March 8, 2005, p. 24.

4. *Ibid*, p. 25.

5. Chanon Ross, "Jesus Isn't Cool: Challenging Youth Ministry," *Christian Century* 122.18, September 6, 2005, p. 24.

6. Jacqueline L. Salmon, "Professor Finds Fulfillment in Emptying His Pockets," *Washington Post*, June 11, 2005, p. A1.

Epiphany 9
Ordinary Time 9
Matthew 7:21-29

What Storms Blow Away

A friend once pastored a church with a beautiful building. On a clear, sunny day, everything looked great: stone facade, majestic cross, and windows that were both shiny and clear. A hard rain exposed a flaw you couldn't see on a sunny day. The clear, shiny windows leaked. Right after a good rain, a dark semicircle of water marked the hallways by the windows. Those water stains were tattletales. The building was brand new. The building leaked, not because of age, but because of shoddy workmanship. The stains on the carpets pointed their fingers at the contractor. Any insistent storm peeled back the curtain and exposed a sin that no one could see in the sunshine.

Matthew closes out the Sermon on the Mount with a parable from Jesus about what happens after a storm. The parable tells us about two men who each built a house. One is wise; one is foolish. As a good rabbi, Jesus draws upon the wisdom tradition of Israel. The sages of Israel often make such comparisons. If we read the book of Proverbs, we see many sayings about wise and foolish people. "Fools show their anger at once, but the prudent ignore an insult" (Proverbs 12:16). The proverb tells us we can respond in one of two ways to an insult. Responding in anger is foolish; responding in serenity is wise.

Just so, Jesus calls one of the house-builders wise, the other foolish. On the surface, the parable seems like a no-brainer. Only an inexperienced fool would try to build a house on sand. Building on sand is easier than building on rock. The guy building on sand could finish more quickly and relax while the other poor guy was

101

still chipping away at the rock. The foolish builder doesn't see any problem with his house. Everything is fine until a storm comes. In just a few seconds, the house built on sand crashes down. The house built on rock, which took more effort, more time, more toil to build, stands fast. The details of the parable seem obvious to us.

What doesn't seem obvious to us is that building our faith is just as hard as building a house on rock. Do we not realize that the storms of life are coming? We should expect storms! The storms of life expose our weaknesses in faith just as surely as the rain exposed the shortcuts in the quality of the church windows. If our faith is shallow, if we have built our faith on sand, when trouble comes, our lives can collapse just as the house of the foolish builder. Nurturing our faith through prayer, scripture, the sacraments, and fellowship with other Christians will build us up to survive the storms that will come.

One of the storms that will come in life is grief. One way or another, grief will intrude into our lives. We will miss out on something that we desperately want. We will lose something we believe we cannot live without. Someone we love will die. Randy Cross, a United Methodist District Superintendent, says that grief can reveal the depth of our faith. After long years as a pastor, he has observed the difference between the grief experiences of those who have a strong faith and those who do not. From the initial impact of the death, through the planning of the funeral, some people have a "deep well" of faith from which to draw in the experience of grief. Cross writes, "The deep well folks still felt profound grief and loss ... but they also expressed trust in God's love and hope in Christ and faith in eternal life. However, families who had no real firsthand experience of faith and spiritual expression were often devastated by death and unable to be consoled."[1] The words of this experienced pastor are not a guilt trip to those who are struggling with grief. If we find ourselves in grief and realize that our faith is not as strong as it should be, we still can turn to God for help.

Storms reveal more than our personal weaknesses. Jesus' parable here seems almost uncannily similar to what happened in Hurricane Katrina. The storm exposed how unprepared and shortsighted the United States had been. We had not heeded the warnings that a storm like Katrina could hit the gulf coast. Even more troubling was the social inequalities that Katrina laid bare. The rich and well-to-do fared much better in the storm's aftermath than the poor did. The racism and classism had been there all along, but the storm forced us to see some things to which we had closed our eyes. If we in this country are wise, we will respond to the devastation of Katrina with the pursuit of justice for all people.

When Jesus tells us that storms are coming, he means not just the everyday storms of life, both real and metaphorical. He holds before us also the storm of God's judgment. That storm is coming. We cannot hold it back any more than we could shoo away a hurricane. In the first part of our passage, Jesus uses the term, "that day." He means the day of judgment. What Jesus says about "that day" sounds even more devastating than the storm. On "that day," the risen Christ may look at us with a puzzled expression — the same one we get when an old acquaintance doesn't recognize us — and claim not to know us. We should be careful here. The ones Jesus doesn't recognize are not the folks who sleep in on Sunday mornings and have no use for the church. The ones Jesus doesn't recognize are the ones who have called him "Lord, Lord!" Calling Jesus "Lord" in the Roman Empire was a risky thing to do. You were claiming your allegiance to Jesus and not to Caesar. These frightening words of Jesus are not merely a warning against simply paying "lip service" to Jesus and his church. The ones Jesus doesn't recognize are the ones who cast out demons. They confronted the evil of the world and won a victory. Still, the risen Christ just can't put name to face for them.

These final words of the Sermon on the Mount warn us about our lack of faith, and about the ways we deceive ourselves about our faith. The sermon has been calling us to a deeper faith. It has been calling us to genuine prayer, to sacrificial giving, to radical love, to tamed impulses. It calls us to forgive those we think we could never forgive. It calls us to shun status and prestige. Some Christians have looked at the demands of the sermon and wondered how anyone could ever measure up. Who can triumph over lustful thoughts? Who can banish anger? Who can forgive those who truly have hurt us? Who can shut off worries about tomorrow, about having enough food and enough money? It seems as though Jesus calls us to do what is impossible, and then threatens us with a storm if we can't do it. Why is Jesus so harsh?

Jesus is harsh with us because Jesus is preparing us for the dominion (or kingdom) of heaven. Jesus is harsh because we are too willing to let ourselves slide. We are too willing to accept easy answers. We are too attracted to a faith that just makes us feel good. Jesus tells the ones with a shallow faith that they will not enter the kingdom of heaven (7:21). We know that the dominion of heaven is available to us because of grace. We do not earn our way into it. Nevertheless, getting in is not all there is to it. Imagine a person who had never studied music, but wanted to enroll in Juilliard, the prestigious music school. If this untrained person had a friend on the admissions committee, perhaps a sneaky admission could be arranged. The first day of class, when the professor asked the new student to sight-read a difficult piece, would expose the fact that the person was not prepared for Juilliard. Preparing for the dominion of God is hard work, like building a house on rock.

We enter the dominion of heaven by grace. Jesus is preparing the church for life in the dominion of heaven and to bear witness to the world about the dominion of heaven. In order to do that, we must live our lives as a reflection of the dominion of heaven. We are the salt and the light. God's grace enables us to live that kind of life, as individuals and as the church. We live in forgiveness, in love, in faith. With God's help, we become those whom Jesus will know. Our faith works on us from the inside out. God recreates us.

What might such a life look like? Reverend Kathleen Baskin-Ball, a United Methodist pastor from Texas, found out in January of 2007 that she had cancer in her chest cavity and liver. Just in her forties, with a young son, Kathleen's faith held firm. Here is what she wrote to her congregation, "My faith does not waver even in the midst of such serious news, and Bill [her husband] and I continue to believe that God, who is always good, will indeed work for good in the days and months ahead. We are saddened and afraid, but no less faithful in believing that God will somehow bring blessing in the midst of cancer."[2] That is a faith that comes from the inside out. It is the faith of a good tree bearing good fruit (Matthew 7:18). It is faith built on rock. It is a faith that stands up to the storms of life. It is a faith preparing us for "that day," when we will see the risen Christ face-to-face. Amen.

---

1. *Adult Bible Studies*, "Living in and as God's Creation," United Methodist Publishing House, 38.3, April 16, 2006, p. 51.

2. From a pastoral letter to Suncreek United Methodist Church, Allen, Texas, dated January 4, 2007.

The Transfiguration Of Our Lord
(Last Sunday After Epiphany)
Matthew 17:1-9

Sneak Preview

How much do we miss when we don't really look? Edgar Allan Poe explores that question in his short story, *The Purloined Letter*. As the story begins, two men are sitting in an apartment in Paris smoking their pipes and enjoying each other's company. They are not much for conversation; they go for an hour at a time without saying anything. One of the two men is the brilliant detective, Auguste Dupin, who had earlier solved the Rue Morgue murders. A police inspector drops by. Clearly agitated and anxious he confides in the two pipe smokers and seeks their help. A thief has stolen a letter from an aristocratic woman. The letter contains information that the woman must keep secret. If the thief were to expose the contents of the letter, the woman would be ruined. She knows who stole the letter because the thief took it right in front of her. She could not stop him because the person from whom she most wanted the contents of the letter hidden was also in the room when the thief pirated the letter. The woman has reported the incident to the police inspector and charged him with retrieving the letter without attracting too much attention. In desperation, the inspector has come to Dupin and his friend, the narrator of the story, to ask advice.

The two men try to help, but the inspector has tried every suggestion they offer. He knows that the thief has hidden the letter somewhere in his own apartment. The inspector has the proper tools to enter the apartment when the thief is away. The methods of the inspector are meticulous. He has examined every brick in the yard of the man's apartment. He has poked needles into the upholstery. He has examined every stick of furniture with a microscope to look for the tiniest clue that indicates the letter might be hidden in a hollowed out chair back. He has looked behind mirrors and under carpets. He has turned each page of every book in the thief's private library. The inspector knows that the thief is playing with him, going out of the apartment frequently to give the inspector another chance to experience frustration. Despite looking in every possible hiding place, the inspector has come away empty-handed. Finally, Dupin and his friend have exhausted every suggestion. The inspector leaves with his shoulders drooping.

A month later, the inspector returns to the apartment of the two pipe smokers to see if they have come up with any new ideas. Dupin asks nonchalantly how much of a reward the inspector would offer for the recovery of the letter. He blurts out the sum of 50,000 francs. With that offer on the table, the brilliant detective replies to the effect that he would like that amount in a check! Astonished, the inspector writes a check for 50,000 francs. Dupin then unlocks a drawer and hands the precious letter to the inspector. At first, the inspector is speechless, but then he stumbles out the door in what Poe calls, "a perfect agony of joy."[1]

Dupin's friend is as astounded as the inspector. Dupin then explains that he knew the character of the letter thief, and suspected what he had done with the letter. Under the pretense of a social call, Dupin had gone to his apartment. He had hired a man to fire off a musket at an agreed upon time. When the letter thief ran to the window to see what the commotion was about, Dupin retrieved the stolen letter, replacing it with a facsimile. The letter was where Dupin had spied it on a previous visit: right out in plain sight. The thief had marked the letter up a bit, torn the envelope, put a few smudges on it, so that it looked like an ordinary letter to the unobservant eye. Dupin recognized that the letter looked too worn, too dirty, compared with the other articles in the plain card rack where the thief had kept the letter. The letter had been there the whole time, but the inspector didn't have eyes to see it.

Do Peter, James, and John have eyes to see God right in front of them? Peter, James, and John are the three insiders among Jesus' disciples. They were three of the first four whom Jesus called. The way Matthew portrays it, they didn't hesitate to follow Jesus when he called (Matthew 4:18-22). All three were busy in the fishing industry when Jesus called, but all three dropped what they were doing to follow when Jesus called, seemingly out of the blue. They have seen and heard enough by this point that maybe the interruption in their careers has been worth the sacrifice. What they see now surpasses all of it.

Jesus leads the three of them up a high mountain. Just from making the climb they know something is about to happen. Surely, they were not prepared for what they saw. Jesus' face shown like the sun and his clothes turned dazzling white. Moses and Elijah show up. Everything added up for Peter, James, and John. They may have been terrified, but everything added up. Jesus' face shone just as Moses' face had shone when he ascended Mount Sinai and spoke with God (Exodus 34). Moses and Elijah appearing on the mountain with Jesus meant that the law and the prophets were represented. Everyone expected Elijah to come back; he had been taken up into heaven. Even the cloud that surrounded the three startled disciples was a sign of God's presence. Here on this mountain, as terrified as they were, the three disciples saw all the evidence they needed that God was working through Jesus. God's presence could not have been more obvious.

God's presence is anything but obvious for most of us. Where is God in the brutality of war, or the political corruption everywhere we look? Where is God when hurricanes and tsunamis wipe out hundreds of lives overnight? Where is God with all of the competing religions, each claiming to hold the truth? Where is God in the everyday dreariness of life? Where is God in our personal grief that never makes it to the headlines?

With all of the things that seem to deny God's existence, or at least our ability to see God, we might wish we could have an experience like Peter, James, and John had. If only God would appear to us in an unmistakable way, leaving no doubt that God was behind the experience. Even if this vision of God terrified us, it would be worth it, just to know God was there. It didn't work that way for Peter, James, and John. This experience on the mountain did not take away the ambition of James and John. They and their mother wanted a special place in Jesus' glory (Matthew 20:20). Having seen Jesus all aglow didn't satisfy them. It didn't take away their hunger for recognition. We know about Peter. Even the transfiguration itself didn't heal his doubt. He cowered in denial at Jesus' arrest as though he had seen nothing (Matthew 26:69-74). For all of its dramatic power, the transfiguration didn't redeem either the ambition of James and John, or the cowardice of Peter. Even the sight of the resurrected Jesus was not a foolproof experience for some of Jesus' followers. Matthew tells us that some of the eleven disciples doubted, even on the mountain where Jesus spoke to them after the resurrection (Matthew 28:17).

The transfiguration was a kind of sneak preview of Jesus' resurrection power. Only three of Jesus' disciples saw the transfiguration. Even that viewing did not solve all of their problems, remove all of their doubts or heal the insecurities that lead to ambition. As much as we might wish for a dramatic display of God's power and presence we will not receive one. We must build our faith on the evidence of God's presence that we have.

We must look for God the way Dupin looked for the purloined letter. We must look for God's presence in what appears to be something ordinary. If we cannot understand how God is present in a world full of violence, maybe we can see God in the people of quiet courage who try to make peace in the midst of war, gang violence, and genocide. If we cannot find God in a world with hurricanes and tsunamis, maybe we can see God in the people who reach out in love to those who have lost everything. If we cannot find God in a world where children die of cancer, maybe we can see God in the courage those children often show. If we cannot find God in a world of competing religions, maybe we can see God in those who choose dialogue to find wisdom in other faith traditions. If we cannot see God because of our own individual pain, maybe we can find God in those who care for us and keep our hopes up. These experiences are not clear and unmistakable evidence of God among us, yet they can be a kind of transfiguration for us. In these experiences we can see God's grace and power shining through the darkness of the world.

All of us in this congregation pray that the church can become a kind of transfiguration. We hope that in our worship, in our service to the world, in our care for one another, we can reveal God more clearly to a world that is searching for God. Poe's inspector had nearly given up looking for the stolen letter. Just so, many have nearly given up hope of finding God. May this church reveal God to them. For those who cannot see God through the fog of their pain, may this church reveal God. For those who have known only a distorted view of God as too judgmental, too punitive, may this church reveal God. For those who think they have no need of God, who think they can get by without God, may this church reveal God. Let us reveal enough of God for people to begin their journey of faith. Let us go out into the world and be the transfiguration for others. Amen.

_____

1. Edgar Allan Poe, *The Purloined Letter, The Murders in the Rue Morgue* (New York: Franklin Watts, Inc., 1966), p. 69.

Sermons On The Gospel Readings

For Sundays In
Lent And Easter

Return To The Lord,
Your God

Lee Griess

Return To The Lord, Your God

Every once in a while a whimsical story makes the news. A couple of years ago, the Associated Press carried a story about a woman in Olney, England, named Dawn Gallyot who defied snow and a biting wind to beat seven other women to the finish line in the annual Shrove Tuesday pancake race. In her first race, the 38-year-old school teacher made the 415-yard dash from a pub in the market square to the Church of St. Peter and St. Paul with a pancake and a frying pan in her hand in 73 seconds. That was 9.5 seconds slower than the previous year's pace. Each woman must flip a pancake in the frying pan at the start and at the finish of the race. The record is 58 seconds. Mrs. Gallyot reportedly wore a traditional headscarf and apron, but opted for modern running shoes.

Shrove Tuesday, known in England as Pancake Day, is traditionally the last day for merrymaking before the start of Lent. Pancakes are thought to be a good way to get in the eggs and fat that faithful church people were supposed to give up for Lent. Legend has it that the Olney race started in 1445 when a housewife, dashing to get to church on time, arrived at the service clutching in her hand a frying pan with a pancake still in it.

The pancake race is but one of many traditions that have grown up around the season of Lent. New Orleans' Mardi Gras is another — one last blow-out before a season of denial. Throughout the years, Lent has become associated with fasting and denial. Even today many people talk about giving up something during Lent.

115

Some stop eating meat. Some give up coffee. For others it's choco-late or desserts. And that's all well and good, but the real intent of Lent is that should we look within. We should change our hearts and not our diets.

That's what Jesus means when he talks about fasting in the passage from Matthew. Remember what he said? "When you fast, don't look somber as the hypocrites do for they disfigure their faces to show others they are fasting. For I tell you, they have already received their reward." God doesn't want an outward display from us. God doesn't want us to change our eating habits. God wants us to change our hearts. God wants a change within. The Old Testa-ment prophet Joel puts it well when he says, " 'Even now,' says the Lord, 'return to me with all your heart, with fasting and weeping and mourning.' Rend your heart and not your garments."

The first task of Lent is not fasting or alms giving. It's not giving up sweets or going off fatty foods. It is repentance — re-pentance that brings us before the Lord with penitent, contrite hearts. That's what Jesus is saying in the passage from Matthew. "Don't put on a show with your acts of righteousness ... Don't even let your left hand know what your right hand is doing ... And when you fast, do it in secret. For your Father who knows what is done in secret will reward you." Lent tells us to repent of our sin-fulness; to look within and purify our hearts. As the prophet Joel says, "Return to the Lord, your God...." Repent of your sinfulness. Turn back, change directions, make a new start from an old life and do so without making a show of it.

As we begin this season of Lent, we are invited to bring our sins and lay them before the throne of God. We are invited to un-burden our souls in repentance. We are directed to come before the Lord our God with open hearts and make a new start within.

Sometime ago, I read an article in the newspaper about a man who walked into the Sacramento Police Headquarters and con-fessed to a crime he had committed fifteen years before. Accord-ing to the article, the police were dumbfounded. They had no record of the crime and certainly no active investigation of it. In fact, the crime was so insignificant that they refused to even prosecute the man. And yet, the man insisted that he be charged with the crime so that he could "do the time." The reason for his confession? He said, "I just haven't been able to get it off my mind." Now here was a man willing to subject himself to punishment in order to restore his peace of mind.

And that's what God has in mind for us when he says, "Return to the Lord, your God...." Return. Turn back. Repent and begin a new life. Lent is a time of repentance, a time for confession and the beginning of a new life. Because, as the prophet Joel tells us, "God is gracious and merciful, slow to anger and abounding in steadfast love."

Now, repentance does little good if its only purpose is to show off. Repentance has no reward if it is done as a public display of our righteousness. That's what Jesus warns us of when he says: "Let your acts of righteousness be done in secret ... Let your fasting be done in private ... For your Father who sees what is done in secret will reward you."

Lent is a time, not only of repentance, but also of forgiveness (the word we use in church is "absolution"). Lent tells us that God so loved the world that he gave up his only Son on a cross for us that through that one man's death, God might grant us forgiveness. Jesus reminds us that our God, who is unseen, will reward our penitent hearts. God will see within.

An old Scottish clergyman once said that the devil really has only two lies to tell us. The first lie the devil tells us comes before we commit a sin when the devil says that it doesn't matter what we do for no one will know. The second lie the devil tells us comes after we've sinned when the devil tells us that no one can forgive us what we have done.

Lent is not only a time of repentance. It is also a time of forgiveness. Yes, Lent tells us that no sin is too little to go without notice, for we have a God who sees what is done in secret. But Lent also tells us that no sin is too great to be forgiven — for we have a God who can see within the heart. Lent is a time for repentance and forgiveness.

And there is one more point. Lent is also a time of renewal. Contrary to most people's opinion, Lent is a time of hope, a time of renewal, a time of refreshment. It is a time to turn over our

117

burdens to the Lord, knowing that God will receive them in forgiveness and love.

In the Musee de Chagall in the Mediterranean city of Nice hangs Marc Chagall's painting of *The Sacrifice of Isaac*, a favorite theme of the Jewish painter. The painting depicts Abraham as he is about to plunge the knife into the heart of his only son, Isaac. But an angel has seized his hand and off to the side of the stone altar that Isaac lies upon a ram has been caught by its horns in the bushes. God provided the sacrifice to take the boy's place. Up in the corner of the painting, however, is another figure. It is Jesus carrying his cross to Golgotha. It's an amazing picture, especially for a Jewish artist, and it is a theme for us in Lent.

Lent reminds us that there is one who bears our sins before the throne of God. There is one who hears the cries of our hearts and receives them. There is one who waits to welcome us home. That is why the prophet's words are so important for us. "Return to the Lord, your God." If we repent of our sins, there is a gift of forgiveness awaiting us. If we turn from our sinful ways, there is a heavenly Father waiting to welcome us home. On this Ash Wednesday when we bear on our brows the ashen mark of our sins, let us heed the prophet's words. Let us turn to the Lord our God that the ashes of our sins be so compressed by the grace of God that we might sparkle like diamonds in the crown of the Lord, our God. In Jesus' name. Amen.

Lent 1
Matthew 4:1-11

Strong In God's Name

A young man was sent to Spain by his company to work in a new office they were opening there. He accepted the assignment because it would enable him to earn enough money to marry his long-time girlfriend. The plan was to pool their money and, when he returned, put a down-payment on a house, and get married. As he bid his sweetheart farewell at the airport, he promised to write her every day and keep in touch. However, as the lonely weeks slowly slipped by, his letters came less and less often and his girlfriend back home began to have her doubts. "Spain is filled with beautiful women," she wrote, "and after all you are a handsome man." When he received that letter, the young man wrote her right back declaring that he was paying absolutely no attention to the local girls. "I admit," he wrote, "that I am tempted. But I find myself so busy with my work that I have no time for such foolishness."

However, in the very next mail delivery, the young man received a package from his sweetheart. It contained a harmonica and a note. "I'm sending you this harmonica," his girlfriend wrote, "so you will have something to take your mind off those girls." The young man wrote her back, thanking her for the gift and promising her that he would practice the harmonica every night and think only of her.

Finally, after months of waiting, the day came for him to return to the States and his sweetheart was waiting for him at the airport. As he rushed forward to embrace her, she held up a restraining hand and said sternly, "Hold on there. First, I want to hear that harmonica!"

119

She was a wise young lady. She knew the power of temptation and the weakness of the human heart. And so did Jesus. Our subject this morning is just that — temptation. The gospel reading for today begins by telling us that "Jesus, full of the Holy Spirit, returned from the Jordan and was led by the Spirit into the wilderness, where for forty days he was tempted by the devil."

We begin with the story of Jesus in the wilderness. We begin our observance of Lent as we always do with the topic of temptation. For it is no stranger to any of us. Temptation is part and parcel of the human condition. Someone once said that, ever since Adam and Eve fell into sin, "forbidden fruit has led to many a bad jam." Temptation. We know what temptation is for we all experience it. And we do ourselves an injustice when we minimize it.

Temptation is like a wedge. In the world of physics, in the mechanical world, there is no more powerful application than the wedge. Once you get it's thin edge in, it's only a matter of time and force how far the wedge can split things apart. The hardest stone, the toughest wood — no matter what it is — nothing is able to resist the power of the wedge to drive it apart.

Many years ago, a large fishing boat sprung a leak. Bringing it in for repairs, the owners discovered that in the depths of its hull, a hammer had been left in the bottom of the boat when it was built. Over the years, the constant motion of the ship had caused the hammer to shift back and forth on the bottom of the hull until it had completely worn the metal away. It rubbed a hole in the boat and sprung a leak that, left unattended, would have sunk the boat. Temptation is like that. It is the wedge of the devil's desires that seeks to wear us down. Its constant rubbing hopes to wear us out. It is the shifting back and forth of sin that threatens to take us under.

But there is good news today. There is hope in dealing with temptation. There is help for those who battle with sin. For there is one who has faced temptation and overcome it. There is one who promises to strengthen us in our battle with the devil. There is one who stands ready to come to our aid.

The remedy to temptation is more than willpower. The key to overcoming the devil is more than to "just say no." It would be so easy if that were true. It would be so simple if that were so. But it isn't as simple as that. It isn't that easy to say no. Perhaps Mark Twain was right when he said: "I can resist anything except temptation."

Did you know that during the years of 1987 and 1990, eight million children disappeared in the United States? However, not one of them was abducted. Not one of them was kidnapped or harmed. No. Rather, in the year 1987 the Internal Revenue Service first began to require proof that children claimed as dependents actually existed. Beginning in 1987, Social Security numbers were required on tax returns when dependents were claimed. And suddenly, eight million children disappeared in America. Temptation. It is a constant companion and very real danger to everyone's life.

Jesus knew the power of temptation. He knew its allure for the human heart, and he knew the solution was not simply willpower. To be sure, it involves our will — the will to resist temptation, the will to do what is right, the will to live more closely with Jesus and be a child of God. For without that will power, without that resolve, there is no hope we can ever overcome temptation.

But the key to overcoming temptation is not our willpower but God's power. It is not our resolve, but God's Spirit. One of the greatest Christians who ever lived, the apostle Paul, knew this. Remember what he said, "Woe is me. I do not understand what I do. For what I want to do, I do not do. But only what I hate, I do ... Wretched man that I am. Who will rescue me from this sinful nature? Thanks be to God who gives us the victory through Jesus Christ my Lord!"

The key to dealing with temptation is not found within ourselves. If it were, Saint Paul would have found it. No. The key to overcoming temptation is found only in God. It is found only in allowing God's Spirit to fill the void within. It is found in allowing God's power to empower us.

In Homer's epic poem, *The Odyssey,* the sirens were mythical, evil creatures, half-bird and half-woman who lived on an island surrounded by jagged rocks. As ships approached the island, the sirens would sing a beautiful, seductive song that would lure the sailors to their death on the rocks. When Odysseus approached the island, he ordered his crew to fill their ears with wax to escape the tempter's songs. This done, he then commanded his men to bind him to the mast of the ship as they passed the island so that he could not change his orders.

That is one way to resist temptation, and it has been tried by many. Bind yourself up. Put wax in your ears. Close your eyes and cut yourself off from the world around you. Sounds great, except for one thing. It doesn't work because nobody wants to live that way and in fact, God doesn't expect us to. Luckily, there is another story from ancient Greek mythology that may be able to help us. It's about Orpheus, the Muse of Song, and about a time when his ship came near the sirens. Instead of putting wax in his sailors' ears and binding himself to the mast, Orpheus sang a song of his own — a song so beautiful and divine that his sailors could not hear the siren's song and be lured to their death. So they, too, passed by safely.

And that is a clue for us in resisting temptation. We need to fill our lives with a song so beautiful and divine that we will not hear the voice of the tempter as he whispers his evil words into our hearts. We need to fill our hearts and lives with the Word of God which is stronger than the devil's tempting. That's what Jesus did, isn't it? To each of the devil's temptations, Jesus relied on God's word to guide him. He centered his heart and life in God.

We can overcome temptation. We can overcome the devil's testing. We can confront Satan face to face and survive. But it starts with the heart, having our heart in the right place and filling our heart with the presence of God. So let me give you some very practical advice this morning about dealing with temptation.

First of all, never deal with temptation alone. That's where the devil wants to get you — alone in the wilderness. Jesus' wasn't alone — the Spirit who led him there to be tempted was there to help him. Never let the devil get you alone. Stay close to the family of God. Whenever you are tempted to let your worship attendance slide, to make commitments that keep you apart from church, resist them. They are the devil's way of pulling you apart and getting you alone. When you begin to think you don't need others, that people at church are just a bunch of hypocrites, or worse yet, when you begin to feel that you can be just as good a Christian without worship and fellowship, cast aside those thoughts. They are the devil's way of setting you up for a fall. Never deal with temptation alone.

Secondly, don't play with temptation. It's real and deadly. I think we often fool ourselves in thinking that temptation sneaks up on us. It can do that but it doesn't usually. Most often, temptation comes right to the front door and rings the bell. We know that it's wrong and we know we shouldn't be doing it. But we tell ourselves it doesn't matter. Or that nobody will know. Or worse yet, we try to convince ourselves that it really isn't wrong at all. Human beings have an incredible ability to rationalize our way into trouble. Recognize temptation when it comes calling and refuse to have anything to do with it. Nip it in the bud and avoid it from the start.

Third and finally, lean on God's help to deal with temptation. Remember that God wants us to live good lives, to do what is right and to experience the fullness of life — not the devil's empty promises. And because of that God stands ready to help in resisting temptation and in returning to God once we have fallen. At the end of the gospel reading today, the Bible tells us that God sent angels to minister to Jesus. They were there to help him and they are here for us as well. Be confident that God will help you. Our God is a God of love — a God who knows our weaknesses and our failings and loves us in spite of them. Trust that God will see you through any temptation that may come your way.

A group of mountain hikers came across an old woodsman with an axe on his shoulder. "Where are you going?" they asked him.

"I'm headed up the mountain to get some wood to repair my cabin."

"But why are you going up the mountain?" they asked incredulously. "There are plenty of trees all around us here."

"I know," he said, "but I need strong timber and it grows only on the highest elevations, where the trees are tested and toughened by the weather around them. The higher up you go, the stronger the timber grows."

And that is what God desires for us — that through the winds of trial and the storms of temptation we would grow strong and live on a higher level — strong to resist the devil's urging, strong to serve God, and strong as we stand together in faith and service to one another. Take my advice — stay close to each other, worship regularly and often, avoid temptation when it comes your way, and fill your hearts with God's word. Because if you do, you will grow strong; in Jesus' name. Amen.

Faith To Follow

How much faith does it take to follow? How much trust in God must we have? What does it mean to be part of the kingdom? How can we be born again? That's the question that Nicodemus asked. That's the theme for our time together this morning. How much faith does it take to follow? I came across an interesting idea this past week. I read an article about businesses that reward their employees when they make a mistake. Have you heard about this new trend?

A temporary office-help agency in Washington DC recently began offering a $100 bonus to the employee who makes the biggest mistake of the month. He doesn't get a reprimand. He doesn't get demoted. He gets a $100 bonus. I read about an executive for a company called Sara Lee Direct who thought he was getting a great deal on a shipment of belts, so he acted quickly and bought a whole warehouse full. Only later did he discover that what he bought was not manufacturing belts for the conveyor system at the factory, but a bunch of those three-inch-wide paisley belts from the 1960s. Instead of getting fired, he was awarded a bronze plaque that proudly commemorated the "Worst Buy of the Year."

When I read these stories, I had two reactions. My first was: Are these businesses nuts? Have they gone crazy, or what? And then my second thought was that maybe I could talk the church council into adopting a similar policy. Maybe there could be a bonus for the worst sermon of the month. I could use some extra cash!

125

Seriously though, there's a strategy behind rewarding mistakes. The president of that temporary help company explained it this way: "The object is to get people to take risks." An official at Sara Lee Direct where the employee got promoted instead of fired for making that terrible purchase put it this way, "If you don't go up to the plate and swing hard, you're never going to hit a home run. If you're not willing to make a mistake, you're not really trying."

The bottom-line is that risk-taking is the only road to success. And companies are finding that it's worth rewarding a few mistakes along the way if it encourages their people to take the kind of risks that can bring huge rewards. And the same is true for people of faith.

How much faith does it take to follow? How much risk are we willing to take? That's the crux of the discussion between Jesus and Nicodemus. That's what Jesus meant when he said you must be reborn. For birth is an inherently risky procedure. And if you don't believe that, ask any pregnant woman entering the labor and delivery room. In spite of the advances in prenatal care, in spite of the wonders of medical science, find me a woman who is not anxious as she is wheeled in to give birth. For every expectant mother knows that birth is a risky adventure. Because giving birth requires commitment. Giving birth requires all that we have.

With that in mind, Jesus tells Nicodemus that being part of the kingdom of God requires the same. Jesus tells Nicodemus that following God takes the same kind of commitment; that being part of the kingdom of God demands giving all that we have. Remember what Jesus said? "I assure you, unless you are born again, you can never see the kingdom of God." In other words, no one can be a follower of God unless he is willing to take a risk. No one can be part of the kingdom of God unless he is ready for commitment. We must be willing to let the old life go and trust in God for a new birth.

"You must be born again" is the way Jesus put it. You must take the risk to start again. For taking risks is the only way we grow — not only in business, but in our personal and spiritual life, as well. Either we take a reasonable risk and expand the horizons of our life, or we become stagnant and, in the end, live a life of regret.

Did you know that when people over the age of 95 are asked in a survey what changes they would make if they could live their life over again, one of the top three responses they always give is that they would take more risks. It seems that at age 95 people are more willing to be born again.

But you don't have to be 95 to look back on life and wish you'd been more of a risk-taker. Think back to high school days. Don't you wish you had taken the risk to try out for the school play or the cheerleading squad or the football team? When you look back on some of your friendships, don't you wish you'd taken the risk of being more honest and open with the people you love? Many of us can look back on businesses or investments or personal ventures and wish we'd hadn't played it so safe at the time.

No one can go back to seize opportunities time has already snatched away. No one can live life again. But we can go forward. We can take a risk of trusting Jesus. We can look to God to lead. So, let's take a moment and look at what risk is all about, and why spiritual risks are so well worth taking.

First, let's ask: What is risk? Well, risk is simply the ability to stretch beyond the usual limits in reaching for a goal. Risk involves facing a fear, chancing failure. Maybe it's the fear of the unknown, the uncomfortable, the unacquainted. Or maybe it's the fear of physical harm or emotional hurt. Whatever it is, risk always involves adventure.

When I was a child, I had a little, old motorcycle. It was primarily designed for off-road use, but sometimes I'd ride it on the streets of the town where I grew up. Going twenty miles an hour (because that's as fast as the old thing would go) down the smooth streets in town was pretty boring. There wasn't much risk involved in that. But when I'd take that old scooter of mine and go zipping off road, into the deep weeds, down twisting dirt trails, dodging trees and bushes — places where there was some risk of falling and going out of control — then riding became an adventure.

The same can be said for living a life of faith. It's when we face our fears and take a risk that we experience the thrill of following

Jesus. For faith and risk are intertwined. It is only when we stretch the horizons of our lives, it is only when we venture away from the comfortable to follow Christ that faith takes on its true dimension. That's what Jesus was trying to tell Nicodemus. You must be born again. You must risk a new beginning. You must trust yourself to a new birth in God to truly be part of the kingdom of God. As long as you hold on to the old, as long as you are afraid to follow, as long as you are unwilling to risk your life for God, you will not be part of God's great adventure.

And that adventure is all around us. For instance, when we follow God's teachings on honesty despite the fear of the price it may cost us, that's spiritual adventure. When we ask God to open doors for us to make a difference in the lives of others around us despite our fear of where that may lead us, that's spiritual adventure. When we talk to someone about our faith, in spite of our fear of what they may think of us because of it, that's spiritual adventure. When we think enough about God to want to be in worship in spite of the inconvenience it may cause us, that's spiritual adventure.

Those are the times when we leave the smooth, paved road, when we abandon the boring residential streets for the adventure of unmarked trails — that's when faith becomes real and that's the new birth that Jesus is promising us. Faith means being born again as a new person, leaving the comfortable behind to adventure with God.

Dear friends, God asks us to be risk-takers for Christ. God calls us to follow Jesus on paths that are unknown. God invites us to venture forth in faith beyond the ordinary and mundane. How much faith does it take to follow? In Matthew 17, verse 20, Jesus answers that question. He says, "If you have faith even as small as a mustard seed, you can say to this mountain: Move from here to there, and it will move. Nothing will be impossible for you." The question is *not* how *much* faith does it take to follow; it is whether we will use the faith we have. It is whether we will put our faith into practice and (ad)venture forth with God. The Bible says in Hebrews 11:6 that "God rewards those who seek him." Rewards come to those who take the risk of faith. Adventure awaits those who decide to follow. New life is ours when we consent to be born again. But the first step begins with us. We must take the risk.

Begin this morning by praying a new prayer to God. Begin by offering the prayer that Nicodemus was unable to make. Begin by saying, "God, I want to take the adventure of faith with you. I want the new beginning that comes with being born again. I want to get serious about my faith. Use me like you've never used me before."

This is the kind of prayer that says, "I want to be part of the action." This is the kind of prayer that says, "I want to grow in my faith." This is the kind of prayer that says, "I want a new birth in my following. I want to adventure with you, O God."

It's a risky prayer, I admit, and a prayer that God will answer differently for each person. For some, it will mean devoting ourselves to beginning a new routine of Bible reading and prayer, deepening our faith through spiritual discipline, committing ourselves to faithfully be present in worship and prayer.

For others, it will mean asking God to use us as a blessing in the lives of others, starting a conversation about values and faith, sharing our faith with others and helping them to new birth as well.

For some, it may mean that God has basic training in mind — time to get serious about Bible study and building a more solid foundation for our faith. It may mean setting aside some bad habit, or being more loving at home.

Friends, it's a risky topic this morning — this question about how much faith it takes to follow. Because it really isn't about how much faith we need to follow, but whether we'll use the faith we have. For when we ask God to use us, God will bring us a new beginning. God will give us a new birth.

Think of the alternatives before us — letting God give us a new birth in following Jesus, risking adventure with a faith that is alive, *or* living a comfortable life, maintaining a non-threatening existence, holding on to the old life that is ours. It's the choice that faced Nicodemus and the choice that faces each of us. But remember the choice we make determines the life we will live. Let me tell you what I mean.

The man looked around and saw people love each other. He saw that love made strenuous demands on them. It required sacrifice and self-denial. It produced arguments and anguish. It involved risk and hurt and the man decided that love cost too much. He decided not to allow himself to be hurt. The risk was too great.

The man looked around him and saw people strive for great goals. He saw men and women pursuing high ideals, but he saw that the striving was frequently mixed with disappointment and the ideals often carried a great cost. And the man decided that great goals and high ideals were too costly for him. He decided the risk was too great.

The man looked around and saw people serving others. He saw them giving money to the poor and spending time in their care. And he saw that the more they served, the more they were needed. He saw ungrateful receivers and tired out workers. And he decided not to waste his life with serving. The risk was too great.

And when the man died, he went up to heaven and offered his life to God. Undiminished, unburdened, unsoiled, his life was free of the hurts and worries of the world around him. The man said proudly to God, "This is my life, safely lived and risk free." And God replied, "What life? That's not life that you lived!"

How much faith does it take to follow? How much are you willing to risk? For however much you risk is how much your life is worth. Remember Jesus said, "I assure you, unless you are born again, you can never see the kingdom of God." In Jesus' name. Amen.

Streams Of Living Water

Streams of living water ... That's what the Son of God offered the Samaritan woman at the well, and that's what he offers us as well — streams of living water — life-giving, life-renewing, life-refreshing water that can satisfy those who drink so that we will never thirst again. We are offered water that satisfies our longings in life, water that nourishes our innermost selves, and water that comes from an active, living trust in God and a passionate faith in Christ.

We need this kind of water. We need this kind of trust in God. We need this kind of faith in Christ because without this living water, our lives are like a desert. The Old Testament prophet Jeremiah knew this and so he wrote in chapter 17 of his book the words of the Lord, saying, "I will condemn the person who turns away from me and put his trust in human things. He will be like a bush in the desert which grows in the dry wasteland on salty ground where nothing else grows. Nothing good will ever happen to that person." Wow! Pretty strong words, huh? Words that reflect the truth that without a living trust in God, without a passionate faith in Christ, our lives are like a desert. Eternally, ultimately speaking, nothing good will ever happen to us.

Living waters! That's what we need and that's what Jesus offers us this morning — living waters that can satisfy our thirst for life. He offers living waters that promise to give life to our faith — living waters that supply us with an endless source of strength and encouragement no matter what we face in life.

Yet, it is difficult for us to admit our thirst. It is difficult for us to admit our need. We are like the mouse in an old fable from India. It seems that there once was a mouse who was terrified of cats until a sorcerer agreed to transform the mouse into a cat. And that solved the fear of cats — until the cat met a dog. So the sorcerer changed the mouse-turned-cat into a dog. And that took care of that. No more worry about dogs, until the mouse-turned-cat-turned-dog met a tiger. So once again the sorcerer turned it into what it feared most. And once again it was content until the mouse-turned-cat-turned-dog-turned-tiger met a hunter and went back to the sorcerer again. This time, however, the sorcerer refused to help. "I will make you a mouse again," he said. "For though you have the body of a tiger, you have the heart of a mouse."

Do you understand what that old fable is saying? Do you see yourself in it? How many of us ignore the thirst within us by pretending it does not exist? How often do we tackle our anxieties or deal with our sinfulness by simply putting on a false exterior. We pretend that these weaknesses don't exist. We refuse to acknowledge them.

But inside of us still lies the heart of a mouse. We avow that our Christian faith is important to us. We say that we trust in God. We go through the motions of being religious, but we refuse to draw close enough to God to allow God to touch us and change our hearts inside. We attend church when we can. We open the hymnal and hold it in front of us. We hear to the pastor's words each Sunday, but inside a thousand other thoughts are running wild. The same self-righteous judging of others still plagues us. The same seeking and striving to be better than those around us continues. The same selfish nature still rules unchecked within our hearts and the seeds of faith planted within us never seem to take root.

We need living water. We need to draw close to God, open our hearts, and allow the waters of God's love to flow within us and nurture that fragile planting of faith into fruit.

For all too many, the choice is to satisfy thirst by drinking from the sugary fountains of the world around us. We dip our cups into the streams of modern life — we try to quench our thirst with the things around us. We try to fill ourselves with the drinks of power, possessions, and popularity. We think that personal pleasure can give us lasting satisfaction. We hope that power and prestige will fill us up.

But if power could produce peace of mind, then there ought to be a lot of contented people in Washington DC. If prestige could satisfy, then there ought to be a lot of satisfied people in Hollywood, California. And if possessions could produce happiness, then our world ought to be filled with nothing but joyful people, because no one can dispute that we have more possessions than any generation ever before us.

But we aren't happy and this world is not filled with satisfied, contented people. Because none of the "p" words — power, prestige, possessions, popularity, or personal pleasure — none of them can truly satisfy the thirst in our souls. Our thirst is for truth and meaning. Our search is for purpose in life that cannot be found in material possessions, carnal pleasure, or worldly power and prestige. Those streams do not contain living water. Those who drink from those streams will thirst again.

Nothing short of living water that flows from a real, living relationship with God can satisfy. Jeremiah knew that as well. In the same chapter, he writes, "Blessed are those who trust in the Lord, whose confidence is in God. They are like a tree planted by the water, which sends its roots out to the stream. It does not fear when heat comes; its leaves are always green. It has no worries in a year of drought and it never fails to bear fruit."

I don't know about you, but that's the kind of life that I want to live, that's the kind of faith I want to have. Those who drink of the living water that Jesus offers cannot fail. We are like a tree by the river that never dries up. The mercies of God are always present — our lives are safe in God.

Streams of living water. That's what Jesus offers us, a faith that is strong and active, a life that is steady and true. It's the kind of life that God wants us to live and it's the kind of life available to those who live by streams of living water.

And yet, how often we fail to do that. How often we refuse to send down roots. Instead of turning our hearts over to God, we just go through the motions. Instead of rooting ourselves in worship, we only come when we feel like it. Instead of disciplining our hearts and minds through scripture reading and prayer, we ignore God's word and only pray when we want something. Instead of flexing our spiritual muscles and exercising our faith through Christian service to others, we refuse to volunteer our time and keep to ourselves.

Streams of living water — we need them as badly as the woman at the well. We need to encounter Christ as badly as she did. Having gone through five husbands (and living with yet another as well) she was in search of something. Her life was empty inside. Looking for happiness in all the wrong places, her encounter with Christ was to be a life-changing event, for he offered her streams of living water. He gave her a new start on life. He offered her love and forgiveness and she was a new woman after having met him.

Streams of living water — that's what Jesus offers us today — streams of living water. There is a source of blessing in our world today. There is hope for every living thing, and it is faith in Christ Jesus. It is the living water he offers us. But we must send out our roots. We must risk and take God at God's word. We must say to ourselves, "Lord, I want that water. God, I want to drink."

I'm going to risk that you know what you say when you tell me to "love my neighbor." I'm going to trust that you know what's best when you tell me to "bear another's burdens." I'm going to believe you know what what's when you say, "It is more blessed to give than to receive."

Friends, it's time for us to take our faith seriously. It is time for us to dedicate ourselves to deepening our faith. It is time to send down our roots and its time to get passionate about our faith.

Jesus says to us, "If anyone is thirsty, let them come to me and drink." For I will give you streams of living waters. That is what Jesus offered the Samaritan woman and that's what he offers us as well: streams of living water that flow from his sufferings and death. Jesus offers streams of living water that bring us blessings and peace. In Jesus' name. Amen.

A God Who Suffers With Us

Sometimes you have to wonder. Sometimes all you can do is shake your head about the things people say and the things people think and the things they reveal to us about them.

A friend of mine has multiple sclerosis (MS), a chronic disease that gradually weakens and paralyzes the body. She tells me the things people say to her, the advice she gets, and you wouldn't believe it. Here a short sampling:

"You must really like being sick; you bring so much of it on yourself." That comment came to her from a close relative who has never so much as sent her a get-well card.

"The reason I have such good health is that I think right; nobody gets sick unless they think wrong." That came from another relative. Wouldn't you like to be in that family?

"I know just how you feel being crippled; I had a bad case of tennis elbow last month." Great, that helps a lot.

"Your present improvement is just wishful thinking." How's that for encouragement? Or, how about this one?

"God must really cherish you a lot to trust you with this burden."

The things people say and the things people think and the things they do reveal to us who they really are. The story from today's gospel reading is no exception. It all began with a question, seemingly a simple inquiry. "Who sinned," the disciples asked Jesus, "this man or his parents that he would be born blind?" A question, which on the surface seems simple enough, but when you think of it, how ridiculous it sounds. What kind of God did those disciples believe in? What kind of God did they follow? Did they really think that God looks down from heaven and says, "All right, fellow. I've seen you cheating on your taxes; I've seen you skipping church. So I've decided to make the precious baby of yours be born blind."

What kind of God would do that? Why would the disciples think that way? And yet as shocking as it sounds, many people view God in precisely those terms. The ancient Jews dealt with illness and suffering much differently than we do. In fact, it was common belief that illness and especially physical deformity were evidence of sinfulness and so upon seeing the blind man, the disciples naturally asked, "Who brought this suffering upon him? Was it something his parents had done that caused God to do this? Or did the man sin himself and cause it?"

To our modern ears, this line of questioning sounds incredible. We wonder who would think such a thing. And better yet, who hasn't? When tragedy strikes or when suffering comes calling, when misfortune hits or when death makes its solemn visit, who hasn't asked the question, "How come?" Who sinned? Whose fault is this? Why would God allow this to happen...?

For (we think):

- if God is in charge, how can this tragedy happen?
- if God is so loving, why must I suffer loss?
- if God is kind and all knowing, why not prevent this from happening?
- if God is almighty, all-powerful, all-loving (or all-whatever else) ... if God is any of these things or even just one of them, why should this happen?

Charles Hall blows up bombs for a living. He is a part of an EOD team — an Explosive Ordinance Demolitions team. He is paid $1,500 a week to walk the sands of post-war Iraq, to patrol the fields of war-torn Bosnia, or to search the killing fields of Cambodia for land mines, discarded grenades, and unexploded bombs. Richard Lowther is another EOD specialist. Together with Hall they have spent years blowing up thousands of deadly devices left

136

behind by the carnage of war. Hall often says, "Every time I pick up a newspaper and read of a war someplace, I think, 'Great. More work for us.'"

Now, you and I have a lot more in common with Hall and Lowther than you may think. Making our way through this world, journeying along the pathway of life can be just as treacherous as any trail through an abandoned mine field. The threat of violence or random crime, the anxiety of illness or suffering, the sudden grief of death and loss are just as much a part of our world as any remnant of war. For like that demolitions team, we often find ourselves in a mine field not of our making, in a battle with sickness that we did not cause, struggling against tragedy that is beyond our controlling.

And all too often when we come face to face with this minefield of life, we find ourselves asking (as did the disciples): How could God have let this happen? Who sinned? What did I do wrong? Today's scriptural question of the disciples is our question as well.

You see, from the time we are children onward, we learn to admire power. We stand in awe of things that are big and loud and mighty looking. We honor the victor. We congratulate the one who outsmarts the system. And with our gift of imagination, we project these images out beyond ourselves, magnify them to eternal dimensions, and call them "God."

- God, the most powerful of all.
- God, the mastermind of everything that is.
- God, the clever controller of everything that happens.
- God, who can do whatever we imagine.
- God, who can fix whatever that's wrong.

Get God on your side (we think) and you can't lose. Get God behind you (we believe) and everything will be all right. When we encounter illness or suffering, when we come face to face with tragedy; when we pray for healing or comfort, and it doesn't happen, out pops the question, "Who sinned?" What went wrong? How could this happen? For after all, if God were on his side, he wouldn't have been born blind.

137

Who sinned, this man or his parents? It's the difficult question of the problem of suffering, perhaps the most difficult question any human being can face. And we must be careful to avoid an easy answer. That's what the disciples did. Who sinned, they asked, this man or his parents? If only the answer were as simple as that. If only we could trace the source of suffering as directly as that. But we know it's not as easy as that. We know the answer is more difficult than that.

I read not long ago about a new digital recording device being marketed that allows the user to program it to record a movie and edit out the commercials at the same time. I'd get one, but I'm afraid I'd goof it up and record the commercials and edit out the program.

And yet, how often we wish our faith were like that digital recorder. We want easy answers for everything. We'd like to program out the unexplainable and attribute the good to God's will. We'd like to have life clearer, more easily understandable. But life is not like that. Bad things happen to good people. Some prayers are answered and others seemingly are not. People suffer. Misfortune happens. Tragedy strikes and we are left only with questions. As Saint Paul says, "We see in a mirror dimly ..." (1 Corinthians 13:12).

In the midst of a life filled with questions, in a world that often confounds us with no answer, we turn to the One whose love we can trust. In this season of Lent, we draw near the cross and there we are comforted. For ours is a God who suffers with us. Ours is a God who embraces our tears. Bishop John Baker says in his book, *The Foolishness of God*, that the only totally accurate picture of God that we have is the crucified Jesus. Or as another theologian puts it, "The only omnipotent power of God that really matters to us is God's almighty power of enduring love."

If God is in Jesus, if we believe that God was present in the sufferings and death of Christ, then we must believe that God is present with us in our suffering, as well. Remember how Jesus answered the disciples? Who sinned, he was asked. "Neither this man nor his parent sinned; he was born blind so that God's works might be revealed in him" (John 9:3). Somehow there is a purpose in this. Somehow God's mercy will be revealed. Now I don't know if the blind man was happy to hear that answer or not or if he even understood it. But I do know this. Jesus' answer can have deep meaning to us.

For when all is said and done, even as suffering, tragedy, misfortune, and loss remain a mystery for us, the source of healing, the source of comfort, the source of strength and hope need not be. For ours is a God who shares our suffering. Ours is a God whose love never ends. And ours is a God who stands within tragedy, who upholds us in loss.

Let me share with you a story that can perhaps help make this clear. The shock of the events of the past few hours overwhelmed Jim. His body was numb and while the world moved on, he felt detached from it. Jim and his wife, Connie, had just lost their beautiful four-month-old son to SIDS — Sudden Infant Death Syndrome.

Just the previous afternoon, Jim had driven to the babysitter's house to pick up Joshua. It was a routine trip he made five days a week after work. Routine, until he arrived and little Joshua could not be awakened from his nap. The next hours were a blur. Wailing sirens, swift-moving paramedics, emergency room doctors, and reassuring nurses. All efforts to revive little Joshua all failed. There was no brain activity and the decision was made to remove life support. Little Joshua was gone. Yes, they wanted all his organs donated. That was not a difficult decision. Other more difficult decisions awaited them.

Telephone calls, funeral plans, notifying family and friends. Strangely, for some reason, this morning Jim felt he needed a haircut and being new to the community, Jim's brother volunteered to call his hairdresser for an appointment. Her schedule was full, but after a few words of explanation, the salon owner said, "Send him right over. I'll work him in."

Exhausted from a night of no sleep, Jim settled into the chair and began to reflect on the events that had happened, desperate to have them make sense. How could this have happened? The questions kept coming; the pain was still there. Just then Jim remembered the words of the hospital chaplain, "Sometimes we just don't know what part we have in God's plans. Perhaps Joshua's part was already done."

The hairdresser expressed her sympathy and Jim found himself relating the events. Somehow it helped to tell the story. Perhaps if he did it enough, some sense would come of it. As Jim mentioned the organ donations, the hairdresser stopped, motionless. After a few moments she spoke, her voice barely a whisper. "You're not going to believe this," she said, "but only an hour ago the customer sitting in this very chair wanted me to hurry so she could get to Children's Hospital. She was so full of joy, said her prayers were answered. Her new baby granddaughter was receiving a desperately needed transplant, a heart valve that would save her life." And at that moment, Jim's healing began.

Jim's story echoes what Jesus tells us today. When heartache comes, as it surely will, when suffering and tragedy befall us as often happens, let us not cry, "Who sinned? Whose fault is this?" But let us by faith be drawn closer to God. Let us remember that we have a God who suffers with us, a God who shares our pain. In Jesus' name. Amen.

Set Free For Life

When the famous agnostic, Robert Ingersoll, died, the printed funeral program left this solemn instruction. It read: "There will be no singing." For without faith, few feel like singing in the face of death. Running, perhaps. Crying, certainly. But not singing. Not in the face of death. For without faith, death steals our reason to sing. Death takes the song off our lips and leaves in its place stilled tongues and tear-stained cheeks.

We know that is true, not only because we have experienced it, but also because we saw it happening in the gospel reading today. There was no singing at the funeral Jesus attended in Bethany, only mourning and weeping. Only wailing and crying, but no singing. The home of Mary and Martha was more like a prison than a home. People shuffled about aimlessly, their faces downcast, their eyes dulled by death. On their lips was no music or laughter, only the grief that reminded them of their loss. Another prisoner of sickness had been visited by the jailer of death. Another person caught in death's icy grip had been taken from them. Lazarus had died. Another was gone.

Shokoi Yokoi spent 28 years in a prison. Not a prison of walls, but a prison of fear. When the tide in World War II began to turn, Shokoi was a Japanese soldier on the island of Guam. Fearing that defeat meant certain capture and death at the hands of the American forces, Shokoi ran into the jungle and hid in a cave. He later learned that the war was over by reading one of the thousands of leaflets that were dropped into the jungle by American planes. But he still feared being taken prisoner, so he remained in his cave.

For over a quarter century, he came out only at night. He existed on frogs, rats, roaches, and mangoes. A few years back, some hunters discovered him and it was only after they sent to Japan for his aged commander to come and talk with him that they were able to convince him that it was safe to come out and return home. Twenty-eight years of living in a cave because he was afraid. Twenty-eight years lost because of fear. What a shame. How could a person be so foolish? How could a person be so imprisoned by fear? A life wasted because he was afraid to come out. A life lost. And it is all too common. The fear of death has filled thousands of prisons. You can't see the walls. You can't see the warden. You can't even see the locks, but you can see the prisoners.

You can see them every day around us as people slip their way through life around us, hoarding all they can get for themselves, grabbing for more and looking for meaning in things that are dead. People imprisoned by fear and hiding from life. Each under the same sentence. Each under the same fate. The Bible puts it this way: "All have sinned. All have fallen short of the glory of God." And all because, "The wages of sin are death."

Death is like a ball and chain tied to our leg. We can try to run from it, but we can't. Its weight is too heavy. It slows us down. We can try to pick it up and carry it with us, but we can not go far. Its burden is too great. We can try to ignore it, but it always drags us down. It may be a sudden sickness or the death of a loved one. It may be the doctor's diagnosis or the CAT-scan's result. Whatever it is, it reminds us that we are all under the same sentence of death.

Mary and Martha faced death that day. Their brother, Lazarus, had been seriously ill. They were two of Jesus' closest friends, so they sent for him. They had witnessed his healing power. They felt their brother would be in no danger if Jesus were near, so they called for him. We can appreciate those feelings, can't we? Who hasn't called upon the Lord in time of trouble? Who hasn't thought, "If only God would help."

But Jesus didn't come in time. In fact, by the time he made it to Bethany, Lazarus was already four days buried. Martha was wondering what kind of friend Jesus was. She had heard he was approaching town, so she stormed out to meet him. "Lord, if you'd only been here." If you'd only come sooner, "my brother would not have died." There is hurt in those words. Hurt and disappointment. The one person who could have made a difference, didn't, and Martha wants to know why.

And so do we. Perhaps we've done what Martha did — called upon the Lord and sought out healing, asked God for help and looked for Jesus to come. We can almost hear Martha, can't we? Surely he will come, surely he will help. Didn't he aide the paralytic? Didn't he cure the leper? Didn't he give sight to the blind and help the lame? And they hardly knew him. Surely he will come. Surely he will help.

But he didn't come. He didn't help. Lazarus got worse and Martha was left to watch and wait. And when Lazarus slipped into unconsciousness, getting weaker and worse, Martha whispered in his ear, "Hold on. Hold on. He will come. He will be here soon." But Jesus didn't come. He didn't help. And finally it was done. Lazarus died and four days later, Jesus came. And Martha is hurt.

And we know how she felt, for her words are our words. They have been echoed in the minds of countless people as they make their way to the graveside. "If only you had been here. If only you had helped ... my brother, my husband, my wife, my child, would have gotten well. If you were doing your part, God, none of this would have happened. If you were doing your part, Lord, we wouldn't be hurting like this."

Like the story today of Mary and Martha, the grave unearths our view of God. Death forces us to look deep within. When we come face to face with death, our view of God is challenged and we are forced to examine our faith. When we face death, we are forced to ask, "Where is God?" And yet, why do we think that when a person is not healed, that God is not near? Why do we interpret the presence of death with the absence of God?

Because that is how we think. As a result, when God doesn't answer prayers for healing, we think God's not near. As a result, when we experience death and sadness, we think that God doesn't care. And that isn't true. Listen to Jesus' conversation with Martha. As Martha rushes out to see Jesus, she says, "Lord, if you had been here, my brother would not have died. But even now, I know that God will give you whatever you ask." And Jesus says to her, "Your brother will rise again." She thinks he is talking about the resurrection on the last day. So Jesus has to clarify for her. He says, "I am the Resurrection and the Life. Those who believe in me, even though they die, will live. And everyone who lives and believes in me will never die." For death has never stood in the way of God. God is present even in the presence of death.

A few years back, after the first Persian Gulf War, Billy Graham held a crusade in Seattle. At the crusade, Shirley Lansing spoke to the crowds about the death of her son. "I come here with a story about my son, Warrant Officer John Morgan." Shirley told the crowd that her son, Jack, had been baptized as a child and had grown up in the church. "I guess he always believed in God but it didn't seem like a big deal until recently. A few weeks ago, two officers came to our door to inform us that he had been killed when his helicopter was shot down by enemy fire."

The most moving moment of Shirley's story came when she said, "I speak to you only from my heart. Only God can give me the strength to stand here before you and say these words. But it's so important that I speak them and it's so important that you listen. Each of you has the same decision to make that my son made — to believe in God or not. And now is the time for you to decide, for none of us knows how long we've got."

Three weeks before her son had been killed in action half a world away, he had written his family a letter to be opened "just in case." After receiving the devastating news of her son's death, Shirley and her family gathered together and read that letter. It was filled with John's reassuring words. He ended the letter with these words, "In case you have to open this letter, don't worry. I'm all right and I know something that you do not. I know what heaven is like."

Standing there before the grave of Lazarus, Jesus wept. He shed tears of sadness for the pain that Mary and Martha felt and he weeps tears for every family who have ever stood at the grave of a loved one. But he also sheds tears of frustration that we cannot see

144

beyond the grave, that we refuse to hear his words of comfort and peace, and that we think that death is the final word.

To prove once and for all that death has no power where he is present, Jesus cries out, "Lazarus, come out." It took only one call. It took only that one word and Lazarus heard his name. His eyes opened and his life returned. And rising from the grave, he came forth alive and well. And Jesus said to them, "Unbind him and let him go." For death cannot triumph where Jesus is present. God has the last word.

God wanted them to know and God wants us to know. Death cannot triumph where Jesus is present. For where Jesus is there is life. Isn't that what he says? "I am the resurrection and the life." Where Jesus is present, there is life. Where Jesus is present, we are set free. The keys to the prison are in Jesus' hand. Where Jesus is present, there is no need to fear. For death has no power over us. Through faith in Christ Jesus, we are set free.

Don Webb is the President Emeritus of Centenary College. He was born in Wales and served in the British navy before coming to America to begin his ministry. In the British navy he was named captain of the *H.M.S. Switha*. As captain, he wanted to impress the crew with how wise and brave he was. And the first assignment was to check the anchors that held the buoys in place and the only way to do that was to send a diver down to the ocean bottom in one of those big suits with the iron helmets and weights.

Webb was told that the previous captain always went down first. He felt he had to do the same. The only problem was that Webb had never gone deep-sea diving and knew nothing about it. However, rather than admit his weakness to the crew, he told them he would go. Scared to death, he put on the heavy suit with its thick gloves, leaded shoes, and huge helmet. As he reached the ocean floor, he began to panic. As he tried to take his first step, he realized his feet were stuck in the mud and instead of striding forward, he fell forward, face down in the muck. And worse yet, he let go of the lifeline. As he lay there in the mud, unable to move, he remembered the last thing the Navy ensign told him. "Sir, whatever you do, don't let go of the lifeline. And if you need help, just give it a tug."

"This is it," Webb thought. "I'm going to die down here, stuck in the mud, face down on the ocean floor. This is how it ends." However, after several minutes, which seemed like an eternity, Webb felt a gentle touch on his shoulder. The crew, sensing that he was in trouble, had sent down an experienced diver to pick him up, unstick him from the mud and get him back on his feet again.

In the same way, Jesus comes to us in our need. Jesus enters our world. He comes down to help us and he says, "I am the resurrection and the life. Those who believe in me, even though they die, will live, and everyone who lives and believes in me will never die." We need not fear death. We need not hide behind closed doors. For we have a friend who has come to help. We have a Savior who can rescue us from sin, the grave, and the power of death. He holds the keys to eternal life. Death cannot imprison us. In Jesus' name. Amen.

A Salvation Army Parade

Different churches celebrate Palm Sunday in different ways. At one church in Chicago, there is a tradition for worshipers to gather outside the church. Palm branches are distributed, and when the time comes, another group of worshipers emerge from the front doors playing instruments and together they march around the block, singing the songs of Palm Sunday. One year as the procession made its way around the block of the church building, a young man living in an apartment across the street, threw open the window and in his pajamas shouted, "What's all this noise? You sound like the Salvation Army." To which the pastor responded in a loud voice, "Son, we *are* the salvation army. Come down and join us!"

What better way to sum up the events of that first Palm Sunday than to call it a Salvation Army parade. A Salvation Army parade with Jesus as the grand marshall, and yet, his purpose in coming was not be the city's honoree. He knew he had a different calling. In the gospel account of the events, one cannot avoid thinking of Saint Paul's description of Jesus in Philippians. Paul writes of Jesus, "... who being in the very nature of God, did not consider equality with God a thing to be grasped, but made himself nothing, taking the very nature of a servant, being made in human likeness."

Even though the people along the parade route hailed Jesus as king, he did not consider himself one. Most Americans are unfamiliar with royalty. We only watch them from afar, fascinated by the pageantry which surround them. For even though we are skeptical of that form of government, we cannot help but be stirred by the majestic strains of "Pomp And Circumstance."

147

There is something overwhelming about power. There's something attractive about the majestic aura that surrounds a king. In fact, whether we agree with their politics or not, there is something awesome about being a president or prime minister or better yet, a king or a queen.

But not so with Jesus. For he knew the reason for his coming. Whereas royalty come determined to rule, Jesus came determined to serve. Whereas most monarchs spend time building their ego with the trappings of office, Jesus came in humility. Remember, this king chose his vehicle of transportation. Whereas royalty come on the back of a mighty stallion or in the luxury of a private jet, the Bible tells us this king came on the back of a donkey colt. Not a horse. A horse stands for war. Now, that may have been what the people wanted. A king to set them free, a leader to help them throw off the yoke of Rome. But this king came on a donkey colt, a symbol of meekness, peace, and humility. While most kings set themselves up to rule, Jesus came facing a cross.

Today is Palm Sunday and that same Salvation Army parade makes its way to us. The king is coming and we must respond. The parade approaches and we must decide. For the choice is ours to make. If we want to be bystanders — parade watchers — we can do that. If we want to be flag-waving Christians who go home after the parade, we can do that. Throw your offering in the offering plate, feel good about yourself, be at ease, and let the world move on. But today is Palm Sunday and the Salvation Army parade comes by. And that parade calls us to decide. We can be bystanders or we can be followers. We can watch from the sidelines or we can step out and follow.

For the king is coming, the parade approaches. That's one thing about this parade. No one can be neutral. We must decide. For the king has come and he brings us a choice. We can stand and wave, join the crowds that cheered him on that day, and watch him pass by. Or we can follow him wholly and stand with him at the cross. Remember: it's easy to shout but it's harder to serve.

Perhaps you've seen the old bumper sticker: "Honk if you love Jesus." Well, I saw a better one recently. It said, "Tithe if you love Jesus. Any fool can honk." Everybody loves a parade. Everybody loves to cheer. But Palm Sunday reminds us that Jesus came with a choice. The Salvation Army parade marches past and we must choose — to stand on the sideline and cheer as he passes by or join the small crowd of followers who marched with Jesus.

The great American humorist, Will Rogers, is said to have said, "Everybody wants to go to Rome to see where Saint Peter is buried, but nobody wants to live like him." The Palm Sunday Salvation Army parade marched Jesus' choice before us, a choice that required our dedicated devotion.

For if we choose to follow, we decide to give him our devotion. That's what it takes to be a Christian in today's world. It was that way in the beginning and it is the same today: twelve disciples with Jesus. And when he asked them to go into the village and find the donkey colt, they went — not as a bunch of tag-a-longs, but as eager followers — not as sometimes servers but as his constant companions. And even though they would sleep when they were told to stay awake, deny him when he needed their loyalty, flee when they were in danger, and even doubt his rising when they were told, they were still his faithful followers, those who had dedicated their lives to him. When Jesus marches past us, he doesn't look for bystanders. He looks for followers.

That's what Palm Sunday requires of us. That's what this Salvation Army parade Grand Marshall desires. If we choose to follow Jesus, we must give him our devotion. We must march to his destination. It's not easy to be a Christian in today's world. It's not easy to be a follower. Daily we are bombarded with a different message. Daily we are urged to march in a different direction. According to the world around us, life's goal is to be happy, satisfied, forever young and beautiful. And the way to achieve that goal is all around us — for a price. If we spend the money, heartache and heartburn need never be ours. If we buy the right product, popularity and success are assured. Daily we are told that our value and worth are easily determined — just look at what we eat, drink, drive, or wear.

But Jesus' parade marches in a different direction. This king offers a dangerous destiny. If we choose to step off the curb and give him our devotion, we could well be headed for trouble. For

149

following Jesus will lead us to service. It will require our love and devotion. It will demand our life and our time. Following Jesus in the Salvation Army parade may mean missing out on earthly pleasures, marching past this world's riches and rewards. For Jesus was on his way to the cross. Jesus was on his way to suffering and on his way to his Father's throne. When we follow Jesus and offer him our devotion, we march with Jesus to the Father's leading. For when we follow Jesus, we must give him our trust and our faith. Remember: it's easy to shout but harder to serve.

There is a story from the days of the Civil War about a woman who sat crying on a park bench outside the White House. Her son, upon hearing of the death of his father, had deserted his post in battle to return home and offer his mother comfort and support. However, upon arriving home, he was arrested and was now to be shot by a firing squad. The woman had come to the capitol to see President Lincoln in hopes that he might intervene on her behalf. However, to her dismay, she had been turned away at the gate. The president was too busy to see her, she was told. Unable to get past the front gates, she sat on the park bench off to the side, crying.

She sat in her tears watching people come and go. After a while, a young boy approached her and asked her why she was crying. Through her tears, she told him of her little boy, now sentenced to death. She ended by saying that all she wanted to do was to see the president, because she knew he was a fair man and her son would be pardoned.

To her great surprise, the little boy asked her to follow. As they approached the front gate, the little boy said to the soldier it was all right for them to enter. "She's with me," he said. To her amazement, they stepped aside and together they made their way into the White House past generals and cabinet officers. Finally, the little boy pushed inside the room, and running, he jumped on the president's lap. "Daddy," he said. "Here's a lady who needs to see you. She needs your help." The little boy who had stopped to talk with the woman was Todd Lincoln and indeed upon hearing the woman's story, President Abraham Lincoln issued a presidential pardon and the woman's son was spared.

150

Like that story from Civil War, God's Son is passing by. At the head of the Salvation Army parade, Jesus approaches, offering to lead us into the Father's presence. Palm Sunday invites us to be followers. There is no such thing as "spectator Christianity." The grand marshall of today's parade invites us to be servants not sideline watchers. For it's easy to shout but harder to serve. But only in serving is our life blessed.

What the people who welcomed Jesus into Jerusalem that first Palm Sunday did not realize was that God was offering them the opportunity to do something more than cheer. God was inviting them to join him in doing a great thing. For Jesus was on his way to the cross to bring us new life and salvation. As Jesus rode to his death that day, as he led that parade and procession, he came freeing us from our sins.

For the ultimate destination of that first Palm Sunday parade was not praise but the cross and salvation. In his book, *Lift High The Cross*, Robert Morgan tells a story about a man named Dave. He was a camp counselor at a Christian camp in Arkansas. In the hills above the camp is the camp's landmark — a large, lighted cross. One winter night, a stranger came to Dave's home to ask Dave if he would take him up the mountain to see the cross. It was an icy, snowy night and Dave tried to put the stranger off, but the man seemed desperate to see it, so Dave reluctantly agreed. As they drove the narrow winding road up the mountain, the stranger told his story.

The night before, the man had set out in his small plane to fly to Little Rock. He was in despair over his chaotic life and the thought of running away from everything or even worse, of flying his plane into the hillside and ending it all, ran through his mind. As he contemplated those two bleak alternatives, a snowstorm suddenly overtook him. He soon became disoriented and began to panic.

When he radioed for help, he couldn't tell the control tower where he was because the snow had blotted out the landmarks for miles around him. Then suddenly from out of nowhere, the man saw a glowing cross in front of him. At first he thought it was a

151

hallucination. But when he described the cross, the traffic controller immediately knew where he was and was able to guide him to safety. "That cross saved me," the man told Dave as they reached the hilltop. "I would never have found my way without it. And now my life is different. I'll never be the same again."

That's what the cross has done throughout the ages. It brings us back to God. That was Jesus' destination; that was his goal. And he invites us to join him. He invites us to march along. Today he comes before us as humble Savior, the head of the parade. Remember: it is easier to shout than it is to serve. Serving is a great blessing. In Jesus' name. Amen.

Brought Together And Sent Forth

There once was a majestic cathedral in Northern Europe that was known for its magnificent organ. Unlike the pipe organs and electronic organs of our day, the organs in the old churches of Europe depended upon air pumped by hand to produce sound. When they had services or wanted to play the organ, an assistant to man the pumps was needed in addition to an organist to press the keys.

There is a story told of one time when a guest organist was scheduled to play a recital featuring the works of Mozart and Mendelssohn. As was the custom, when the organist appeared at the organ bench, he turned and bowed to the crowd and announced the music he was going to play. "For my first selection today," he said, "I will play a piece by Mozart." With that he turned to the organ and after a moment, with great flourish, put his fingers to the keys. But when he pressed the keys, no sound came out. A bit flustered, he arranged himself again and pressed the keys a second time. Still nothing. Aggravated, he stood and faced the crowd again and in a louder voice said, "For my first selection I will play a piece from Mozart." He returned to the keyboard and pounded it again, but still no sound. Just then he heard a voice from behind the organ. It said, "If you don't say *we*, I ain't going to pump." Standing once again, the organist addressed the crowd another time. This time, however, he said, "For *our* first selection, *we* will play a piece from Mozart." With that he returned the organ, pressed the keys, and great music was heard.

The church always plays its best music when we realize the church is a *we* and not an *I*. And this is why our Lord Jesus made holy communion one of the great sacraments of our faith. Because holy communion teaches us that we are brought together as a community of faith. We gather as God's family to receive the bread and wine. At the communion table we are brought together as the family of God.

A few years ago, my wife and I took some vacation time off and went to San Francisco. We'd been there for our honeymoon and wanted to go back. One of the places we wanted to see again was Muir Woods, a secluded forested place not far from the Golden Gate Bridge. It is a special place. In the windswept barren hills of the California coast, the road dips suddenly into a valley of redwood trees. There you enter another world altogether — a world of giant trees, ancient coastal redwoods hundreds of years old which tower hundreds of feet into the air.

When we were there, the National Parks Service guide said something I will never forget. She said, "You know, of course, that you never find a redwood in isolation. It cannot survive. These towering trees can only survive in forested groups together. Their root systems are too shallow. By themselves they cannot withstand the wind. They will blow over. They survive only together because the root system of each tree is interwoven and connected to those of its neighbor. This is where they get their strength and together they are able to grow tall and survive for so long. There is no individualism here."

One of the greatest threats to our Christian faith is our own individualism. Too often we think we can be just as good a Christian on our own. We think we can read our Bibles on our own. We can pray on our own. We can even worship on our own, and we think we can get along without anyone else. But that's not what the story from the gospel of John tells us. That's not what Jesus says. In fact, the story shows us just the opposite. Like the redwood tree, we cannot survive by ourselves. We need each other. God knew that and so did Jesus, and that's why before going to the cross, Jesus gave an example of Christian love for us to follow. He knelt down and washed the disciple's feet.

In Jesus' day, the washing of feet was a task reserved not only for the servants, but for the lowest of all the servants. Every circle has its pecking order and the circle of household workers was no exception. The servant at the bottom got the "worst" jobs and in this case it meant getting down on his hands and knees and washing other people's feet.

But in this case, the author of the universe, the most high king of creation is the one on his hands and knees. Imagine it. The same hands that fashioned the universe, the same hands that cast the stars in their places, now wash feet! The one to whom all nations kneel, now kneels before the disciples. Just hours before his death, our Lord turns his concern on those nearest and dearest to him. And he leaves them an example of the Christian life together, and it is service and love for one another.

This moment of service, this act of washing the disciple's feet, is the key to understanding everything that follows. Before going to the cross, Jesus stooped in service to others. There in the midst of his last supper, there in the context of holy communion, Jesus put his stamp on all that he taught. By washing the disciple's feet, Jesus was saying that selfless love and servant-like living is what characterizes those who follow.

Many years ago, a sticky situation happened. It occurred at the wedding ceremony of the Duke of York. All the guests and wedding attendants were in their place. The sound of the majestic organ at Westminster Abbey filled the air. Everything was perfect for this royal wedding of some of the highest in British society. Except for one thing. As part of the wedding ceremony, the duke and his bride were supposed to kneel on a cushioned bench to receive a blessing.

A nervous whisper spread through the congregation as guests noticed that one of the cushions from the kneeling bench had fallen on the floor. The attendants standing near the kneeling bench were of royal blood and part of the "upper crust" of British society. To reach down and pick up the pillow would have been beneath them. So rather than do it, they all pretended they did not see the misplaced pillow until finally the Prince of Wales, who was a groomsman, picked it up and returned it to the bench.

Now, that example may not impress us much here in America where we pride ourselves on the equality of every person, but in a class-conscious society like Great Britain, that was an extraordinary act. However, it is not one that can even begin to parallel what Jesus did that night in the upper room. In kneeling to wash the disciple's feet, Jesus bowed down to our mortal creation; he lowered himself to the role of a servant, and not just a servant, but the lowest of all servants and in doing so, showed how deep our love for one another must be.

In holy communion we are brought together. But it is a meal that does more than that. It brings us together — yes — but it also sends us forth as God's servants. When we come to receive holy communion, we are sent forth to serve the lowest and the least.

Pastor Bill Hybels is the pastor at one of the largest churches in America — Willow Creek Community Church. He is also a servant of God, someone who understands reaching out to others with God's love. Where did he learn that? At school, at seminary? Well, perhaps. But he also learned it at home. For Bill's father was not only a highly productive and successful businessman, he was also a Christian. And as such, for 25 years without fail, Bill Hybels' father spent one afternoon a week with a group of mentally disabled women at a local hospital. Every Sunday afternoon, the senior Hybels led a song service for the women there. He knew each woman by name and he treated them all with respect. Those women had no interest in his business. They could do nothing for him. He did it just for the joy he had in serving them, and that example rubbed off on his son.

It is that kind of example of selfless service that Jesus gave the disciples in washing their feet and it is the example he gives us. We come together in holy communion. But we are also sent forth to serve. There is no pecking order here. There is no higher or lower among those who serve the Lord. We are all equal. We are all servants of our God and king. Jesus has made that clear — we are called to "love one another," to be selfless servants of God.

A group of four- to eight-year-olds was asked what love means. Here are some of their answers:

"Love is when you kiss all the time," one little boy said. "Then you get tired of kissing and you just talk with each other. My mommy and daddy are like that. They look gross when they kiss."

Another little boy said, "Love is when a girl puts on perfume and a boy puts on shaving cologne and they go out and smell each other."

But one little girl summed up best what Jesus means when he tells us to love one another when she said, "When my grandma got arthritis, she couldn't bend over any more and paint her toenails. So my grandpa does it for her now, even though his hands got arthritis, too. I think that's what love is."

Before going to the cross, Jesus gathered his disciples around him and shared a last meal with them. And as they gathered for that meal, Jesus gave them an example to follow: he washed their feet; he bowed down in service before them; he showed them what real love was like in the hopes that we would follow his example. In holy communion we are brought together as one family of God and we are sent forth in service. Let us do that now. In Jesus' name. Amen.

The Cross No One Wants To See

Garbage truck driver, Craig Randall, brings his work home with him sometimes. There was that old-fashioned sewing machine he found. There were some books he rescued from the trash. And then there was that soft-drink cup that just happened to be worth $200,000. Neither Randall nor his fiancée really believed it until he drove his garbage truck up to the restaurant and picked up the check. Twenty-three-year-old Randall said he lifted the cup from a pile of trash while he was on his route in south Boston. He can't remember exactly where he found it (or he won't say). He began taking notice of those cups after he pealed another sticker from another cup earlier in the week. "I won a chicken sandwich off that one," he said, "so I thought maybe I'd get some fries to go with it." This time, however, the sticker said, "$200,000 winner." A treasure lifted from the garbage heap. It seems like an appropriate thought for our worship today. A treasure from the garbage heap — for after all, it was from the garbage heap of humanity that our salvation was lifted.

In his book, *Lift High The Cross*, Robert Morgan tells about a most unusual cross that stood on the lawn of a Dallas church one Lenten season. The cross, which was about ten foot tall, created such a stir that pictures of it were carried by newspapers across the country and a television station in Dallas filmed it. It was an ugly thing — made from weapons of violence and crime, most of which had been confiscated by the Dallas Police Department. There were guns and pistols, knives and bayonets, bullets, bombs, and broken glass. The cross rose out of the remains of an automobile that had

159

been involved in a drunken driving fatality. An ugly barbed-wire enclosure, like they use at prisons, surrounded the whole thing. It was an ugly sight — a thing of violence and death and it caused quite a controversy. The neighbors hated it — in fact, they started a petition to have it removed. The congregation's members were repelled by it. They thought it was sacrilegious and had no place on the church grounds. The pastor just commented, "The reactions to our Lenten display are understandable. No one wants to be reminded of our inhumanity toward each other. But isn't that indeed the basis for the cross?"

It was a cross no one wanted to see. Much like the cross of Christ — not a cross of guns and knives, bayonets and bullets. But a cross of suffering and shame. A cross of derision and death.

Matthew, in his gospel, simply writes that after the soldiers had whipped and flogged Jesus, "They took him away to crucify him." Matthew goes on to say, "Then they came to a place called Golgotha (which means The Place of the Skull)" and there they crucified him. "Above his head they placed the written charge against him which read, 'This is the King of the Jews.' Two robbers were crucified with him also, one on his right and one on his left."

You know, it is ironic. Calvary is not that far from Bethlehem. The distance is really not more than seven miles. In fact, you could walk it in a couple hours, probably less time that it took for the events on the cross to be over that fateful Friday. The journey of a lifetime — over in the span of a few hours. It was a cross no one wanted to see. And yet, we must join those faithful women and the disciple John and stand near the cross and see it.

For the first thing we need to see as we stand at the foot of the cross is that the cross was a place of shame. And even though in life throughout his ministry Jesus identified with outcasts and victims, the cross was a place of shame. And so it was intended to be. Those being crucified were the objects of derision. Led through the city streets, the Roman soldiers intended the experience to be physically exhausting and emotionally insulting. Made bloody by the whipping and flogging, prisoners were marched through the streets to the cries of the crowds. And for the crowd, it was great

160

fun, a diversion in an otherwise unentertaining existence. No, a crucifixion was great excitement. Like a bull-fight, blood was in the air.

And so it was for Jesus that fateful Friday. As he climbed the hill of Golgotha, as he ascended that "place of the skull," the cries of the crowd were filled with anger. The mocking intended to shame. "You saved others. Save yourself if you are the King of the Jews." Once at the cross, the soldiers nailed the condemned to the beams and a brutal, painful death awaited them. Stripped naked, exposed for all to see, the cross was a place of shame, for so it was intended to be.

Pastor Wayne Rouse tells the story of a friend of his wife — a friend named Alice. Wayne's wife grew up with Alice in a small town where Alice's mother and grandmother had quite a reputation — they were known for being the "worst of the worst." Drinking and sleeping around, they lived a terrible life of addiction and immorality and made life miserable for Alice and her brothers and sisters. One afternoon while in a drunken state, Alice's mother had all the children in the car and, crossing the town's railroad tracks, stalled the car. Suddenly, off in the distance a form appeared. It was an approaching freight train. Sitting in the backseat, Alice could hear the train's warning whistle but she realized that her mother was too drunk to sense the danger that faced them. So Alice took things into her own hands, as any child of an alcoholic knows well to do. She began pulling her brothers and sisters out of the car to safety. When they were out, she went back for her mother. Just as she had gotten her to safety, the train hit the car at sixty mph. Alice's love had saved her family, but unfortunately it cost her own. As the train smashed into the car, Alice was too close. It was thrown from the tracks right into her and she died instantly. Pastor Rouse recalls that story in telling the story of the cross. For like Alice, Jesus' extravagant love for the unlovely, his compassion for the wretched and the worst of the worst enabled him to endure the cross. He was hung on the cross no one wants to see. And there he saved our lives by giving up his own. He endured the shame.

But there is more. The cross was also a place of suffering and so it was intended to be. An upright wooden post with a crossbeam near the upper part of the post, it was an instrument of torture, a cruel form of death reserved for rebels, robbers, and criminals of various kinds. So cruel and painful was the practice that Roman law forbade its use on any Roman citizen. And even though the practice seems grisly to us today, crucifixion was commonplace in the ancient world, and death by the cross was made even more degrading by the fact that in many cases, the victim was left to hang on the cross in public view until the body rotted away.

The cross was a place of suffering — it was designed to be so. That is the meaning of the cross itself — an instrument of capital punishment, an executioner's device, like the electric chair or a hangman's noose. Death on a cross was a slow, agonizing, humiliating form of death, intended to torture its victims as much as kill them.

Only lowest of criminals were put to death on a cross — thieves, murderers, and rapists. For it was anything but a noble death. Nails were driven through the hands and feet and, more often than not, the person being crucified died of asphyxiation as the very weight of their body crushed the lungs. It was a horrible thing, a thing of torture and pain of suffering and death.

And so it was for Jesus that fateful Friday. Bloody and bruised, mocked and derided, stripped naked and nailed to the cross, he endured the suffering and felt the pain. And the death he died was a death for you and me.

For the cross is more than a place of shame and suffering. It is also a place of love — love divine, all loves excelling. And how we need that kind of love. Love — not in abstract terms; love — not in silly songs or rhymes. Love — made real for everyone. Love — for all to see. For even though this is the cross we don't want to see, at the cross we see God's love for you and me. The cross is love made concrete. The cross is love made real.

In the hit film, *In the Line of Fire*, Clint Eastwood plays Secret Service agent, Frank Horrigan. Horrigan is an elderly, nearing retirement age agent, assigned to protect the president. For more than three decades he has served in this role. But he is haunted by the memory of what had happened thirty years before. As a young agent, Horrigan had been assigned to protect the president on a visit to Dallas in 1963. There in the motorcade, Horrigan froze in shock when he heard the gunshots. And now, thirty years later, he wrestled with the ultimate question: Would he freeze again? Could he take a bullet for the president if so required? In the climactic scene of the movie, Horrigan did what he had been unable to do earlier: he threw himself into the path of an assassin's bullet to save the chief executive.

At Calvary, the scene is reversed. The "president of the universe" takes a bullet for us. The Son of God endures the suffering and shame for you and me. Such is God's love. For if we are able to look at the cross, there amid the repulsion, the loathing, and the disgust, there underneath its ugliness, is beauty divine.

As Jesus hung there on the cross that fateful Friday, he experienced it all — the shame and humiliation, the suffering and pain, the weight of our sins and wrongdoings. And through it all, he also knew that by his wounds we would be made well.

Somehow he knew that his death was a death for us all. Somehow he knew that his innocent suffering would free us from ours. Perhaps he had read the words of Isaiah, 550 years before he was born, "He was wounded for our transgressions, he was bruised for our iniquities: the chastisement of our peace was upon him; and with his wounds we are made well."

In Stroudsburg, Pennsylvania, there is a tomb dedicated to an unknown Union soldier who died fighting in the Civil War. When President Abraham Lincoln heard of it, he had the tomb inscribed, "Abraham Lincoln's Substitute. He died that I might live." And so we might inscribe the cross that no one wants to see; so we might say of the cross of Jesus, "He died that we might live." And that is why we must go to the cross that no one wants to see and there discover the wondrous love God has for us. In Jesus' name. Amen.

The Rest Of The Message

On June 18, 1815, the combined forces of Austria, Russia, Great Britain, and Prussia under the leadership of the British General Arthur Wellesly Wellington, engaged the army of the French Empire under Napoleon Bonaparte in a climatic battle to decide the outcome of the war for the European continent. There, near the Belgium town of Waterloo, those two armies collided in fierce combat. By prearranged agreement, the British army at the end of the day was to signal back to the coast the outcome of that battle through a series of smoke signals. The message would then be communicated across the English Channel and hand delivered to the King of England in the city of London.

As evening approached at the end of that day's fierce fighting, in which more than 25,000 men lost their lives, English communication experts on the coast awaited the smoke signals declaring either victory over that dreaded foe or defeat of their army — either hope for the future or despair in their battle for freedom for the entire European continent.

Soon their wait came to an end. Over the top of a distant hillside, they were able to make out the distinctive smoke signal message from Waterloo, and they began to translate it. The first word was unmistakable: "Wellington." The second word also soon followed, and it said, "defeated." However, as soon as those two words were received, the wind suddenly shifted and the sky was filled with dark, low clouds. It was impossible to determine if there was any more to the message or not. They were left with the message,

165

"Wellington defeated." In great sorrow, they turned and communicated that fact across the English Channel and on to King George and the people of England.

That night, all of England lay in deep sorrow, heartbroken to receive the news that their general, Arthur Wellington, had been defeated by the French emperor, Napoleon — for now it seemed that there was no hope of stopping the expansion of Napoleon's power and no hope for them for the future. They had only but to wait until Napoleon's forces crossed the channel, invaded their homeland and placed them as well under the cruel slavery of his rule.

After a dark night of despair, the following morning British soldiers once again searched the skies for messages. And once again they saw the word, "Wellington," signaled to them. The next word was also the same, "defeated." But this time, in the bright blue skies of a morning sun, a third word appeared, a word that made all the difference in the world, a word that changed their sadness into joy, their grief into rejoicing. For the third word read, "Napoleon." You see, the correct message, the complete message that they were unable to receive the night before read "Wellington defeated Napoleon." And the rest is history. Napoleon's army was conquered and freedom for the European continent was secured. For Napoleon had met his Waterloo.

May I suggest to you that something like what happened at Waterloo so many years ago happened in Jerusalem at the death of Christ. The scriptures tell us that early in the morning on the first day of the week, Mary went to the tomb of Jesus to grieve his death. The spices and embalming items indicated her intention. Her tears spoke her anguish. The message on her heart was: Jesus defeated. Death had done him in. Death had won over the Savior. For he was dead and gone.

Now, I suppose that's an understandable feeling. I suppose we can forgive her mistake. Religion says that death is a passage to a new life. But when death comes to a loved one, when death visits someone near, when it is the death of a friend we cherish, its hard to see the whole message. Death obscures our sight. Death clouds our vision. Death puts us in a fog and keeps us from seeing. That's how it was for Mary — and even worse. For Jesus was more than friend to her, more than just a loved one. He was the one she believed in. He was the one she hoped was the Savior. So when Mary stood outside the tomb, she was convinced that it was over. She was certain it was done. Gone were her hopes for the future. Gone was her faith in God — for Jesus was defeated.

Perhaps that's why when she got to the tomb, things really got confusing. For when she arrived at the tomb, the stone had been rolled away. And when she didn't find a body inside, she assumed someone had taken it. What more must she endure? First, the arrest in the garden; the trials before Herod and Pilate, then Jesus' flogging and whipping, and his cruel death on the cross. It was more than she could stand, so she fled away. Running quickly back to the disciples, Mary told them what she had seen. "They have taken Jesus' body and I don't know where to find it." Peter and John went running to the tomb to see what happened and Mary came along behind. Completely forgotten, Mary arrived at the tomb, overcome by grief.

For she could not believe it. For her the message was clear. Jesus was defeated. Jesus was dead and gone. No one expects the dead to rise. No one believes it can happen. In this fallen world, the dead don't get second chances. Death is final. DEFEATED is what it says.

Friends, we are much like Mary. Before we criticize her on her unbelief, let us look at ourselves. We are much like Mary. We see all the signs and yet fail to believe. We can be surrounded by people in whom faith abounds in deeds of kindness and love, and yet fail to understand what faith can mean for us. We can sit in sanctuaries with lovely crosses. We can sing hymns of praise and prayer. We can join in Easter celebrations and go home unchanged, untouched by the miracle. For we are much like Mary, slow to believe and unable to see the rest of the message.

Don't believe me? Then look at your checkbook, see how you spend your money. Do you pay more for cable television, spend more on a cell phone, make a car payment larger than your offering to the church? How about what we read? Did you open a newspaper more often than the scriptures? Do you read other books more intently than God's word? Or how about the music on your lips? Do you know the latest advertising jingle better than you know any song in the hymnal? We are much like Mary; slow to believe, slow to change, hearing only part of the message. Like Mary, we can stand at the mouth of the open tomb and still can not see. We hear the words of the angels and let our lives be untouched by the miracle of Jesus' resurrection from the dead.

Dear friends, the good news of Easter is that God knows how hard it is for us to believe. God knows how tightly our sinful, human nature clings to this world. God knows how easily our hearts drift from faith, how quickly our lives betray us. And because of that God sends us another message. Easter proclaims, "Jesus defeated death." That's the rest of the message. That's the whole story. Because he lives, we shall live also.

The message of Easter is that life is not over at the grave. The dead do rise in Christ, for Jesus defeated death. The message of Easter is that life does not end in darkness; life is not over when we die. For Jesus defeated death. That is the message we believe, the words that we hold true, our hope for the future, our joy of life with God. Jesus defeated death. And because he lives we shall live also. His victory is our victory. His resurrection is our resurrection. His rising to new life is new life for us as well.

In the fifth chapter of the gospel of John, Jesus says it this way, "I tell you the truth whoever hears my word and believes in God who sent me has eternal life and will not be condemned. He has crossed over from death into life."

It was not until Jesus spoke Mary's name that she believed. It wasn't until he said, "Mary," that she recognized him. And that's an important thing for us to remember. Faith always comes from hearing. Faith is ours when God speaks our name. Faith is dependent upon God's word for us. It is God's action in our lives and God's grace in our hearts. Faith is born when we hear God; it is ours when God speaks.

Want to grow in faith? Then draw nearer to God's people in worship and allow God to speak to you. Want to experience the presence of Christ more fully? Then stand closer to him and listen for him in prayer. Join us in worship, open the Bible, read it more

168

faithfully and bow your head more often in prayer. Stretch your spiritual muscles by reaching out in love to someone in need. For Jesus defeated death. That is the glorious message of Easter. Through the death and resurrection of Jesus, we are set free, free from death's cold grip, free from our sins and wrongdoings, freed to live as children of God. When Mary heard Jesus speak her name, she knew the rest of the message. That's why she fell at his feet in worship. And that's where we belong as well.

His name was Tigyne. He belonged to the Wallamo tribe in the interior of Ethiopia. In the years just following WWII, missionaries carried the message of Christ to this people, and one of the earliest converts was Tigyne. Raymond Davis was the missionary who knew him and freed him. For you see, Tigyne was a slave and his decision to follow Jesus displeased his master, who refused to allow Tigyne to attend Bible studies or go to church. In fact, his master frequently humiliated Tigyne for his faith. But for this young Christian, it seemed a small price that he was willing to pay.

There was another price, however, he could not pay. He could not purchase his freedom. His master only wanted $12 for him. But for a slave who has no salary, it might as well have been a million dollars. However, when Davis learned that Tigyne's freedom could be purchased, he saved his money and gave Tigyne back his life.

Tigyne was now free — both physically and spiritually. Not long after his received his freedom, the government in Ethiopia was overthrown and all foreign missionaries were expelled from the country. Twenty-four years passed before Raymond Davis was allowed to return to Wallamo. However, through all those years, Tigyne had not forgotten and he longed to see Davis again.

When he heard that his friend was returning to Africa, he went to the mission station to greet him. Because dates on the calendar and times on the clock didn't mean much to Tigyne, he just kept coming back day after day. Finally, Davis arrived, riding in a car driven by a native pastor. When Tigyne saw the vehicle come round the corner, he ran to the window and took Davis' hand and began to kiss it over and over. The black pastor slowed the car so Tigyne could run beside it. As he ran, he yelled to his friends, "Behold. Behold. Here is the one who redeemed me. Here is the one who set me free. He has returned as he promised."

Finally, the car slowed to a stop. And as Davis stepped out, Tigyne dropped to his knees, put his arms around the legs of the missionary he had not seen for 24 years and began to kiss his dusty shoes. Davis reached down to bring him to full height and there they stood, their arms around each other, tears of joy running down their cheeks.

Dear friends, such is the joy God has for us when we hear the rest of the message. Such is God's grace for us. The message is not "Jesus defeated." The message of Easter is that God's grace has triumphed. Death's power is gone. Death's rule is over. For Jesus defeated death. He is triumphant forevermore. He is the Lord of Life and the Savior of our soul. And this is the message that God speaks to our world today — Jesus defeated death. May God bless us this Easter with hearts full of joy. In Jesus' name. Amen.

Behind Closed Doors

There are some jokes that are just too terrible to tell from the pulpit. A pastor would have to be nuts to try to slip such a story by his congregation. For example, there is a story of a man who went to a psychiatrist one time with a sleep disorder. "Doc," he says, "I've been having trouble sleeping because of weird dreams. For example, last night I dreamed that I was a wigwam."

"Oh yes," the psychiatrist said. "That is terrible. Yes, yes indeed ... Please try very carefully to remember more and come back and see me next week."

So the next week the man returned. "Doc, it's gotten worse. Now I dreamed that I was a teepee. It was awful."

"Oh yes," the psychiatrist said. "That is terrible. But I do know now what your problem is. You are two tents."

Get it? Two tents — a wigwam and a teepee. Aren't you glad that I'd never start off a sermon with such a terrible joke?

Well, the disciples of Jesus that first Easter Sunday were not just too tense — they were downright terrified. The picture we have of them from the gospel writers is of a frightened, discouraged, downhearted group of DISbelievers! The crucifixion of Jesus had done them in and no matter what anybody said to them, they could not be shook out of their grief and sorrow. Look at what the Bible says.

Early in the morning, Mary and the women visit the tomb of Jesus and are greeted by angels who announce to them that Jesus is alive. The women return to the disciples and tell them the news and how do the disciples respond? Luke tells us in chapter 24, verse 11, "But they [the disciples] would not believe the women because their words seemed to them like nonsense." Peter rushes to the tomb to see for himself and Luke says, "Peter went away wondering to himself what had happened."

John picks up the story for us today in the second half of chapter 20. He begins by saying, "When it was evening on that day, the first day of the week and the doors of the house where they met were locked for fear of the Jews." *For fear of the Jews.* Did you hear that? This is a timid, frightened group of followers. Everything has happened too fast for them. One moment the crowd is welcoming Jesus. And then just a few days later, he is arrested, put on trial, and crucified on a cross. The picture the Bible gives us is of a shell-shocked bunch of disciples who gather in hiding to mourn the death of their leader. They are living in fear of the dreaded knock on the door that will signal that they are next.

Fear shut them out and anxiety locked them up. A few years ago, W. H. Auden wrote a poem about modern life and called it, "The Age of Anxiety." That poem's name stuck. It soon became a byword for our modern times — The Age of Anxiety — because it is so true. Ours is a world that is anxious and afraid. Older people are afraid their health will fail them and their savings will run out. Younger people are afraid they won't have any savings for old age and they could care less about health. Some fear the future and others dread the past. College students are afraid they won't have a job when they get out and parents are afraid they'll never get out. Middle-agers wonder if their lives have amounted to anything and young people wonder if there's anything to strive for anyhow. And all of us live in an age of terrorism and random violence.

On a personal level, we fear sickness and the gnawing concern that as we grow older our bodies will give out. We fear diseases that have no cure and cures that have no effect. There are those who fear the new and others who dread the old. Some long to return to the past and others struggle to be free from it. But this is nothing compared to what the disciples faced that first Easter evening!

Their lives were in ruins. For three years they had devoted their lives to Jesus. They had left home and family, jobs and security, to follow him. They had seen him do wonders and cure the sick, raise the dead and proclaim the love of God. And what did it get him? A death on the cross! The worst of their fears had come true and now they found themselves caught in a whirlpool of anxiety. He was dead — their leader, their teacher, their rabbi, their Lord! They were left with only a nightmare of memories — a Passover meal that had become a nightmare with the revelation that one of their own would betray him. There was the dreamlike time in the Garden of Gethsemane that ended when the high priest's soldiers came with weapons to arrest him. Even Peter, the boldest of them all, even Peter's brave vows of loyalty were followed with words of denial. The mocking, the beating, the horror of his death had left the disciples a shell-shocked, frightened, disbelieving bunch whose worst fears seemed reality now.

Then suddenly, that first Easter evening everything changed. Suddenly, Jesus was with them, among them to soothe their fears — not with the knocking at the door that they so feared — not with a plea to be let in or a request that they open it for him. With all due respect to Holman Hunt and his famous painting of Jesus knocking on the door, Jesus didn't knock. He just came in. He loved these men too much to wait for them to open the door for him. As the old saying says, "Love laughs at our locks." He loved them with an undying love and no lock could keep him out. Boldly, persistently, powerfully, the risen Savior came back into their lives.

Now, think with me for a moment about what could have happened in those next few minutes. Jesus could have coldly surveyed this frightened bunch and could have begun a sarcastic review of their recent words and actions. "Let's see, Peter. Let me hear again what you said. 'Though the world deny you, yet I will not.' Isn't that what you said? So what happened, big guy? How about you James and John? Can you drink the cup of suffering that I drink? Can you? Where were you guys?" He could have pierced each and every one of their hearts if he had wanted to. He could have thrown their cowardice in their faces. He could have held their denial up

173

to them. He could have seared their hearts with their cowardly deeds, their faithlessness, and failure. But he didn't.

He didn't. Instead, he said, "Peace be with you." For that's what they needed most. That's what they lacked. They knew their failure. They knew how they had deserted him. They knew their denial, their cowardice, their sinfulness and they didn't need reminding of it. And he knew that, too.

What they needed was their lives, their thoughts, their hopes and dreams back again. They needed to be made whole. They needed to be released from their fears and set free from the guilt and anxiety that locked them in. They needed what only the Christ could give them — forgiveness, new hope, and a reason for living. And that's exactly what he did. He gave them peace. He set them free. He made them whole again. That's what the peace of Christ is all about — being restored to the goodness that God created us in, being made whole to dream about the future, being restored to live and love and laugh again. That's what Christ gave them because that's what they needed the most.

Fear not, he said. Fear not. How many times do we need to hear that? How many times do we find ourselves in the clutches of fear? Did you know that one Bible scholar has counted up the number of times the Bible says that exact phrase (Peace be with you.) and it is exactly 366 times — one time for every day of the year and even another left over for Leap Year! Fear not! That's God's message to us today. Fear not — for my peace is with you, too.

Remember, these are not atheists or agnostics that Jesus recruited. Now, they weren't religious scholars by any means, but surely they had some familiarity with the Hebrew scriptures. They would certainly have grown up reciting the words, "The Lord is my shepherd." They would have known about Joshua and Moses and the other heroes of the Old Testament. They would have been schooled to know that Lord is the rock of their salvation — and yet, when fear closed in upon them, they forgot all that. They had been with Jesus for three years, but when the anxiety of the cross came upon them, they acted as if he never existed.

In Charles Dickens' famous novel, *A Tale of Two Cities*, there was a man who had worked as a shoemaker in prison. After being released from prison, the injustice of his sentence was discovered, and he was reinstated as a nobleman, rich and secure. However, later in life whenever he ran into problems, he would retreat to his home, go down to a little dark room in the basement and make shoes. Under stress, he reverted to his old self.

And so it is with us. When troubles beset us, when difficulties come our way, we revert to our old selves, forget God's promises and act as if Jesus never existed. That's why a regular habit of worship, of scripture reading, and prayer is so important. By making it a regular part of our life, we imprint on our hearts the words of Jesus so that when troubles come our way and we are surrounded with difficulties, we will not flee from Jesus but run right back into his loving arms.

Peace be with you, Jesus says. Peace be with you. I have conquered death and the grave. Is there any bigger obstacle than that? I am the Lord of life and death and I will always be with you. Henry Ward Beecher once said, "Every morning has two handles to open the new day — one is the handle of anxiety and the other the handle of faith." The disciples grabbed anxiety and found themselves closed in behind locked doors, afraid and abandoned. Jesus opened the door of faith for them.

More than anything else, when Jesus appeared to the disciples behind those closed doors, he was saying to them, showing them, telling them in a way they could not misunderstand that there were no doors that could keep him out. There was no way they could ever be separated from him. There was no circumstance in which they would ever be alone.

That's the good news that God brings us today. There is no closed door that can keep the love of God away from us. There is no lock that can shut us apart from God. There is no dark room that God will not enter and there is no one that God does not love. That's the answer to any fear and the antidote to all anxiety. "Peace be with you," Jesus says. I don't care how bad tomorrow looks, how gloomy the prospects may seem, how dreadful the problem

175

is, or how hopeless everything seems. Jesus says to us that with his presence, peace is possible.

Immediately after World War II, the well-known German pastor, Helmut Thielicke, stood to preach a sermon on the rubble of his bombed-out church in Berlin. He knew about fear. He knew about huddling behind closed doors. He himself had barely escaped the wrath of Adolf Hitler. Death was all around him. And yet, even in the midst of this despair and devastation, Thielicke could rejoice in God's love and say, "Where Christ is king, everything is changed. Eyes see differently and hearts no longer beat the same. And in every hard and difficult place, his hand will never let us go and he will always uphold. For the voice of Jesus is there to say, 'Peace be with you.'"

There is hope for all of us in this Age of Anxiety. There is help when we feel like giving up. There is courage when we are tempted to hide. For there is one who can enter any room. There is one who can overcome any problem. There is one who can bring peace to every anxious heart. In fact, today he holds out his hands to us and shows us his side and says, "Peace be with you. Do not be doubting. But believe." In Jesus' name. Amen.

Hope To Carry On

It is perhaps one of the most compelling narratives in all of the scriptures. So fascinating is this scene, in fact, that the gospel writer Luke includes it in detail near the end of his gospel writing. It is a story known well and beloved in the church — the story of two disciples walking down a dusty road to the village of Emmaus, the evening of that first Easter day.

Their talk centers around the crucified, dead Jesus. Their words come out slowly, almost painfully, as they trudge their way along, their feet heavy and their hearts broken. "I can hardly believe it," one of them says. "In fact, I wouldn't believe it if I hadn't seen it with my own eyes. He is dead. He is really gone." "What should we to do now?" the other asks. "Life seems hopeless." And just then a stranger joins them — perhaps he has come up from behind, unknown to them. Perhaps he has walked along with them for a while without their noticing. But suddenly he is there. "I'm sorry," he says, "but I couldn't help but overhear you. What are you talking about?"

They stop and turn to him. Other travelers step around them, anxious to reach their destination before night falls. The three of them stand there in the middle of the dusty road and talk. "Where have you been the last few days," one of the disciples asks the stranger. "How is it you haven't heard anything about Jesus of Nazareth?" And so the two of them tell the stranger what they know. Listen to what they say from chapter 24 of the gospel of Luke.

177

He was a prophet, powerful in word and deed before God and all the people. The chief priests and our rulers handed him over to be sentenced to death, and they crucified him; but we had hoped that he would be the one who would redeem Israel. And what is more, it is the third day since all this took place. In addition, some of our women amazed us. They went to the tomb early this morning but didn't find his body. They came and told us that they had seen a vision of angels, who said he was alive. Then some of our companions went to the tomb and found it just as the women had said, but they did not see him. — Luke 24:19c-24

I don't know about you, but this story has always fascinated me — this scene between two beloved disciples of our Lord, filled with sadness and despair, grieving at the death of a friend, telling that stranger how the last nail has been driven into their hope for the future. And our Savior himself, unknown to them, patiently listening to them, his nail-scarred hands undoubtedly buried deep within his robe to keep them from recognizing him. As he heard those words of grief and sadness, no doubt his heart must have been touched by their pain.

Do you hear what they are saying? Can you understand what is happening here, for there is a message for us today? Listen to what they say: "He was a prophet, powerful in word and deed before God and all the people. The chief priests and our rulers handed him over to be sentenced to death, and they crucified him; and we had hoped that he would be the one who would redeem Israel."

"We *had* hoped," they said. They might as well have said, "We *used to hope* but not anymore." Because that's the way they felt. He was dead and gone. He had died a cruel death on the cross and it was now over.

For those without a resurrection faith, those who have not yet heard and believed the good news of Jesus' resurrection, for those who do not believe the good news of Easter, death is a terrible thing. For it puts to an end our hopes for the future and seems to erect an eternal barrier between our loved ones and themselves.

Without a living hope, without a living faith in the resurrected Christ, like those disciples on the Road to Emmaus we are left to trudge our way along the dusty, dark roads of life, dragging our feet, wondering what we could have done to avoid this. But it need not be that way.

Because as children of God, as those who know the rest of the story, as those who have been to the empty tomb and have met the risen Christ, we know that death is not the end. We know that there is an eternal hope that is ours through faith in the living Christ.

There is a certain city in Romania which has a "burying ground" which is called "The Merry Cemetery." The crosses that serve as tombstones are decorated with carvings, paintings in bright colors, and even amusing epitaphs. They express, of course, the Christian belief in the resurrection. However, the former Communist government which wrote the travel folders describing this cemetery and its unique tombstones, until recently, described that Christian hope expressed on the tombstones as merely "the expression of a certain philosophy regarding a way of facing death."

"A certain philosophy regarding a way of facing death." As Christians we know there is more to our faith than that. Our faith in Christ is more than just a "philosophy about facing death." It is a living hope, a living trust in God and a certain faith in a risen Savior regarding the very nature of life and death itself. As people of God, our faith rests on our relationship with the crucified and living Lord Jesus Christ who says to us, "I am the resurrection and the life; if anyone believes in me, even though he dies yet shall he live."

That's why the apostle Peter can say, "Praise be to the God and Father of our Lord Jesus Christ. In his great mercy he has given us a new birth into a living hope through the resurrection of Jesus Christ from the dead." Our hope as Christian people comes from God and resides in Jesus Christ, who died for our sins and won the victory over sin and death when God the Father raised him from the dead. This risen Savior alone can say, "I died and behold I am forevermore; I am the resurrection and the life. If anyone believes in me, though he were dead, yet shall he live. And whoever lives and believes in me, shall never die."

The story of those two disciples on the Road to Emmaus is the story of faith reborn. It is the record of hope restored. That's what makes it so lovely. That's what makes it one of the greatest stories ever told. For it reminds us that we have a pledge and promise from our God, a word of hope, a living trust in our risen Savior that we can hang on to.

Young Helen Keller was a prisoner of her own circumstances. She could not see or hear. She could feel with her hands, but without sight or hearing, how could she know what she was feeling? One day her teacher, Anne Sullivan, took Helen down the familiar path in front of her house to an old hand-pump well. Someone was there drawing water. Anne took Helen's hand and held it under the water and in sign language spelled on her other hand the letters — W - A - T - E - R. And suddenly, something happened. Suddenly her life changed. In danger of making a bad pun, we could say, suddenly her eyes were opened! It was just a little five letter word. It was just the splashing of common water. But now Helen knew what it was. Now she had a name for it — water. And if that experience had a name, others must also. It was suddenly as if the world had opened up for her. Now she could begin to reach out to the world and experience it in spite of her handicaps.

My friends, a breakthrough of equally breathtaking importance happened to those two disciples of Jesus that first Easter night. Just as Helen Keller's life was changed, just as her eyes were opened to a whole new world outside of herself, in the same manner Jesus came to those two disciples and revealed himself to them and their lives were never the same. Such is the nature of faith. Such is our resurrection hope. Because he lives, we shall live also — and he will walk and guide and comfort us through life.

In 1847, a young doctor in Edinburgh, Scotland, made an amazing discovery — one that changed the course of modern medicine. He discovered chloroform, and in doing so he found a way to take the pain out of surgery. Now, everyone who has ever had surgery ought to thank God for Dr. Simpson. For even though we don't get chloroform for surgery any more, the concept of taking the pain out of surgery was born then. Give a person an anesthetic and they will avoid the dreadful pain of surgery.

One day while lecturing at medical school at the university, a young student raised his hand and asked, "Dr. Simpson, what in your opinion, is the greatest discovery ever made?" It was one of those questions that students sometimes ask to cater favor with their professors, for the student was aware of Dr. Simpson's discovery of chloroform and expected a certain answer. But do you know what Dr. Simpson said? He replied, "In my opinion, the greatest discovery a person can ever make is to find the grace of God."

And he meant it — not just out of a sense of humility — but he meant it from personal experience. We know that because Dr. Alexander Simpson and his wife had a little girl — a child they dearly loved and one day she was taken ill and all the medicines in her father's black bag could not help her. And she died. They buried her in a cemetery in Edinburgh. A few months later, they placed a stone at her gravesite and on the stone they had inscribed her name "Faith Simpson" and below the name the dates of her short life. But there was more they put on that stone. There, above the place for her name, they had inscribed the words, "Thank God for faith — Faith Simpson and faith in God."

The poet writes:

> The stars shine down upon the earth;
> And the stars shine upon the sea.
> The stars look up to a mighty God;
> The stars look down on me.
>
> The stars will shine for a million years,
> A million years and a day.
> But because of Christ, I live and love
> Even when the stars pass away.

Such is the hope that is ours in the resurrection of Christ; such was the trust we have in God; and such is the faith that we live with — a faith, hope, and trust that those two disciples discovered on the Road to Emmaus that day. In Jesus' name. Amen.

181

The True Shepherd

It's no wonder that the image of the shepherd was so frequently on the lips of our Savior. It's no surprise he used that illustration so often. For the image of a shepherd and the sheep was very much a part of Jesus' heritage and culture. Abraham, the father of the Jewish people, was the keeper of great flocks of sheep. Moses was called by God to be God's deliverer of the ancient Jewish people while living as a shepherd and tending the flocks of his father-in-law. And David, the greatest king of the Jewish nation, was a shepherd boy called from the fields when God selected him for service.

The imagery of the shepherd is deeply rooted in the history and tradition of the Jewish people and imprinted in the literature of the Israelites that Jesus studied. As a good Jewish boy, Jesus would have learned the Hebrew scriptures and there among those writings were example after example of God's love for God's people, often using the image of a shepherd and the sheep. Among the words Jesus would have known and treasured are the words we read today from Psalm 23. "The Lord is my shepherd, I shall not want. He maketh me to lie down in green pastures. He leadeth me beside still waters."

In fact, when the Old Testament prophet Isaiah spoke of the coming of the Messiah, he portrayed the Savior with the same image when he said, "He will feed his flock like a shepherd! He will gather his lambs into his arms." Yes, the tradition of the shepherd was very much a part of the heritage of Christ.

This picture of God as a shepherd who cares for the flock comes even more clearly into focus in the New Testament. Jesus once told a story about a shepherd who had 100 sheep, but one of them went astray. In our way of thinking, a 99% return on our investment would be fine, most desirable, in fact. But not for the shepherd. In Jesus' teaching, the shepherd leaves the 99 alone in the wilderness to go in search of that one lost sheep. Later, when Jesus was speaking to the crowds who flocked to him, the gospel writer, Mark, tells us that Jesus had compassion upon them because they were "as sheep without a shepherd."

Throughout the scriptures, this image of the shepherd and the sheep is scattered throughout. In our reading for today, the same picture is held up in front of us. Jesus again taps into this imagery when he refers to himself as the gate for the sheepfold — as the one who leads the sheep to safety. For the next few moments, I'd like to have us ask ourselves: What does Jesus have in mind here? What is Jesus trying to teach us this morning with this talk of the true shepherd and the false shepherd? Well, the first thing we discover as we look at Jesus' words again is that we have a shepherd who cares for us.

United Methodist Pastor, Reverend Larry Daniel, is a well-known writer of Civil War novels and he tells a story on himself. He says, "I will never forget when I got my wife's engagement ring. Even as a college student, I was fascinated with the Civil War. In fact, during my senior year, I'd been saving up all the money I could to buy an antique musket, an 1864 US Springfield rifle. Oh, was it a beauty! Well, all that changed when I met my future wife. Instead of buying the gun, I decided to buy an engagement ring. The Bible verse that comes to mind is, 'Greater love hath no man than that,' because it wasn't an easy choice. I really wanted that gun, but I knew that if I didn't get her a nice ring, she'd be the one buying a gun!" After he had bought the ring, Pastor Daniel said to the jeweler, "Now, be honest with me. The deal is made. I can't back out of it. Can you really tell the difference between a real diamond ring and one of those cheap rings you see on the shopper's channel on television?"

184

"Well," the jeweler said, "come around here and look at this. I want to show you something." He put two rings under the jeweler's light — the one that Larry had just bought and a cheap phony ring from a box below the counter and gave Larry his jeweler's eyeglass. "Look," he said. "Look at the cheap ring and then look at what you just bought." When he did, Pastor Daniel was amazed. The real diamond ring sparkled while under the light, under closer examination, while the counterfeit ring was dull and had no luster.

In the gospel reading, Jesus compares two shepherds. Outwardly they may seem the same. The skin of both is bronzed by the sun and weathered by the wind. They both wear a coat of sheep's wool to keep them warm at night. Both carry a shepherd's staff. But only one is a genuine shepherd and the other is a counterfeit. One is a shepherd in his heart; the other is a shepherd for hire.

On an ordinary day, you would never tell them apart. But let trouble approach, or let a pack of wolves appear, and the difference comes out. The counterfeit runs, because it is only a job to him. He has no ownership of the sheep. But the real shepherd stays. The real shepherd risks everything to protect his sheep. The real shepherd lays down his life for them. Isn't that what Jesus says in our text? "I am the true shepherd for I lay down my life for the sheep." For that is the difference between the real shepherd and the false one.

Now, this is good news. Here is God's word of grace for us today. Jesus says, "I don't care how much trouble comes your way; the good shepherd will never leave you. I don't care how difficult times become, the good shepherd will never desert you. I don't care how helpless, how hopeless, how hapless your life may seem, the good shepherd will always be at your side. He will not desert you in time of need. For the true shepherd lays down his life for the sheep."

But that's not all. As we look at this text, we see more. Jesus says the true shepherd knows his sheep. Sir George Adams Smith, the great Anglican church leader, tells of touring the Holy Land many years ago. One day on his travels, he saw several different groups of sheep converging together on a watering hole. *Now, there*

185

will be trouble, he thought. *They'll all get mixed up. The shepherds won't like this.* But to his amazement, the shepherds gave it no thought. All the sheep came together and formed one big flock of sheep. They all looked alike — a big mass of white wool. *What will they do now?* Smith thought. *How will the shepherds ever separate them out?* To his amazement, when they had finished drinking, each shepherd gave out a cry. Each let go his unique call, and almost by magic, the sheep divided back into their original folks. Jesus says to us, "I am the good shepherd. I know my own and my own know me."

Tony Campolo loves to tell the story of a particular census taker who went to the home of a rather poor family in the mountains of West Virginia to gather information. He asked the mother how many dependents she had. She began, "Well, there is Rosie, and Billy, and Lewella, Susie, Harry, and Jeffrey. There's Johnny, and Harvey, and our dog, Willie." It was then that the census taker interrupted her aid said: "No, ma'am, that's not necessary. I only need the humans."

"Ah," she said. "Well, there is Rosie, and Billy, and Lewella, Susie, Harry, and Jeffrey, Johnny, and Harvey, and...." But there once again, the census taker interrupted her. Slightly exasperated, he said, "No, ma'am, you don't seem to understand. I don't need their names, I just need the numbers." To which the old woman replied, "But I don't know them by numbers. I only know them by name."

It strikes me as a rather comforting thought that the creator of the universe, the almighty God, and Father in heaven above knows me by name. He knows my situation. He knows my worries and cares. He knows my joys and sorrows. Oh, I know there may be those who scoff at this idea. There are those who would question the thought that the God of all creation would also be a caring shepherd. But isn't that what Jesus is telling us this morning? Isn't that what he means when he says, "I am the gate for the sheep. Whoever enters through me will be saved."

About a year ago, a murder took place in a small Mississippi town. The neighbors who were interviewed on the news were all shocked. It seemed impossible to them that the man next door would have done such a thing. "We knew these people," they said. "We knew what was going on in their lives. Or at least we thought we did." You see, that's the difference between God and us. God knows. We only think that we do.

But Jesus says more than that. Remember what he says? "The man who enters by the gate is the shepherd of his sheep. The watchman opens the gate for him and the sheep listen to his voice." Did we hear that? "The sheep listen to his voice." So the question before us today is, "Do we?" Do we listen to his voice? Do we know the voice of the shepherd? Are we reading his word? Are we speaking to him in prayer?

Have you ever seen the painting done in the 1930s of a dog, looking with a cocked head, at an old gramophone? The name of the painting is *His Master's Voice*, and it's a symbol of what Jesus is saying to us. "The sheep listen to his voice. He calls his own sheep by name and leads them out."

Now, I know there have been times in my own life when I haven't recognized the master's voice as I should have. There have been times when I've been too busy, too preoccupied, too centered on my own concerns. And frankly, there have been times when I was afraid to hear his voice; for I figured he'd have something to say that I didn't want to hear. Maybe you're like that, too. That's why Jesus says, "The sheep listen to his voice. He calls them by name and leads them out."

Some people know the sound of high finance. Others don't miss a word spoken by their favorite politician. Young people know the voices of rappers and all the lyrics from their favorite songs. But do we know the voice of the shepherd? In the verses that follow our text for today, Jesus makes it clear when he says, "I am the good shepherd. I know my own and my own know me." This is a great word of promise and a great blessing for us. But we dare not hear it only in the *Reader's Digest* version that says only, "I know my own." Because the whole blessing of this verse comes in saying it through to the end, "I know my own and *my own know me*." Do not miss that! *I know my own and my own know me*. We cannot know the voice of the shepherd if we do not listen for it. We cannot recognize the Father in heaven if we do not spend time in his house here on earth. We will never be sure of the good shepherd's presence if we do not live our lives with his flock. If the church is always just an option to us, just another activity in our busy schedule — if worship is something we do only when there is nothing else scheduled — if we do not set aside time in our daily living for prayer and Bible reading — the voice of Jesus will always be the voice of a stranger and the promise and blessing of the shepherd will never be ours.

That's what Jesus' illustration of the gate is all about. It is by following the true shepherd into pastures of blessing that we truly find peace. It is by hearing his voice and following his leading that we go the right way. That's why Jesus says, "All who came before me were thieves and robbers, but the sheep did not listen to them. I am the gate; whoever enters through me will be saved." For the true shepherd lays down his life for the sheep.

Isn't that what Easter is all about — a shepherd who lays down his life for the sheep? A Savior who dies for the sinner? In using this illustration, Jesus points out the true nature of the cross. He reminds us that this is no exchange between equals. A shepherd dies for the sheep. A person sacrifices his life for an animal. The God of creation dies to redeem the wayward ones, and a Savior offers up himself for the world. That's what he means when he talks of being the gate through which the sheepfold passes.

A true shepherd comes that we might have life and have it in fullness. Through his leading we are saved. Through his death on the cross, we are redeemed and made children of God. For it is not enough that we simply remain sheep. It is not enough to wander about in life like a bunch of stupid lambs. Jesus calls us his children and asks us to be shepherds. He invites us to be the shepherd of the sheepfold in his place. He wants us to share God's love with one another and offer up our lives for something worth living.

Remember these words. I am the gate for the sheep. Whoever enters through me will be saved. For the Lord is my shepherd. I shall not want. In Jesus' name. Amen.

The Way And The Truth And The Life

The great American humorist, Will Rogers, had the reputation that he could make anyone laugh. President Calvin Coolidge, on the other hand, had the reputation that he never laughed. Want to know what happened the time those two met? Rogers was invited to visit the White House and as was the custom, the president's assistant brought Rogers into the Oval Office. As was the custom as he entered, the assistant said, "President Coolidge, this is Will Rogers. Mr. Rogers, this is President Coolidge." To which Rogers leaned forward and said, "I'm sorry. I didn't catch the name." With that, President Coolidge cracked up and started laughing.

Don't you wish you were as quick on your feet as he was? Quick with a comeback, quick with just the right thing to say. Well, of all the things that Jesus said, some of the most significant are the words in today's Gospel reading, when Jesus says, "I am the way and the truth and the life." There is an absolute nature to those words, isn't there? There is completeness to that saying. Perhaps that's why they are so powerful and so controversial as well. For among all the words that Jesus spoke, these are also some of the most debated. Notice — Jesus did *not* say, "I am one of the ways." He did *not* say, "I am one of the truths among others." He did not say, "I am a life among many others." No, he said, "I am *the* way and *the* truth and *the* life."

The great Catholic theologian, Thomas à Kempis, caught the meaning of Jesus' words and said this about them, "Without the *way*, there is no going; without the *truth*, there is no knowing; and without the *life*, there is no living. For Jesus said, 'I am the way and the truth and the life. No one comes to the Father except by me.' "

This passage from chapter 14 of John is part of a great discourse, a body of teaching material that Jesus spoke to the disciples in the upper room. The end of his earthly ministry approaching, the cross looming before him, Jesus gathered his disciples around him and to help them understand his life and work, his approaching death and resurrection, he spoke to them these words, which include him saying, "I am the way and the truth and the life."

Let us pause a few moments this morning in our busy lives to give these words some thought. Let us take a few minutes today to pull them apart and examine them more closely for in them there is a great blessing. In them there is eternal meaning and truth.

Jesus begins by saying, "I am the way." When God created us, he didn't put us permanently in a set of revolving doors, like those that go around and around in the front of big buildings. Even though life may at times seem to be just going in circles, even though there are those who say that life is one cycle after another and that everything that comes around goes around, and even though there are theories about life that say that life is one reincarnation after another, Jesus does not say that. God has created us with a purpose. Life has a goal to it. We are created to travel through life toward an end. And the way to that end, Jesus says today, is through him.

We don't find the way by wandering. We don't stumble across it by gosh and by golly. It's not enough to live life by just doing it. There is a way. And Jesus tells us today it is through him that we find the way. The safest, most secure, most dependable way through life is by Christ. That's why Jesus says, "I am the way." If we want to find our way to the place God has created for us, we must follow Christ. For Jesus leads us to God. The apostle Philip learned that. After Thomas had questioned Jesus on where he was going, Philip came to Jesus and said, "Lord, show us the Father and we will be satisfied." Show us God, Philip asked. Help us understand who God is and that will be enough for us to understand where you are leading.

190

And to that request, Jesus responded by saying, "Have I been with you all this time, Philip, and still you do not know me? Whoever has seen me has seen the Father." Imagine that! When Jesus says, "I am the way," he tells us that he is the way to know God. "Whoever has seen me has seen the Father." God need not be a mystery to us. If you know me, Jesus says, you know the Father.

So let's see what we know about Jesus. First of all, we know that Jesus is love. No one would dare argue against that. When we see Jesus, we see love in action. We see love reaching out a hand of care. We see love healing the leper, accepting the outcast, rebuking the hate-filled. We see love restoring the fallen, welcoming the prodigal, freeing the captive, and giving new life to all. Remember what Jesus said to the disciples of John the Baptist when they came to him asking if he was the Messiah, sent by God? In Matthew the eleventh chapter, Jesus says, "Go tell John what you see and hear: the blind receive their sight, the lame walk, those who have leprosy are cured, the deaf hear, the dead are raised, and good news is preached to the poor." There is no doubt about it — when we look at Jesus, we see love in action.

Jesus' words, then, are an invitation to know God as well as an example of how to live our lives. They are intended to invite us to draw closer to God as well as give us a model to pattern our lives after. In fact, in verse 12, that's exactly what Jesus says. "Very truly I tell you, the one who believes in me will also do the works that I do." Again in chapter 15 of John, Jesus repeats this saying, "This command I leave with you: that you should love one another as I have loved you."

It is important to remember that for Jesus, love was not primarily a feeling. For Jesus, love was much more concrete than that. That's why Jesus said, "You are my friends, when you *do* what I command." For Jesus, love was expressed in actions. Love was the words and deeds of our lives, our attitudes and actions toward others. The path through life to the place where God has created for us is found through love — love for God and love for one another.

Now, we are not only travelers through life, we are also called to be learners, and for that reason, Jesus went on to say, "I am the

191

truth." We are created for the truth, and seeking and living the truth is what we are called to do. However, when you think about it, it is rather ironic. While more books have been written about Jesus than about any other person who ever lived, Jesus never wrote a book. He didn't sit down and write about the truth or anything like that. In fact, there is only one instance in the gospels when Jesus wrote anything and that was in the dust at his feet and we have no record of what he wrote.

But that's okay. Because instead of writing about the truth, Jesus lived it. His life was a witness to the truth. And the truth of his life is seen through the eyes of the blind man who now sees. The truth of his life is seen in the leper who returned to give thanks, the dancing feet of the lame made well, and the dead now raised to life. For Jesus is truth in the flesh — truth incarnate — truth able to say, "If anyone sees me, they see the Father."

For when we look at Jesus, we see the truth about God. We learn that, first and foremost, God is love. It is God's nature to love. It is God's nature to show mercy. It is God's nature to forgive and accept the outcast, welcome home the prodigal. In Christ, we see the very nature of God whose love for us is unearned, unwarranted, and most unexpected. And when we look at Jesus, we learn the truth about the life God wants us to live. We, too, are to love, to forgive, to show mercy, and welcome each other, and in doing so, be part of the truth about God.

The New Testament puts it another way in 1 John 4:7, when John writes, "Dear friends, let us love one another for love comes from God. Everyone who loves has been born of God and knows God." He also says, "If anyone says, I love God, and yet hates his brother or sister, he is a liar. For anyone who does not love his brother or sister, whom he has seen, cannot love God whom he has not seen."

When we look at Jesus, we also see the truth about ourselves. Maybe that's why it's so hard to look at Jesus sometimes, because when we look at Jesus, we see ourselves — the ugliness of our lives, the sinfulness of our thoughts and deeds, the blemishes of selfishness and pride, and our failure to love. When Jesus says, "I am the truth," he confronts us with our failures to forgive, our re-fusals to show mercy, and our self-righteousness pride that puts others down.

That is why it is so important that Jesus not only say, "I am the way and the truth" but also say, "I am the life." For without Jesus, there is no life in us. Left to our own, judged by our own thoughts and deeds, there is no hope for us. And, in fact, that, too, is the message of scripture, isn't it? How does Paul put it? "All have sinned and fallen short of God's glory." And "The wages of sin is death." Without Jesus there is no life.

That's why these words are so sweet to our ears because Jesus also says, "I am the life. No one comes to the Father except by me." These words remind us that Jesus is our life. Rather than get bogged down in a discussion on the exclusivity of Christianity and the exclusive nature of these words; rather than engage in a the old argument about who is and who is not saved, these words of Jesus are meant as gospel to us. They are Jesus' invitation to us to come to him, to receive in him the gift of life that God created for us.

In his book, *The Magic of Believing*, Charles Allen says just that. As a newspaper reporter, Allen covered a lot of stories and as he covered those stories and met a lot of people, he began to ask himself what the tangible difference between people really was. In hospitals he saw some people die while others get well. He watched some football teams win while others lost. He studied the lives of great men and women in all lines of human endeavor. And after years of study, he wrote this book in which he said, "Gradu-ally, I discovered that there is a golden thread that runs through Jesus' words that makes them work for those who sincerely accept and apply them. And this golden thread can be named in a single word: faith."

It is faith that brings God's blessings to life for us. It is faith that puts us on the path that leads to God. It is faith that enables us to see the truth about our lives and to embrace the truth about God. And it is faith that brings God's gift of life to us. Faith comes from trusting in Jesus' word, following his example, and living with God. And with all deference to Charles Allen, it is not magic nor is it a secret.

Because Jesus tells us plainly, "I am the way and the truth and the life." Throughout John's gospel this has been the theme. In Jesus, we have life. In fact, in the very beginning of his gospel that's what John tells us, He writes, "In the beginning was the Word ... and in him was life and the life was the light of men." And again at the end of his gospel, John says that same thing. "These things are written that you may have life in his name."

That is God's promise to us. In Jesus, we have the way and the truth and the life that God creates us to be. In Jesus, we find the blessing that God has ready for us. In Jesus, we find the power for living and the essence of life itself. That's why he tells us. "I am the way and the truth and the life." In Jesus' name. Amen.

Always With Us

On a hot southern night, some 150 years ago, a weary slave sat before a tar-paper shack and lifted his voice in a song of lament — a mournful, deep song whose words gave expression to the pain of having been taken from home, separated from family, and subjected to slavery. With hurt and longing he sang these words:

> *Sometimes I feel like a motherless child,*
> *Sometimes I feel like a motherless child,*
> *Sometimes I feel like a motherless child,*
> *A long ways from home.*
>
> *Sometimes I feel like I'm almos' gone,*
> *Sometimes I feel like I'm almos' gone,*
> *Sometimes I feel like I'm almos' gone,*
> *Way up in de heab'nly land.*[1]

There's a story told of a rookie baseball player just up from the minor leagues who was sent up to bat against the great Hall of Fame pitcher from the St. Louis Cardinals, Bob Gibson, in his prime. Just off the bench and as nervous as someone on his first date, the rookie stepped up to the plate and took a couple of tentative practice swings as the great right-hander, Gibson, glared down at him from the mound. Then, with a great windup and pitch, Gibson blew two consecutive fastballs right down the center of the plate, so fast that the poor rookie didn't even have time to swing his bat. With that, the rookie turned on his heels and started back to the

195

dugout. "What're you doing?" his manager shouted at him as he approached the steps. "Get back out there. You've got another pitch coming." "Let him have it," the rookie said. "I've seen enough already."

Have you ever felt that way? Outmatched by life? Up against what seems to be impossible odds? Depressed? Downhearted? Hopeless and helpless, overpowered by life? What do we do when life bullies us into a corner? Where do we turn when trouble traps us? Well, there is good news. As we gather here today, we encounter the resurrected Christ, the one who has triumphed over the cross and the grave; the one who stands eternal before the throne of our heavenly Father, our Lord Jesus Christ, who says to us as he did to the disciples, "I will not leave you as orphans." I will not leave you alone. I will not abandon you.

Orphans ... Now that's a word we don't hear very often any more. It's not a popular word. In fact, we try to avoid the thought that orphans even exist any more. And yet, it is estimated that the South China Sea tsunami that struck at Christmas time a couple of years ago left as many as 1.5 million children orphaned. Just think — one point five million children left without parents from that one tragedy. And there's more children like them who are made orphans each day.

And yet, we know that it isn't just children without parents who are orphans. There are countless others who feel abandoned, who feel alone without help, who are left without guidance or comfort who feel like orphans as well. They can be like the following people.

The 55-year-old factory worker is laid off when the plant closes leaving him with no prospect of another job. Too old and too weary to consider re-training, without skills that can be retooled, he feels alone. Unemployed and living off of pension funds that will soon run out, who is there to say to him, "I will not leave you as orphans"? I will not abandon you.

Or how about the eighty-year-old, alone at home after fifty years of marriage? Her spouse no longer with her, she nods off in front of the television set, a half-eaten frozen meal cold in front of her. She is alone in a house too big for her, children with lives of their own in different towns. Who is there to say to her, "I will not leave you as orphans"? I will not abandon you.

Or the AIDS ravaged youth of Africa. His errant lifestyle has brought shame on his family and driven his friends away. His body is dying and he lies alone in pain. For him and for the millions of others throughout the world who face this dreaded disease, who is there to say to him, "I will not leave you as orphans"? I will not abandon you.

It may be the teenager who is different from the rest, the wife or husband whose spouse has left them, the businessman whose business is failing, or the parent whose child has rebelled and left home. Or any of the countless others in the world around us who feel alone and without hope, rejected and lonely, like that rookie facing Bob Gibson. To them and to us, there is good news this morning. For there is one who is here to say, "I will not leave you as orphans." I will not abandon you.

In the gospel reading today, Jesus sits with the disciples in the upper room. The candles of the Passover meal have burnt short and it is time to go. One disciple has already fled the gathering, his betrayal a shock to all of them. Another disciple's denial is predicted and the pain of the cross awaits them all. And in the midst of this uncertain gathering, Jesus reaches out to them in love. Listen again to what he says in various verses.

> *I will not leave you as orphans. I will come to you. In just a little while, the world will not see me again, but you will. For I will live again and you will, too. And I will ask the Father and he will give you another counselor who will never leave you — a Counselor who is the Holy Spirit.*

I will not leave you. I will not abandon you. I will send you a counselor, an advocate, a comforter, a friend who will care for you, who will offer you hope when there is none to be found, help when you are helpless, comfort when you can find none, and life in the face of death. The Holy Spirit is God's gift to us in our baptism. The Holy Spirit is God's presence in life. The Holy Spirit is Christ's gift to us and the promise to all the faithful.

197

The Holy Spirit sends us forth then as messengers of God's love to the poor, the unemployed, the young and the elderly, the sick and rejected, the unhappy, the sorrowful, the lonely and the dying. Who is there to say to them, "I will not leave you as orphans"? I will not abandon you. Well, God says it can be us. For we are the ones whom God entrusts with the good news. We are the ones sent forth with his love.

One of the themes that dominate this passage of scripture is the theme of love. "If you love me," Jesus says in verse 15, "obey my commandments. And I will ask the Father and he will give you another counselor, who will never leave you." In his great love for us, Jesus promises us help. He promises us the Holy Spirit. He promises us one whose presence will comfort us.

One could easily make the case that where there is no love, there is no comfort. That is what Jesus says. "If you love me...." For all too many of us, our Christian faith is centered eighteen inches too high, for that is the distance between our head and our heart, between knowing about God and knowing God, between understanding the presence of God and experiencing it.

You see, ideas are powerful things. But an idea has no power to heal a broken heart. An idea cannot take away the pain of heartache or fill the void of a loss. An idea can bring no comfort in the face of tragedy or peace in the wake of death. An idea is no substitute for experiencing the love of Jesus Christ. That's why Jesus says, "I will not leave you as orphans." I will not abandon you. You will have my love to strengthen you.

One of the most famous of all the English poets was a woman by the name of Elizabeth Barrett, an invalid for many years, her illness so severe that in the end, she was so weak, in fact, that she could not even raise her head from her pillow. One day, she was visited by a man by the name of Robert Browning, who had come to meet the author of the poetry that had inspired him so. After his first visit, an amazing thing happened. He left Elizabeth with such joy and happiness that she was able to lift her head. On his second visit, she sat up in bed. And on their third, they eloped and were married. Today she is known as Elizabeth Barrett Browning, the greatest of all of the English love poets.

198

Such is the power of love. Love has the power to heal. It has the power to make well. It has the power to lift drooping heads and fill empty hearts. No wonder people were healed just by coming into the presence of Jesus. Did you ever wonder about that— those stories in the New Testament that tell of someone who just came to Jesus and with just a touch or with just a word were made well? There's no secret to that. If we believe that Jesus was God's love incarnate, God's love in the flesh, why shouldn't people be healed by just coming into contact with him? For love has the power to do that. Love has the power to heal and that's what Christ can do.

But we must come into his presence. We must draw near to him. That's why we open God's word. That's why we study the Bible. That's why personal time of devotion and prayer are so important. For in them we come close to Christ. In them, we draw near to our Lord. And in coming to him, we enter the presence of God and God's love makes us well.

For he can heal the broken heart. He can fill the emptiness of loss. He can comfort the lonely and strengthen the weak. Sometimes we do feel like a motherless child. Sometimes we feel overmatched by life. But we have a Father who loves us. We have a Savior who triumphed over death. We have the Holy Spirit, God's presence, to bring faith to life. And because of that we have the peace of God that passes all understanding to keep our heart and mind in Christ Jesus. Amen.

---

1. Traditional Negro spiritual, author unknown.

Connected To God

It's one of those stories that circulates around the internet. I don't know if it's true or not but it's so interesting that I have to share it with you. It seems that a woman came home to find her husband in the kitchen, shaking frantically with what looked like a wire running from his waist toward the electric outlet in the wall. Intending to jolt him away from the deadly electricity, she grabbed a piece of wood that was leaning by the back door, and gave him a good whack, breaking his arm in two places. It was a shame. He was not being electrocuted at all. He was merely listening to his new iPod.

Well, what would you have done? You walk in the kitchen and think your husband is being electrocuted. You can't touch him for fear of being electrocuted yourself. So this woman grabbed a board and hit him. How was she to know that he was just dancing to the music coming out of the tiny headset? She had to make an instant decision. And who knows? Maybe he deserved a good whack anyhow!

Decisions — we are all faced with them and so were the disciples. Forty days had passed since the resurrection. The disciples of Jesus have finally come to believe that he is truly alive. The scriptures tell us that Jesus appeared to the disciples on numerous occasions. But it is now time for him to return to heaven.

And so once again, Jesus appears to the disciples. He joins them in worship and announces to them that he will soon send the Holy Spirit to them and when the Holy Spirit comes, they will be his witnesses in Jerusalem, Judea, and Samaria, and even to the ends of the earth. And after he has spoken these words to them, after he has given them the assurance of his presence, he is lifted up before them to heaven. Literally, physically, lifted up before them and taken into heaven above.

What an exit. What a conclusion to his ministry on earth. Before their very eyes, Jesus ascends to heaven with the promise that the Holy Spirit will come upon them. Instead of Jesus being bodily present with them, they will become his body. Instead of his words to guide them, they will speak his word for him. Instead of his physical presence, they will have his Spirit and be his presence in the world. And with that Spirit, they will truly experience Jesus' promise in Matthew 28. Remember how that goes. We call it the Great Commission — the great command Jesus gives us — "Go and make disciples of all nations, baptizing them in the name of the Father and of the Son and of the Holy Spirit. And lo, I am with you always, even until the end of the age."

Luke, in his account of the Ascension of Jesus, concludes the story by telling us what happened next.

> It was not long after he said this that [Jesus] was taken up into the sky while they were watching, and he disappeared into a cloud. As they were straining their eyes to see him, two white-robed men [two angels] suddenly stood there among them. They said, "Men of Galilee, why are you standing here staring up at the sky? Jesus has been taken away from you into heaven. And someday, just as you saw him go, he will return!"
> — Acts 1:9-11 (NLB)

And at this the disciples returned to Jerusalem. Upon entering the city, they went back to where they had gathered and (Luke tells us) "they were of one accord and devoted themselves to prayer."

It is the first picture we have of the church of Jesus Christ. It is the first mention of what the disciples did when Jesus was no longer with them. "They were of one accord and they devoted themselves to prayer." Imagine the effect the ascension must have had on those disciples! They had seen Jesus physically ascend into heaven. And they were told that they would be his witnesses. They would be his presence on earth.

Author Liz Higgs tells an amusing story of when her young daughter was baptized. Like many, after getting married, Liz had drifted away from the church. Even the birth of her daughter hadn't brought them back. It wasn't until her mother's death and the ministry of the church at that time that Liz decided it was time for them to reconnect with God. Because she hadn't been baptized as an infant, Liz's daughter, Lillian, was four when she was baptized. The pastor met with them and spoke about baptism, telling the little girl that in baptism, Jesus enters into our heart and lives within us.

Everything went fine until after the baptism. As they gathered in the entry, Lillian seemed troubled and refused to talk. "What's wrong, honey?" her mother asked. With pursed lips, Lillian replied, "Nothing. I just have to keep my mouth closed so Jesus won't get out." She was worried that if she opened her mouth too wide, Jesus might escape.

And yet the opposite is true, isn't it? In baptism we receive the Holy Spirit. Jesus' presence comes within us and we become his witnesses. Like the disciples at the ascension, we are sent forth to be his voice. We are told to speak for him because we are connected to him.

The disciples knew Jesus had ascended into heaven to be with God, the Father, and that was good news for them, because they also knew that they were connected to Jesus. Through his appearances to them after the resurrection — popping in and out of their lives — the disciples knew they were connected to Jesus. And because they were connected to him, they were also connected to God — not just to him physically as they had been to Jesus, but in Spirit.

It must have been a scary time for them. Jesus had been crucified for preaching his message of God's love. And now, he leaves and tells them to finish the work he has begun. You would think they would be afraid! But they weren't! The historical account tells us that just a few days later, at Pentecost, the Holy Spirit indeed was given to the disciples and they went forth into the world as his witnesses. Connected to Jesus, they were connected to God. And no matter what the future held for them, they were okay. For even though they did not know what the future held, they knew who held the future. And that was enough. That sense of being connected to Jesus enabled them to face persecution and suffering knowing that God was on their side. They could trust God because they knew Jesus.

It is said that the wife of Albert Einstein was once asked if she understood her husband's theory of relativity. She replied, "No, but I know my husband and that's enough." The disciples knew Jesus. They knew that he could be trusted with their lives and because they were connected to him, they were connected to God.

When you and I face difficulties and troubles in life, when life deals us a "bum hand" or the future looks bleak and hopeless, we need something to hold on to. We need to be connected to God. And we are!

The same Lord Jesus who welcomed the little children into his arms, the same Lord Jesus who healed the lepers and opened the eyes of the blind, the same Lord Jesus who offered himself up on the cross for our salvation, now sits at the right hand of God the Father and rules over all things. He can be trusted with our days. We can depend upon him to care for us. For Jesus rules over all creation and he is the head of the church.

The disciples knew that. That's why they responded the way they did. Remember: Luke tells us that when returned to Jerusalem, they were all of one accord. When you think about the diverse personalities that were part of that circle of disciples, that in itself is a minor miracle. The disciples' hearts were bonded together by the resurrection. It's almost as if the experience of the cross had shown them their own weaknesses — their shared failure to stand with Jesus in his hour of need, the betrayal of one of them, and the outright denial of Jesus by another — had shown them where they all stood — each a weak, sinful human being. But more than that, Jesus' forgiveness of them, his understanding and acceptance of them, and his willingness to receive them inspite of their failures and his promise to use them as his witnesses, had welded them together into a great unity. A unity that is a symbol of what the church of Jesus Christ is called to be.

Connected to God — that's what the Ascension of Jesus tells us. We are all connected to God. In our baptism, we are made children of God. Jesus enters our hearts and lives and comes out in our words and deeds. And we are given a great "commission" — a great purpose for living — to share the caring love of Christ.

As the church of Jesus Christ, we are called to welcome one another, to forgive, to love, and accept each other with the same forgiveness, love, and acceptance we have received from God. We are called to be those who speak of God's love to others, who bring family and friends to worship with us, who speak of God's love for him.

The disciples knew that. They returned to Jerusalem from the Mount of Olives after the Ascension of Jesus with joyful hearts, of one accord, devoted to prayer and to one another. That's what the Bible tells us. That's their example for us. They didn't know what awaited them. They didn't know the persecutions and hardships that lay ahead. They didn't know that of them, only the apostle John would live to old age. All the rest of them would meet a martyr's death. As they returned to Jerusalem, there was much they did not know.

What they did know, however, was that they would need each other. And the picture that we get of those disciples in the early days of the Christian church is one of joy. They joyfully gathered in worship with each other. They joyfully devoted themselves to prayer. And they joyfully accepted Jesus' mission to take the news of his resurrection to all the world. It was a privilege for them to represent him in the world because they knew they were connected to God.

We focus this morning on the Ascension of Jesus to remind us that we are connected to God. We are connected to God through faith in Christ Jesus. And like those first disciples, we have the same mission ahead of us. Jesus has ascended to God the Father in heaven. He is no longer bodily present in this world. But before he left, he gave us the same promise. God will fill us with his Spirit

205

and send us forth as witnesses of his love. We are now the presence of Jesus in this world — his word that is spoken and his love shared with others. May we be faithful in fulfilling this mission. In Jesus' name. Amen.

One In Faith And One In Service

A few choice words — that's what Jesus gives us this morning — a few choice words about our lives and faith. Just hours before being arrested, just hours before being tried and condemned, Jesus gathered his disciples around him and in all sincerity bowed his head and prayed for them and for us. These words from John 17 are part of a great discourse recorded by the gospel writer John, part of a great priestly prayer that Jesus offered up to his heavenly Father. These are words that unite us to God. And in them Jesus petitions his heavenly Father to protect us. He prays that we may continue his work and his prayer. In this prayer he prays for heavenly protection as we go forth one in faith and one in service.

Back in the days of King Arthur, a young knight would be invited to the banquet feast set for the Knights of the Round Table. He would be wined and dined. But he would not receive his golden spurs of knighthood until he went forth on a quest to serve his king and to help someone in distress. In much the same way, we are gathered in Christian community, and Jesus prays that his Father would protect us, for we, too, are sent forth one in faith and one in service.

There is a delightful old story about a certain Mexican bank robber by the name of Jorge Rodriguez, who operated along the Texas border around the turn of the century. He was so successful in his forays across the border that the Texas Rangers put an extra posse along the Rio Grande just to try and stop him and recover the money he stole.

Sure enough, late one afternoon, one of those rangers saw Rodriguez sneaking back across the border and trailed him at a distance back to his home village. The ranger watched Jorge mingle with the people in the town square and then go into a cantina to relax. The ranger came up with a plan. He waited until later when most of the people had left the cantina, slipped in through the back door and managed to get the drop on Rodriguez. With pistol in hand he confronted the bandit. "Tell me where you have the money hidden or I'll fill you with lead," he said. The ranger thought he had Jorge dead to rights. However, there was just one flaw in his plan. The ranger spoke no Spanish. And Jorge understood no English. So there they were, caught in a verbal impasse.

But just at that moment, an enterprising little guy stepped forward. "Ranger, sir," he said, "I am bilingual. Let me act as a translator for you." The ranger nodded and proceeded to tell him to ask Jorge where he had the money hidden or suffer the consequences. Nervously, Jorge responded, "Tell the big Texan not to shoot. I have the money hidden at the bottom of a dry old well. It's exactly one mile north of town at the abandoned old mill."

The little translator got a very solemn look on his face and said to the Texas Ranger in perfect English, "Jorge Rodriguez is a very brave man. He would rather die than tell you where the money is." It's absurd to say that what we don't know won't hurt us. Tell that to Jorge. It's equally absurd to say that what we believe doesn't matter, as long as we are sincere about it. What we believe does matter. How we live does make a difference.

As Jesus prepares to go to the cross, as he prepares to offer up his life for the world, he prays for his followers. He prays that God would protect us as we go forth one in faith and one in service.

As children of God we are united one in faith — faith in a living God who has revealed himself to us in the life, death, and resurrection of our Lord Jesus Christ. We are united in faith in Christ whose word unerringly fills us with faith and faith in the Holy Spirit whose presence guides us through life. As children of God, we believe that God speaks to us in the holy scriptures. That's why we call them God's word. We believe that we can rely upon the Holy Spirit to guide us in our understanding of that word and unite us in faith and in service to God. That's what Jesus prays for in the passage this morning. "I pray for them because they are yours." We are God's children and our lives demonstrate that as we are one in faith and one in service.

Jesus prays for himself and for us. He prays that God would protect us, as we go forth in this world. We are one in faith. But we must put that faith into action. I read somewhere about a father who had decreed in his will that he would provide $50,000 a year living expenses for his son while he was still in college. And you know what? That boy was in college for 46 years. He accumulated eleven degrees. But he never put a one of those degrees into practice. He spent his whole life going from one class to another never amounting to anything. He did no great evil, but he didn't do any good either.

In his prayer, Jesus makes it clear that we are God's. He offers us up to God's protection, and then he prays that we would be one in our faith in God. But Jesus expects more from us than that. We are also called to be one in service. It is in serving that our faith becomes real. It is in serving that our lives become what God intends for them to be. When we go forth from the "Round Table," we receive the blessing that God has in store for us.

Because when we serve one another, we serve Christ. He is the inspiration of our lives. He is the living example of faith in action. He is the Lord and Master of our lives, the heartbeat of our faith. And that faith becomes real when we go forth one in service.

I read recently about an advertisement campaign for the humane society in one city that pictured a dog and cat seated side by side on a beautiful couch. The caption over their heads read, "A Couple of VIPs — Very Important Pets." And at the bottom, a second line read, "What makes them important is who owns them."

If you and I are VIPs, there is only one reason — who owns us. We are children of God, followers of Christ, Jesus' own children — and it is in his footsteps that we follow. We are one in faith and one in service — all children of God and followers of Christ. From the prayer this morning it is clear that there is a purpose for our lives. And that purpose is that we go forth in serving, bringing the message of God's love to light.

We are one in faith and one in service. I'm sure you've heard the old story of the conversation between a pig and a cow. The pig is complaining to the cow that nobody ever has a kind word for him. "Look at the way I give of myself," he says. "I produce bacon, ham, and pork chops. The bristles of my skin are used for brushes, my hide for luggage. Why, some people even pickle my feet and consider them a delicacy. Why is it then that everyone speaks more kindly of you, the cow, than of me?" To which the cow replied, "My friend, perhaps it is that I give of myself while I am still alive."

We are one in faith and one in service and in serving those around us, our faith becomes real and the message of God's love is shared with all. In the early 1800s, there was a New Englander by the name of John Chapman. One morning he appeared in Licking Spring, Ohio, and taking some seeds from a burlap bag slung across his shoulder, he began to plant them. When he was finished, he quietly left town and moved on to the next town, where he did the same. You see, Chapman had read that there were few fruit-bearing trees in the midwest and he decided to do something about that. So John Chapman, alias Johnny Appleseed, set out and in giving of himself in service to others, left a lasting legacy of himself for generations to come.

God calls us to be spiritual Johnny Appleseeds, sowing the word of God's love in the hearts and lives of those around us. We are one in faith and one in service when we offer ourselves, our lives, and our hearts, in service to God. That's what Jesus' prayed for, and that's what we do.

The year was 1939 and trainloads of Jewish children with pale, thin faces and sunken eyes were piling into Sweden. These boys and girls, mostly only three or four years old, would file off the trains with nothing except a large tag around their necks stating their name, age, and hometown. Most of them had already seen and experienced more than anyone should see or experience in a lifetime.

Swedish families were taking the children in for the duration of the war. One of the Swedes who opened his home to them was a man by the name of Johann Erickson, a middle-aged man who had no children of his own. When he learned that a frightened nine-year-old named Rolf needed a home, he responded and the little Jewish boy began to adjust to life in his new Swedish Lutheran home. At first, any knock on the door or loud voice outside would drive Rolf to the closet where he would hide and cover his head, but slowly the warmth and love of his new Swedish home began to change him. He put on weight and a spark of life returned to his eyes. Eventually, he even began to laugh and trust again.

Later after the Nazi invasion of Sweden, men at the machine shop where Johann worked warned him that he would lose the boy, that the Nazis would come and take him away. "They'll never take a child of mine," Erickson declared. "Not as long as I'm alive."

In keeping with the promise the Swedish government had made, Johann tried his best to respect Rolf's religious heritage. Even though he took Rolf to Lutheran services with him, he also saw that the boy learned his Jewish traditions and when the time came, he arranged for Rolf to be bar mitzvahed. For when the war ended, Johann wanted to be able to return to Rolf's parents a son who had been raised as closely as possible in the way they would have raised him themselves.

But when the war ended, the family was not reunited. Rolf's parents and all of his brothers and sisters had perished in the Holocaust, their fate one with the millions of others who had not survived the war. Rolf did not leave Sweden. Instead of returning to Germany — to the hometown scribbled on the note around his neck, Rolf remained in Sweden and became part of Johann's family. He was the son Johann never had. And over the years that followed, Rolf became a successful businessman and whenever Johann needed someone, Rolf was there. He took him to the doctor. He cared for him when he was ill. And when he lay on his deathbed, there was Rolf at his side to comfort him still. For in his time of need, Johann had offered him the love of God — and they were one in service.

211

As the candles of the Passover meal are burning short, as the meal draws to a close and his time on earth quickly fading, Jesus gathers the disciples around them and prays for them in the time to come. He prayed that God would protect them and he prayed that they would be one. He prayed for them and he prayed for us.

We are one in faith and one in service — sent forth to serve our loving God. We are called to share the love of God with others and to care for those near us in need. In his prayer to his heavenly Father, Jesus prayed that God would protect us. He prayed that we would serve and love. The apostle John says it well in his first letter, "We love because he first loved us." Therefore, let us be one in faith and one in service. In Jesus' name. Amen.

Sermons On The Gospel Readings

For Sundays
After Pentecost
(First Third)

Jesus' Vision
Of A Fun, Free Life,
Not Driven By Purpose

Mark Ellingsen

To Betsey
With love

Introduction

By the time you get this book, some of the steam created by Rick Warren's best-seller, *The Purpose-Driven Life*, will have cooled. Nevertheless, the book's impact will be with us for some time, given the large number of people it reached (perhaps some of our parishioners) and in view of the numerous congregations (perhaps your own) which sponsored study groups about it.

There is a lot in the book to like. It starts out so well.

> *It's not about you.*
> *The purpose of your life is far greater than your own personal fulfillment, your peace of mind, or even your own happiness ... If you want to know why you were placed on this planet, you must begin with God.*[1]

But the stress on purpose and being driven by one's sense of God's purpose can lead to problems and misunderstandings in everyday life. The idea of being *driven*, even if it is God's purpose that does the driving, is likely to be experienced as a new set of demands, as a living under the Law of God. And long ago, Saint Paul taught us what a curse that is (Galatians 3:10).[2] When you feel like you have to do something, have to live a certain way, even if it is being driven by God's purpose, you never find contentment. You are never sure you have done it right or done enough. The gospel according to Rick Warren and a lot of other megachurch pastors can very easily lead to a life of guilt and feelings of inadequacy or failure.[3] Purpose-driven living is not much fun. I think that Jesus, Saint Paul, and the Protestant Reformers offer us a vision of a life that is a lot more fun and more free than the lifestyle Warren proposes. You have more fun when you don't take yourself and what you do so seriously. Cutting-edge neuroscience bears that out, too. My sermons try to provide you and your flock a chance to experience this alternative reality.

The whole idea of a life driven by purpose makes the Christian realist in me uncomfortable for other reasons. Though there is a sense in which I can agree, that God does have a plan for all our lives, that purpose is very often hidden under all sorts of mundane, even contradictory events in life, including our own stubbornness and narcissism (Deuteronomy 32:39; Psalm 30:7). To his credit, Warren is willing to admit the mundane character of much that God calls us to do, and he even concedes that we have weaknesses. But he gives the distinct impression that we can get over these problems, making points which overlook how chronic our self-seeking, sinful ways are (Romans 7:14-26).[4] In fact, Rick Warren's idea of a purpose-driven life can easily lead the faithful to take themselves too seriously, to forget that it is not their own sense of purpose that realizes good in life, that any good that emerges out of the things you and I do is a kind of "divine accident," a miracle of God's grace despite our self-seeking pride. We indeed need some healthy antidotes to purpose-driven living, less grandiose and self-aggrandizing visions which understand life more modestly as nothing more than a life devoted to "glorifying God and enjoying him forever" (as the Pilgrims taught us) or as a life of "brave sinning" (as Martin Luther taught us).[5] These sermons try to move us in those directions.

We need this biblical and reformation countervision to Warren, but not just because of the impact of his book. Despite how commendable his intention is to get us away from narcissistic preoccupation with the self and more centered on God, much of the reason for the popularity of his vision is that it reinforces unfortunate cultural trends in twenty-first-century American life. I've already been lamenting about how, probably contrary to his intentions, Warren wants us to take ourselves a bit too seriously (for we have a God-given purpose). Granted, we all have a God-given purpose, but we also need to be reminded how easy it is to justify what we do by invoking God. Besides, Americans, caught up in all the self-seeking narcissism and passion for self-fulfillment that our society teaches us to chase, take themselves seriously enough

216

— too seriously. They don't need another dose of it on Sunday in church. We need to get free from those hang-ups. What we need is more humility, a deeper awareness of our selfishness and of how such sin mars even the good we do. Likewise, Americans are task-oriented enough. Many of us are on the job 24/7 and are working more hours with less vacations per year than our counterparts in other Western industrialized nations. We do not need a vision of the Christian life which is more about what we should do, as Reverend Warren proclaims.[6] We could use a little more fun in our faith, along with more freedom. That's what these sermons are all about. They are really more a critique (Jesus' critique) of contemporary American society, only secondarily of Warren and his purpose-driven model.

Preparing sermons of the genre I have planned is just another way of preaching about the unconditional love of God, the way that Saint Augustine, Martin Luther, and John Calvin taught the Church to read Saint Paul and Saint John. They all believed that when you experience God's unconditional love, it sets you free and gives joy. It also helps in proclaiming that vision to others if you've been nurtured like I have, since the cradle, by penultimate expressions of unconditional love. Two women in my life come to mind. My mother, Edna (along with my father, the late Emil), Ellingsen introduced me to no-strings-attached love. And I have experienced it daily for nearly 35 years with the wonderful lady I've lived with, Betsey. This is thirteenth time I have written a dedication page like this one, and I am not very original at this point. In different words, I have just been communicating the same thing to her: "You're very special, and I love you."

Love, especially when it is a reflection of the unconditional love of God, is a potent thing. I can attest, and I hope that these sermons will help you experience it too, that the unconditional love of God does not drive you to anything — not even a purpose. This is a love that sets you free really to be yourself, no longer hung up on what others expect of you. That kind love makes life a little happier, a lot more fun. Amen.

1. Rick Warren, *The Purpose-Driven Life: What On Earth Am I Here For?* (Grand Rapids, Michigan: Zondervan, 2002), p. 17.

2. *Op cit*, Warren. It is no accident that a survey of the biblical texts Warren cites in his book (pp. 327-334) rarely includes references to the books of Romans and Galatians, and the pericope noted here as well as other texts which stress the unconditional grace of God are never cited.

3. I have in mind here Prosperity Gospel preachers like T. D. Jakes, Paul Crouch, Kenneth and Gloria Copeland, Eddie Long, and Joel Osteen.

4. *Op cit*, Warren, pp. 212-213, 219-220, 260-264, 276.

5. Martin Luther, *The [Puritan] Shorter Catechism* (1646), Q.1; Martin Luther, *Letter To Philip Melanchthon* (1521), in *Luther's Works*, Vol. 48, ed. Gottfried G. Krodel (Philadelphia: Fortress Press, 1963), pp. 281-282.

6. *Op cit*, Warren. For examples of how Warren's task (law)-orientation tends to compromise the primacy of grace, see pages 212 and 201.

Life And Forgiveness Come Easy When You're Filled With The Spirit

It's Pentecost Sunday, a day when we celebrate the birth of the Church and the giving of the Holy Spirit, as our lesson from Acts (2:1-21) reports. But the Bible makes it clear that it was not just on that first Pentecost that the Holy Spirit was given. It happened to some in Old Testament times (Judges 6:34; 1 Samuel 11:6; 16:13). However, the Spirit was also given during Jesus' own life on earth. Here's the story.

The disciples were still pretty much in despair that Sunday evening over the events of Good Friday, over the loss of their dear friend and, with his apparent failure, the withering of all their hopes and dreams. Yes, there had been some fantastically hopeful news relayed by Mary Magdalene (whatever you may think of her). She had seen, as Peter and John did later, that the stone in front of Jesus' tomb had been removed. They had both even found the linens that had wrapped the body! Then to top it off, Mary Magdalene even reported that she had seen Jesus. But, at least as John tells the story, she seems not really to have understood what it was all about.[1] So the disciples were hoping, but not yet certain, not really understanding, and still in despair. I'm not always sure I understand the resurrection, and am not always confident in its reality. How about you?

Then it happened that evening. The doors of the house were locked, because the disciples were under suspicion by Jewish leaders, as followers of Jesus. But then suddenly he stood among them, saying "Peace be with you." Showing them his hands and his side

219

led the disciples to rejoice. They had seen the risen Lord! (John 20:19-20).

The story continues. Jesus reassured the happy disciples with another blessing of peace. (Do not forget that to offer such a blessing in ancient Hebrew culture connoted a wish for "completeness," for the total well being of those being blessed. In John's linguistic tradition, the Greek term translated "peace" here is a wish for complete concord and unity among all those blessed.) Jesus comes to wish the best for his people as well as to offer them unity and harmony with himself and with each other. That's what he wants for you and me.

The risen Lord continues to address his followers. He told his disciples he was sending them, as his Father had sent him (John 20:21). Christ is sending you and me! And then, John says, Jesus breathed on them; he gave them the Holy Spirit! (John 20:23). There you have it. According to John's version of the gospel, the disciples had the Holy Spirit even before Pentecost.

So what? What's the point of all this talk about the Holy Spirit? If you don't believe in speaking in tongues like the Pentecostals do, what does the Holy Spirit have to do with everyday life? Our Bible lessons for today and the title of this sermon tell you. After Jesus had given the Holy Spirit to his disciples, he added, "If you forgive the sins of any, they are forgiven; if you retain the sins of any, they are retained" (John 20:23). By giving us the Holy Spirit, Jesus gives his followers, gives you and me, the authority to forgive. The point here is to remind us that forgiveness is a big part of Pentecost. It's like Martin Luther and the fourth-century African theologian, Saint Augustine, said, "Forgiveness of sin is what the church is all about."[2]

Certainly, forgiveness is a central aspect of Christian living, and so it makes sense that the church would be all about this reality. Indeed, Rick Warren, in his best-seller, *The Purpose-Driven Life*, asserts that restoring broken relationships, forgiving, is an aspect of our purpose as Christians. He tells us that we need to become peacemakers in order to get God's blessing, that if we pray first about the conflict, we will discover that God will change our hearts or the heart of the person who did us wrong.[3] It's like we have to do something first in order for God to bless us or before God gets involved in forgiving. Forgiveness, like life itself, is a burden, if Reverend Warren is correct. I understand the sentiments of Rick Warren here to stress the importance and value of forgiveness, but I wonder what happened to the Holy Spirit and the grace of God, I wonder what happened to Christian freedom and the joy of living.

Remember Jesus' emphases. He linked the Holy Spirit to forgiveness. He wanted to make it clear in so many ways, that forgiveness and Christian living are *works of God.*

During the Reformation, Martin Luther preached several sermons on the very gospel lesson that the church has assigned for Pentecost. On two occasions, Luther tried to make very clear how God is involved in the forgiveness of our sin. He started by pointing out how Jesus approached the disciples on that first Easter in the locked house. It is how he approaches you and me today.

When Jesus came to the disciples, Luther claimed, he showed them his hands and his feet, and then his side. Just like I was trying to get you to see when we told the story again, this meeting the disciples had with Jesus that first Easter is like the way he comes to you and to me today. You see, Martin Luther contended, while preaching in Borna, Germany, in 1522, that "the Lord's hands and feet really signify nothing but his works ... And the showing of his side is nothing but the showing of his heart, in order that we may see how kind, loving and fatherlike his mind is toward us."[4]

In another sermon preached over a decade later, probably just for family and houseguests, Luther elaborated on these points. Commenting on Jesus' appearance to the disciples that Easter evening, the first Reformer pointed out that Christ does not wait for his disciples to go after him. In fact, he goes after them (and us) through locked doors. (You and I have a way of putting up locked doors for Jesus, don't we? That's one of the reasons that it is hard to believe in his resurrection sometimes.) But Jesus breaks though those locked doors of our lives. And when he comes, he comes in a warm friendly manner. That's what the offer of peace is all about.

Luther goes on to add that with this example Christ presents his heart, who he is and what kind of heart he bears to us. Christ treats his disciples and us so tenderly, not reproaching anyone for unbelief and sin. Instead he comforts, strengthens, and lifts them, and us, up. This was done for our good and comfort.[5]

Isn't this a comforting word? You and I can be confident, certain of a loving God, because he keeps coming back. Jesus will not leave us alone. Our gospel lesson says that the disciples rejoiced when they saw the Lord Jesus (John 20:20). You and I can celebrate; his presence among you and me can make us happy!

When you realize that God, that Jesus, takes the initiative in your life, then you better understand how the Pentecost message of the giving of the Holy Spirit can make a difference in your life, how forgiveness and life come easy. The Spirit is Christ's presence among us (Galatians 4:6; 1 Peter 1:11), and so forgiveness and the good works of life are his work.

I like the way another great sixteenth-century Protestant Reformer, John Calvin, explained the Holy Spirit. He called the Spirit the power of God.[6] The Holy Spirit as God's power gives you and me the power, the strength, and the ability to do God's work. Think of it: If you and I do any good, if our lives have purpose, it is only because God has given us the power, the ability, to do them. That is what the giving of the Holy Spirit is all about.

Our gospel lesson makes this point in another way. It helps here if you know the Hebrew which the Jews spoke. Sometimes the Hebrew word for "breath" (*nephesh*) gets translated as "Spirit" in our English. And the other Hebrew word for "Spirit" (*ruach*) gets used interchangeably with *nephesh*. Get the point? When John says that Jesus gave the Spirit by breathing on his followers (John 20:22), his point was to make clear that the Spirit is the breath of God! When you understand the Holy Spirit in that way, then the Holy Spirit's role in your life becomes a little clearer. Why as the breath of God, the Spirit is as essential for our doing good works, as essential for us when forgiving others, as the air we breathe is necessary to keep us alive! When you see it that way, life is not as hard.

Forgiveness, like life, does not always come easy. It's so hard to forgive the son-of-a-gun who did you dirty, right? It is so hard sometimes to face another day. But it is not so difficult if you believe Jesus, that you are filled with the Holy Spirit. Because if you believe that, then you can also start to believe that you and I do not do the forgiving, do not give meaning to our lives, do not even have to find our purpose. It's all God's work! After all, his Holy Spirit is the one who has the power to do these things. His Holy Spirit provides the breath, the oxygen we need to live.

Once again, Martin Luther had it just right in a 1540 sermon that he preached in Dessau, Germany on our gospel lesson for today. He noted that only God himself has the power to forgive sins. That's good news, the Reformer claimed, because now we can be certain of our forgiveness. You can be certain of God's forgiveness, even if you are not quite sure that the one who says you're forgiven really meant it, because God gave it.[7] Get the point? When somebody says he or she forgave you, believe it! It's not theirs to give. The words of forgiveness are God's, even if the human speaker had some reservations. Take it as if God himself had spoken these words to you!

In the same 1540 sermon, Martin Luther went on to claim what a great treasure it is to hear that you are forgiven, since it is God himself forgiving us.[8] That's a blessing for you and me when we are called to exercise the power of the keys, when the opportunity is there for you or me to forgive the troublemaker and difficult person. Maybe we're not quite sorry enough, not quite sure we can forget along with the words of forgiveness. In this same sermon, Martin Luther reminds his hearers and us that our attitudes don't matter, because our attitude will never be sufficient. Forgiveness is God's work, not yours and mine![9]

I don't know about you, but that is a wonderful, freeing insight. It takes the pressure off me when it comes to my relationship with God, when it comes to my relationship with you and with others. Forgiveness, like most things pertaining to God, is not a matter of feelings.[10] Forgiveness depends on God; forgiveness is a work of the Holy Spirit whom Christ has already given to you and me. What a wonderful, freeing word. It takes the pressure

223

off, makes life a little easier, a little more fun. That is why our gospel lesson says that "the disciples rejoiced when they saw the Lord" (John 20:20).

In the 1522 sermon by Martin Luther that I have already noted, we find Luther summing up the essence of this joyful, Spirit-filled life just right. He was commenting on Jesus' word in our gospel lesson when he gave us the power of the keys to forgive sins and gave us the Holy Spirit. He said, "As the Father has sent me, so I send you" (John 20:21). Some preachers we noted before see this as an assignment of purpose by God, an expectation that if you do not give such proofs of your purpose you don't have faith. Luther wrote in response: "Not that good works are commanded us by this word; for where faith in the heart is right, there is not need of much commanding good works to be done; they follow of themselves."[11] When you have been filled with the Holy Spirit like you, I, and the disciples have, forgiveness and living come easy. Because they are God's job, such good days and purpose just "follow of themselves." Friends, the next time you have a tough task to do, have difficulty forgiving, enjoy it! God, the Holy Spirit, is going along, and he'll do all the heavy lifting for you! Amen.

---

1. For an example of scholarly consensus regarding how John diminishes the testimony of Mary Magdalene, see R. Alan Culpepper, *Anatomy of the Fourth Gospel: A Study in Literary Design* (Philadelphia: Fortress Press, 1983), pp. 144, 147, 161.

2. Martin Luther, *The Small Catechism* (1529), II.III.6, in *The Book of Concord*, ed. Robert Kolb and Timothy J. Wengert (Minneapolis: Fortress Press, 2000), p. 356; Augustine, *On The Creed: A Sermon To the Catechumens* (n.d.), p. 16, in *Nicene and Post-Nicene Fathers*, First Series, Vol. 3, ed. Philip Schaff (2nd printing; Peabody, Massachusetts: Hendrickson Publishers, 1995), p. 375.

3. Rick Warren, *The Purpose-Driven Life: What On Earth Am I Here For?* (Grand Rapids, Michigan: Zondervan, 2002), pp. 153 ff.

4. Martin Luther, *Of True Piety, The Law and Faith, and of Love To Our Neighbor* (1522), I.24, in *The Complete Sermons of Martin Luther*, Vol. 1.2, ed. John Nicholas Lenker (Grand Rapids, Michigan: Baker Books, 2000), p. 373.

5. Martin Luther, *First Sermon for First Sunday After Easter* (1534), pp. 2-5, in *The Complete Sermons of Martin Luther*, Vol. 6, ed. Eugene F. A. Klug (Grand Rapids, Michigan: Baker Books, 2000), pp. 55-56.

6. John Calvin, *Institutes of the Christian Religion* (1559), ed. John T. McNeill (4th printing; Philadelphia: The Westminster Press, 1960), I.XIII.18, pp.142-143.

7. Martin Luther, *The Fruit of Christ's Resurrection and the Authority and Office of the Keys Christ Exercised* (1540), II.27-31, p. 35, in *The Complete Sermons of Martin Luther*, Vol. I.2, pp. 390-391, 393.

8. *Ibid*, II.50, p. 401.

9. *Ibid*, II.51.

10. See Martin Luther, *Of Christ's Resurrection* (n.d.), I.13, in *The Complete Sermons of Martin Luther*, Vol. I.2, p. 244, where he claims that "feeling is opposed to faith and faith is opposed to feeling."

11. *Op cit*, Luther, *Of True Piety, The Law and Faith, and of Love To Our Neighbor*, II.28, pp. 374-375.

225

Having Fun With
The Great Commission

I find it interesting that today as we commemorate the Trinity doctrine, the church assigns the Bible reading that includes Jesus' Great Commission — Jesus' mandate to go and make disciples of all nations (Matthew 28:19). You can't do evangelism without believing in the Trinity, proclaiming the Triune God in whose name we baptize. And to believe in the Trinity, it seems, is to be an evangelist. That's the way it's supposed to work, but it does not feel that simple when you hear these words as calling you to be an evangelist. Let's face it, doing evangelism does not come easy for most of us.

I am right about our problems with evangelism, am I not? Most laity feel that that's the job of the pastor with a little help from the evangelism committee. Most of us say we do not have those gifts. Part of the problem is that it is a matter of our lack of confidence, a feeling that we do not know enough or do not feel comfortable approaching strangers. Another problem is that much of the purpose-driven talk we hear in churches these days is about the "mandatory" character of the mission of the Great Commission to do evangelism.[1] If doing evangelism is mandatory, and we're not doing a very good job about it, what does that say about our relationship to God? What does that say about being a Christian and doing evangelism? It doesn't sound like much fun, more like a burden. Is that what Jesus intends? It seems a little strange, insofar as according to Matthew these were Jesus' last words to his disciples before leaving them at the Ascension to return to the Father, that he would lay that kind of burden on his followers. Let's see.

Our gospel lesson's account of Jesus' commissioning the disciples is unique to Matthew, and so we need to get clear on the point Matthew seems to have been trying to make. There is a general consensus among biblical scholars that a core commitment of Matthew is to believe that the earthly Jesus and the exalted Christ are one. This seems implied in our gospel lesson today, as Matthew only reports in verse 18 that Jesus "came up" (*proselthown*) — language which is just as conducive to a heavenly appearance as it is to an earthly, bodily appearance.[2]

Why does it matter? This point seems to be Matthew's way of drawing us into the story. Because if there is a thin line between Jesus' post-resurrection earthly appearances and his heavenly communications since that time, then time itself is blurred. This entails that Jesus appeared to the disciples in a manner not different from the way in which he comes to you and me today. As a result of his fusing the time of Jesus and the time of the church, Matthew is effectively communicating to us that the disciples represent all future generations of believers. They represent you and me![3]

What does Jesus say to us? Because all authority in heaven and earth has been given to him, we are to "Go therefore and make disciples of all nations, baptizing them in the name of the Father and of the Son and of the Holy Spirit ..." (Matthew 28:18b-19). You and I have been commissioned, to do the work of evangelism. But wait, there are some nuances to Matthews' version of this commission that put some new, happy light on how to do evangelism.

New Testament scholars like to point out that because Matthew is the most Jewish of all the gospel writers, he tends to focus more on obedience. This is evident in his version of the Great Commission, as it is not so much preaching or the conjuring of the Spirit that is to be done in evangelism (Luke 24:46-48; Mark 16:15-18; John 20:22-23), but instead evangelists are to teach to the targets of evangelism "to obey everything ... [Christ] commanded ..." (Matthew 28:20).[4]

Does that mean evangelism is commanded? It is not insignificant to remind ourselves that before Matthew had Jesus tell his disciples and us that we were to teach potential converts to obey what Christ commanded, he refers to baptism in the name of the

Triune God. Again we are reminded that evangelism and the Triune God are inextricably linked. Let's also not forget that if evangelism includes obedience to what Christ commanded, the first point Matthew wants readers to know about Jesus' way of living was to tell the story of how Jesus began his ministry after his baptism by John by dealing with temptation (Matthew 4:1-11). And the main point of that temptation was to provide Jesus with an opportunity to testify that we are to "Worship the Lord ... God and serve only him" (Matthew 4:10; 6:33 cf).

Get the point? The heart of the obedient lifestyle to which evangelism aims is to focus on God alone. We are back to the main point I have been trying to make in this sermon. Evangelism comes easy, and it's a lot more fun, when you're focused on God.

Let's start with the nature of that God on whom we are focused. We have talked all along about the Trinity and the celebration of that mystery today. Contemplate that mystery with me for a moment.

What does it mean to say that God is Triune? It entails that God is a relational or communal God. He is always in a relationship with himself. The Father relates to the Son and to the Spirit, and the Spirit relates to the Son. Think of it. Forever and ever God has been in relationship. He is no solitary God.

You and I are created in the image of God, the Bible teaches (Genesis 1:26-27). That has implications for evangelism, for community life, and for doing justice in society. Carl Henry, the famous American Conservative Evangelical theologian and long-time editor of the Right's premier magazine, *Christianity Today*, had it right. He once wrote, "Trinitarian religion involves all men's relations to God and to society; the social relationships within the Trinity call out against any antisocial interpretation of personal religion."[5] In other words, to live your life in solitude without social relationships is to be out of harmony with the social creature God made you to be by creating you in his image. Relating to other people comes naturally to folks created in the image of our social God. Evangelism, making new friends in Christ, comes natural! It's only tough when you forget that you are God's creature, forget that you have a God who is naturally social and who has made you

229

that way. It is kind of hard to be unconcerned about society and the things of the world when you know who you are. People created in the image of God are not loners. They are people passionate about social relations as God originally created them.

There is another aspect to the nature of the Triune God that is relevant here. Yes, God is *three*, and is always socializing. But do not forget that he is also one. His communal character is also concerned to bring about unity. Well, evangelism is not just about cultivating social relationships. It also aims to facilitate unity, to bring all whom we contact into unity with us in the body of Christ. Just as God's sociality brings unity, the aim to facilitate such unity in Christ with all human beings through our social engagements with them is built into our genes. Can't you see? When it comes to doing evangelism (and seeking justice in society), you're a natural!

We are not only naturally equipped and gifted for evangelism and seeking just social relations. We have been wired by God to have fun with these commissions. That becomes clearer when we combine our recognition that, for Matthew, the heart of the obedient lifestyle to which Christians are called is to focus on God alone, along with the latest cutting-edge research on the brain.

Here's the story. For some time, pollsters have noted that religiously inclined people seem to have higher levels of happiness than the population as a whole.[6] The latest cutting-edge research on neurology tell us why this is the case.

It seems that when we are engaged in spiritual exercises like prayer and contemplation, the front part of our brains, specifically the frontal lobe (the part of the brain which is the seat of concentration) and the limbic system (the part of the brain where powerful feelings are created by pleasurable neurochemicals), become very active. The neurochemicals (also called monamines) released in prayer and meditation create pleasurable feelings of self-transcendence. Of course, it is not surprising that you would feel that you are getting beyond yourself when all this is happening, because when the front part of your brain is in overdrive as it is in prayer and meditation, the back part of your brain, the parietal lobe which is the seat of your awareness of yourself and its circumstances, grows dim.

230

Got it? When you become single-mindedly focused on God like Jesus was, and live the obedient lifestyle to which evangelism directs converts, then you forget yourself! You also experience these pleasurable, drug-like chemical reactions transmitted by the neurochemicals that are released in your brain.[7] It feels good to be caught up in God.

It gets more interesting. The part of our brain that is in over-drive when we are involved in spiritual activity contains within it the prefrontal cortex, which is a region of brain gray matter that is the seat of human emotions. It seems that feelings of happiness are to a great extent related to our activating this outer layer of gray matter in the front part of the brain, which then in turn becomes bathed in other neurochemicals, specifically dopamine and endorphins (which are like natural narcotics that numb pain and create feelings of euphoria).[8] In other words, when you are focusing on some activity that's bigger than you are and forgetting your particular circumstances, be it falling in love, parenting, music, play, service, prayer, yes even evangelism, you get a natural high! Dedicating your life to something bigger than you are, and so even focusing on God, makes you happy.

Modern neurobiology confirms the insights of Martin Luther, which he articulated over dinner table and perhaps some German beer in 1531. He provided his own formula for happiness.

> *Prayer helps us very much and gives us a cheerful heart, not on account of any merit in the work, but because we have spoken with God and found everything to be in order.*[9]

Immersion in spiritual matters, like focusing on God in prayer, makes you happy.

When we keep in mind how natural it is for us human beings to do evangelism, since we are socially oriented naturally just like the Triune God in whose image we have been made, and when we also keep in mind how much fun and happiness scientists now tell us we can find in spiritual undertakings and in getting focused on projects bigger than we are, then engaging in the Great Commission, doing evangelism, seems like a winner! Nobody has to tell you it's your purpose and require you to do it. It comes naturally along with a lot of good feelings and happiness from a Christian life focused on God.

Of course, there is still that ingrained inertia among lay people and even among some pastors about evangelism, a feeling that it is just not our gift. Neurobiologists would remind us that those feelings of insecurity emerge because we're too focused on the personal agendas that activate the back of our brain, not focused enough on thinking about the big picture part of our brain that gets the dopamine flowing. Getting focused (especially on spiritual matters), remember, makes you happy. Get focused on the Great Commission, forget yourself, and it won't be so bad. When you get that focused on God, then you see that he's your all-in-all, and that all you do is his work. When you lose yourself in that big picture, the dopamine, which stimulates feelings of pleasure and happiness, will start to flow. You'll enjoy it.

These brain dynamics and an appreciation of how God and his love permeate all you do also help us understand the sort of teaching or modeling of righteous living we are to do with potential converts. When they see you and me single-mindedly dedicated to the things of God and our (Great) Commission, a little of Jesus' single-minded devotion to God, a sense that grace surrounds you in all you do, will become theirs. And of course when that happens and they begin to activate the part of the brain exercised in concentration, the dopamine will flow. This life of obedience, like doing evangelism in that spirit, with an awareness that God is with you in dominating all aspects of your life, leads to happiness. The Great Commission and evangelism: It's a lot of fun! Amen.

1. Rick Warren, *The Purpose-Driven Life: What On Earth Am I Here For?* (Grand Rapids, Michigan: Zondervan, 2002), p. 283.

2. Brevard S. Childs, *The New Testament as Canon: An Introduction* (Philadelphia: Fortress Press, 1985), pp. 65-67; Eduard Schweizer, *Good News According To Matthew*, trans. David E. Green (Atlanta: John Knox Press, 1975), p. 528.

3. *Ibid*, p. 67-69.

4. *Op cit*, Schweizer, pp. 535-536.

5. Carl F. H. Henry, *God, Revelation and Authority*, Vol. V (Waco, Texas: Word Books, 1982), p. 213.

6. The Gallup Organization, "Americans' Personal Satisfaction" (2005), at www.gallup.com/poll/content/default/aspex?ci.

7. See Dean Hamer, *The God Gene: How Faith is Hardwired into Our Genes* (New York: Doubleday, 2004). Also see Antoine Lutz, Lawrence L. Greischar, Nancy B. Rawlings, Matthieu Richard, and Richard J. Davidson, "Long-term meditators self-induce high-amplitude gamma synchrony during mental practice," *Proceedings of the National Academy of Sciences*, Vol. 101, No. 46 (Nov. 16, 2004), pp. 16369-16373.

8. See Michael D. Lemonick, "The Biology of Joy," *Time*, Jan.17, 2005, pp. A12-A19; Stephen Braun, *The Science of Happiness: Unlocking the Mysteries of Mood* (New York and Chichester: John Wiley & Sons, 2000), esp. pp. 71-76.

9. Martin Luther, *Table Talk* (1531), No. 122, in *Luther's Works*, Vol. 54, ed. and trans. Theodore G. Tappert (Philadelphia: Fortress Press, 1967), pp. 17-18.

Proper 4
Pentecost 2
Ordinary Time 9
Matthew 7:21-29

With A Firm Foundation,
Application Is Second Nature

Practice makes perfect. If you do these things for Jesus, the Lord will bless you. Much Prosperity Gospel preaching advocates these themes. It's a word that America wants to hear. Even Reverend Rick Warren of the California megachurch, Saddleback Church, has said that:

> I must apply its [the Word of God's] principles. Receiving, reading, researching, remembering, and reflecting on the Word are all useless if we fail to put them into practice. We must become "doers of the word."[1]

Let's get Jesus' "take" on this.

Jesus was concluding his famed Sermon on the Mount. You have heard about that famous discourse many times during your life in the church. Among its gems include The Beatitudes (Matthew 5:3-12 — where Jesus refers to the blessedness of those who mourn, are pure in heart, and are peacemakers). Matthew also reports that Jesus taught The Lord's Prayer as well the Sermon on the Mount (Matthew 6:9-13).

In Matthew's version, the sermon as a whole is a summons to a way of life. This emphasis fits the first gospel's orientation to making Jesus' teachings more important than any of the other three gospel writers do, presumably because some church leaders after the resurrection were not doing so.[2] This seems evident in verses 21 through 23 in today's gospel lesson. New Testament scholars have concluded that the references to the judgment against those who have had charismatic experiences and performed healings are critiques of leaders of the post-Easter church who were not living in accord with the teachings of Jesus.[3]

So far it sounds like Pastor Warren is right about Matthew's version of Jesus — that an emphasis on practicing, on doing the word and living our purpose is the heart of the gospel. But wait, there is another wrinkle to the agenda of the author of the gospel of Matthew. Its author seems to have been identified with a community of Christians which was still very much in dialogue with the church's Jewish roots. But while maintaining this continuity, while still desiring to affirm that the message of Jesus did not nullify God's law (5:17-19), the author of Matthew still sought to distinguish the gospel of the kingdom from rabbinic thinking.[4] We can see this at several points in the gospel. For example, it becomes very clear in chapter 23 where Matthew has Jesus criticizing the scribes and the Pharisees, even to the point of contending in contrast to the rabbinic thinking of his day that one can observe all the precepts of the law and still be guilty before God (Matthew 23:28).[5]

This same concern to distance the gospel from Jewish and all other forms of preoccupation with the law and application through practice is evident at several points in Matthew 7 and in our gospel lesson for today. Pastor Warren and the other purpose-driven, Prosperity Preachers of the airwaves do not quite have it right. At the very beginning of Matthew chapter seven, Jesus warns in a very non-Pharisaic way that we are not to judge — that the log in our own eye is likely bigger than the speck you see in our neighbor's eye. We are all sinners, in need of grace.

But later in verses 7 through 9 we hear the famous words of comfort, that when you and I knock, the door will be opened. The Father in heaven is there to give good things! Of course that's the way it is to be a Christian. We're receivers, not doers!

Martin Luther put it this way in a sermon on the gospel of Matthew.

> *To make good people does not belong to the gospel, for it only makes Christians ... So one is not called a Christian because he does much, but because he receives*

*something from Christ, draws from him and lets Christ
only give to him ... If you look at what you do, you have
already lost the Christian name.*[6]

If you spend too much time fretting about application, doing, and
the living out of your purpose, be careful. You might lose the Christian
name, Luther says.

Mathew and Jesus seem to agree. We see this quite clearly in
verses 24 through 27 of today's gospel. Matthew reports that our
Lord claimed that everyone who hears and acts on Christ's Word
is like a wise man building his house on a rock. For such a believer, even if the rain falls, floods come, and winds blow, the house
will not fall on account of its firm foundation. By contrast, everyone who hears these words, but does not act on them, is like a
foolish man building a house on sand. People like that fall, their
faith shatters when the hard times come, just like when rain falls,
floods come, and winds blow, the house built on the sand will fall.
The moral of the parable: No matter how spiritual you try to be,
you need to be sure you have built the foundation of your faith on
Christ. He is your firm foundation, the rock!

Let's talk about foundations. Foundations are the chief means
of supporting a building, supporting the loads (the weight) of the
building. If the building were constructed on surface soil, any
movement of the earth might topple the structure. The issue, then,
is not how you apply Jesus' words, what you do, but where you
"settle" with your life. No act guarantees salvation if it is not based
on the foundation of Jesus (Matthew 7:22).[7]

There are rich implications for everyday life in this insight.
Realizing that only Christ can provide your foundation makes living the Christian life, makes living in everyday American life, a
lot easier. After all, I never saw a building sweat and agonize about
how it is going to withstand the storms of life. If the foundation is
firm, it may sway a bit in the wind (especially in the big thunder-
storm or the hurricane), but it still stands tall and proud in the
midst of the storm. What is the cause of the building's strength?
Not the windows, walls, not even the columns and beams get the
credit. No matter how strong these parts of a building are, they are

not sufficient without the firm foundation. That is why these parts of the building are not what keeps things intact. That is sort of the status that your and my activities and practices have with regard to maintaining ourselves in life. No matter how many grand things you do, no matter how well you apply the teachings of Jesus, no matter how firm your faith and sense of purpose, it all tumbles down if you are not rooted in Jesus. He is the one, then, who gets all the credit! And because the foundation is firm, the other parts of the building do their thing effortlessly, just like our application of Jesus' teachings. Our carrying out and living out our divine purpose comes spontaneously, without much effort. Just like the windows, walls, columns, and beams do not keep the building erect and do not agonize over their tasks, so you and I have been set free from agonizing. Life is a lot less stressful, a lot more fun, when you are rooted and settled, in Christ.

Who gets the credit for this lifestyle? The foundation of course. Commenting on this text, the man who was probably the greatest, most influential theologian of the last century, Karl Barth, has claimed that "... the righteousness which the Sermon [on the Mount] exacts is inseparable from the one who exacts it. It is his righteousness. It does not consist in the greatness and splendor of what man himself achieves ... Everything depends on the fact that the required righteousness does not now consist in a self-assertive grasping a promise, in a self-willed desire to fulfill the law, as though this were an independent law...."[8]

Yes, Martin Luther was correct: Christians are receivers, not doers. In one of his sermons, a man widely recognized as perhaps the great preacher of the early church, John Chrysostom, wrote: "Wherefore both against our will He befriends us often, and without our knowledge oftener than not."[9]

This appreciation that we do nothing when it comes to Christ's benevolence to us, that the foundation of your life does all the work, will change your perspective on what you do with the gifts he has given us. It makes you grateful for what you have, not just grateful for the big things but even for the little, seemingly ordinary things you have, like friendship, family love, the food you eat, and the job you have. Again the "golden-mouthed one" John

Chrysostom (this is what the Greek word *Chrysostom* means) said it well. Elsewhere in the sermon we noted, he wrote:

> *Let us therefore continually give thanks, for our own blessings, and for those of others, alike for the small and for the great. For though the gift be small, it is made great by being God's gift.*[10]

This sort of gratitude will make another difference in your life. Again we turn to the latest scientific research on happiness, on what makes people happy. A University of California psychologist, Sonja Lyumbomirsky, has noted that satisfaction with life is boosted in most people who savor life's joys and count their blessings. This is hardly surprising, since other research on the brain has indicated that the more focused you are on projects and insights greater than you are, the more the pleasurable brain chemicals saturate the brain.[11] With a firm foundation (in Christ), life and application is a joy. Even temptations do not shake faith when your faith has the firm foundation in Christ. That's what the great Reformation theologian, John Calvin, said in a commentary on our gospel lesson for today.[12] Doing Christ's thing is both natural and joyful when you've got your foundation rooted in him.

Of course, there are still forces which try to pull you away and take away your peace and joy. It is still very possible to be pulled away from this insight, and instead focus on all the impressive activities, like the growing megachurches and the wealth accumulated by or promised to their members, which are said to be happening within certain Prosperity Gospel circles. Contemporary American social trends want to lure you away from where you are planted, providing instead its promises of self-fulfillment and novelty. To cling to a firm foundation seems to make you a "stick-in-the-mud." What is new and fresh and customized to your needs is what attracts us and makes us yearn. America and a lot of its religious convictions teach us that you've got to be flexible and think about what's in your own self-interest, about acquiring or being in the presence of what makes you seem like a winner.[13]

Martin Luther put it just right one time while explicating today's gospel lesson. It is as if he understood contemporary American dynamics:

> *I am convinced that if someone were to arise here today and perform just one sign, whole crowds would fall for it. That is how the crazy mob behaves. If someone pulls out something new in front of them and makes them stare, they forsake everything, the Word and God and doctrine, and go gaping after that.*[14]

Those with a foundation in Christ, those caught up in his overwhelming love, are tempted to follow the crowd, to chase after what is novel and sensational. Those with Christ as their foundation do have to struggle, may sway in the wind. But the good news of our gospel lesson for today is that our firm foundation, Christ, will not give way. Take heart, friends, and rejoice. You and I are reminded today of his authority (Matthew 7:29), an authority that will not let you or me go! No matter how strong and turbulent the storms of this life blow, keep in mind the firm foundation of our lives that will not be shaken, will not let all our feeble efforts to apply his insights to become burdensome or to fail. Thank God for our foundation. Whatever purposes we are to have in life cannot ultimately fail when you are rooted in Christ! Amen.

---

1. Rick Warren, *The Purpose Driven Life: What On Earth Am I Here For?* (Grand Rapids, Michigan: Zondervan, 2002), p. 191.

2. For these observations about the gospel of Matthew I am indebted to Eduard Schweizer, *Good News According To Matthew*, trans. David E. Green (Atlanta: John Knox Press, 1975), pp. 179-180.

3. *Ibid*, pp. 178-179.

4. *Ibid*, pp. 16, 188.

5. *Ibid*, p. 189.

6. Martin Luther, *The Gospel and Christ, Or Jairus' Daughter Raised and the Woman With an Issue of Blood Healed* (n.d.), pp. 5-6, *The Complete Sermons of Martin Luther*, Vol. 3.1, ed. John Nicholas Lenker (Grand Rapids, Michigan: Baker Books, 2000), pp. 329-330.

7. *Op cit*, Schweizer, p. 191.

8. Karl Barth, *Church Dogmatics*, Vol. II/2, ed. G. W. Bromiley and T. F. Torrance (Edinburgh: T. & T. Clark, 1957), p. 692.

9. John Chrysostom, *Homilies On the Gospel According To St. Matthew* (pp. 386-388), XXV. 4, in *Nicene and Post-Nicene Fathers*, First Series, Vol. 10, ed. Philip Schaff (2nd printing; Peabody, Massachusetts: Hendrickson Publishers, 1995), p. 175.

10. *Ibid.*

11. See page 233, notes 7-8. Also see Sonja Lyumbomirsky, as summarized in Claudia Wallis, "The New Science of Happiness," *Time*, January 17, 2005, pp. A8-A9.

12. John Calvin, "Commentary On a Harmony of The Evangelists, Mattew, Mark, and Luke" (1555), in *Calvin's Commentaries*, Vol. XVI.I, trans. William Pringle (Grand Rapids, Michigan: Baker Books, 2005), p. 370.

13. For such an analysis of American social dynamics, see my *Blessed Are the Cynical: How Original Sin Can Make America a Better Place* (Grand Rapids, Michigan: Brazos Press, 2003), esp. pp. 22-23, 114-115; Richard Sennett, *The Corrosion of Character* (New York and London: W. W. Norton & Co., 1998), pp. 55-63, 101-102; Robert D. Putnam, *Bowling Alone* (New York: Simon & Schuster, 2000), esp. pp. 241-245.

14. Martin Luther, *Commentary on the Sermon on the Mount* (1532/1533), in *Luther's Works*, Vol. 21, ed. Jaroslav Pelikan (St. Louis: Concordia, 1956), p. 280.

Sick People Like Us Will
Always Need The (Divine) Doctor

Jesus spent a lot of his time hanging around undesirable folks, not with "good" people like us. I mean here in today's gospel lesson we have the story of his calling Matthew, the tax collector (Matthew 9:9). Of course, most of us have our hang-ups with taxes. But in the eastern part of the Roman Empire in Jesus' day tax collectors were notorious for overcharging the taxed, often with harassment, and keeping the difference between what was actually owed and what was collected, for themselves. In short, they were regarded by many who lived in the Roman Empire as robbers, as crooks. Another problem was that such tax collectors violated Jewish tradition, because not only did they defile themselves in dealing with Gentiles, but also because they were actually employed by Gentiles like the Romans and the Herodians.[1] No, tax collectors were undesirable people.

Associating with a sleaze like Matthew is not all Jesus did. Not only did he associate with Matthew, just one tax collector, he went and had a meal with a bunch of them and other sinners (Matthew 9:10)! It was scandalous for a good man like Jesus to associate with that crew. It was all the more scandalous from a Jewish perspective, given the fact that Jesus was eating with people who had already been polluted by association with those Gentiles.

What does all this have to do with you and me? I mean, we are not like that low-life with whom Jesus associated. You and I are good, decent people. Gee, we are a lot like the Pharisees who chastised Jesus for eating with the tax collectors and other sinners (Matthew 9:11). You know the answer he made: "Those who are

243

well have no need of a physician, but those who are sick ... I desire mercy, not sacrifice. For I have come to call not the righteous but sinners" (Matthew 9:12-13).

These are hard words for good American Christians like us. After all, Americans think of themselves as basically good and decent people. In fact, there is a widespread consensus in America that we are all too healthy most of the time for a doctor. This message is even in the church. Poll data bears out the validity of this conclusion. A 2000 *New York Times* poll revealed that 73% of the American public believe that we are born good. Another, much more recent 2005 poll of American Christians conducted by the Barna Research Group revealed that only 54% of the public believe that works do not get us into heaven.[2]

Are you clear about what this means? About seven in ten Americans think that we are good, so good that we can contribute to our own salvation by pleasing God. There is no reason to think that these numbers have changed much in the past few years. "Good" folks like us are likely to avoid sinners and other low-life. Deep down, though we might not admit it, we sort of wish our Lord would avoid that type, too. After all, we don't welcome many of them into our church, and if they come in from off the streets or come from good backgrounds like us but get in trouble or get involved in affairs, we are quite likely to gossip about them. So had we been around Jesus when he sat down and ate with all those tax collectors and other sinners, you and I probably would have joined the Pharisees in complaining about the sort of folks with whom Jesus hung around. Of course, you will say that you are no Pharisee. But how welcoming are you and I to the sort of folks Jesus accepted? In fact, you and I are no better than they are.

In the church, there is another way of reinforcing these Pharisaic propensities. We speak of growing in grace. One of the most popular religious best-sellers in history, dealing with our purpose in life, tells readers that "God wants you to grow up ... It takes an intentional commitment."[3] "We can get better," the most influential preachers in America say. What do you think? I'll tell you what it does to me. It lays guilt on me, and yet the American in me who wants to do for myself and improve myself likes it. In a way, those are sentiments not unlike the Pharisees expressed in the confrontation with Jesus.

The desire to suppress the seedy side of our human nature, to act as if we were not really that bad, or at least that we could get better, is part of the baggage you and I carry as a result of our fallen human nature. In his commentary on this text, the great Protestant Reformer, John Calvin, pointed out why we do not want to hear this message.

> *Hypocrites, being satisfied and intoxicated with a foolish confidence in their own righteousness, do not consider the purpose for which Christ was sent into the world, and do not acknowledge the depth of evils in which the human race is plunged ... The consequence is, that they are too stupid to feel the miseries of men, or to think of a remedy. While they flatter themselves, they cannot endure to be placed in their own rank, and that injustice is done them, when they are classed with transgressors.*[4]

These are pretty harsh words. Calvin says that you and I are hypocritical and stupid, inclined to flatter ourselves. We think that we are so good that it is down-right insulting to be grouped with sinners.

He is right, isn't he? I do not want to hear this message. I want to hear words about my potential, about my purpose, about what I can do, with a little help. I have had this experience in ministry in the last 25 years or so, and similar experiences are commonly reported among my colleagues. I and they have been requested, even warned, to "stop beating up" on the congregation, because "people come to church to feel good about themselves."

That is precisely the problem. You and I want to think that we are basically decent, at least that we are on the way to self-sufficiency, because that will demonstrate to ourselves that we are capable and have self-worth. We do not like being needy. We do not want to admit that we are in need of a physician, or we would remain forever dependent. And that is where our sin becomes diabolically apparent. We really do not want Jesus! The great

American Puritan preacher of the eighteenth century, Jonathan Edwards, said it so well in what was perhaps his second most famous sermon, *God Glorified in Man's Dependence.*

> *Hence these doctrines and schemes of divinity that are in any respect opposite to such an absolute and universal dependence on God, derogate from His glory ... Now whatever scheme is inconsistent with our entire dependence on God for all ... is repugnant to the design and tenor of the gospel....*[5]

You and I are really telling God that we do not need him if we fail to confess our insidious selfish sinfulness. The next time you do not want to make that confession, keep in mind that in our gospel lesson, Jesus told us Pharisees that he only came for sinners, not for the righteous (Matthew 9:13). Keep in mind that insight and how selfish you are in wanting all the credit for what you do.

Sin is selfishness. The essence of sin is selfishness, what the great African theologian of the early centuries Saint Augustine called concupiscence.[6] You and I, he contended, are so starved for satisfying our needs, that we are almost like sex addicts, looking to please ourselves in everything we do. I really like what Martin Luther said about this matter. While lecturing on the book of Romans before the Reformation, he wrote:

> *For man cannot but seek his own advantages and love himself above all things, and this is the sum of all his iniquities. Hence even in good things and virtues men seek themselves, that is, they seek to please themselves and applaud themselves.*[7]

There is no such thing as a good deed or sinless action. That is why we need Jesus, our spiritual doctor, throughout our lives.

In the same lecture series, Luther described the problems that emerge when we are unwilling to admit our sin. He told his students:

246

This is like the case of the doctor ... who wishes to heal his patient, but finds that he is a man who denies that he is sick, calling the doctor a fool and an even sicker person than himself for presuming to cure a healthy man. And because of the man's resistance the doctor cannot get around to recommending his skill and his medicine. For he could do so only if the sick man would admit his illness and permit him to cure him....[8]

But we all want to be great and good. What of those parishioners of mine and my colleagues who wanted to be built up in church? I want that for them, too. The gospel is about the good news of God's affirmation of us, of our true greatness. You need to be clear, though, what it is that makes you and me great.

The renowned seventeenth-century French intellectual, Blaise Pascal, has written:

Man's greatness comes from knowing he is wretched; a tree does not know it is wretched.
Thus it is wretched to know that one is wretched, but there is greatness in knowing one is wretched.[9]

How does knowing that you are wretched make you great? It is a healthy antidote to that selfishness which has been with us since the fall into sin, the selfishness with which you and I have been cursed since birth. But hanging around that doctor (Jesus) can make you healthy, pure, and well. Martin Luther put it this way one time in one of his 1535 lectures.

Thus if I look at Christ, I am completely holy and pure, and I know nothing at all about the Law; for Christ is my leaven. But if I look at my flesh, I feel greed, sexual desire, anger, pride the terror of death, sadness fear, hate, grumbling, and impatience against God.[10]

An awareness of our ongoing need of Christ is really the essence of the gospel, what it takes to be truly wrapped up in God. In the very sermon of his that I noted earlier, the great colonial-era

247

American preacher, Jonathan Edwards, put it this way: "Faith abases men, and exalts God; it gives all the glory of redemption to him alone."[11]

Edwards has in a nutshell what is at stake for you and me in believing that we will always need the divine doctor (Jesus). If it were true that we could grow out of that dependence, presumably by our commitment, then you and I would be really exalting ourselves, not giving God all the glory. What do you want with your life? Jonathan Edwards and the entire Puritan tradition tell us that life is all about glorifying God and enjoying him forever.[12]

Enjoyment. That is wonderful thing about realizing your sickness, and not being so concerned about your growth in grace and level of commitment. Knowing that you are sick, that doctor Jesus is treating you, regards us as holy and pure, takes the pressure off you and me. That's what makes life enjoyable, an appreciation that no matter how much sicker we get with our crazy ventures, no matter our failures to get better, we have this wonderful, caring doctor working to heal us.

No two ways about it: In a paradoxical way, there is something wonderfully freeing, even comforting and inspiring in becoming aware of how (spiritually) sick and selfish you are. It helps you become more self-critical, perhaps more socially and politically alert, and certainly more tolerant, less Pharisaic, about other's foibles. Someone like that, always in need of the spiritual doctor, is likely to become more alert to the miracles in life, as we marvel that our beloved doctor and Lord can make any good emerge from our sinful, selfish motives. Life is truly miraculous and joyful when you continue to feel the need for our spiritual doctor! Amen.

1. For more details on tax collectors in the Roman Empire, see Eduard Schweizer, *The Good News According to Mark*, trans. Donald H. Madvig (Richmond, Virginia: John Knox Press, 1970), p. 65.

2. *New York Times* magazine, 7 May 2000; Barna Research Online, "Beliefs: Salvation" 2005, at www.barna.org.

3. Rick Warren, *The Purpose-Driven Life: What On Earth Am I Here For?* (Grand Rapids, Michigan: Zondervan, 2002), pp. 179 ff.

4. John Calvin, *Commentary On a Harmony of The Evangelists, Mathew, Mark, and Luke* (1555), in *Calvin's Commentaries*, Vol. XVI.I, trans. William Pringle (Grand Rapids, Michigan: Baker Books, 2005), pp. 401-402.

5. Jonathan Edwards, *God Glorified in Man's Dependence* (1731), in *The Works of Jonathan Edwards*, Vol. 2 (Peabody, Massachusetts: Hendrickson, 1998), pp. 6-7.

6. Augustine, *On Man's Perfection in Righteousness* (415), XIII.31, in *Nicene and Post-Nicene Fathers*, First Series, Vol. 5 (Peabody, Massachusetts: Hendrickson, 1995), p. 71.

7. Martin Luther, *Lectures On Romans* (1515-1516), in *Luther's Works*, Vol. 25, ed. Hilton C. Oswald (St. Louis: Concordia Publishing House, 1972), p. 222.

8. *Ibid*, pp. 202-203.

9. Blaise Pascal, *Pensees*, 114, trans. A. J. Krailsheimer (Harmondsworth, UK and Baltimore: Penguin Books, 1972), p. 59.

10. Martin Luther, *Lectures On Galatians* (1535), in *Luther's Works*, Vol. 26, ed. Jaroslav Pelikan (St. Louis: Concordia Publishing House, 1963), p. 350.

11. *Op cit*, Edwards, p. 7.

12. Martin Luther, *The Shorter Catechism* (1646), Q.1, in *The Book of Confessions* (Louisville, Kentucky: The Office of the General Assembly, Presbyterian Church [U.S.A.], 1996), 7.001.

Proper 6
Pentecost 4
Ordinary Time 11
Matthew 9:35—10:8 (9-23)

Wonderful Opportunities For Mission

Jesus' ministry and mission was shifting into high gear. Matthew reports that Jesus had gone about all the cities and villages teaching in their synagogues. But he had not just been preaching the gospel of the kingdom (Matthew 9:35a). It seems that Jesus had compassion on the crowd because they were harassed and helpless, like sheep without a shepherd (Matthew 9:36). Matthew reports that Jesus cured every disease and sickness he encountered (Matthew 9:35b).

Our Lord was clearly trying to make a point about his own mission and that of his followers with these deeds. He called the disciples together after claiming that he needed laborers to bring about a harvest he had planned (Matthew 9:37-38). And then Jesus gave the twelve "authority over unclean spirits, to cast them out, and to cure every disease and sickness" (Matthew 10:1). He did not say a word about preaching and saving souls at this point.

Similar emphases are apparent in what follows in chapter 10. Jesus gives more instructions, and again the focus is caring for those in need. He does get around to telling the disciples to preach the good news that the kingdom of heaven has come near. But they are to "cure the sick, raise the dead, cleanse the lepers" (Matthew 10:7b-8). This is the essence of mission, and at least in these verses, Jesus wants it done close to home, not to be targeting Gentiles or even those half-breed Samaritans, but only for the "lost sheep of the house of Israel" (Matthew 10:6).

What is the point of this story? New Testament scholarship has discerned that the context of Matthew's gospel is the experience of persecution, and that such persecution is a sign of the end which is not far away (Matthew 10:23, 7). One of Matthew's main concerns, it has been noted, is that because the earthly Christ and the heavenly Christ are one, time is blurred with the approaching end of the world.[1] As a result, it follows that what Matthew reports is intended to paint a picture of our day. Jesus' word in the gospel was addressed to Matthew's contemporaries long after the resurrection, just as it is addressed to us. "Expect persecution," Matthew's version of Jesus says. "It won't be so easy carrying out the mission I have for you. But it is urgent! Don't dawdle, for the end of all time is coming." Mission is a challenge, but let's get to it, church. It's urgent!

The church, if it is to be the church, must be all about mission. Perhaps the greatest, most famous Christian theologian of the last century, a Swiss Reformed Christian named Karl Barth, has written: "The church is either a missionary church or it is no church at all."[2]

Granted, mission is important. But what is it? The first reaction of most Christians is to think in terms of foreign missions. Mission involves evangelism. It is interesting that the most popular presentations of the faith today also tend to perpetuate this understanding. Best-selling author and megachurch pastor, Rick Warren, sees mission mostly in this way.[3] Though to his credit of late, he has begun to immerse himself in a mission to help in the struggle against the AIDS Crisis in Africa, in his best-selling book on purpose-driven living. Warren never expressly talks about mission to the poor, sick, and oppressed that Jesus urges here.[4] That is a very problematic omission given the great impact his book has had and is still having on Christians.

Today's gospel lesson account corrects this view of mission so prevalent in many parts of the church. Mission is not about traipsing off to foreign lands. Start "where you're at" is a core message. That's why Matthew has Jesus instruct the twelve to "Go nowhere among the Gentiles, and enter no town of the Samaritans, but [to] go rather to the lost sheep of the house of Israel" (10:5-6).

Of course, Jesus did not preclude a witness to the Gentiles. He sees it happening in the course of the mission to the Hebrews (Matthew 10:18). We may learn from Jesus' instruction in our gospel that mission happens right here in our community, that when missionary activity brings us to foreign shores it needs to happen as an outgrowth of what is happening right here. The real missionaries are not just those in Africa, Asia, and South America. You and I are missionaries right here in this community when we are doing mission as Jesus wants it done!

The gospel lesson for today also makes it clear that mission is not just preaching. Remember the points I was making as I told you the story again. Very little of Jesus' instructions were about preaching and evangelism. The special bias that God has for the poor and hurting is obvious in Jesus' instructions.

Jim Wallis, a well-known Evangelical political activist, wrote a best-selling book titled *God's Politics*, which pointed out that there are several thousand verses of the Bible which deal with the poor and God's response to injustice. One of every sixteen verses in the New Testament, he contended, is about the poor.[5] In view of the weight that the Bible gives this theme, I wonder why we don't have more focus on addressing poverty in American Christianity. I wonder why more talk about this mission is not incorporated in discussions of our purpose. A little of it has to do with the fact that significant segments of American Christianity have gotten more concerned about abortion and homosexuality than with poverty and justice. We have also become more preoccupied with wealth (with attaining prosperity) than with poverty.

Jesus' words in our lesson even provide us with clear and unambiguous evidence for why Christian mission must include, indeed must prioritize, concern for the poor and outcast, why that mission is so wonderful. In chapter 10, verse 8, after urging the twelve to "Cure the sick, raise the dead, cleanse the lepers, cast out demons," Jesus talks about giving away freely to those in need just as the disciples "received without payment." Get the point? Since all that you and I have is given freely by God, it is just logical to engage in a lifestyle of giving away what was never ours.

The love of God begets love. How can you and I be stingy with it since God is so generous?

I love the way that the ancient Christian theologian from Africa, Saint Augustine, once put it. In his view, life is best seen as a wayside inn. Christians are people who are then never captive to money and the world, because like travelers in an inn use tables, cups, and couches for the purpose of not remaining but of leaving them behind, that is the way we are to regard money and other things of the world.[6]

The spiritual father of the Methodist church made an observation in the same sprit in the eighteenth century, one which perhaps better addresses the spirit of modern capitalism. About money, he wrote, "Earn all you can, save all you can, give all you can."[7]

If Christian mission were a matter of something you and I had to do, it wouldn't get done. One of the reason we have so few takers is because we are not making it clear that this is not our work. John Calvin, the Reformer of sixteenth-century Geneva, Switzerland, offered a penetrating observation in response to Jesus' remarks about the disciples receiving freely in order to give freely (Matthew 10:6). He eloquently described the dynamics which make it so difficult to try to alleviate poverty as a mission of Christ.

> We know how unwilling every man is to communicate
> to others what he considers to belong to himself, and
> how any one who excels the rest of the brethren is apt
> to despise them all.[8]

Do you get the point? You and I do not want to see what we have as belonging to God, as belonging to the hotel in which we are staying. What I have is mine! And since you and I have more than the poor, there is a subtle despising and patronizing we feel toward them, even as we undertake or contribute to some project on their behalf. That's what "charity" is; it is not mission. Charity is selfish love. It is selfish because it is giving to the poor on our own terms, giving them what you and I think is really ours.

John Calvin's observations are right in line with the insights of a twenty-first-century French scholar, Alain de Botton. He has done of nice job explaining how contemporary society impedes our generosity. Botton points out how we are driven to succeed in order to attain status in society. We are likely to have anxiety if we do not conform to the ideals of success laid down by society.[9] In our context, where the accumulation of money counts for so much, there are all kinds of reasons not to give the impoverished and others in need too much. Not only will it result in less wealth, but the less wealthy I am, the less successful I will seem to be or feel.

How can we get out of this mess? Botton contends that because self-esteem is a matter of both success and pretensions (or expectations), what needs to happen when you experience status anxiety is to change your expectations. In this instance, we need to challenge our society's expectations that you really are not somebody unless you have a fortune. Personally, though, I do not think that you and I have enough gumption on our own to make that happen.

The good news this morning, and every morning, is that we Christians have been changed, have a different set of expectations which allow us to challenge society's expectations of us. It's like our second lesson says, "God's love has been poured into our hearts" through the Holy Spirit, given to us in salvation by grace (Romans 5:5). Our gospel lesson implies this point when Jesus says to the disciples that what they have is from him (salvation has been free, by grace [Matthew 10:8]) and that when they face the harshest challenge imaginable, the Holy Spirit will speak for them (Matthew 10:20). You are not the same anymore, not like what society expects. That is why mission comes easy, is a wonderful opportunity. There is a security in the midst of our insecurity, for you know that the work to be done in mission is not yours, but God's. That is a security that makes mission possible. That is the security and confidence everyone needs in order to do mission.

Doing the works of mission is no burden for Christians. Undertaking a mission to the poor and the needy is not a burden for those of us caught up in God's love in Christ and the Holy Spirit. We are no longer burdened by the dynamics John Calvin and Alain de Botton describe, the hesitancy about sharing what we think belongs to us, because now we have in Christ the assurance that

255

we are already valuable. As a result, you and I no longer need all those commodities to prove anything. We no longer even need to do good deeds to prove to ourselves and others that we are religious. Martin Luther put it so well in one of his 1522 sermon series. He wrote:

> ... If someone desires from me a service I can render him, I will gladly do it out of goodwill ... All our works should be of such a nature that they flow from pleasure and love ... since for ourselves we need nothing to make us pious.[10]

Think of it, friends. With the gift of salvation by grace, from a God who gives all the goods we could ever want without payment (Matthew 10:8b), you are probably going to forget about yourself. And when that happens, keep in mind how cutting-edge medical science concerning research on the brain has shown that the front part of your brain gets more active when you forget yourself to concentrate on God and projects bigger than you are, and then the neurochemical dopamine (and the natural "highs" it gives) starts getting secreted.[11] Get focused on Jesus, be overwhelmed by God's love, when you get inspired by his compelling love to focus on the opportunities for mission right here in our community, out there in the streets, jails, and hospitals, and you will begin to experience for yourself how wonderful and how much fun doing mission is. Amen.

---

1. Brevard Childs, *The New Testament as Canon: An Introduction* (Philadelphia: Fortress Press, 1984), pp. 65-69.

2. Karl Barth, *Church Dogmatics*, Vol. III, ed. G. W. Bromiley and T. F. Torrance (Edinburgh: T. & T. Clark, 1976), p. 64.

3. Rick Warren, The *Purpose-Driven Life: What On Earth Am I Here For?* (Grand Rapids, Michigan: Zondervan, 2002), pp. 283-288, 300-302.

4. *Ibid*, pp. 259-260.

5. Jim Wallis, *God's Politics: Why the Right Gets It Wrong and the Left Doesn't Get It* (San Francisco: Harper San Francisco, 2005), p. 212.

6. Augustine, *Tractates on the Gospel of St. John* (c. 406/421), XL.10, in *Nicene and Post-Nicene Fathers*, First Series, Vol. 7, ed. Philip Schaff (2nd printing; Peabody, Massachusetts: Hendrickson Publishers, 1995), pp. 228-229.

7. John Wesley, *The Use of Money* (n.d.), L.III.1, in *The Works of John Wesley*, Vol. 6 (3rd edition; Grand Rapids, Michigan: Baker Books, 1996), p. 133. See the use of this citation by Warren, p. 259.

8. John Calvin, Commentary On a Harmony of The Evangelists, Mathew, Mark, and Luke (1555), in *Calvin's Commentaries*, Vol. XVI.I, trans. William Pringle (Grand Rapids, Michigan: Baker Books, 2005), p. 442.

9. Alain de Botton, *Status Anxiety* (New York: Pantheon Books, 2004), pp. vii-viii, 36-37.

10. Martin Luther, *Sermons On the First Epistle of St. Peter* (1522), in *Luther's Works*, Vol. 30, ed. Jaroslav Pelikan (St. Louis: Concordia Publishing House, 1967), pp. 78-79.

11. *Ibid*, see pages 230-231 as well as nn.7-8 of that sermon for details.

When You're Free (In Christ), Sacrifice Is No Burden!

It takes a lot to be a Christian; you have to make your share of sacrifices. That is the popular version of Christianity. Megachurch pastor, Rick Warren, teaches, on the basis of our gospel lesson for today, that "each of us will have to give a personal account to God." Eternal rewards are at stake if we have served others with our lives.[1]

That is only part of the story. Those concerned with purpose-driven living make it too hard, but also too easy. The whole story is evident in today's gospel lesson.

Jesus was continuing what we read last week — his commissioning and instruction of the disciples. Keep in mind that most New Testament scholars have concluded that the context of Matthew's gospel is the experience of persecution. The church that Matthew was addressing as being harassed by the Roman establishment. It was interpreted by Matthew as a sign of the end which is not far away (Matthew 10:23).

Of course this comes as no surprise to you and me. Being a Christian is never easy. So far it sounds like the purpose-driven scenario for Christian living. The onus is on you to endure the sacrifices for the sake of others.[2] But Matthew has Jesus add another point about why Christianity involves its trials and sacrifices. In verses 24 and 25 of chapter 10 at the start of today's gospel lesson, Jesus says that the disciple is not above, but is like the teacher. It's the same with regard to the relationship between master and slave. And then Matthew has Jesus say, "If they have called the master of the house Beelzebul, how much more will they malign those of his household?" The point seems to be that to be a

Christian is to get what Jesus gets. And since he endured suffering and needed to make sacrifices, that's the baggage we can expect.[3]

In the context of the persecutions and suffering, Jesus is concerned to offer comfort from our fears. In verse 26, he comforts his disciples with words of assurance, that they need to have no fear. In fact, he wants everything about the gospel message to be public, to be proclaimed boldly despite the persecution and the suffering that is all around.

In verse 28, Jesus proceeded to offer reasons why his followers need not fear in the midst of hard times and suffering. He tells us that we need not fear even those who would kill us, because while they may kill our bodies, they will never harm our souls. Christians are set free from threats to their physical well-being. They cannot destroy us.

Jesus next proceeded to offer further comfort, more liberation. Recall that Matthew is a gospel, like many narratives, which abolishes a sharp distinction between the time of Jesus and the time of the church, our own time.[4] The comfort Jesus offers is his attempt to comfort you and me. I need that comfort. You need it too, right? That word of comfort sets us free. Start there. Nothing else about our purpose, about living as a Christian, makes much sense, if you forget this word of comfort and the freedom it affords.

Jesus proceeded with another word like that. In verses 29-31, he reminds the disciples and us that God the Father is in control of all things, even in control of where sparrows fly. But Jesus adds if God watches the sparrows that closely, he will certainly do the same for you and me, because we're more valuable to the Lord than the sparrows. If God so carefully follows the course of the sparrows, imagine what he will do for you and for me. In fact, Jesus claims, God the Father even knows how many hairs are on your head. He's counted them. That is how valuable *you* are to God! What a comfortable, liberating word. Trials, hardships, and sacrifices cannot take away the assurance and joy that Jesus' word of comfort affords. Oh how we need such comfort when we encounter life's hard times. When you have that comfort and confidence in God, you can face all the hard times.

Jesus' next comments involve applying this liberating, caring word to everyday trials and challenges. In Matthew 10:34, he makes references to not coming to make peace, but to bring a sword. This comment challenges Jewish expectations of the Messiah. It is Jesus' way of making it clear that God's acts convulse and alter the entire world. Since Jesus' entry in to the world, nothing is the same. You and I are not the same; we no longer share the world's ways.[5]

From this point, our Lord made some very controversial, almost troubling comments. He claims in verse 35 and what follows to have come to set men against their fathers, daughters against their mothers, to the point that your enemies will be members of your family. In fact, Jesus even goes on, "Whoever loves father or mother more than me is not worthy of me ..." (Matthew 10:37). Whatever happened to family values? How can you and I live that way. What does Jesus want?

At least one prominent New Testament scholar contends that Jesus' words about setting men against their fathers, daughters against their mothers, is an emphatic, provocative way of affirming that nothing, not even family, may get in the way of our obedience to God. Conflict with one's family over loyalty to Jesus was likely to happen in the Jewish Christian context in which Matthew wrote.[6] The message for us today is clear: Be willing even to sacrifice your middle-class values, the hidden lie that to be American, middle class, and Christian are synonymous. In fact, be ready to sacrifice *everything* to Jesus. But if you keep in mind Jesus' words of comfort and liberation, it will come more joyfully. It will be no burden!

The great French scholar, Blaise Pascal, described the human condition concerning this topic of sacrifice.

The true and only virtue is therefore to hate ourselves,
for our concupiscence makes us hateful, and to seek
for a being really worthy of love in order to love him.[7]

We can only be virtuous, truly sacrifice our selfishness for the sake of others, if we have an object worthy of love. Isn't that caring compassionate God of ours worthy?

261

I do think that Rick Warren, the influential spokesman for purpose-driven living, has a point in contending that "We are only fully alive when we're helping others."[8] Where he's got it wrong, it seems to me, is that he hasn't appreciated how profound and radical the sacrifice we are called to make is. It is a total renunciation, which we can't really execute. Who can give up mother, father, child, and spouse the way Jesus teaches? It is not natural. It can only be done when your self is totally saturated by the only one who is worthy of love, whose love has so overwhelmed you that you forget about and get free from yourself.

God clearly does not intend our sacrifices to be so burdensome that there is no joy. I have shared with you previously that we are biologically geared to happiness when we find ourselves concentrating on projects bigger than we are. Concentrating on a holy object "worthy of love," gets the front part of the brain (the frontal lobe and prefrontal center) working in high gear. As a result, the back of your brain, the part that orients you in space and time, goes dim. You forget yourself, but there are psychic rewards. The front part of your brain releases pleasurable neuro-chemicals that give you a high, make you feel good and happy.[9]

Forgetting yourself, being caught up in God's grace to sacrifice yourself, feels good. This is just old-fashioned Christian thinking. Martin Luther put it this way in 1531 over a good meal:

> *God wants us to be cheerful and he hates sadness. For had he wanted us to be sad, he would not have given us the sun, the moon, and the various fruits of the earth. All these he gave for our good cheer.*[10]

In a sermon in the late 1530s, Luther was describing what living like a Christian is like.

> *The life of such a person and whatever he does, whether great or small and no matter what it is called, is nothing but fruit and cannot be without fruit; for in Christ he has been born into a new existence, in order that he may constantly be full of good fruit. Everything such a person does becomes easy for him, not troublesome or*

vexatious. Nothing is too arduous for him or too difficult to suffer and bear.[11]

Doing good, making sacrifices, comes easy when God's freeing grace takes over in your life. There is no need to be so serious about your purpose in life. God will give it meaning. His all-consuming love and grace, so full of comfort and assurance, takes care of all your and my business. Amen.

---

1. Rick Warren, *The Purpose-Driven Life: What On Earth Am I Here For?* (Grand Rapids, Michigan: Zondervan, 2002), p. 232.

2. *Ibid.*

3. For these insights I am indebted to Eduard Schweizer, *Good News According to Matthew*, trans. David E. Green (Atlanta: John Knox Press, 1975), p. 245.

4. See page 256, n.1, for references.

5. *Op cit*, Schweizer, p. 251.

6. *Ibid.*

7. Blaise Pascal, *Pensees*, 564, trans. A. J. Krailsheimer (Harmondsworth, UK and Baltimore: Penguin Books, 1972), p. 222.

8. *Op cit*, Warren, p. 232.

9. See pages 230-231 as well as nn.7-8 of that sermon for details.

10. Martin Luther, *Table Talk* (1531), No. 124, in *What Luther Says*, comp. Ewald M. Plass (St. Louis: Concordia Publishing House, 1959), p. 689.

11. Martin Luther, *Sermons On the Gospel of St. John* (1537-1538), in *Luther's Works*, ed. Jaroslav Pelikan (St. Louis: Concordia Publishing House, 1961), p. 230.

Proper 8
Pentecost 6
Ordinary Time 13
Matthew 10:40-42

If Your Sense Of Purpose Ever Becomes A Burden, Remember Your Value

Do you ever wish you counted for something, that you had value? All the talk about purpose in church circles these days tries to respond to the natural human desire to count for something, to be somebody. But I worry about that way of thinking. If your value is all about your purpose in life, what if you fail? Are you then without any value?

Today's gospel lesson is Jesus' final words of instruction to his disciples, as he commissioned them to undertake their mission and continued instructing them about their purpose. He starts out his final words of advice in verse 40 at the beginning of our gospel for today by noting that whoever welcomes his team of leaders welcomes him, and so also welcomes God the Father. Keep that observation in mind when you think about your purpose, about God's purpose for you. We can get a little clearer about our sense of purpose, more clearly recognize that it is not a burdensome task but a joyful response, if we delve a little more into the full background of Jesus' remarks.

Move on to verse 41. Here Jesus speaks of welcoming prophets. These remarks indicate that among Jesus' followers (at least among the first post-Resurrection church) included charismatics. For prophets, according to Saint Paul who wrote before Matthew, spoke in tongues, were charismatics (1 Corinthians 14:39). Well, Matthew's Jesus would have Christians of the day welcome these charismatics and also "righteous men," that is followers of these prophets who offer more practical instruction, even though many of them seem to have been nomadic.[1]

265

Matthew has Jesus say we are to welcome these nomadic church leaders "in the name of prophet" or "in the name of a righteous person" (Matthew 10:41). I like the way the great Protestant Reformer, John Calvin, put it in a commentary on this biblical passage. He claimed that Jesus' point was to have us pay these wanderers respect and give them hospitality for the sake of honoring what they taught or what sort of faith they had.[2]

Think of it! To the world, these nomadic leaders of the church did not look like much, were not worthy of the hospitality usually extended to important and distinguished people in ancient times. But Jesus tells his disciples and us that a core element of living the way of Christ (living with a Christian purpose) is to extend hospitality even to these wanderers, not because of how they seem to be, not because of what they look like, but because their teachings and actions were of God! In short, Christians see and hear Christ in these motley-looking leaders, experience God in Christ when they encounter these leaders. Keep in mind whom you are meeting the next time a pastor comes knocking at you door or casually meets you in town.

But it is not just these special leaders of the church in Matthew's day and today who warrant our hospitality. Today's gospel teaches that Jesus has so thoroughly identified himself with any of his people that whoever welcomes such a member of the church, not just the leaders, but any Christian, whoever offers such believers just a cup of cold water, has offered it to our Lord, has encountered God entering into his or her life. Think of it, friends. Jesus Christ, God himself, is at your door, making small talk with you, in need of your assistance! Will you give him what he wants. Who could say, "No," to him as he stands before you? This must truly be the meaning of Christian life, our purpose, the opportunity to serve God.

It seems like a natural, something Christians should be pleased to do. But we know that it does not happen that way an awful lot. Christ comes to our door many times in the person of our pastor, other church leaders, and those in need — and we turn them all away. I think it has to do with the fact that too often the Christian

266

life — living our purpose — is a burden. And I think that that is because we have missed how valuable you and I are to God. We have not heard Jesus' exhortations here, not heard the call to live according to the divine purpose in the broader context of these exhortations and call. Let's do that now.

Keep in mind that today's gospel lesson that we have been considering is part of Jesus' instruction to and commissioning of the disciples. Just a little before today's gospel lesson begins, in verses 29-31, Jesus reminds the disciples and us that God the Father is in control of all things, even of where the sparrows fly. Then Matthew reports that Jesus added that we should imagine how much God attends to guiding us, "for surely we are worth more than the sparrow." Think of if it friends: You and I are highly valued to God! The Lord, the king of the universe, values you.

Let's celebrate this wonderful insight with a little more reflection. Ancient Greek, the language in which the New Testament was written, gives us some interesting food for thought. The Greek word that is translated "value" here in verse 31 is *diafero*. What is neat is that this Greek word shares a root with another Greek word, *diaferonta*, which translates "thing that really matters." So when God tells us that we have value, he is also saying that we matter. You and I matter — matter to God. Your and my lives matter. According to the French intellectual, Alain de Botton, you and I have what all yearn to have.

According to Botton, every adult life is defined by two quests — the quest for sex and the quest for status. These two quests fall under the category of love, and in both cases they have to do with desire, the desire to be noticed. We yearn to have respect, to be the object of others' concern, to have our views heard, and even to have our failings indulged.[3] This is precisely what Jesus is announcing we have when he declares that we have value! You and I matter. And Botton says that when people like us experience this kind of attention, we flourish.[4]

To flourish: What a good word. We Christians, valued by God, have been set free to flourish. To flourish, the dictionary tells us, is a verb that describes the reality of blossoming, vigorous growth, and thriving. With Jesus' proclamation of your value, that you matter to God, you and I are now set free to flourish, to blossom, and to thrive. God's love leads to flourishing, blossoming lives.

Are you valuable to God, do you matter to him? Martin Luther had a wonderful way of describing how much God values you and me. He claimed that we are lords of all, subject to none. In one of his famous treastises written in 1520, he claimed, "The Christian is perfectly free lord of all, subject to none."[5]

Luther's vision of the Christian life (it is really Saint Paul's vision — see Galatians 3:10-13) entails that there is nothing we *have* to do. We are no longer subject to the Ten Commandments, not even to Jesus' mandates in our gospel lesson. The purpose God has for you is not something that binds you. It is not a burden! See yourself as God sees you, and you will begin to feel your "somebodiness," your royalty (lordship), that you matter. When that happens, your life will begin to flourish — to blossom and to thrive. That's how you will begin to perceive your purpose in life, your call to serve your neighbors, not as burden, but as opportunities to flourish and thrive.

When you begin to see yourself as God sees you, then just as you matter to him, he will matter a little more to you. You will yearn for him. That will make it easier to see him, just as Matthew's audience was called by Jesus in our gospel lesson to see him, in the wandering preachers and followers of the law, to see them as righteous people, as prophets, not as the uneducated, lower-class Hebrews that they were. When you see your fellow human beings as God sees them, when you see Christ in them, as if Christ himself were coming into your presence, then fulfilling God's purpose in bringing them into your life, comes a lot easier. After all, you are somebody, a lord who is subject to nothing, but these visitors in your life passing through are pretty special, too. Who would not want to serve them joyfully? Caught up in the love of God, revelling in how he has noticed me, the opportunity to serve these neighbors feels like an opportunity to flourish, to blossom, to thrive.

The best-selling Christian author, Rick Warren, is moving in the right direction when he reminds readers in one of his bestsellers that we may "accept and enjoy our shape," for they are

God-given. The people who come into your and my life are God-given, too; they are Christ himself! Unfortunately Pastor Warren does not clearly affirm Jesus' proclamation of our value. As a result, his rhetoric still makes that acceptance of the shape of *your* life as your task, not God's, and then adds the burden of having us work to develop ourselves.[6]

There is a side of you and me that finds this rhetoric attractive. We want a role in our salvation. We want to have a say in our purpose. We want to prove ourselves. But that is really the pride and selfishness that are the essence of original sin. We really know better. You have known all along what Jesus, Matthew, and I have been saying today, that we can only live the Christian life, only live out our purpose, after hearing and believing that we matter to God.

The great, ancient African theologian, Augustine, sheds further insight about the dynamics of living the Christian life, of living your purpose with joy. A little more than of 1,600 years ago, Augustine was reflecting on how much God values us, so much that great rejoicing in the heavens transpires when just one is saved. Then he prayed that God would inflame us, excite us so that we would come to delight in praising God.[7] People who delight in praising God will spontaneously, and with delight, long to serve their neighbors when Jesus comes to them in the person of these neighbors. Christian living, living out your purpose, is no burden. When you're clear about your value to God, Christian living is a wonderful opportunity to flourish and thrive.

Of course, a touch of humility is also relevant here. Rick Warren does not seem to have heard this point, as he makes what you and I do as Christians a bit too important in contending that a Christian's mission has eternal significance, that it continues Jesus' mission on earth.[8]

Let's get real. Much of what we do in life seems mundane, routine, not really important in the big picture, in the grand scheme of history. It is common these days to hear the media talk about the "legacy" of the deceased. That sort of rhetoric is to be heard in ordinary conversation these days, at funerals or in family conversations about the recently deceased. But the truth is probably none of us will be remembered in 200 years. The book of Ecclesiastes told the truth centuries ago: "A generation goes, and a generation comes ..." (Ecclesiastes 1:4). Pastor Warren is correct that what we do has eternal significance in the sense that it is not forgotten by our Lord. But what you and I do is not eternally significant in the sense that it unambiguously contributes to Christ's mission. That's too arrogant, too much of a burden, and not biblical enough for me.

I don't know about you, but if I thought that my words must contribute to Christ's mission, that my interaction with others must contribute to that mission, the pressure would be unbearable — a guilt-trip. Besides, such a view would contradict Saint Paul's contention that we remain trapped by sin (Romans 7:17-20) and the book of Ecclesiastes' reminder in chapter 4, verse 4 that "all toil and all skill in work come from one person's envy of another." All we do is vanity. I sure hope that what I do on my own is not of eternal significance. All I do is marred by sin.

But the good news is that you and I are forgiven, have been declared to have value. As a result, God can and does miraculously use at least some of our vain, feeble actions and skills to work good.[9] I don't know about you, but that is freeing, liberating news. It entails that my life is not so much purpose-driven, as it is a life that is more like the vanity of children's activities, more like play. But because you and I are like the beloved children of a loving family, the play in which we engage is joyful, and even, thanks to the indulgence and care of our beloved divine parent, somehow contributes feebly to the aims of our parent. That grace-filled perspective on life makes living a joy! Amen.

---

1. Eduard Schweizer, *Good News According To Matthew*, trans. David E. Green (Atlanta: John Knox Press, 1975), pp. 179, 181.

2. John Calvin, *Commentary on a Harmony of the Evangelists, Matthew, Mark, and Luke*, in *Calvin's Commentaries*, Vol. XVI.I (reprint edition; Grand Rapids, Michigan: Baker Books, 2005), p. 476.

3. Alain de Botton, *Status Anxiety* (New York: Pantheon Books, 2004), pp. 5-7.

4. *Ibid*, p. 6.

5. Martin Luther, *The Freedom of a Christian* (1520), in *Luther's Works*, Vol. 31, ed. Harold J. Grimm (Philadelphia: Muhlenberg Press, 1957), p. 344.

6. Rick Warren, *The Purpose-Driven Life: What On Earth Am I Here For?* (Grand Rapids, Michigan: Zondervan, 2002), pp. 252-255.

7. Augustine, *The Confessions* (399), VIII.IV.9; I.I.1, in *Ante-Nicene Fathers*, First Series, Vol. 1, ed. Philip Schaff (Peabody, Massachusetts: Hendrickson Publishers, 1995), pp. 119-120, 45.

8. *Op cit*, Warren, pp. 282, 284.

9. This exposition draws upon the concept of "brave sinning" which I will develop further in the final sermon. The concept is indebted to Martin Luther. See page 294, n.10, for the references.

How Jesus' Friendship
Makes Your Burdens Light

Jesus was teaching about the kind of authority he has. We need authority in our context, because to Jesus' mind we are a very confused, wayward generation. There was nothing to compare the people of his time to, nothing to compare us to.[1] They and we are wayward, hardened, confused people. Inappropriate behavior seemed to be the order of the day in Jesus' view. The people of Israel were like children who were playing, but could get none of the other children to celebrate, even when they played music. But when the same children played funeral, the other kids were celebrating (Matthew 11:16-17). Stubborn, fickle children. Is that not the way it is with us? We complain about how burned out we are while enjoying the highest standard of living in the world, along with all the conveniences that minimize work, despite all our squawking about how email never lets us get off the job. And when the rap music is lamenting about the meaninglessness of inner-city life and the degradation of male-female relationships, we have a party and dance.

The people of Jesus' day had other perverse ways of living and thinking, attitudes which even permeated their religious life. It is sort of how we take our business values (the sort that created Enron) and try to incarnate them in church life. Like we take the values of the modern media and make them the criteria for organizing worship (contending it's got to be "entertaining" and "soundbite short"). Jesus reports that the people of Israel in his day had complained about John the Baptist for living a life-denying (almost monastic-like) life, and then gossiped about Jesus for eating

273

and drinking, and even eating with sinners (Matthew 11:18-19). No pleasing some folks. It's like today: We criticize some people who are too "extreme" in their religion, and then we gossip about those who seem to be too life-affirming to be "religious." Oh how nit-picking and inconsistent we are.

Jesus then continued his remarks by giving thanks that his teachings are hidden from the wise and intelligent (Matthew 11:25). In the final sermon he preached, Martin Luther explained why this has been necessary. He pointed out that the wise and intelligent in the world are always asserting themselves. In the Church they do things the way they want. They feel that they just improve everything God does.[2]

If you and I are going to submit to Jesus' authority, as he was endeavoring to have us do in his remarks in today's gospel lesson, then we need to be alerted to the sins of our times. You and I need to be made aware of the sin in ourselves. The other great Reformer of the sixteenth century, John Calvin, put it this way.

> He [Jesus] tells us that the reason why most men despise his grace is, that they are not sensible of their poverty ... Let our miseries drive us to seek Christ; and as he admits none to the enjoyment of his rest but those who sink under the burden, let us learn, that there is no venom more deadly than that slothfulness which is produced in us, either by earthly happiness, or by a false and deceitful opinion of our own righteousness and virtue.[3]

Only when we know how sinful and twisted you and I are will we appreciate grace, God's forgiving love, and our need for it.

Despite some economic hard times and the poverty that surround us, America continues today to be the wealthiest nation in the history of the world. And wealth can be a cross to bear. The great German theologian of the World War II era, Dietrich Bonhoeffer, who died as a martyr in the cause of resisting Hitler, spoke of the loneliness and inward suffering of the wealthy. Their wealth cannot buy the most important things in life — inner peace, love in marriage, he claimed. Bonhoeffer believed that even those intoxicated with life, rushing from day to day, wildly plunge into their supposed happiness because they do not want to admit that they are unhappy and burdened, too.[4]

This great German theologian is right about us in our context today, isn't he? There is a lot of unhappiness out there. That is why people send much time seeking happiness, wanting to be entertained. Those have even become reasons for picking churches. Concerns about keeping parishioners entertained and happy have even come to set the agenda in many congregations.

When we become burdens to ourselves, Bonhoeffer says in a sermon on the very biblical text we are talking about today, then we need a person we can fully trust without reservation, a person who understands, hears, and bears all things.[5] In other words, you and I need a friend, someone to make the burdens we are encountering right now a little lighter.

Our gospel lesson moves in this same direction. In verse 27, Jesus makes it clear that it is only through him that we can really know God. God is only truly known in Christ. This knowledge is given to all, even the poor, uneducated, and spiritually immature.

In this regard, Jesus is a real friend. He is the one who makes God known to us, and in a way that demands so little of us, just as true friends make few demands of their friends.

The idea that Jesus is your friend is a popular theme again in a lot of popular Christian literature. An entire chapter of Rick Warren's best-seller, *The Purpose-Driven Life*, is devoted to "Developing Your Friendship with God." But the whole idea of *developing* a friendship, that you "must work at developing" it, seems to make friendship with God in Christ something that you do.[6] That has not been the way friendship has worked in my life. Has it been that way for you? In my experience, friendship is an unearned, joyful gift. It is that way in our friendship with Jesus. After all, he says in verse 30 that his "yoke is easy, and [his] burden is light." Developing friendship makes that yoke heavy, it seems to me.

While preaching the sermon on this gospel lesson that I noted previously, Dietrich Bonhoeffer said of Jesus that our Lord is "The one who thinks and lives for Others." In this text, Bonhoeffer claims,

Jesus puts us in the awkward position of having to admit that his invitation was meant for us, too.[7]

What is it like to have a friend who thinks and lives for you? To some extent, friends can think and live for you and know you better than you know yourself. In Jesus, you and I have that sort of full-time intimate friend. And of course, in view of the way in which we twenty-first-century Americans are messing things up, wayward and confused that we are, we need someone to make us sane. With all our squawking despite all the things we have to make our lives easier, our moaning when we should be rejoicing and rejoicing (laughing at the Reality TV shows) over things that warrant mourning, we need a sane friend (the Lord himself) to do some thinking for us. I need a friend who will exercise authority, take charge, and lighten my burdens. How about you?

There is great comfort in having this Jesus as your friend. In a 1525 sermon on this text, Martin Luther put it this way.

> *Therefore every Christian, if he has accepted the gospel, may well rejoice that he is in the hands of this Christ and need not be troubled by his sins, if he has accepted the gospel, for Christ, under whom he lives, will carry on from there.*[8]

Later in the sermon Luther made a related point about friendship with Jesus:

> *Moreover, he [Christ] not only refreshes us in the anxiety and assaults of sin, but he will be with us in all other troubles; in hunger, war, famine, and whatever other tribulations which may come he will not leave us....*[9]

Our friend, Jesus, takes care of the big social problems for us, not just our own individual sins and trials.

Jesus says more about what kind of a friend he is at the end of our gospel lesson. Besides telling us that his yoke is easy and his burden is light, he wants to remind you and me that he is "gentle and humble in heart" (Matthew 11:29), that in him we can find rest. He wants to give you rest from your burdens. Again, Martin Luther in the same sermon I shared with you says it so well about this gentle Lord of ours.

> *And Christ makes a special point of saying here that he is gentle. It is as though he were saying: I know how to deal with sinners. I myself have experienced what it is to have a timid, terrified conscience (as Hebrews 4:15 says, "He in every respect has been tempted as we are, yet without sinning"). Therefore let no one be afraid of me; I will deal kindly and gently with him. I will not jump on him or frighten him. Let him come boldly to me, in me he will find rest for his soul.*[10]

Friendship with Christ is not burden. He makes all the burdens you and I have feel so light. It is like we sing in the old hymn at several points:

> *What a friend we have in Jesus. All our sins and griefs to bear! ... Do your friends despise, forsake you? ... In his arms he'll take and shield you; you will find a solace there.*[11]

How does having Jesus for your friend make the burdens light? Not only does Christ take away our sin and give us companionship as we grapple with our personal problems and with the big social issues of the day. As Martin Luther put it, "All this Christ takes from me and gives me the Spirit, through whom I cheerfully, willingly, and gladly, do everything I should do."[12]

Did you catch this point? Our friend, Jesus, makes life even more bearable, a little more fun, by giving you and me the Holy Spirit. Because to have the Spirit with you in the trials, challenges, and duties you encounter is on Luther's grounds to have what makes you cheerful and glad in facing them. Friendship with Christ and the Holy Spirit make life a whole lot more fun.

The first Reformer had more to say about the joy that comes with your friendship with Jesus:

> *And it is called gentle, sweet, and easy because he him-*
> *self helps us carry it, and when it grows too heavy for*
> *us he shoulders the burden along with us. The world*
> *looks upon it as heavy and intolerable, but it is not, for*
> *then one has a good companion and, as the saying goes:*
> *With a good companion the singing is good. Two can*
> *carry a burden easily, though one alone may not carry*
> *it well.*[13]

Singing is more fun, life is better, when you do it with a friend. Life is like a song. I told you, Jesus gives as a vision for a fun, free life. Life is play!

In the final sermon of his life, Martin Luther put these words in the mouth of Christ our friend. We can imagine him saying them to you and me.

> *If things go badly, I will give you the courage even to*
> *laugh about it; and if even though you walk on fiery*
> *coals, the torment shall nevertheless not be ... so bad*
> *and you will rather feel that you are walking on roses.*
> *I will give you the heart to laugh....*[14]

Hanging out with Jesus and the Holy Spirit makes life fun. That sure shatters a lot of stereotypes about Christian living, but then Jesus was a fun guy. At least that was the gossip about him we hear in verse 19. His critics said he was a glutton and drunk who hung with a rough crowd. Well, he's still hanging with a bunch like you and me. Let's go party with him. And get the word out about this friend of ours. Why we might just get more converts if everyone knew him like we do. Amen.

---

1. For documentation of this point, that since Matthew abolishes the distinction between the time of Jesus and the time of the church, between his time and ours, so that the comments of Jesus in the gospel pertain to us, see page 233, nn.2-3.

2. Martin Luther, *The Last Sermon, Eisleben* (1546), in *Luther's Works*, Vol. 51 ed. and trans. John W. Doberstein (Philadelphia: Fortress Press, 1959), pp. 383-384.

3. John Calvin, *Commentary On a Harmony of The Evangelists, Mathew, Mark, and Luke* (1555), in *Calvin's Commentaries*, Vol. XVI.II, trans. William Pringle (Grand Rapids, Michigan Baker Books, 2005), p. 43.

4. Dietrich Bonhoeffer, *The One Who Thinks and Lives for Others* (1934), in *A Testament to Freedom*, ed. Geffrey B. Kelly and F. Burton Nelson (New York: Harper San Francisco, 1990), p. 248.

5. *Ibid*, p. 249.

6. Rick Warren, *The Purpose-Driven Life: What On Earth Am I Here For?* (Grand Rapids, Michigan: Zondervan, 2002), pp. 92 ff.

7. *Op cit*, Bonhoeffer, p. 247.

8. Martin Luther, *Sermon On St. Matthias' Day* (1525), in *Luther's Works*, Vol. 51, p. 128.

9. *Ibid*, p. 130.

10. *Ibid*, p. 131.

11. Joseph Scriven and Charles C. Converse, "What a Friend We Have In Jesus."

12. *Op cit*, Luther, *Sermon On St. Matthias' Day*, p. 132.

13. *Ibid.*

14. *Op cit*, Luther, *The Last Sermon*, Eisleben, p. 392.

It's Not About You;
It's All About God

Jesus left the house (which one we are not sure). He went to the Sea of Galilee and great crowds gathered around him. He began to teach in parables. What followed was the famed parable of the sower.

Most of us think we know the point of the parable. After all, Jesus himself explained its meaning (Matthew 13:18-23). But did he? In its present form, the parable is about our response to the seed (the word of God) which has been sown among us. But was this really Jesus' point? The consensus among most New Testament scholars is that this was not Jesus' point, that the explanation of the parable in verses 18-23 was not part of the original parable!

The general consensus among these scholars is that if you study the parable, it is not about us, not about what kind of soil we are, but about Jesus, about God, about why his kingdom is not fully realized and does not bear fruit, but that when the kingdom is realized it will happen suddenly and without warning, just as much of the work of the sower seems useless, the interpretation of the parable with which most of us grew up was a later addition of the church in order to determine what has happening in its daily life, the different levels of membership commitment.[1] Do you get the point? We have been missing the boat with this parable for centuries. It's all about God, not about you and me! There is an important lesson for life in that insight.

Let's look at the parable in this new (it's actually the original) way. It is all about this sower, God, who went out to sow seed, but only some of it takes root. Many of the seeds took no root, failed to yield fruit. Much that God does seems not to fruit. Yet, the Bible reports that there was a rich harvest, despite the false starts, that God the sower brings about a rich harvest, in some cases a hundredfold yield! (Matthew 13:8). And it is all God's work, for you and I are nothing but passive soil.

Can we agree that soil is passive? Since when does soil actively receive seed and take actions to ensure that the seed flourishes? I mean, I have never observed a single piece of agonized soil, in despair over whether it will provide a good home for seed. Of course, that is absurd. It is nature (God) that grows the seed, along with the sower (who is represented as God in the parable). In other words, the parable is all about what God does, not what we do or must do. It's not about you and me; it's about God!

It's all about God; it's not about you and me. That's a valuable lesson for living. The problem is that we don't quite believe it, or don't practice it. Too often in my life it's about me, and God comes in somewhere around second place or lower.

How about you? Are you not inclined to look to yourself, your friends, or some human endeavor like science, politics, or education for answers to life's tough questions? There is nothing wrong with looking to these resources for help in life, if they are understood as gifts of God, as tools used by God to give us all good. Unfortunately, though, too often it does not work that way, and you and I engage in the most heinous forms of idolatry. Hear that again. You and I bow down to idols we have built no less than any of the most ancient idolaters. The first Reformer, Martin Luther, helps us to see that.

The issue, Luther claims in his *Large Catechism*, is who we make God to be — whether we let God be God or try to become god ourselves. As he put it, "A 'god' is the term for that to which we are to look for all good and in which we are to find refuge in all need. Therefore, to have a god is nothing else than to trust and believe in that one with your whole heart."[2]

All of us have a god. But far too often, what we look to for refuge in need, what we trust, are the things of this world — wealth, status, job, self-esteem, friends, even family. Those things are too often our gods. Too often you and I illicitly shift the focus, get our priorities messed up. We make it all about ourselves, and not God. It's true. Too often we are not God-centered enough. I really like what Rick Warren said in his best-seller when he contended that "it's not about you" and then proceeded to remind readers that "we must begin with God."[3] He's also on target in my book when he tries to give comfort to his parishioners at his California mega-church. He is correct in lifting the burden from them regarding the feeling that no one is good enough to do God's work. But he does this with an attitude that it does not have to be perfect, just "good enough" for God to use and bless it.[4] I would say that this gets the focus off God and Christ's work on the cross, shifting the attention instead on to our good intentions and efforts. God does demand perfection, but accepts us anyhow, not because we are "good enough."

What happens to you when you don't get so hung up on yourself, when life is more about God than about yourself? We can get some helpful ideas from the giants of the faith — both with regard to how it feels for Christians and how to think about God permeating every aspect of our lives. Here is how the famous American Puritan pastor, Jonathan Edwards, put it in one of his famous sermons.

> *There is an absolute and universal dependence of the redeemed on God. The nature and contrivance of our redemption is such, that the redeemed are in every thing directly, immediately, and entirely dependent on God: They are dependent on him for all, and are dependent on him every way.*[5]

Feel dependent on God, and you'll make your life be more about him.

The sixteenth-century *Heidelberg Catechism* makes a strong, moving affirmation of our total dependence on God. In response to the question of "What is your only comfort, in life and in death?" the catechism reads:

That I belong — body and soul, in life and in death —
not to myself but to my faithful Savior Jesus Christ ...
[to] expect all good from him alone ... and honor him
with my whole heart.[6]

Expect all good from God.

Martin Luther said something very similar in his *Large Catechism*. He claimed that "creatures are only the hands, channels, and means through which God bestows all blessings."[7] As I said before: Use the things of the world, but be sure that God is getting the credit for using the knowledge, the technology, and the friends who help you. It really is all about God.

Back to our parable. The soil may help the seeds to grow. But it is just a channel (like the rain). God makes the growth happen.

The ancient North African bishop who greatly influenced Luther and John Calvin, a man named Augustine, has a compelling image for explaining how God can be the source of all good while using earthly channels. He compared God to a vast, infinite ocean, one larger than the seven seas combined. Think of the whole cosmos as a tiny sponge thrown into the immense sea.[8]

What becomes of the sponge? It is totally saturated by the ocean's water. That is the way your and my life, the way the whole cosmos, is! We are in that sponge thrown in the infinite ocean. It is not that God is in us. You and I are *in* God, totally permeated by him!

Filled with God, with his love, you might think about God along with Martin Luther as an eternal, inexhaustible fountain who overflows with pure goodness.[9] Think of it: you and I are being saturated by the goodness of God, and that soaking will never end. It really is all about that wonderful fountain called God.

Saturated by God. What is it like to experience that reality? In his famous 1520 book, *The Freedom of a Christian*, Luther speaks of our being so saturated by God that it is like we were drunk with God, and when that happens we have peace and freedom.[10]

Drunk with God — out of your mind with peace and freedom. It happens when your life is all about God. Gee, what a fun way to live! Who needs a purpose? It will happen spontaneously. Christians, let's get high on God. His love is saturating you and me. He has authority. The things of the world don't stand a chance. Amen.

---

1. Joachim Jeremias, *The Parables of Jesus*, trans. S. H. Hooke (2nd rev. ed.; New York: Charles Scribner's Sons, 1972), pp. 149-151; Rudolf Bultmann, *History of the Synoptic Tradition*, trans. John Marsh (New York and Evanston, Illinois: Harper & Row, 1963), p. 187; Eduard Schweizer, *The Good News According To Mark*, trans. Donald H. Madvig (Richmond, Virginia: John Knox Press, 1970), p. 96; Eduard Schweizer, *The Good News According to Matthew*, trans. David E. Green (2nd printing; Atlanta: John Knox Press, 1977), p. 297.

2. Martin Luther, *The Large Catechism* (1529), I.1, in *The Book of Concord*, ed. Robert Kolb and Timothy J. Wengert (Minneapolis: Fortress Press, 2000), p. 386.

3. Rick Warren, *The Purpose-Driven Life: What On Earth Am I Here For?* (Grand Rapids, Michigan: Zondervan, 2002), p. 17.

4. *Ibid*, p. 260.

5. Jonathan Edwards, *God Glorified in Man's Dependence* (1731), in *The Works of Jonathan Edwards*, Vol. 2 (Peabody, Massachusetts: Hendrickson, 1998), p. 3.

6. *The Heidelberg Catechism* (1563), Q.1, in *The Book of Confessions* (Louisville, Kentucky: The Office of the General Assembly, Presbyterian Church [U.S.A.], 1996), 4.001, 4.094.

7. Martin Luther, *The Large Catechism* (1529), I.26, in *The Book of Concord*, ed. Robert Kolb and Timothy J. Wengert (Minneapolis: Fortress Press, 2000), p. 389.

8. Augustine, *The Confessions* (399), VII.V.7, in *Nicene and Post-Nicene Fathers*, First Series, Vol. 1, ed. Philip Schaff (2nd printing; Peabody, Massachusetts: Hendrickson, 1995), pp. 104-105.

9. Luther, *The Large Catechism*, III.55-56, p. 447.

10. Martin Luther, *The Freedom of a Christian* (1520), in *Luther's Works*, Vol. 31, ed. Harold J. Grimm (Philadelphia: Muhlenberg Press, 1957), p. 349.

Life's Purpose Is Often Hidden!

Life is a messy affair. Our purpose is often hidden. We have a parable today that originally may have tried to explore these mysteries — the parable of the weeds in the field. But once again the explanation that Mathew provided of this parable is probably not original, not something Jesus himself taught.

No, it is more likely, New Testament scholars increasingly agree, that Jesus' original point in the parable was to affirm the messiness, hiddenness, of life in a context where sectarian sentiments were dominating in the church to be more like the Pharisees and other devout groups of Jews in the era. Like the Pharisees and others, like the community of Jews responsible for the Dead Sea Scrolls and the group of Jews planning a military revolt against the Romans (the Zealots), Christians in Matthew's community were contemplating purging their less devout members. But Jesus makes clear that matters are murky enough that human beings in this context, even faithful ones, are not able to discern the weeds from the wheat.[1] The point of the parable, as Matthew understood it by adding the interpretation in verses 36-43, seems to be that since the end is coming, the judgment is at hand, and we need to get on the stick and live faithfully or suffer the consequences.[2]

But that is not the Jesus we know, not a threatening judge. No, our Jesus, the one who seems to have taught the Parable in its original form, is a wonderful Savior.[3] And his original point seems to have been that life is messy, even in the church, that God's purpose, that our purpose, that the purpose of life is often hidden. Let's take another look at Jesus' own point.

287

One point about which several New Testament scholars agree is that even Matthew's interpretation of the original parable did not intend to focus solely on the future, but to portray the reality described about the end times as having relevance to our present context. The kingdom of the future has continuity with the way that God rules in the present.[4] This entails that God's kingdom is being realized right now, is present among us; the plants are bearing grain, even as the weeds surround the grain-bearing plants.

Yes, God is creating little seeds of the kingdom right now among us. There are a lot of good, beautiful things happening in life that God has given you and me. But with all the weeds growing around them, it's often hard to see the good things. There's a lot of confusion. The good things in life, our purpose, are often hidden.

The guru of purpose-driven living, Rick Warren, and some Prosperity Gospel preachers do not seem to have heard this point. Pastor Warren makes what you and I do as Christians a bit too important in contending that a Christian's mission has eternal significance, that it continues Jesus' mission on earth.[5] I think you have to get more real about life! If you are not, you are likely to rob God of the glory he deserves.

You have to get real about life, what will be accomplished by all our human strivings. The great twentieth-century New Testament scholar, Rudolf Bultmann, put it this way one time:

> ... man forgets in his selfishness and presumption ... that it is an illusion to suppose that real security can be gained by men organizing their own personal and community life. There are encounters and destinies which man cannot master. He cannot secure endurance for his works. His life is fleeting and its end is death. History goes on and pulls down all the towers of Babel again and again. There is not real, definitive security, and it is precisely this illusion to which men are prone to succumb in their yearning for security.[6]

Because of our sin, there is no security in life; nothing lasts forever. Contrary to all the talk about "legacies" you hear these days in the media, no one will remember you and me someday. As the preacher said in Ecclesiastes 5:15-17, it all amounts to a toiling after the wind. Even Christians come naked from their mother's womb and return naked to the ground in death with nothing they can take with them. In between, there is darkness, spent "in much vexation and sickness and resentment."

The preacher of Ecclesiastes is right, is he not? Much of our lives are spent with aggravations, with health problems, or resentment about other people, even the ones who live with us. And if none of those things are happening we spend time worrying that they might happen. In the end all there is is that grave someday, when it all won't matter anymore. The New Testament scholar, Bultmann, is on target. It all has to with our selfishness and presumption. That is what occasions sin and all the meaninglessness of life, the striving after the wind. As I noted recently, all the mess we are in is occasioned by trying to make life all about ourselves, instead of all about God. But that is the reality on this side of the fall into sin until Christ comes again. It's all meaninglessness, vanity, and a striving after wind for the present.

Of course, God still continues to work miracles. Lots of good things emerge out of our twisted, self-serving motives. Children are created from the satisfaction of their parents' lust. People are edified by books and other media creations brought about by the ego and quest for fame of their creators. Life-giving food is given to us by those who farm and sell it in order to make a buck. Yes, good gets done in the world, but it is often hidden. What are we to do in the interim? How are we to do good, to make decisions? What good is life under these circumstances?

The great American theologian and social ethicist, Reinhold Niebuhr, claimed that "human history is a mixture of wheat and tares. We must make provisional distinctions, but we must know that there are no final distinctions."[7] Moralists, Niebuhr claimed, may urge us to make war on the tares, on the evil that is in us and is exhibited by our fellow human beings. True, much evil comes from human selfishness. But Jesus suggests, Niebuhr contends, that perhaps more evil comes from premature judgments about ourselves and each other. Creativity and selfishness are mixed in life. So are love and self-love.[8]

Niebuhr's point is that we dare not be too judgmental in assessing the difference between good and bad. Recognize that there is ambiguity in life. What we have, the people with whom we associate, the good things in life, even what you and I do and think deserve praise — but not without some qualifications. There are still a lot of weeds, and bad motives associated with those good things. So be realistic. What you got ain't perfect. What's good about what you got is not the result of the goodness of the thing or the person. It is good because God used that person, used that thing, to make an imperfect good. Only God is good.

On the other hand, don't be so darn judgmental about those weeds — about those difficult people, about those hard-to-live with family members, about the problems with the job and your congregation, about the imperfections of your own life and the material possessions you have. I don't care how many fights you have had with those people, how many problems the job or the church have caused you, there is still some healthy grain-bearing plant hidden in there. Open your eyes to the good in the midst of the bad! This is still a world in which God is in control.

Similar sentiments were expressed back in the sixteenth century by Martin Luther as he preached one time on our gospel lesson. He noted that life and the realities of the church are a little like the human body. Just as the body is not free from impurities like waste matter, sweat, and saliva, but were they eliminated we would become weak, so with absolute purity in life we would not heave health and a true, vibrant church.[9] No, I say, you would not have a healthy life and a vibrant church without an awareness of all the things that are selfish and sinful in and around us, because then you would be missing God. You and I might not turn to God and the church for all good if we thought that we could do it all ourselves. And when you think you have to do it all yourself, that's a lot of pressure. You just set yourself up for failure, and more failure.

Could it be that the reason that many churches like ours are losing members, why many Americans are unhappy and feel burned-out, is because we don't have this perspective on life? Many twenty-first-century Americans think that they can do it all themselves.

How can you and I live our everyday lives with an awareness of the hiddenness of the good among the weeds, without getting unhealthy in our cynicism, without going crazy? Again Martin Luther offers a profound insight. He put it this way once in a letter to his friend, Philip Melanchthon.

> *If you are a preacher of grace, then preach a true and not a pretended grace; if grace is true, you must bear a true and not a pretended sin. God does not save people who are pretended sinners. Be a sinner and sin bravely, but believe and rejoice in Christ even more bravely....*[10]

Sin bravely. The weeds, our selfishness, our sin, will always surround the good that you and I and everyone else do. So fess up about it. See it. Confess the sin in your own life. Instead of setting aside some dimension of your life as good and sacred, like your love for your family, your vocation or your purpose, fess up about how selfishness typically motivates the things you do in those contexts. Folks who don't admit the weeds in those segments of their lives are what Luther calls "pretended sinners."

What does this all mean for the way you live? The first Protestant Reformer says that you will see grace more clearly, be a preacher of a true grace. That is in line with the original version of the parable of the weeds. Its point, recall, was to proclaim that God is realizing his kingdom, is working good among us, despite all the weeds.

The pressure is off people who live the life of brave sinning. Brave sinners no longer need to cover their base motives, agonize over whether they are doing good for the right reasons. Brave sinners also do not need to justify their lives with high-sounding names like "purpose" or "calling." For the brave sinner, life is play! Brave sinners know that what they do will not bring in God's kingdom, is not of eternal significance in and of itself. Good will only come out it if God intervenes with his miraculous grace. And so brave sinners see God in action, bringing about his kingdom in the most mundane of events.

I see this dynamic in my own vocational life quite often (at least when I do not let the "weeds" of my own sloth get in the way). A casual word of encouragement, and unthinking deed of politeness, can change a parishioner's or a student's life or sense of vocation. I meant nothing cosmic by those comments or actions. I am confident that you can point to times in your life when someone came back and said what you had done for them or said to them meant so much. Perhaps like me, in those instances, you cannot even remember the act of kindness for which you are so profusely thanked, or if you remember it, perhaps your motives in doing the deed were not too good. Like me, you were sinning when you did them, caught up in your own agenda more than that of the person you helped. Your purpose was really ego-gratification, nothing high flown. But in retrospect, is it not magnificent to see know that in a hidden way you were used by God? Gee, life is truly magnificent, miraculous. You and I count for something after all, even with all the weeds growing in our lives.

Okay, let's say that is the reality. How do we live with this hidden purpose? Enjoy life along with honoring God, the preacher in Ecclesiastes (2:24; 12:13b) says. In our parable, Jesus says that the harvest time will come, so in the meantime don't let the weeds trouble you (Matthew 13:30). Live with no illusions about the importance of what you are doing. Your life's work as well as that "important" project you and I have undertaken, even if it is for the family's good, the community's good, or the church's good, is just play. We are just indulging our sinful egos with it. So fess up about that. That is what "brave sinning" is. And then the pressure to succeed will be off.

God and the world are not depending on you and me. We have too many weeds growing in our lives, are too sinful. But maybe, just maybe, God will do something with your life and mine, with those random deeds of ours, with what we do with our lives. Maybe it is God's plan in a hidden way to use of feeble actions, to take the all too flawed lives you and I lead, and in a hidden way make something out of them. So play on, friends, sin bravely, but keep

292

your heads up for the miracles. We have God's promise in this morning's parable that these miracles will happen. After all, the plants are still bearing fruit despite all the sinful weeds that lie around you and me. Life has meaning and purpose, even if it is hidden. Let's celebrate! Amen.

---

1. Rudolf Bultmann, *History of the Synoptic Tradition*, trans. John Marsh (New York and Evanston, Illinois: Harper & Row, 1963), p. 187; Eduard Schweizer, *The Good News According to Matthew*, trans. David E. Green (2nd printing; Atlanta: John Knox Press, 1977), pp. 302-305; Joachim Jeremias, *The Parables of Jesus*, trans. S. H. Hooke 2nd rev. ed. (New York: Charles Scribner's Sons, 1972), pp. 81-85, 226-227.

2. *Ibid*, Schweizer, pp. 310-311; Brevard Childs, *The New Testament as Canon: An Introduction* (Philadelphia: Fortress Press, 1984), p. 73.

3. For this opinion, see Martin Luther, *Promotion Disputation for Cyriacus Gerichius* (1533), in *What Luther Says*, comp. Elwald M. Plass (St. Louis: Concordia Publishing House, 1959), p. 185.

4. Jack Dean Kingsbury, *Matthew As Story* (Philadelphia: Fortress Press, 1986), pp. 62-63.

5. Rick Warren, *The Purpose-Driven Life: What On Earth Am I Here For?* (Grand Rapids, Michigan: Zondervan, 2002), pp. 282, 284. For examples of the sort of visible, material prosperity that is promised by Prosperity Gospel preachers like Gloria Copeland and Paul Crouch, see Bill Press, *How the Republicans Stole Christmas* (New York and London: Doubleday, 2005), pp. 221-222.

6. Rudolf Bultmann, *Jesus Christ and Mythology* (New York: Charles Scribner's Sons, 1958), pp. 39-40.

7. Reinhold Niebuhr, "The Wheat and the Tares" (1960), in *Justice and Mercy*, ed. Ursula M. Niebuhr (Louisville, Kentucky: Westminster/John Knox Press, 1974), p. 59.

8. *Ibid*, pp. 55-57.

9. Martin Luther, *Sunday After Epiphany* (1528), 10-11, in *The Complete Sermons of Martin Luther*, Vol. 5, ed. Eugene F. A. Klug (Grand Rapids, Michigan: Baker Books, 2000), p. 268.

10. Martin Luther, *Letter To Philip Melanchthon* (1521), in *Luther's Works*, Vol. 48, ed. and trans. Gottfried G. Krodel (Philadelphia: Fortress Press, 1963), pp. 281-282; cf. Martin Luther, *The Pharisee and the Publican* (n.d.), 44, in *The Complete Sermons of Martin Luther*, Vol. 2.2, ed. John Nicholas Lenker (Grand Rapids, Michigan: Baker Books, 2000), pp. 367-368.

Sermons On The Gospel Readings

For Sundays
After Pentecost
(Middle Third)

Political Religion

Wayne Brouwer

To the people
of Harderwyk Ministries
who shared the journey
for eleven years

Preface

One cannot read the gospel of Matthew without quickly running into the kingdom of heaven. Jesus is born of royal stock (ch. 1), announced to the world as a supranational king (ch. 2), declared kingdom business as his message (ch. 4), assumed the allegiance of others to him as a rightful expression (ch. 9), and commands the powers available only to a king (ch. 10). He engages in conversations that suppose his royal identity (ch. 12), speaks openly about the character of the kingdom (ch. 13), and reveals himself as king (ch. 17). He legislates the moral ethos of the dominion (chs. 18-19), is identified and received by others as king (ch. 21), is challenged about his kingship (ch. 27), and announces his royal rule (ch. 28). The kingdom of heaven is clearly a major theme of Jesus' identity and its expressions through the gospel of Matthew.

We who live in democratic societies twenty centuries after Jesus' life in Palestine read the words "kingdom of heaven" and hear sermons about Jesus' teachings, but we typically theologize them until we de-politicize their meaning. We do not live with kings or royalty. They are odd anachronisms of bygone eras in European and Asian histories, which have never functioned in North American society. So we think that our "separation of church and state" means religion has little to do with politics. At most, it may be something which informs the consciences of people who then might lobby to enact certain forms of legislation that salve our uneasy consciences about our social obligations. But religion as such is or ought to be apolitical.

We need to clean out our ears and take the pious cataracts off our eyes in order to hear and see again the very essential political character of the religion of Jesus. Jesus did not assume he could speak to and about the political affairs of his day; he assumed he had a right to declare the true character of politics precisely because he spoke religiously. Any power is religious power. Any kingdom is a reflection of or a challenge to the one real kingdom. Religion is political or it is not religion at all.

In the pages that follow, something of the political religion of Matthew's gospel reemerges. Perhaps we can set aside our spiritual reductionisms enough to be captured by a cause and a king who deserves our attention and allegiance.

— Wayne Brouwer

Why We Need The
Pledge Of Allegiance

When I was in high school, a new music teacher came to town. He was fresh out of college and full of ambition. But here he was, stuck in a very rural community where people didn't put up with (as they called it) "long-haired music," either from the Beatles or Beethoven.

Still, he was determined to teach us good music. We were going to sing selections from Handel's *Messiah* for our Christmas concert. Most of us had never heard of George Frideric Handel, and when we first tried to sight-read through the selections we became convinced we didn't like his music. It was too hard, too complicated. More than that, Handel wouldn't allow us to sing simple harmonies; no, he created different parts for each voice, and we in the bass section weren't able to hide all our typical mistakes when Handel and our new director demanded that we sing alone.

Our fearless leader did his best, but half-way to Christmas, it was obvious that we were all losing: We in the choir had lost our places, he as director and new teacher on the block was about to lose face, and Handel had long ago lost interest in all of us. Still, we had gone too far to turn back, and with a grace we didn't feel we stumbled through the first part of our concert. Our parents smiled politely, while our little sisters and brothers squirmed restlessly. Some of our grandparents with hearing problems even managed to smile.

Finally, after too many minutes of painful lapses and a competition between ourselves and the piano, which neither won, we

299

came to our last section, the one we knew best. As we raced through the opening lines, a few people actually stood up! At first we thought they were walking out on us, but they just stood there beaming until we had shouted our last "King of Kings, and Lord of Lords! Hal - le - lu - jah!"

Later, of course, we learned why these few fearless folks had risen to the occasion. When the German prince, George II, became king of Great Britain, he had a special fondness for Handel's music. At the premier concert of the *Messiah* in 1743, the king and the crowds were deeply moved by the glory and grace of the masterpiece. When the musicians swelled the "Hallelujah Chorus" and thundered those mighty words "... and he shall reign for ever and ever!" King George, whose English wasn't all that great, jumped to his feet thinking that they sang about him.

The whole crowd, naturally, followed suit, although they were standing more out of ceremonial habit, and thinking about a different king. Since that day, though, people have continued to stand for the "Hallelujah Chorus" to worship the glory of God whose kingdom shall know no end.

Rethinking The Kingdom

But what kind of kingdom is it? How, among the many nasty dictatorships and the autocratic tyrannies and the changing number of troubled democracies of this world, do we think about the kingdom of God, especially when it plays such a large part in the teaching of the Bible? Matthew 13, for instance, is a profound collection of parables by Jesus whose primary focus is the kingdom of heaven. Writing to a primarily Jewish-Christian community, Matthew honors the devout tradition of minimizing public use of the name of God by using the term "kingdom of heaven." Elsewhere among the gospels and throughout the New Testament the equivalent idea, "kingdom of God," is dominant.

Some of us have the notion that the kingdom of God is primarily a secret and personal rule of God in individual hearts. God is no earthly ruler whose fortunes are dictated by the latest research poll. His name won't appear on the ballots when we vote in November. *Time* magazine is not likely to declare God as a list topper in one of its annual collections of "most powerful leaders in the world."

God doesn't have his own political party, though a few small groups attempt to lay claim to him as leader. Back in 1951, shortly before he was forced from his throne by a military coup, King Farouk of Egypt confided bitterly to British Lord Boyd-Orr, "There will soon be only five kings left — the kings of England, diamonds, hearts, spades, and clubs."

That is sometimes the way we see the kingdom of God, sifted through the world like the kings in a deck of cards. The king of heaven may have a kind of power when we play a certain game called religion, but for the most part it is a rather invisible and private authority, one held closely in your hand so no one else sees, and played as a trump card when you run out of other options.

Perhaps there is some reason for this view. Didn't Jesus himself tell Pilate, "My kingdom is not of this world"? (John 18:36 NIV). And another time, when the Pharisees came to Jesus and asked him about the kingdom of God, Jesus told them, "The kingdom of God does not come with your careful observation, nor will people say, 'Here it is,' or 'There it is,' because the kingdom of God is within you" (Luke 17:20-2 NIV). Even the apostle Paul seemed to echo that when he wrote about the rule of God as being "in your heart" (Romans 10:8).

Another thought we sometimes have about the kingdom of God is that it is really the same thing as the church. One of the great hymns puts it like this:

I love Thy Kingdom, Lord, the House of Thine abode;
The Church our blessed Redeemer saved with His own
precious blood.

These words tie the kingdom of God directly to the church. While national governments may wield temporal power of armies and economies, the church claims spiritual power and a moral sway over values and behavior. This view sees the world in two parts: a "secular" life of week days and business and family and school,

301

and a "sacred" life of the church and spirit which sneaks in now and again like the weekend "religion" pages of the newspaper.

A third view of the kingdom of God reacts strongly to the individualism and private spirituality of a privatized religion, and sees in Jesus' words a socially transforming message. In 1917, while the kingdoms of this world were at war, while revolution stalked Russia and set up a dictatorship of the proletariat, while labor strikes were sweeping across North America, Walter Rauschenbusch delivered four addresses at the Yale School of Religion. He had been pastor at the Second German Baptist Church in a suburb of New York City politely called "Hell's Kitchen." He had seen children working fourteen-hour shifts in dark and dirty factories. He watched pregnant women hemorrhage to death while standing at their industrial posts. He said funeral prayers for men who died in tragic accidents, whose families would be turned out into streets at the loss of income and lack of insurance or pensions.

He was supposed to preach the love of God, the grace of God, the providence of God from his pulpit, week after week, Sunday after Sunday. But where was God on Monday, while the bosses treated their workers like slaves? Where was God on Tuesday, when pollution took the life of a sickly child? Was the gospel limited to things "sacred"? Was salvation only for people's souls, while their bodies could rot in Hell's Kitchen?

Rauschenbusch searched the scriptures and prayed as Jesus taught, "Thy kingdom come!" Then he challenged Christians to look for a kingdom that was bigger than the church, a kingdom that stepped into the world on Monday and organized labor unions, that fought political battles on Tuesday, and demanded social justice on Wednesday. He called for people of God who took a piece of heaven and set it to grow here on earth.

A fourth possibility, when we look for a way to read these parables of the kingdom, is that Jesus is primarily focusing our attention on the future, and keeping our eyes trained toward the skies. We know that some day the Lord who spoke these parables will come back again, and then the fullness of his kingdom will become a glorious reality. Now, however, we live in the kingdom of Satan, the prince of this age, the ruler of the powers of darkness, as Paul put it. So we hide ourselves into our corners and protect our little ones as best we can, until someday we will see Jesus return and then we will live in his kingdom. The old gospel song testified to it like this:

This world is not my home, I'm just a-passin' through;
My treasures are laid up, somewhere beyond the blue.
The angels beckon me from heaven's open door
And I can't feel at home in this world anymore.

An All-Encompassing Citizenship

We have all been touched by each of these views of the kingdom of heaven. Yet today, as we read Jesus' parables again, it is important to hear the undercurrent of what he is saying. First of all, the idea of "kingdom" implies citizenship, or at least allegiance to a governing authority. This is Jesus' theme in his parable of the treasures (Matthew 13:44-46). Among the pieces of properties that we collect in this life, says Jesus, we may someday suddenly stumble upon a treasure that collects us. It possesses us. It demands allegiance from us.

It is the kind of thing that J.R.R. Tolkien tried to picture in his powerful trilogy *The Lord of the Rings*. Writing in the recovery years after World War II, Tolkien imagined what powers there are in this world that can possess peoples and nations, for good or for ill. His tale of the struggles of Middle Earth allegorically reflected the biblical idea of kingdoms in conflict.

Either, as Jesus indicates, we play games with little treasures, buying and selling them on world markets, and moving among commercial districts that hold our attraction for a while, or we are sold out to a greater power. We sell all and buy it. We give up our claims in order that we might be claimed.

Our youngest daughter was born in Nigeria while I was teaching at the Reformed Theological College in Mkar. Because the Nigerian government does not automatically grant citizenship to all who are born on its soil, Kaitlyn was truly a person without a country in her earliest days. Until I could process her existence with the United States consulate in Kaduna, she had no official identity, no traveling permissions, and no rights in society outside of our home. We took a picture of her at five days old, sleeping in my hands, and this became the photograph used on her passport for the first ten years of her life. The snapshot may have become outdated quickly as she grew through the stages of childhood, but the passport to which it was affixed declared that she belonged to the United States of America. She had rights. She had privileges. She had protection under the law. When the time came for us to leave Nigeria and travel through three continents to get back to North America, that little passport opened doors and prepared the way for her. She had never lived in the US, but the US knew her by name and kept watch over her.

So it is and more with the kingdom of heaven, according to Jesus. It becomes the badge of identification for us, as well as the symbol of our protection and care. When we choose other pearls, or dig around for treasures in our own backyards we get from them what we are looking for — things that we can possess. But when the great prize of the hidden treasure comes our way, or we stumble onto the pearl of great price, we realize that our little hordes are insufficient. It is not enough to own a piece of fading substance; we need to be owned by something which transcends our time. We need God to lay hold on us.

This is why, in many of the earliest liturgical forms for baptism, those were newly coming into the fellowship of believers were asked if they renounced the devil and all his works. Early on, it was recognized that entering the kingdom of God was more than just adding another spiritual talisman to the mix of superstitious hex warders; it was a fundamental commitment of identity that could not be shared. No dual passports in this kingdom! The truly great treasure demands that one sell everything else. It is exclusive. And when it is purchased, it actually purchases you.

Living On A Battlefield

A second implication of Jesus' parables in this chapter is that we are under orders. Not every citizen in most realms is thereby automatically also a soldier preparing for battle. A few times in history it has been close to the truth — when the modern state of Israel was founded, for instance, and all of its neighbors made a concerted effort to drive it into the sea. Suddenly everyone was under military orders; there was no other way to survive. While this is not a typical occurrence of our citizenship experiences, it does in fact mirror the urgency of Jesus' view of the kingdom of heaven.

Certainly, of course, we have to be careful with battlefield images as we communicate Christianity. Too often our world has experienced bellicose religion in forms that have destroyed civilizations, dehumanized societies, degraded value systems, and diminished piety. We have had enough of religious groups battling for domination at the expense of God's honor and human dignity.

Yet, one cannot read both Old and New Testaments without appreciating the challenge of transformation that places citizens of the kingdom of God under orders. Jesus speaks to that in his parable of the net (Matthew 13:47-52). The kingdom of heaven is like a net that catches fish. It is not like a hook thrown carelessly into the water in case a silly fish might be stupid enough to nip at it. No, the kingdom of heaven, says Jesus, is a network of citizens who together are constantly under orders to bring in others.

Some time ago, I talked with a pastor of a large congregation in a major city. He was pleased with the worship and the ministries of his church. Everything seemed to operate with care and good taste and competence. He had the right staff in place, and they all were able to find dedicated, trained volunteers to shape a marvelous network of programs. Yet, something didn't sit right with him. In his words, it was a very, very nice church. And therein was the problem. It was a church that looked after itself so well that it had forgotten that it was under orders to be about the missionary business of the kingdom of heaven.

If people wanted wonderful worship, all they had to do was join the congregation on Sundays. If they wanted terrific children's ministries and youth programs, all they had to do was drop their sons and daughters off at the right times. If anyone wanted a little diaconal assistance, just stop by the office and a secretary would arrange for a modest handout.

But the onus was on others to come and find the church. The congregation itself had little use for going out to search for the lost and the last and the least. It had given up being a net. It had lost its marching orders. It had gained the corner on "nice" but was losing the ability to call itself church.

C. S. Lewis knew the battlefield connection underlying Christianity. He came about that insight in a very personal way. When he was nine years old, his warm and loving mother contracted cancer. Within a very short time, she was confined to bed, enduring harsh treatments, in terrible pain, and stinking because of the sores and horrible wasting of her body. At night she would cry out in anguish, and young Jack (as he was known) hid in terror under his covers. He had heard the minister say that God answers prayer, so he begged God for his mother's deliverance. But to no avail. She died gasping and screaming, and his belief in God went with her.

Years later, when as an Oxford professor he began to rationally think through the possibility of Christian belief, Lewis finally understood what was going on in his mother's painful illness. He came to see that this world is a battlefield between the kingdom of God and the powers of evil, and that Christianity was true precisely because it took this conflict seriously. The religion of the Bible was not a streamlined Santa Claus story of a jolly old grandfather figure who always brings gifts, whether you are naughty or nice. Rather, it is an acknowledgment of the struggles present in this world and the necessary reality of God's intervention. Lewis' mother died not because God didn't grant a child's wish but because the evil one had twisted God's good world in such a way that even the very cells of her body no longer worked as they should. But though healing did not come in that instant of boyish spiritual lisping, the prayers did not go unheard, and his mother was not lost forever or forgotten.

So the parable of the net reminds us of our marching orders in the kingdom of heaven. We are not saved so that we may politely pat ourselves on the back and smile at one another in the tiny corners we occupy. No, we are part of a net that seeks and engages the fish of this world who might be swimming to their own destruction.

306

Confidence

③ Finally, Jesus' stories in this chapter remind us that we are on the winning side in the battles of life. When Jesus tells the parables of the seed and the yeast (Matthew 13:31-35), he presents a picture of the kingdom of heaven that grows and dominates until it is the primary factor shaping the world. The tiny mustard seed morphs into a tree that provides a home for the birds, and the bit of yeast transforms the entire loaf until it is utterly and completely changed. And, it is important to note, these things happen rather automatically. The change takes place from within the seed, and from within the grain of yeast.

In other words, the kingdom of heaven has the winning power within itself, and invites us along on the journey. We do not create the kingdom, but the kingdom creates us. Even though it appears to be insignificant at the start, the essence of greatness and the confidence of success lies within.

Scripture is filled with testimonies to this. One in particular from the Old Testament is the scene in Jeremiah 32 where the prophet buys a field. Normally, this would seem like an ordinary transaction, just another day at the real estate office. But Jeremiah and the salesperson are both holed up inside the walls of Jerusalem, and the battering rams of Babylon's armies are pounding the gates and walls to rubble. What is more, in the prolonged siege of Jerusalem, the invading armies have killed and burned every living thing for miles, and made waste of whatever farmland there might have been in the region. Added to that is the sure promise of God, spoken through Jeremiah himself, that this time Babylon would be successful and the city, along with the temple, would be destroyed.

If there was ever a bad time to invest in real estate, this was it. The land itself was worthless, the currency inflated, the threat of destruction obvious and the future about as grim as any could be. Yet, Jeremiah buys the field. Why? Because he knew the power of the seed of the kingdom of God. He knew that God would have his way, even beyond the threat of Babylon. He knew that in spite of the waywardness of the people, God's kingdom would rise again and thrust itself to the heavens until even the Babylonian vulture would nest in its branches.

When we hear Jesus tell us about the kingdom of heaven we recover our sense of values and outcomes in the quagmire of daily events. We carry the passport of heaven. We live as those who are under orders to be and do and make a difference. And we know who writes the last chapter, because the kingdom of heaven is growing tenaciously around us in spite of reports to the contrary.

When we were very young we learned the "Pledge of Allegiance" to the flag of the United States of America. We were taught to understand and respect the symbol of our country, and to renew our commitments to its well-being. Far more significant, as Jesus reminds us in these parables, is our need as Christians to regularly and repeatedly stand together and recite the greatest pledge of allegiance of all time, and even eternity:

> *I pledge allegiance to the Christian flag and to the Savior for whose kingdom it stands. One Savior, crucified, risen, and coming again, with life and liberty for all who believe.*

Amen.

Proper 13
Pentecost 11
Ordinary Time 18
Matthew 14:13-21

Hunger And Politics

Yogi Berra, the great baseball player of an earlier age, was known for his unusual and creative use of the English language. In giving directions to his home, for example, he often told people, "When you come to the fork in the road, take it." His formula for success, as some heard it, was this: "Ninety percent perspiration, and the rest mostly just plain hard work." Then there was the time he went to a restaurant by himself and ordered a large pizza. The waitress asked if he would like it cut into four or eight pieces. "Better make it four," he replied. "I'm not hungry enough to eat eight."

Yogi Berra may have had a few things to learn about food service, but those who followed Jesus into the Galilean hillsides were very pleased that Jesus was able to cut five loaves and two fish into enough pieces to satisfy a huge crowd. They were certainly hungry enough to eat more than just the original seven or even Yogi Berra's famous eight.

Of course, as Matthew tells the story, he has some particular thoughts in mind which go far beyond merely the miraculous event itself. After all, he does not give as many details as John would in his later gospel — talking about the boy who brought the food, or the extended dialogue Jesus has with those who introduced the lad to their master. Here Matthew spits out the story quickly and moves right on to another miracle. But that's the way he does it, over and over again. Matthew had lived with Jesus long enough to find what others might call unusual made ordinary, and things that most considered spectacular to be almost commonplace.

309

But that doesn't mean Matthew is telling us about an event with no consequence. Much to the contrary, Matthew has some very important ideas he wants his readers to pick up.

Who Serves In The Wilderness?
First of all, we have to remember that Matthew is writing to a community that is primarily composed of Jewish Christians. He makes this clear in the way he opens the gospel. Most other biographies don't start out with a wander through a cemetery, but that is how we encounter Jesus here. Verses 1-17 of Matthew 1 move in stages through the memorial gardens of Israelite history, stopping briefly to read the grave markers on nearly forty sites. These are representatives of the major eras of Hebrew history, Matthew tells us.

This, of course, makes us immediately aware that Jesus enters a particular history. He does not appear without a context, like a stone skipping across a pond that happens to flit and hit in some random manner, and then dive into the pool at a chance spot. Jesus, according to Matthew, is the "son of David" and the "son of Abraham." This is quite a loaded statement, for those two great figures were called by God to establish the character of the nation of Israel. Abraham received the first great covenant promise of God when God picked him out of the crowds of Mesopotamia and sent him on a journey to what would become the promised land (Genesis 12:1-2). Out of this transforming event was born the people of Israel. Their beginnings and the name of Abraham were forever linked.

Then, generations later, the great King David was divinely assured that he would always have a son of the family ruling as king (2 Samuel 6-7). Throughout the centuries, even though the Israelites lost huge tracts of their land to foreign invaders and were diminished in numbers until only a remnant remained, they kept tracking the descendents of David. One day, they knew, a child would be born from this blood line who would reassert home rule and re-establish national hope.

So when Matthew marks Jesus' entrance into the human arena, he reminds those who own this particular portion of history that

Jesus is one of them, that Jesus came as a member of the family, and that Jesus is heir to the unique promises announced to their forebears. Moreover, Matthew goes on in chapter 1 to describe Jesus' unique birth. The child doesn't show up in the usual way, Matthew declares. For Jesus' parents it was not to be a prayed-for pregnancy in the first year after marriage, the kind that brings the family together for a big celebration party.

Instead, Mary finds herself with child in a manner and at a time that appear unquestionably scandalous: she is pregnant without Joseph's help, and begins showing before their marriage has been publicly confirmed. Embarrassment and suspicion would entirely overshadow both the baby and the family were it not for the arrival of a divine messenger who announced this as God's deliberate interruption of all their lives. While people from other traditions who read this gospel may not easily catch it, for devout Jews it was a brilliant revelation. They would immediately place this birth alongside those of Samson and Samuel, two of the greatest deliverers their history had produced. In each instance a boy was born under unusual circumstances, and on each occasion an angel came to clarify God's designs. Obviously, this child was destined for greatness, and in his wake would flow deliverance and restoration.

To make the point unmistakable, just a few lines later in chapter 2, Matthew calls to mind the ancient conspiracy of Pharaoh to get rid of the male babies in Israel by relating King Herod's plot to slay the infants of Bethlehem. While the other boys died, Jesus, like Moses, was divinely protected. Once again Matthew's Jewish Christian audience would draw out the parallel. In fact, Matthew reaffirms this comparison by relating that when Jesus began his public teachings (ch. 5) he first climbed a mountain, and then delivered an updated version of the covenant stipulations which were earlier mediated by Moses to Israel at Mount Sinai. Jesus must be the new Moses for this new age in which God's people find themselves.

In other words, Matthew wants us to know up front and all the way through that Jesus is the uniquely birthed and commissioned Messiah of the Jews. With this in mind we are helped to

311

understand why Matthew can quickly toss off to us the story of Jesus feeding the crowds in what might appear at first to be an almost cavalier way, from our point of view. If Jesus is indeed the Messiah, as all the signs indicate, he obviously wields divine power and purpose. Therefore, if the God of ancient Israel made it a concern to feed those who came out into the wilderness to experience God's leading and provision, people in Jesus' day could expect the same thing from him. In the deserts of the Sinai Peninsula God provided manna to the hungry tribes of Israel; Jesus, as God's agent, makes sure there is food enough for the famished Jewish crowds. It's a no-brainer.

Anybody Hungry?

But that only leads us to the second and more important thing Matthew wants us to think about. Who are these people that Jesus feeds? Who would be so foolish as to go unprepared out into the wilderness running after Jesus? Why would anybody do that in the first place?

I find a clue to that in books like John Hull's autobiography, *Touching the Rock* (New York: Random House, Inc., 1992). His is both a personal story and a spiritual saga. At age seventeen, Hull began to go blind in his left eye. One day he realized that the only way he would ever see his left shoulder again would be by turning to his side and catching his reflection in the mirror with his right eye. Later the blindness spread, and eventually John's sight was gone entirely.

Hull writes that for a while he energetically tried to remember what he looked like. He thought about old photographs of himself and struggled to recall the face that peered back at him from the bathroom mirror when he shaved. After a while, though, his memory banks gave out and he couldn't remember his own face anymore.

"Who am I?" he thought, with a wash of panic. "If I don't even know my own face, who am I?"

Worse still, however, was his daughter, Lizzie's, question. She was only four years old when she asked him, "Daddy, how can a smile be between us when you can't see my face?"

It was Lizzie's curious questions that prompted Hull to write his book. He wanted to remember himself and repicture the times and circumstances that made it important and unique. More than that, he wished for Lizzie to know him in his sighted and unsighted years. His biography was a journal to restore the smiles between them.

But then, as he surveyed his life in its spiritual dimensions, Hull took his daughter's query to a level higher. "How can a smile be between us and God if we cannot see *his* face?" he asked.

As he reflected, Hull came to realize that the only way we can see God is when we take what little God gives us to work with and use it as a kind of tarnished mirror to seek out God's distant face. In other words, said Hull, we are all somewhat blinded, and we need to use things like the scriptures and the person of Jesus to help us take first steps toward making a smile happen between ourselves and God. In this, he echoed Matthew's design in writing the gospel. Those of us who did not originally stand with Jesus in that ancient wilderness are no less hungry than they were. We are all looking for meaning in our lives. To a person we are searchers on a quest for purpose or identity. The hunger is in every belly, and each of us finds ourselves in strange wilderness places as we look and seek.

But what will we find? And how will it become visible to us? Where will we see the smile between God and us? However it will happen, according to Matthew, it will be when we first believe that Jesus has what it takes to satisfy our cravings.

A friend called me one Saturday. He was a perennial student, far away from the town that shaped him, and mostly at odds with his family. There was good reason for his mother to chide and nag and scold, for my friend had lost his faith, and his parents were worried. But the more they pushed the certainty of their beliefs on him, the more he chafed and backed away. He could no longer live in the simplicity of their dogma, even if it gave them shelter and safety.

So now he wandered in the wilderness of academia, hoping in each class to find a glorious utopia or a grand dream or at least a tiny map that might point toward some secularized Holy Grail.

Every term, he called me to describe his latest faculty mentor, a true savior, finally, who was worthy of his devotion. But this Saturday, something was different. There was wistfulness in my friend's voice, and a trembling uncertainty in his words. What if there was no big picture or all-encompassing thesis or unifying meaning? What if we were tripping with stumbling paces through the wilderness and there was no limit or signpost or way out? What if he was on a quest, but there was nothing to find?

"I'm lonely," he told me, and I was left to imagine his cosmic, spiritual aloneness, a void where both heaven and hell were silent and he was left in awful communion with only his inadequate self. There was no dream here; only an incessant heart hunger kept awake by an unrelenting nightmare.

Generations ago, George Herbert penned a brilliant picture of the aching in each of our souls. In his poem, "The Pulley," he portrayed God at the moment of creation, sprinkling his new human creature with treasures kept in a jar beside him. These were God's finest resources, given now as gifts to the crown of his universe: beauty, wisdom, honor, pleasure.... All were scattered liberally in the genetic recipe of our kind.

When the jar of God's treasures was nearly empty, God put the lid on it. The angels wondered why God did not finish the human concoction, leaving one great resource still in its container. This last quality, God told the angels, is "rest." But God would not grant that divine treasure to the human race.

Restless Spirituality

The angels, of course, asked why. Herbert was ready with the divine answer regarding the best mix for the human spirit.

> Let him be rich and weary, that at least,
> If goodness lead him not, yet weariness
> May toss him to my breast.

Herbert saw well that the strong talents and marvelous abilities of humankind would make us like impatient children, eager to strike out on our own and find our self-made destinies. Only if

God would hold back a sense of full satisfaction from our souls would we search our way back home.

This remains a perennial theological paradox: It is the creative act of God that gives us freedom. Yet, when we use our abilities for our own ends we tend to lose what is best in ourselves and often demean it in others, and push like adolescents away from our spiritual parent. Only if we become restless to find the face of God in some longing for home will we regain a glimpse of our own best faces reflected back toward us in the kindness and smile of God.

Here is where the hunger found in Matthew's story connects with us. We are the people who go out into the wilderness seeking something to give us meaning. And like the crowds in Jesus' day, we lack the resources to take along anything of lasting value. We would die in the wilderness, left to our own devices. As with the crowds around Jesus, there is no food to keep us alive unless God does a miracle. Desire leads us on the quest, but only a miracle of grace will keep us from dying there.

Food is a very big part of our lives. Hunger can be a time clock ticking inside, regulating the hours of our days with calculated passion. Or it can be a biologic need, demanding fuel stops on our restless race. Even more, hunger functions as a psychological drive, forcing us to crave chocolate when we lack love, or driving us to drink, drugs, and sex.

But deeper than all of these things is our search for meaning beyond the drudgery and repetition of our daily activities. It is the spiritual need each person has to know that she is not alone in this gigantic and sometimes unkind maze of life.

Hunger is what the writer of Ecclesiastes meant when he said that God has "set eternity in the hearts of men" (Ecclesiastes 3:11 NIV). Hunger is the pilgrimage of the soul. In other words, the old adage is true: "You are what you eat."

So life beckons us to follow the latest fad, to search for the newest fulfillment, to seek the richest treasure. We consume and devour until we are fed up with life, so to speak, and still we want more.

315

You are hungry, and you are what you eat. The cravings of your soul will not be stilled. A meal will reset the alarm of your biological clock. Food will keep your hungry body going. Potato chips and a soda will stop the munchies for a while. But what are you feeding your soul?

Augustine reflected on the spiritual character of our race. "Man is one of your creatures, Lord," he said, "and his instinct is to praise you. The thought of you stirs him so deeply that he cannot be content unless he praises you, because you made us for yourself and our hearts find no peace until they rest in you."

What are you eating today? Tomorrow and next week those who are close to you will know whether there was any eternal nourishment in your diet. Amen.

Ecological Politics

One of the greatest military campaigns ever conducted was the Persian invasion of Greece in 480 BC. King Xerxes (the ruler featured in the pages of the Old Testament book of Esther) set out to redress the humiliation suffered by his father's army at Marathon, where a small Greek force had worn out the massive Persian onslaught and whimpered it into retreat. While the previous force had been huge, Xerxes' collected battalions were massive. Historians who traveled along to document the planned Persian victories claimed that it took seven days for the entire company to pass by any one point.

When the Bosporus waters stalled the entourage, Xerxes commanded his engineers to float a bridge over the gap. But when their temporary pontoon structure was ready, the fickle European weather turned and a grand storm piled up the waters until they swallowed the link.

Xerxes was livid. How dare the god of the deeps challenge him? In a rage, he ordered the waves to be lashed with whips, tied with chains, and sunk beneath the surface. While this may have placated the king, in reality it failed to harm the deeps one whit. They would rise again and again to challenge others who dared to test their uneasy face.

Dangerous Waves In Galilee
Like the disciples of Jesus, out that lonely night on the Sea of Galilee, the storm that rose was a double whammy for them. Only hours before they had been front and center in another of Jesus'

amazing magical acts. The crowds had followed this young rabbi out into the wild places where he was wandering, just to listen and look for miracles.

He certainly gave them a good one — it had been well past meal time, with no fast-food restaurants in sight when Jesus took the lunch a mother packed for her young son and turned it into a feast that everyone could share. That's when they, Jesus' special deputies, were put in charge of the distribution. No one among the milling men could fail to notice that these fellows were important. They were hand-picked agents of this great man, and got to spend all day every day with him. Envy skittered around them as they moved with humble pride to serve these poor folks.

But then Jesus had left them. He had just walked away and gone off into the hills by himself, as if he didn't want to be around them, as if they didn't really matter that much to him. They retaliated and ran from him in the other direction, shoving off across the lake in a boat. Conversation among them, over the waters, must have skittered between rehearsals of their afternoon greatness and pouty uncertainties about Jesus.

They were fisherman, though, and this rowing across Galilee was good therapy. They knew these waters well. Some, like James and John, could probably see the lights in the windows of their parents' home over in Capernaum. Fickle fortunes may challenge them, but they could always come back to the sea. It was their home. They were masters of these acres.

And that's when the second wallop hit them. Their friend, Galilee, rebelled. It caught them by surprise. The winds changed. The horizon melted and sky merged with sea in a toxic soup. They thought they could play this lake like a dance partner, but she kicked them in the shins and was coming back with a kidney punch. They turned the boat into the wind and rowed with passion. They were more than a little scared, even if they wouldn't admit it.

Terror And Tightrope Walking

Then, suddenly, their fear turned up the volume. Like the bow of a ghost ship emerging from a fog bank, something was aiming for them out of the storm. A phantom? Another boat about to be

318

thrown at them by the wicked winds? A premonition of death? They were terrified. And amazed as well, for there was an eerie calmness surrounding this apparition. No waves bounced it, no breezes billowed whatever rags it might own. Swirling about it were the claws of death, but they could neither claim nor impede this water walker.

And certainly it seemed to be striding across the surface, for there was no question now that it was headed toward them. Between gasps of futile rowing and spits to get rid of the spray, they began to make out the form of a man. "It's Jesus!" cried one, and the breathing of their oarsmanship hiccupped. Peter yelled out, "Is it you, my Lord?"

A familiar voice cut through the tempest, as if it were on a different frequency altogether. "It is I! Don't be afraid!"

Things like this don't happen every day, even for disciples of Jesus who are getting used to a winning string of miracles. Surprised by his own giddiness, Peter called out, "Is it really you, my Lord?"

Then, to confirm his passionate boldness, he begged for a chance to find the footing Jesus knew atop the waves. "Come!" commanded Jesus, and Peter stepped gingerly out of the boat.

It was amazing and intriguing to feel the cold softness against his bare feet form in place like a shoe's gel insert. He suddenly had an unusual place to stand!

He tested his left foot against the flood and found he could walk! Gingerly, he shuffled toward Jesus, wondering when he would come to the edge of the wet precipice. But the terra aqua held firm.

Still, the storm had not abated. In fact, it seemed almost as if the wind packed a new punch in its insistence that these strange events not take place. Peter was pummeled by gales that sneaked in from every direction without pattern. He bobbled and turned to beat back his enemy. It was then that his feet slid. The water became slippery, with pockets and holes that no longer supported his footfalls. He felt himself tipping and twisting, and groped the air for non-existent supports. The deep knew his name and was laying claim to his body heel upward.

319

"Lord, save me!" he cried in panic. And Jesus took his hand. Jesus took his hand and the footing was firm. Jesus took his hand and the waves were tamed. Jesus took his hand and the winds calmed.

They chatted together as if it were a walk in the woods, nothing unusual. Jesus chided his friend for losing focus so quickly, and the two of them stepped into the boat together. Around them the others gaped wordlessly. What do you say when nothing makes sense and yet everything is okay?

More quickly than it had blown in the storm whimpered away. Suddenly the skies were clear, the stars bright, the air fresh and the sea shimmering as it reflected sentinel fires on the shore.

Living With A Story Too Big

What were the disciples to make of this? Nothing, really. You just get on with your life, and tell the tale over drinks every chance you get. For a while at least. But then you begin to hold it and review it and wonder at it. Not so much the freak storm, or even the strange thing Peter did, although, looking back, you wonder how it ever happened. Who, in his right mind, would get out of a boat on a stormy sea and think he could walk on water?

But the recounting of the story would begin to feel weird, as if you were violating some sacred trust. Because you told the story at first out of sheer exhilaration at the experience, and then later because it was such a good story and it made you kind of proud to have been there. But now you know that the story can't be about you. It was always about Jesus. The storm came because Jesus was not there. The winds blew in because the disciples were becoming overconfident in their Superman status. The seas rebelled because, for a moment, everyone and everything had lost focus when Jesus stepped up into the hills by himself. Without Jesus at the center everything becomes dark and brooding and chaotic.

This, then, is why Matthew made sure to tell the story as he did. Not with great embellishments of flair or excitement, but in straightforward simplicity. For the meaning is not to be found in the extraordinary things that occurred, but in the place Jesus must have at the center of every picture.

I think of Madeleine L'Engle's fine story, *Dance in the Desert*. It begins with a caravan of people traveling in hurried fear through a trackless wilderness. They seem to be running from something, and turn furtively to check the movement of shadows at the edge of their peripheral vision. Particularly noticeable among them is a young family, a husband and wife along with their tiny boy.

Night falls and the travelers establish a camp. All gather around the huge bonfire which is lit as a repellent to the darkness and whatever beasts and demons it might hold. From huddled security near the flames, the community shivers at growls and hisses that emanate from the unseen world beyond the licking of the fire. Now and again the piercing reflection of strange eyes looks at them out of the black void and they quickly turn back to comforting small talk which helps them pretend at safety.

But they will not be left alone. The shrieks and warning snarls edge closer. Then a paw appears, or a sniffing nose, only to be withdrawn before spears can poke or arrows be aimed. More fagots are thrown on the fire.

Yet, the beasties and wild things will not be stopped. Growing more daring, a bear steps into their circle and a bold viper slithers in from the other direction. There is panic in the camp as all scatter and leap and search for weapons. In the commotion, the young husband and his younger wife are separated, each believing the other has grabbed their little boy to safety.

But the child was left behind. He faces the wolf and the lion and the bear and the snake and the other wilderness creatures alone. Only there is no distress in his voice, no panic in his cry. Instead, he coos and clucks with delight at these mighty furry and scaly toys that have come to play. He claps his hands and bounces his feet and giggles with animation.

As the caravansary is suddenly pulled from its panicked zigzagging by the tinkle of the child's good humor, all the adults stop and turn, expecting the wild things to tear limb from limb and demolish this human plaything they have abandoned. But it is not so. Instead, the child has brought some kind of intelligent direction to its strange play. His chubby arms are actually orchestrating a symphony of animal cries, and his hands are directing the chore-ography of a marvelous beastly dance. The bear is on its hind legs, not to swipe and strike but to gyrate with the tempo of the child's clapping. The snakes slither in pairs forming artistic designs in the desert sands. Above, the vultures and hawks swoop and turn and bank and dive in aviary formation. The lions and tigers nod their heads as if in rhythm to celestial instrumentation.

Slowly, and with mesmerizing fascination, the adults creep back to their places by the bonfire. They become the audience in the greatest show on earth. The child whoops and tips and giggles and sways and claps his hands in time with the music of heaven, and the animals of earth dance around him with delight. Even the big people begin to hear transcendent melodies, and the night has become as friendly as dawn or daylight.

Eventually the child tires, as all children do, and the cooing stops, the clapping ceases, and the animals slink away. But they are no longer predators, and the fear of both man and beast has vanished. All that is left is the child. And those who linger in awe know that there is a new center of gravity in the universe.

I cannot reflect back to all of you today what storms and beasts and dark places you are fearing. You know them all too well. They have become, for some of you, a house of horrors from which you would move if you could but you can't. You step out into the weather of each morning wearing a facade of faith and trust, believing you are able again to walk on water. Yet too often, before the day is half finished, and often in full sight of your friends and coworkers traveling with you, you slip and slide and sink.

I do not have any quick-fix solutions for you, no faith waders, no emergency life rafts, or instant pontoons. All I can say is what Matthew, in recounting this story for us, wished to affirm. You've got to keep your attention focused on Jesus, not as an iconic talis-man, but as the center of meaning around which everything else begins to revolve and resonate.

At The Center, Jesus

A friend of mine had a wonderful dream some years ago. As he slept, his subconscious imagined him walking along a wide chasm with vertical sides and no means to cross. The footpath was safe enough, but like all of us he was drawn to the edge of the gorge.

Up ahead he noticed a peculiar sight. There seemed to be something yellow billowing just at the overhang of the cliff. Intrigued, he strode ahead to take a better look.

Soon he noticed that it was actually a tent made of yellow fabric. Most fascinating, however, was that it appeared to be hanging in space immediately beyond the limits of terra firma.

As he came close, a man emerged from the tent and greeted him personally, like a dear friend. He knew he recognized the man, but he was unable to remember how or why, or even the man's name. So he played along, fudging his way through a seemingly familiar round of greetings and pleasantries.

The man noticed that my friend was glancing often toward the tent, still amazed at what kind of contraption this might be. "Do you want to try it?" the man asked.

"What do you mean?" my friend responded.

"Well, just come on in," the man said, and stepped into the tent, pulling my friend along.

The floor of the tent was as yellow as the rest, and felt spongy as they went in. My friend dreamt that he was very nervous, and almost pulled back. But the man radiated confidence and drew him along.

As they moved into the tent it bobbed and swayed a bit, and my friend stumbled against his guide. The man steadied him however, and soon my friend got his "sea legs," or whatever it was that one needed to walk easily on this strange surface.

Then they began to fly. My friend didn't know how it was possible, or what propelled the tent along. All he knew is that they were flying and soaring and gliding and sailing. It was awesome.

Quickly my friend lost his fear. Then his curiosity needled him until he had to ask, "How does it fly? What makes it go?"

Instead of answering directly, the man said, "Would you like to try it?"

"What do you mean?" responded my friend.

"Just think about where you would like it to go," came the reply.

So he did. At first there were some jolts and abrupt shifts and dizzying ups and downs, but soon he got the hang of it. They were flying, and he was piloting the tent!

After what felt too short a time but could well have been many dream hours, the man guided the tent back to its place along the cliff. But my friend was not yet ready to relinquish the freedom of the craft, nor his power to control it. So he scuffled with the man, and threw him out onto the cliff. "There!" he cried in victory. "Now I can go wherever I want!"

Immediately, however, the tent began to collapse in on itself and started to plummet into the abyss. No matter how my friend tried to think and force his will on it, the craft dropped like lead.

In spite of his urgent fear my friend knew instantly who the man was. It was Jesus!

"Help me, Jesus!" he cried.

Immediately, Jesus was in the tent with him, and it billowed out and steadied. The fall ended as quickly as it had begun, and they were flying again.

"What happened, Lord?" my friend asked. "Why couldn't I make it go?"

"My child," said Jesus, "didn't you understand that all along I was its energy and its guide? I wanted you to share the flight with me, but it was always propelled along by my will."

So it is wherever we might find ourselves. Unless Jesus is at the center of it all, no craft will convey us along safely. If we try to row the boat without him, all hell eventually breaks loose. But once he comes to us across the waters of our fears, the storms and the beasts are tamed. Amen.

Proper 15
Pentecost 13
Ordinary Time 20
Matthew 15:(10-20) 21-28

Religious Balkanization

As a seminary intern in St. Louis, Missouri, I was part of a Jewish-Christian Dialogue group. We were seeking to understand one another's traditions, work together for the good of our neighborhoods, and promote tolerance and respect in society. I had been invited into the group by a member of the church at which I was serving. She grew up Jewish, and in recent years had, in her words, "completed my faith" by gaining an understanding that Jesus is the Messiah foretold by the prophets of Israel.

One of the dimensions of religious life that we all found we had in common across faith traditions and denominational lines was the incessant divisiveness that split our seemingly monolithic communities into dozens of similar yet tenaciously varied subgroups. A Jewish professor of psychology said of his tradition, "If there are ten Jewish males in a city, we create a synagogue. If there are eleven Jewish males, we start thinking about creating a competing synagogue."

A Baptist police officer had a similar tale. He said, "One Baptist family in a neighborhood witnesses until they bring another family to Christ. Then they form a church, and start witnessing to the rest of the community. When another family joins, they have a schism and form a rival church."

According to a Presbyterian homemaker, her communion was a little like vegetable soup. "We have," she said, "the OPs, RPs, BPs, and Split Peas!"

And a Methodist businessman complemented these tales with an apocryphal tale of a man from his faith community who had

325

been shipwrecked for years on a small island. When found by a passing ship, rescuers asked him why he had constructed three huts, since he was there by himself. "Well," he replied, "that one is my home, that one is my church, and that one is my former church."

Religious Bigotry?

Religious life in our world is like that. We call it "Balkanization." The term comes from the history of the Balkan Peninsula in Eastern Europe where centuries of fierce clannish self-preservation have defied the creation of stable broadly encompassing nation states. Large identities, like huge denominations, may expand rapidly for a time, but inevitably splinter groups form and secede, often at the price of vitriolic rhetoric and great emotional pain.

Groups living in an area may have much in common with one another, yet they often become unusually antagonistic in their expressions of contempt for each other. That was certainly the case between the Jews and some of the other communities in the larger Palestinian world of the first century. In Matthew 15, Jesus is confronted by that bias and seems, at first, to buy into it.

Jesus' fame at working miracles has spread, and a woman from the north, beyond mostly Jewish Galilee, has come seeking his favor. She is from Tyre, now part of Lebanon. Her ethnic lineage could have been any of a dozen local varieties, but it is certainly not Jewish. Jesus and his disciples recognize that immediately. When she requests that he heal her daughter, Jesus comes back with the standard segregationist rhetoric announced day by day in the streets and shops and synagogues. "You seek help from someone from your own kind and we'll look after ours."

Did Jesus mean it? Was he as bigoted as all the rest?

There are dozens of other texts that say otherwise. Think of his camaraderie with the Samaritan woman in John 4. Samaritans were even more despised by the Jews than were folks from this woman's background, and Jesus showed no aversion to that woman at all. Or remember Jesus' tenderness with the Roman Centurion (Luke 7) whose servant was dying. Jesus praised the man for his faith, and treated him as a colleague and friend.

326

A Teaching Moment

So Jesus' initial conversation with this woman is unlikely to have arisen from deep ethnic prejudice on his part. Instead, it seems to have had two targets. First, it appears to be offered for the benefit of Jesus' disciples. They carried with them the attitudes of their day, including the racial paradigms and hierarchies that were taught through marketplace conversations. When Jesus at first voiced their judgments it probably took them by surprise. They knew that Jesus did not limit his behaviors to the conventions of the time in other respects. Furthermore, they were well aware that that Jesus had initiated this journey into a foreign territory, so he must have wanted to be in that setting in the first place.

As they listened to the words emerging from his mouth, the disciples must have cringed a little. Prejudice may feel right in the mind and it may breathe with the bellows of the emotions, but when it is voiced it has a way of losing its rich timbre and echoes tinny and hollow.

I remember a Saturday evening when I was already in bed and the telephone rang. I had often told my elders and ministry staff not to call me after about 8 p.m. on a Saturday evening unless there was a really severe emergency. By that time, my mind was leaning heavily into Sunday morning worship preparations and I needed my rest and sleep in order to be well prepared. Furthermore, we had so often told our daughters that they could not have friends over on Saturday night, and that if they had to be out, to come in quietly so as not to disturb Dad.

But this Saturday night, the phone rang at 11:10. Worried, I rapidly answered it. Our oldest daughter, then a freshman away at college, was on the other end. She was sobbing. My heart clenched. What could have happened? Was she hurt? Did I need to rescue her?

Quickly she assured me that she was not in any danger. Then she asked one of those unanswerable rhetorical questions, "Dad, why do we treat each other the way we do?" She asked it with such passion and vehemence that I knew I needed to wait for a better explanation of her mood, and not too abruptly try to fix things.

327

She had just gotten back to her residence hall after going to a movie that was shown on campus. It happened to be *American History X*, the biting story of a prejudiced family and the unfolding horror of the way this bigotry destroyed their lives and their communities. The main character kills someone of another race at the beginning, and proudly goes off to jail as a triumphant martyr for the white supremist cause. Flashbacks show how his father indoctrinated ethnic stereotypes and warlike blood pride into the family over mealtime monologues.

But in prison, the only person who defends this tough skinhead against an even crueler world of torment and dehumanization is a black man. Suddenly, the old prejudices lose their punch and moral worlds collide. The inmate gets an education he never expected, and sees color and ethnicity in new ways. He emerges from jail far more reflective, and his boastful prejudices and racial slurs have been virtually wiped clean from his lexography.

Yet, the problem of racism grows tenacious roots in a family or community. When the main character returns, he finds his younger brother welcoming him like a god, ready to fight at his side in the next genetic clash over turf and social dominance. The story winds to a tragic conclusion in which all of the prejudices come back to haunt and bite and disrupt.

So that's the movie my daughter had been viewing. And now, in tears, she needed to talk to me. "Why do we treat each other the way we do?" she asked. What could I say? What would you say? What answer is there to give?

The reality is that we all harbor peevish prejudices, but most of the time we keep them internalized in order to live politically correct lives. What would others think of us if we really told them how we felt about so-and-so or such-and-such? So we parade around in the dignity of refined culture.

Yet, the bigotry remains underneath. And only when it is voiced in all of its ugliness, like my daughter faced from the movie screen, or the disciples of Jesus heard reflected back to them from the uncharacteristic words that shot at this woman, is there the start of a revulsion that may bring healing.

A Test

There is a second reason why Jesus might be using these cruel words, and that is to clarify the issues at stake in this moment of teaching and healing. Jesus is not a magician doing tricks. He is not a spiritual shaman with a few spells in a bag. He is not an itinerant medicine man who fixes up elixirs to sell in a scheming con game.

So it is important that this woman and all who will be part of the aftermath of his healing miracle recognize that Jesus is from Israel; that he is a Jew; that he is appearing in history in a given context that clarifies his identity and mission. Jesus is the Messiah promised by the Hebrew prophets. To ask for his miracles without having that understanding is to play silly religious games which have no purpose. Jesus must be recognized as the one sent by God to turn human history around.

So Jesus' words of challenge to the woman are in part a test. Will she understand that salvation is channeled to the world through Israel? Will she acknowledge that Jesus is more than genie in a bottle for whoever next finds the lamp?

The issue is not so much whether Jesus can deliver on the request given, but whether the request itself matches the true need. On that basis Matthew sets next to one another this story and the preceding short teaching. In verses 10-20 Jesus wrestles with the disciples to identify the values that underlie our actions. Do we act on the basis of external demands, like the peer pressure of the Pharisees in their codes of conduct? Or do we express our actions as the outcome of the values we have internalized?

The latter is more true, Jesus says. Our actions reveal what we have come to believe inside. And because of that, too often in life we get what we deserve. The Pharisees valued a particular kind of religious political correctness, and their behaviors matched. Unfortunately, what they lost in the process was a need for grace. If they could define their own needs and then fulfill those needs through a particular set of actions, there was no longer any room for grace.

Leo Tolstoy wrote a brilliant little story about such desires and the quests they lead us on. He told of a man who had found

329

favor with the governing powers of his society in a Russia now historied, and was allowed to select a parcel of ground as his own possession. The only limitation on this field's size was the requirement that the man be able to plow a furrow around the property in a single day.

Early one morning he set out, drawn by the lure of free land and excited about the small farm he would stake out and claim as his own. He didn't need much, of course — just enough to make a simple living for himself and his family.

By mid-morning he had moved a great distance. Still, when he looked back, the area seemed terribly small. So, since the day was still young, he decided to angle out a bit more. After all, a larger farm would make him a wealthy man. In his mind scenes flashed of his children, robust because of the fine meals they would take off this land. He could see his wife gliding at the ball adorned in a Parisian gown. Men would sidle up to him and seek his opinions; women would giggle with delight as he tipped his hat to them. He was becoming a person of importance!

As noon approached the plowman grew impatient with his slow progress. The circle of land now seemed much too insignificant. He must have more; so once again he widened the sweep of his plow.

Throughout the afternoon he fantasized of kings and princes calling him to court, and the fever for more acres burned in his soul. He plowed with a passion, forgetting to watch the sun as it slipped in the western skies.

Too late he realized that he might not make it back to the starting stake by dusk. In panic, he whipped his horse, pushing at the plow handles as the furrow began to zigzag madly. His heart pounded, his stomach churned and his muscles tightened in desperation. He *must* make it!

But his desire had overextended itself, and inches short of a complete circle he fell to the earth he so desperately coveted, dead of a heart attack. Ironically, wrote Tolstoy, the man was buried on all the land he really needed: a plot of ground three feet by six — a farm for the dead.

We get what we deserve unless we seek grace. The Pharisees plowed their furrow around the field of ritual cleansing, and in that field they themselves would be buried. But this woman knows she has nothing to plow around in order to earn healing for her daughter. She pleads for mercy: just a few crumbs from the master's table.

Whose Table Is It?

Her understanding is more than mere perceptions about herself and what she might or might not have a right to expect; she is also defining the perspective for any reality that surrounds Jesus wherever he goes. No table belongs to those who sit at it. The table is always the master's table. Whoever presumes to own it thereby forfeits a right to draw up a chair or stool.

This brings us back to the religious balkanization nurtured by our ethnic and religious bigotries. When we claim to own the table and determine who we will eat with, the first person to be sent away is Jesus. Think of Matthew's stories again. He tells about the table manners of the Pharisees. They get upset with Jesus. The next thing you know Jesus shows up in Tyre, a foreign nation according to the Pharisees and outside of the care of God. There Jesus has a conversation with an outcast about who gets to eat at the master's table. Wherever Jesus goes, the table is always his. Whoever would approach the table must acknowledge that no child and no dog have a right to eat there. Only those who receive an invitation from the master of the table are welcome. And these invitations are not hard to get. They come freely to those who know who owns the table, and then come seeking grace.

Our participation in the present humanity of this world drives us often toward distinctions, separations, bigotry, and racism — even in the church. That was powerfully brought home to me during our time as missionaries in Nigeria. We were received with openness and love by our friends in the Church of Christ in the Sudan among the Tiv.

But one of their practices really bothered us: on Communion Sunday, everyone was expected to wear white. Now, in itself, wearing white to symbolize purity before God is a great idea. But if a

331

person in those neighborhoods didn't wear white on Communion Sunday, regardless of her spiritual condition, she was physically directed to the back of the church building. And when the loaf and cup of communion were passed, those whose shirts were yellow, or whose skirts had pink designs on otherwise white backgrounds, or those who were too poor to buy a white blouse — these were served the bread and wine last, as if they were second-class citizens in the kingdom or inferior members of the church.

As a bit of a protest, we never wore white on Communion Sunday, and we always sat at the back and received communion last. Even though we were treated nicely enough, we felt the pressures of racism and the horrors of pride and judgment.

That experience taught me the meaning of the old spiritual, "I Got Shoes." While the richly dressed white folks in the old South of the United States marched off to their churches wearing their polished Sunday shoes, the black slaves, with their bare feet, were left to gather for worship as they could. And while white folks were singing about the worldwide church of Christ, black folks were singing:

> *I got shoes! You got shoes! All God's chillun got shoes!*
> *And when de angel Gabriel calls us home, Gonna walk*
> *all over God's heab'n!*

For they knew that God takes care of God's children, and when God brought them finally to glory, God wouldn't check to see the color of their skin, or the whiteness of their clothes, or even the place where they were born. Instead, God would simply ask them if Jesus was their brother. And then, like the only begotten Son, they too would receive a pair of shoes, the sign of people who were no longer barefoot slaves of others but cared-for children of God. Amen.

Mistaken Identitiy

Appearances can be deceiving. John Wayne, for instance, acted the part of a genuine cowboy in dozens of motion pictures and fired make-believe rifles and revolvers hundreds of times. Even his last starring role in *The Shootist* had him portray an aging western gunslinger. Yet, here is what Wayne had to say about his skills with a firearm: "I couldn't hit a wall with a six-gun, but I can twirl one. It *looks* good!"

Appearances can be deceiving. Still, we often trust what we see more than what we read or hear. That is one of the reasons why television is so captivating. "Seeing is believing," we say.

Sometimes appearances can even change the way we think about things, and "deceive" us into a whole new attitude. Consider, for example, the report of Dr. Maxwell Maltz, a former New York cosmetic surgeon, who tells of a magazine contest to find the ugliest young woman in the United States. Cruel as such a competition may seem, the magazine editors actually hoped to change the life of this unfortunate person for the better.

Photos poured in from all over North America. The editors selected a young woman with poor features, terrible grooming, and appalling clothes as the "Ugliest Girl in America." For her prize, she won a plane ticket to New York City. There a team of specialists went to work on her. Dr. Maltz reshaped her nose and built up her chin. Others gave her a new hairstyle, an elaborate wardrobe of the latest fashions, and grooming instructions. In a modern Cinderella story, the "ugliest" became quite beautiful almost overnight. Within a few months, she was married.

In fact, says Dr. Maltz, the young woman's whole attitude toward life changed. Before the cosmetic transformation she had been shy and inhibited. She felt foolish and ignorant and out of place in almost any company, but once she had tasted what she could become, her personality also exploded with new possibilities. She became confident and poised, articulate and informed. She attracted people to herself in any crowd.

Appearances can be deceiving. But who among us would be able to say which appearance was the deceptive one — the young woman whose photos won the "Ugliest Girl" contest, or the young woman who waltzed in beauty?

School On The Run

Faith is a matter of appearances as well. It is important that we understand who Jesus is, not just in our sometimes mistaken notions of who we would like him to be, but who he is by his own testimony and actions. That seems to be why Jesus challenges his disciples to read the appearances well as they walk one day in the north country of Palestine. "Who do people say I am?" he asked them.

The setting was quite appropriate for such a question, even if it does not immediately strike us that way from our first reading of the text. They were wandering in the region of Caesarea Philippi, we are told. This was a relatively new city built near the site of an ancient gathering place of spiritual significance on the slopes of Mount Hermon.

Mount Hermon is the highest point in Galilee, a striking conical dormant volcano that provides the only significant ski slopes in modern Israel. Because of its high altitude and its position in the northern regions of the land, Mount Hermon receives more rain on its slopes than do many parts of Palestine. The waters not only run down in creeks and streams, but they also sink below the surface to produce springs on the lower skirts of its foothills.

Near Caesarea Philippi there are springs and streams that create an exceptionally well-watered area. Trees grow in abundance and provide a shaded canopy filled with the sounds of gurgling and trickling waters, and a chorus of bird song. It is no wonder that Jesus would take his disciples there for a strolling Socratic teaching session.

But the place held more than just pleasant park-like settings. Because the waters bubbled and gurgled up from caves at the base of the mountain, area residents had long believed this to be the doorway into the underworld. Here, they thought, the spirits of the deep tried to communicate with creatures on the surface. Sometimes sulfuric gasses were emitted, and these only confirmed the presence of other-worldly voices and the breath of Hades.

Over the centuries, a variety of religious sects had used the place as a cultic shrine. They cut niches in the rock walls of the mountain just above the burbling caves and set up statues of gods they thought might be resident there. They even gave the place a spiritual name. They called it the "Gates of Hades." Here, they believed, was the doorway between the realm of the living and the abode of the dead. Those with keen faculties would be able to hear the whispers of the departed and the voice of the underworld gods. It was considered to be a very holy place.

But appearances can be deceiving, so Jesus comes with his disciples to test their perceptions. "Who do people say the Son of Man is?"

We ought not read too much into Jesus' self-identification here. Some think he is making a divine claim already in the question that he asks his disciples. But it is more likely that Jesus is using the term "Son of Man" in a manner similar to that found in the prophecy of Ezekiel. According to Ezekiel, when he was approached by heavenly messengers to form a link in the communication process between God and God's people, the angels called him "Son of Man." The designation was more of a representational term than anything else. In effect it was an acknowledgement that Ezekiel was truly human, but that he was being used in these settings as the conduit between the celestial and the terrestrial.

The "Son of Man," thus, was someone who had no unusual powers in himself, but who had been entrusted with a special revelation that was now supposed to be passed along to others. If

Jesus used the term in this manner, he was merely asking his disciples what people thought about him, now that he had become a point of contact between them and God.

Identity Options: John?

So the answers came. "Some say John the Baptist," they told him. This was Herod's favorite and fearful line. Herod had long been fascinated with Jesus' cousin John, a wild man who lived outside the system. But John was also a prophet who criticized the system and those who ran it, and no one came under more of John's judgmental tirade than did Herod. Herod's forebears had taught him how to survive in politics: it was a matter of deception, bribery, murder, and power plays. When Herod dared to kill his brother and marry his brother's wife, it surprised few. After all, they had been carrying on an openly "secret" affair for years. Moreover, the new alliance produced political benefits for a variety of courtiers and solidified Herod's rule in territorial acquisition and the conferring of titles.

Herod wanted to get rid of John, but he hesitated to kill the man. For one thing, John was a popular figure, and Herod didn't want to build too much resistance. After all, he fancied himself a true "King of the Jews," even if his ethnicity made that a huge stretch, and his religious devotion announced it to be a farce.

Fear of a popular uprising wasn't the only reason Herod didn't want to execute John. Herod was also superstitious enough to believe that John actually spoke for a powerful divinity. So Herod was trying to play it safe. He was not about to garner more ire than necessary, especially if it came from transcendent sources. To have a powerful God against you was an unwise political bargain.

Still, John's public indignation against Herod, especially after Herod stole his brother's wife, was more than the king could tolerate. Herodias, too, disliked the man. She was at least as cunning as her new husband, and would not dismiss John quietly like some quack or minor irritation. Together, they had John put in prison. Even there, however, the prophet refused to be silenced. Herod himself made many secret trips to see the man, now that he was so close at hand. And others who claimed to be John's disciples had ongoing access to their leader through sympathetic guards. The martyr-like John in prison was almost more powerful than was the former wild man of the Jordan valley. His mystique only grew larger.

So Herodias devised a plan to push Herod into the executioner's chair. Using her daughter's beguiling dancing as a lure, she created a scenario where Herod had to buckle. At a heads-of-states banquet where Herod hosted his powerful friends, Herodias got her daughter to serve as entertainment, and then coaxed out of Herod a drunken public promise to reward her seductive whirling in any way she wished. Herod realized too late his wife's part in the plot when it was John the Baptist's head the young woman demanded as payment (Matthew 14:1-12).

Herod followed through on the recompense, for he had made a kingly vow. But since that time he had not slept well, believing that John would come back to haunt him. One may connive and kill others in the royal household, because that is the price of playing with power and living in its vortex. But John was an innocent from outside the system, and there would surely be divine retribution stalking Herod until blood was satisfied with other blood.

So when Jesus showed up looking like John, sounding like John, and running an itinerant school of prophets like John, Herod was sure John had come back to do him in. This new John was probably even more powerful than his previous incarnation — hence the many miracles Herod had heard about — and was probably building a broad base of support to take Herod down in a very painful and public way. Herod believed Jesus was John reborn, and had great reason to fear.

But Jesus wasn't John, and the disciples knew it. They had seen John and Jesus together, and knew the one from the other.

Identity Options: Elijah?

There were other rumors about Jesus' identity floating around, of course. "Elijah" was a favorite among the scribes. They copied scripture and knew it well. Since every manuscript was a hand-written, labor-intensive work of faith, the scribes were committed

337

to knowing every detail of the holy books and transcribing them accurately.

Among the many prophetic notes they painstakingly reproduced was the one left by Malachi. Five hundred years before, when some of the Jews returned from Babylonian exile, three men had stood to communicate God's new challenge to the restored community around Jerusalem. Haggai, the first of the prophetic trio, gave a divine word that was quick and specific. "Build the temple," he shouted to Zerubbabel, "for the Lord your God is with you!" In a few brief motivational speeches on two separate occasions Haggai served as the inspired cheerleader for this ragamuffin crew trying to pretend more strength than they felt in the face of overwhelming circumstances.

Zechariah was the second of the three most recent prophets. By way of apocalyptic visions, Zechariah declared these days to be the harbinger of the end times. With smoke and fire and judgment God would soon come down to destroy all evil and to usher in the glory of the Messianic Age. It would happen right in and around Jerusalem, so those who had recently returned from exile should watch and wait and hope and pray.

The final member of the post-exilic band of prophetic brothers was Malachi. His very name meant "my messenger," so he spoke unabashedly with the voice of God. When Malachi interacted with the crowds of Jerusalem what emerged was a dialogue in which God accused, the people responded with rhetorical questions, and God preached sermons of indignation against them. One of the questions the people asked of God was why God did not return to this temple they had rebuilt? After all, when Solomon created the temple that used to stand here, God showed up at the dedication service and flooded the place with God's own Shekinah glory presence. It was obvious that God had come to live in the temple.

But this time around God didn't seem interested in moving in. An earlier prophet, Ezekiel, had declared visions in which he saw the glory of God leaving Solomon's temple before the Babylonians finally destroyed it. Ezekiel had also predicted that the temple would be rebuilt, and firmly asserted that God's glory presence

338

would re-enter the place. Now the temple was resurrected, however, and still God had not shown up.

Malachi boomed the opinion of God that the people did not really want God in the neighborhood. God would show up when the people were really ready to have God around. As a sign of God's good intentions, intoned Malachi, God would send another messenger to prepare the way. God would raise up Elijah of old, the first of the great prophets, and he would make things ready. Elijah would appear with stern speeches and mighty miracles. The people should get ready, for when Elijah came, God would follow quickly on his heels.

That is why some people thought Jesus was Elijah. Especially among the scribes who copied the prophetic writings this idea took hold. Jesus spoke with divine authority. He performed miraculous healings, just like Elijah had done. Maybe this was the occasion for God to fulfill Malachi's prophecies. If so, Jesus was the new Elijah.

But Jesus' closest disciples knew that was another case of mistaken identity. After all, Jesus had recently spoken clearly about the matter (Matthew 11:14). He said emphatically that John the Baptist was the person that Malachi had written about. John was the new Elijah.

Identity Options: Jeremiah?

So who, then, was Jesus? The disciples reported a couple of other rumors floating about. "Some say you are Jeremiah or one of the other prophets."

Jeremiah was a fitting possibility. More than any of the other prophets, Jeremiah entered scripture with a well-developed personality and a clearly articulated identity. He often reflected introspectively on his divine calling and the painfulness of his vocation. Jeremiah's friend, Baruch, added to the mystique by including biographical information into the record that contained Jeremiah's prophetic tirades.

Moreover, Jeremiah did not disappear from the scene easily. At the end of his prophecies he urged the remnant remaining in Jerusalem to stay there and rebuild. But they were fearful of a return visit from the Babylonian armies, so they kidnapped Jeremiah and forced him to march with them to Egypt. It was at that point that Jeremiah slipped into the hazes of history. Many believed that soon he would recover and roar again out of the fog of time. So when Jesus quoted Jeremiah's prophecy on several occasions, many were quick to pin the ancient seer's name on this new man of God.

Yet, Jesus knew better than anyone else that he was neither John nor Elijah, neither Jeremiah nor another of the prophets come back to life. So he put the matter squarely to those who shared his meals and his snoring and his daily dusty walk, "But who do *you* think I am?"

It was Peter, of course, who answered. Peter is like that boy who sat in the front row of our third grade class. Our teacher would treat us as if we obviously knew what she was talking about. The problem was, we usually didn't. But none of us dared admit our ignorance, believing we would be the butt of every ridicule for the rest of the year.

Not so the boy in the front row. He was already out to lunch in our books and we loved to hate him for it. When our teacher told us things she expected us to know, he would raise his hand and ask her why or what she meant. She would patiently explain everything again more elaborately, and we were in our childhood glory — we got from her what we needed but were too afraid to ask, and we got from our naive classmate someone to razz for being so stupid.

So with Peter. The rest of the disciples don't really know what to say. Can they call Jesus a miracle worker? Should they say he speaks with a prophet's voice? Dare they admit they think he might be Messiah?

All their fears of communication faux pas are put to rest when Peter jumps too quickly into the embarrassing silence and blurts out that Jesus is the Christ, the Son of the living God. But there is no satisfaction here, for the answer is more troubling than the question. As long as Jesus was merely interested in public opinion this discussion was a pleasant way to pass time and share a place in the spotlight of success. But now that Jesus has demanded clarification from them, they cannot hide behind other skirts.

The Familiar Stranger

What should they say? How do you live with someone in the intimacy of the kind of relationship they have had with Jesus and yet linger on the fringes of mistaken identity? As the song put it some years ago:

The greatest man I never knew lived just down the hall
And everyday we said hello but never touched at all
He was in his paper, I was in my room
How was I to know he thought I hung the moon

The greatest man I never knew came home late every
*   night*
He never had too much to say; too much was on his
*   mind*
I never really knew him, and now it seems so sad
Everything he gave to us took all he had.

Jesus is their familiar stranger. He is the man who lives down the hall, yet remains an enigma. The disciples know they don't really know him, yet they are willing to live with the tension as long as nobody has to name it. We are not that different from them.

One of the college courses I often teach is called "Which Jesus?" In it I take my students through Jaroslav Pelikan's book, *Jesus through the Centuries* (Yale, 1999) and the writings of the New Testament, and reflect on the variety of ways in which people think about Jesus. Each time I teach this course, I ask my students to write a paper which requires that they talk with their parents about how Mom and Dad view Jesus. Invariably, I get some papers still wet with tears from students who never before knew the Jesus of their parents' religious devotions. Too long they had passed by one another snickering at the religious folly of others while never having to face the question of Jesus' identity themselves.

Somehow Peter had learned enough during his time as a student in Jesus' rabbinical school to get the answer right on the oral

341

exam. Somehow he managed to sift through the files of mistaken identities and come up with the declaration that Jesus is more than a prophet, more than a religious curiosity, more than a spiritual guru superstar. Jesus is the Christ, the Son of the living God. Jesus brought heaven to earth and earth to heaven. Jesus is the link between imminent and transcendent, and all of us need to know that if we are to get firm footing on the rock that really matters.

With the wall of religious trends there at Caesarea Philippi framed in the background, Jesus affirmed Peter's testimony. None of these other superstitions, commonly known as the "Gates of Hades," spanned the gap between heaven and earth. They never do. We reach and hope and hedge our bets and pray. But unless we know the identity of Jesus, our religious actions are like bad gas burping from the caves of an old volcano.

So the question Jesus asked back then is always relevant. "Who do you say I am?" Do you know? Amen.

The Road No One Wants To Travel

Some time ago, I was riding a train through central England and a man boarded at one of the stops. As he looked for a seat, he saw my face and beamed at me with great joy. "Hi, Will!" he said brightly, in a wonderful British accent.

Unfortunately, I'm not Will. When he sat next to me and I opened my mouth to protest his mistaken notion of who I was, my flat American English paved the way for his embarrassment. Obviously, I was not the person he expected. Nevertheless, we got along "brilliantly," as the British put it, and I am no longer either Will or a stranger to the man.

Mistaken identity is not all that uncommon, especially when there are only so many variations to our same facial features. After both Albert Schweitzer and Albert Einstein gained worldwide fame, and had their pictures printed in a variety of media, some mistook the former for the latter. Once Schweitzer was approached hesitantly by a mother and daughter duo who asked if he was the great scientist, Einstein. Rather than disappoint them, with more magnanimous grace than he felt, Schweitzer signed an autograph, "Albert Einstein, by way of his friend, Albert Schweitzer."

Or take the case of Queen Elizabeth II of England. She was stopped on one occasion in Norfolk as she entered a tea shop. Two women were exiting carrying baskets of cakes and breads. One commented to her that she looked remarkably similar to the queen. "How very reassuring," said the modest royal personage, and moved on. Her daughter, Princess Anne, had a similar encounter. At a

343

sporting event, she was approached by a woman who said, "Has anyone ever told you that you look like Princess Anne?"

She replied, "I think I'm better looking than she is."

Mistaken identities may be commonplace, but on some occasions they are more serious than others. Certainly that is true in Matthew 16. Just before these verses Jesus had asked his disciples what people were saying about him. Did they get it right? Did they know who he was?

They gave back a variety of answers, and Jesus didn't seem too surprised. But to his disciples' chagrin, neither did he drop the matter there. Instead he pressed the query home in a very personal challenge. "Who do *you* say I am?" he demanded.

There was no room for fudging on this exam. Jesus had made it intense and immediate. No time to go back to the books for a night of cramming.

Fortunately for the others, Peter blurted out an answer: "You are the Christ, the Son of the living God." Fortunately for Peter, he got it right. Jesus praised him on the spot.

Strange Reaction

And that only made this next scene so weird. First, Jesus changed the mood of the conversation too quickly. One moment they were grinning and enjoying that moment when friends reach a new level of insight, commitment, and trust; the next Jesus was rambling on about death and dying. It didn't fit. Peter, certainly, wanted to bask in his celebrity status for a while. After all, he had managed to give the right answer to the toughest, most embarrassing challenge Jesus could have thrown at them. It was like winning an Oscar and a Grammy all at once, and Peter wanted to spend more time at the podium receiving the accolades of both Jesus and the others.

But Jesus steps up to the microphone and starts recording his martyr's testimony. He is going to Jerusalem, he says. He knows his enemies are waiting for him there. He is certain they will arrest him and beat him and make him suffer. And he is confident that the outcome of their actions will result in his death.

There was clearly some kind of incongruity here. Peter had just voiced the great testimony that made Jesus seem invincible. Now, in the next breath, Jesus was breathing defeat and disaster. How do these match up? Where is the connection?

Stranger Response

And if that wasn't enough, things only took a more eerie turn. Peter knew he had to deal with this. After all, Jesus had just identified him as the leader among the twelve. Furthermore, he was still confident about knowing the right answers. So he pulled Jesus aside and started to talk him out of this morbid reflection. "Look here, man; you're scaring us. Do you hear what you're saying? You better get it together, Jesus. This is getting out of hand."

At that moment Jesus roughly pushed Peter away and started shouting at him. "Get away from me, Satan!" he yelled. "You're standing in my way! You're blocking my path! You're fighting against God!"

The disciples were in sudden shock, and Peter most of all. He was so taken aback that he didn't know what to do with himself. What could have caused this sudden tirade?

Everyone stood around for a bit, looking kind of dumb. Then Jesus broke the silence, but with a different demeanor. He poured out his heart. He gave them a sense of what was ahead for him, and for them. And in those moments of conversation Jesus spoke to them about the meaning of life. It is a strange and paradoxical word, but one of the truest things they would ever come to know, and we with them.

Don't Stop Here

For one thing, Jesus told them that life is a journey, not a destination. You see, when Peter made his testimony, his confession, his blubbering statement about who Jesus was, there was a sense of euphoria in the group.

You know how it is. Remember when you first said to someone that you loved her? Remember how those words changed everything? You didn't know if you should say it. You wanted to, but then again, you didn't want to.

But suddenly the words blustered out and smashed into the open space between you. They took over. They stopped the conversation. There was nothing more to be said. You just sat there and looked at one another. It was like time stood still. This is the moment! Make this moment last!

That is what Peter and the others were feeling when he blurted the words for the first time. "We think the world of you, Jesus! You're the Son of God! We love you! We didn't know who we were until you came along!"

When they talk that way, they want to sit around for a while and just smile at each other. The moment was intense and it begged to consume all those in it.

Rabbi Harold Kushner remembered a scene from a television program that he saw years ago. He said it showed a young man and a young woman leaning together against the railing of a ship at sea. The winds tousled at their hair. The sprays showered them now and again. But they didn't notice any of it, because their eyes were glued on each other. The world disappeared around them as they murmured their love.

"If I should die tomorrow," he said softly to her, "I'd have lived an eternity in your love."

She nodded her head in bashful intimacy and leaned over to kiss him. Their lips lingered and they became one as the bustle around them faded. Finally, they slipped away, arm in arm in the waltz of passionate lovers.

Behind them, in the void left as they shuffled, the slow two-step to the left, the camera caught a life preserver hanging on the galley wall. It carried the name of the ship: *Titanic*.

Maybe, in our soap-operish television viewing, that is enough for them: one night of romantic passion. That is the stuff of legends and fairy tales, where everything is compressed to the great hour of heroism or the night of intense love. Prince Charming kisses Sleeping Beauty and everything else gets summarized in a single line: "... and they lived happily ever after." Or the heir to the kingdom finds Cinderella and the rest of the story is just one sentence: "... and they lived happily ever after."

346

That is often the way we want it, in our books and movies and television programs. We want to linger in the critical moment. We want to feel the emotional high of the kiss in slow motion. We want to sit in the experience of the warm fuzzies and then go get a burger.

But Jesus says, "No." Jesus says that life isn't found in the moment, not even if it is a moment of insight or love or passion. Life is a journey, not a destination.

It is always tempting to settle down into that special moment, though, and try to make it last. When Phil Donahue wrote his autobiography, he told of something that had happened to him decades before, in his early years of broadcasting. He was a reporter for CBS at the time, and they sent him to Holden, West Virginia, in the heart of the Appalachian Mountains. Holden was a coal town where everybody worked the mines. News media were gathering that day because a mine shaft had collapsed trapping 38 men underground.

Rescue teams rushed down as the clock ticked out the anxious limits of human survival. The weather turned bitterly cold. It took three days to clear the passageways and get within striking distance of the ensnared men. Finally, at 2 a.m. on the morning of the fourth day, the first of the desperate miners cleared the surface and stumbled out of the mine entrance.

Families gathered tightly to hug each new survivor. Snow fell over them in the circle of temporary lights as the local pastor called them to huddle around a little fire. He led them in a prayer of thanks for the rescue. Then they held hands and sang "What A Friend We Have In Jesus."

Donahue said it gave him goosebumps. It was *so* beautiful. He told the cameramen to roll the film. But the sub-zero temperatures had frozen the mechanism and they were not able to record anything.

Phil Donahue is not a man to let a golden opportunity to slide by, so he grabbed the pastor aside and asked him to do it all again — the prayer, the song, the spiritual passion. Donahue wanted to make the feelings happen all over again. "We've got 206 television stations across the country," Donahue told him. "Just let us get another camera and you can share this moment of faith with millions."

What happened next astounded the fledgling reporter. The pastor shook his head and said, "Son, I can't do that. We've already prayed to God. We can't do it again. It wouldn't be right."

But that's what Peter wanted, wasn't it? That's what the other disciples desired as well. With Phil Donahue they wished the moment of truth to linger. They craved for the passion to last. They wanted to hold hands and speak kind words and sing those songs of love. They begged for the cameras to roll, and then they hoped to play the video over and over and over again. That's when Jesus reminded them that life is journey, not a destination.

That can be frightening for us because we get used to a moment of great beauty and then want to hold on to that moment. We try again and again to recapture it in some way, and relive it as if it were more real than the rest of our humdrum hours.

It is for that reason that traditions latch onto us. They can become for us reminders of a moment in the past when things seemed so right in our world: a Currier & Ives Christmas, for instance, or an illuminated Thomas Kinkade painting glowing with just the right moment of sunset perfection outside and the warmth of faith and family shining through the windows of a still life home. G. K. Chesterton called tradition "the democracy of the dead." He said that when we fell in love with tradition we handed the current moment over to voices and times from the past. Let them tell us what to do. Let's try to relive the good old days. "The democracy of the dead."

But life is a journey, says Jesus. "If anyone would come after me he must deny himself and take up his cross and follow me."

That means traditions alone cannot keep our faith strong. It means that life and society and the church will always be changing. It can be frightening to us. How often I have had conversations with people who wished to turn back the clock, to put the pages back on the calendar, to relive the past once again. Then everything would be right and good and true and noble.

But it cannot happen. Soren Kierkegaard put it straight when he wrote that if we are really honest, we experience fear when we read these words of Jesus. "Follow me!" he calls. But where? And how? And in what way?

Why can't we just stay in the little huddle, feeling good about ourselves? Why do we have to hit the road with him?

Kierkegaard said that we should really collect up all our New Testaments and bring them out to an open place high on some mountaintop. There we should pile them high and kneel to pray, "God, take this book back again! We can't handle it! It frightens us! And Jesus, go to some other people! Leave us alone!"

Still Jesus stands next to us, sandals on his feet, staff in his hand, and says to us, "Time to go, folks." Life is journey, not a destination, and we know he is right.

Journey With Purpose

There is something more, as well. Jesus tells us that life is a pilgrimage, not a tour.

You know what a tour is, don't you? It's where you let someone else do all the planning. They take care of your luggage. They put you on a big, air-conditioned bus and ferry you around to all the right sights. They pay the entrance fees for your tickets so you don't have to stand in the heat or the sun by the booth. You can stay safe and comfortable and dry, while others do the sweating for you. That's a tour.

When I studied for a semester in Israel, we watched tour groups come through in regular fifteen-minute intervals. We were studying history and archaeology and biblical geography, so we walked and hiked and followed paths that weren't paved. But the tour busses swept by with tourists who saw Palestine from their windows and never breathed the air or felt the wind or sneezed the dust. Clean in, clean out.

A true pilgrimage, however, isn't like that. A pilgrimage is always personal, always firsthand, always something you have to do yourself. That is what Jesus says to his disciples. With Peter they want him to watch God's plans work themselves out from a safe distance. They wish for him to rest with them on the sidelines, to take the tour on the big love boat instead of swimming with sharks.

But Jesus says, "No." Life is a personal journey. He cannot avoid it. He cannot have someone else stand in for him. He has to make the pilgrimage himself.

Walter Wangerin Jr. put it powerfully in his allegory of Jesus as the Ragman. Wangerin pictures himself in a city on a Friday morning. A handsome young man comes to town, dragging behind him a cart made of wood. The cart is piled high with new, clean clothes, bright and shiny and freshly pressed.

Wandering through the streets the trader marches, crying out his strange deal: "Rags! New rags for old! Give me your old rags, your tired rags, your torn, and soiled rags!"

He sees a woman on the back porch of a house. She is old and tired and weary of living. She has a dirty handkerchief pressed to her nose, and she is crying 1,000 tears, sobbing over the pains of her life.

The Ragman takes a clean linen handkerchief from his wagon and brings it to the woman. He lays it across her arm. She blinks at him, wondering what he is up to. Gently the young man opens her fingers and releases the old, dirty, soaking handkerchief from her knotted fist.

Then comes the wonder. The Ragman touches the old rag to his own eyes and begins to weep her tears. Meanwhile, behind him on her porch stands the old woman, tears gone, eyes full of peace.

It happens again. "New rags for old!" he cries, and he comes to a young girl wearing a bloody bandage on her head. He takes the caked and soiled wrap away and gives her a new bonnet from his cart. Then he wraps the old rags around his head. As he does this, the girl's cuts disappear and her skin turns rosy. She dances away with laughter and returns to her friends to play. But the Ragman begins to moan, and from her rags on his head the blood spills down.

He next meets a man. "Do you have a job?" the Ragman asks. With a sneer the man replies, "Are you kidding?" and holds up his shirtsleeve. There is no arm in it. He cannot work. He is disabled.

But the Ragman says, "Give me your shirt. I'll give you mine."

The man's shirt hangs limp as he takes it off, but the Ragman's shirt hangs firm and full because one of the Ragman's arms is still in the sleeve. It goes with the shirt. When the man puts it on, he has a new arm. But the Ragman walks away with one sleeve dangling.

It happens over and over again. The Ragman takes the clothes from the tired, the hurting, the lost, and the lonely. He gathers them to his own body, and takes the pains into his own heart. Then he gives new clothes to new lives with new purpose and new joy.

Finally, around midday, the Ragman finds himself at the center of the city where nothing remains but a stinking garbage heap. It is the accumulated refuse of a society lost to anxiety and torture. On Friday afternoon, the Ragman climbs the hill, stumbling as he drags his cart behind him. He is tired and sore and pained and bleeding. He falls on the wooden beams of the cart, alone and dying from the disease and disaster he has garnered from others.

Wangerin wonders at the sight. In exhaustion and uncertainty he falls asleep. He lies dreaming nightmares through all of Saturday, until he is shaken from his fitful slumbers early on Sunday morning. The ground quakes. Wangerin looks up. In surprise he sees the Ragman stand up. He is alive! The sores are gone, though the scars remain. But the Ragman's clothes are new and clean. Death has been swallowed up and transformed by Life!

Still worn and troubled in his spirit, Wangerin cries up to the Ragman, "Dress me, Ragman! Give me your clothes to wear! Make me new!"

We know the picture. It is the one that Jesus described to the disciples that day on the road. It is an allegory of the pilgrimage he is on, the journey that is always personal, the path that cannot be watched from a distance. Jesus is the Ragman who has to touch lives, who must heal wounds, who is bound by necessity to bring relief. This is the pilgrimage of the Ragman to the center of the city, to the garbage heap of society, to the hill called Golgotha — the Skull! The Place of Death! The Mountain of the Crucifixion! There he must go — personally.

No Spectator Sport

But so, too, those who are with him. Religion is no spectator sport. Harry Emerson Fosdick remembered a storm off the Atlantic coast. A ship foundered on the rocks and the Coast Guard was called out. The captain ordered the lifeboat to be launched, but one of the crew members protested. "Sir," he said in fear, "the wind is offshore and the tide is running out! We can launch the boat, but we'll never get back!"

The captain looked at him with a father's eyes, and then said, "Launch the boat, men. We have to go out. That is our duty. But we don't have to come back."

So it is, in one of the strangest things about life that Jesus tells us here. The one who wants to protect himself, the one who wants to hide herself, the one who wishes to guard himself carefully, will never find the meaning of life. "Whoever wants to save his life will lose it. But whoever loses his life for my sake will find it" (Matthew 16:25 NIV).

That is why Jesus was so angry with Peter. Peter wanted Jesus to take the easy way out. He wanted Jesus to save his own life, to guard his own safety, to keep his body intact. But how could the Ragman not be the Ragman? How could the Son of God not be the Son of God? How could Jesus not do what only he could do?

Do you know what the early church leaders said about Peter? They had a legend about him, and something that happened in his later years. They said that at the time of the great persecution under Nero, the Christians of Rome told Peter to leave. "You're too valuable," they said. "Get out of town! Find your safety! Go to another place and preach the gospel."

According to the legends, Peter is supposed to have gone from the city. Yet only a few days later, Nero had Peter in custody. Soon afterward, he was sent out to die. When the soldiers took Peter to the site of execution, Peter begged of them one last request. He asked that he might be crucified upside down. He said he wasn't worthy to die in the same way as his Lord. So they nailed him to his cross inverted.

Then, according to the stories, the crowds of Christians gathered round. They wanted to be with their beloved leader as he

352

died. "Why," they asked him as he hung there upside down on the cross, "why did you come back, Father Peter? Why did you return to Rome? Why didn't you flee into the hills?"

This is what Peter is supposed to have said. "When you told me to leave the city, I made my escape. But as I was going down the road, I met our Lord Jesus. He was walking back toward Rome, so I asked him, 'Master, where are you going?' He said to me, 'I am going to the city to be crucified.' 'But Lord,' I responded, 'were you not crucified once for all?' And he said to me, 'I saw you fleeing from death and now I wish to be crucified instead of you.' Then I knew what I must do. 'Go, Lord!' I told him. 'I will finish my pilgrimage.' And he said to me, 'Fear not, for I am with you.' "

That is the end of the story for us today. Peter's great confession, Peter's great denial, and Jesus taking both into his great heart, turning them into great grace. Life is a journey, he tells us, not a destination. We cannot sit down at one spot, however lovely it might be, and hug ourselves into some "... happily ever after."

Moreover, life is a pilgrimage, Jesus tells us, not a tour. It is lived in the footsteps of the Master. It is pursued in the purposes of the Ragman and his associates. It is carried out in the mission of the church.

Here is the road no one wants to travel. Yet, if you choose not to walk it, you will never find yourself.

What does this mean for you personally? I don't know. I can't know for you and you can't know for me. But this I do know: I know that you will know what it means for you if Jesus has spoken to you today. Amen.

Personal Politics

Thomas Browne said that "the vices we scoff at in others laugh at us from within ourselves." More than any other relational failure this is true of hurt and vengeance.

When the great nineteenth-century Spanish General, Ramon Narvaez, lay dying in Madrid, a priest was called in to give him last rites. "Have you forgiven your enemies?" the padre asked.

"Father," confessed Narvaez, "I have no enemies. I shot them all."

Too often that is the story of our lives, and Jesus knows it. Lewis Smedes wrote a book we can hardly step around when thinking about Jesus' words in Matthew 18. Smedes' book is called *Forgive and Forget: Healing the Hurts We Don't Deserve* (HarperSanFrancisco, 1996), and in it he wrestles with us about the commonplace pains we experience in our relationship. One of his stories, based upon true incidents, is about two people he calls Jane and Ralph Graafschap.

Hell Defined

This couple, says Smedes, had been married for more than twenty years. They had three children who had all grown well, and were just in those stages of getting married or leaving for college. Ralph and Jane were about to be empty nesters, and though they loved their offspring, they were secretly anticipating a new time of redeveloping their intimacy as a couple. Jane had given up her personal career goals in order to be a full-time mother and homemaker for these last decades, and she began to plan for reasserting her skills outside their home.

But then tragedy struck. Ralph's younger brother and wife were killed in a horrible car accident. They left three children as orphans, aged eight, ten, and twelve. The community rallied for a short while, providing all kinds of assistance and relief, but Ralph knew that he was the big brother, and to him fell the lot of caring for those kids.

So Ralph and Jane took the three into their home, and Jane started all over again — clothes to buy and clean and mend; groceries to stock for voracious appetites; nighttime cuddling with scared and lonely little ones; Christmases and birthdays to plan for ... Jane's life settled right back into its old routine for another decade.

Ralph was well established in his career, and at the height of his business skills. So he traveled a lot and made deals, and spoke about the sacrifices a family makes when tragedies, like that which happened to his brother, happened. But Jane was left to shuffle three more teenagers through their changing identities and raging hormones. She had hoped to travel some with Ralph, but this new family required all her attentions. Even her biological children were not able to get all the doting they had hoped from their mother as they married and had kids of their own.

By the time nine years had passed, the toll of raising two families had robbed Jane of her vitality and sidelined any chance of another career. Only the youngest of the second tribe was at home, and he was seventeen years old. When he left for college the following fall, Jane would be relieved but emotionally spent. Ralph's rocket had been soaring, however, and Jane couldn't wait to join him for the ride.

That's when Ralph came home from a business trip and broke the news. His secretary, Sue, was a woman of great personality, huge skills, and a lot of good looks. She had made it possible for Ralph to be the man he had become, while Jane was too busy with the children. Sue had time for him. In fact, they traveled often together, something that Jane never seemed to make opportunities for. More than that, Sue absolutely doted on Ralph in a way that he couldn't count on at home. Sue really understood Ralph, while Jane didn't seem to anymore.

Ralph filed for divorce and married Sue. They were both deeply committed Christians, so they joined a church where they could sing and pray and get fed and contribute their considerable skills and money. They were welcomed by the pastor and the leadership team as if God has just sent a wonderful blessing to the church. Jane, of course, felt cheated on so many fronts. Even in her own church she had become an outsider. Her social life grew very small, and her children didn't know what to do with a single parent. Ralph and Sue were always great fun, but Jane was becoming a bitter tag-along nobody cared to have around.

Ralph was truly a nice guy. Even as he slipped easily into his second marriage, he realized his responsibility before God to make things right with his former wife. So one day he called Jane and told her of his happiness. While he was still a bit unsettled as to the manner in which it had all come about, he could definitely feel God's blessing in all of this. But he also was aware that through the process Jane might have felt hurt at times, so Ralph wanted to ask her forgiveness for whatever pain he might have caused. If Jane could just give Ralph and Sue her blessing, he knew God would be pleased.

What could Jane do? What would you advise her to do? What would you do, if you were in her shoes?

"I want you to bless me," Ralph had said. And before she even knew what she should do, the words spat out of Jane's mouth. "I want you to go to hell!"

"I want you to go to hell." That's really what a relationship that has moved into conflict without forgiveness amounts to, doesn't it? Hell is the place where justice is never tempered by mercy, where relationships are never mended, where grudges grow and grace takes a holiday. Hell is eternity apart from God's forgiving love, and hell is the prison of our unforgiveness into which we lock both our enemies and ourselves with no parole hearings. It's a bit like playing Monopoly and landing on a square that forces you to pick up a card which reads: "GO TO JAIL! GO DIRECTLY TO JAIL! DO NOT PASS GO! DO NOT COLLECT $200!"

Prickly People

Jesus' words to his disciples in Matthew 18 about conflict resolution and forgiveness are wonderful on paper. We read them and nod with understanding and trust. Yet, they are some of the most difficult words of challenge that face us anywhere in scripture.

We've all heard of Gilbert and Sullivan, the dynamic duo of the stage. They created fun-filled musicals and light operas a generation ago, giving high school drama departments and community theaters plenty of material to dazzle and delight. Their names always appeared in tandem on the programs: Gilbert & Sullivan's *H.M.S. Pinafore*; Gilbert & Sullivan's *Patience*; Gilbert & Sullivan's *The Mikado*; Gilbert & Sullivan's *The Pirates of Penzance*.

It was as if they were a married couple. Indeed, much of their career felt like that. It was only right that their names be wedded together in common speech.

At the height of their success, they even purchased a theater together so that they could exert full creative control over their new works. Then came the nasty disagreement. Sullivan ordered the installation of new carpets. But when the bill arrived, Gilbert hit the roof at the cost and refused to share in payment. They argued and fought about it, and finally took the case to court. A legal judgment settled the claim, but it did nothing to heal the breach between them.

These grown men never spoke to one another again as long as they lived. When Sullivan wrote the music for a new production he would mail it to Gilbert. Then, when Gilbert finished the libretto, he would post it back to Sullivan again.

One time they were requested to make a curtain call together. Although they normally refused such things because of their ongoing animosity, this time it was a benefit honoring their joint work, and they couldn't get out of it with grace. So they stayed at opposite sides back stage, entered from the far edges of the curtain, ensured that there were props in between them so that they could not see one another on the platform, and waved in isolation to opposite portions of the gathered audience.

Gilbert quarantined Sullivan in the prison of his mind, and Sullivan banished Gilbert from his social continent. Eventually, they each became warders for the prison of the other. Yet, like the guards who traveled to Australia on the first convict ships, it became apparent all too soon that there was little difference between the jailer and the jailed. Both came ashore onto a deserted island in the middle of an alien sea with no way to escape.

Jesus' words are necessary. We are social creatures who cannot live in isolation. Yet, because of the sin and stupidity that trouble our human condition, we do not live well with those around us. The German philosopher, Schopenhauer, compared us to porcupines trying to nest together on a cold winter's night. We crouch toward one another because we need the heat of other bodies to survive. Yet, the closer we huddle, the more we prick each other with our porcupine quills. And, as Jesus indicates, it is most often those who are closest to us, our "brother" or our "sister," who feel the pain of our presence and we theirs.

Jesus outlines a strategy for addressing our troubled relationships with one another. It is important to follow him down this difficult path in our attempts to restore relational glue to our fractured worlds, for the alternatives are much more destructive.

Keep It Personal

First, Jesus reminds us that we have to make the process of restoration a very personal matter. When we are hurt and when our pride has been damaged, we often become vindictive and belligerent. We charge about and spew venom and seek to build polarized communities of those who are for "us" and against "them." The weapon of response most readily available to us is gossip and rumor. If I can send a toxic word to poison the atmosphere around the person who has hurt me, I hold a new advantage over her or him.

In so doing, of course, I demote the other person from humankind and relegate her or him to animal status or lower. She is no longer my equal; she is a slut or a witch or a bimbo. He has become a pariah or a jackass or a scoundrel.

When my friend becomes my enemy, I feel the need to degrade him or her until they no longer deserve respect and have ceased to be bound with me by the rules of gentlemanly conduct or even the combat and prisoner of war stipulations of the Geneva Convention. Then I can blast them with excessive force and hit below the belt.

After the tragedy of September 11, 2001, our nation experienced something of this intentional projected dehumanization. Those who hijacked the planes, according to many speeches and articles, were not humans, but terrorists. They did not play by the rules. They did not value life as we did. They were schooled in barbarianism. For all these reasons and others like them our nation uttered cries for vengeance, many of which exceeded limits of human respect. It was General Philip Sheridan who gave us the striking reflection in 1869 that "The only good Indian is a dead Indian." Post 9/11 there were many voices that seemed to echo his advice in the new and painful context.

But Jesus demands that we keep our hurting relationship and all its parties personal. "If your brother sins against you go and show him his fault, just between the two of you" (Matthew 18:15 NIV). This instruction strips me of my most destructive weapons and forces me to rehumanize the very one from whom my heart wants to pull away in disgust. Jesus does not claim it will be an easy thing to do. No psychologist would pretend the process is a lark, or carries us along like a carnival ride. Hurt is painful, and so is restoration.

Keep It Communal

Second, Jesus challenges us to keep these matters under the eye of the community. It is hard for us to think communally in our highly individualized societies, yet this is precisely what we need to do. To keep these matters under the eye of the community means to place ourselves in submission to at least some form of group identity. This is not easy. Our consumerist way of life constantly tells us that all of reality revolves around us and our tastes and schedules and desires. In stark contrast, to enter a community means that I give up some of my personal agenda for the sake of the greater good. We must be absolutely clear here. The Bible never suggests that our individual lives and personalities and desires and actions are of no value. Nor is a complete commitment to communal living the biblical norm. Significantly to the contrary, the scriptures raise high the importance of the individual and the responsibility of the person. In fact, much of economic capitalism, psychological personhood, and political democracy are rooted in and supported by serious reflections on theologies and philosophies drawing on orthodox Christian perspectives.

Yet, our strong obsession with personal rights and self-absorbed experientialism turns our attention too much toward myopic self-interest and away from group dynamics or social interdependence. After years of reflection on the human condition in books like *The People of the Lie* (Touchstone, 1998), *The Different Drum* (Touchstone, 1998), and *The Road Less Traveled* (Touchstone, 2003), M. Scott Peck came to believe that one of the primary maladies of our age is our resistance against community. In his book *A World Waiting to Be Born* (Rider, 1993) he claimed that religious submission was the only cure for the incivility of our age. When we stop being submissive to some form of higher power, he said, we invariably become gods to ourselves and degenerate into a mad world of petty power brokers who are limited only by the striking range of their swinging fists and demanding fingers.

In the church, at least, we must become more aware of what Body Life means. How is it that Jesus has a stake in multiple lives, and what does this mean for our connection to the head of the body? What is the implication of the church's role in multi-ethnic relations for international politics? How do we allow the leadership of the church, empowered by the Spirit and ordained by the community, to speak into the tensions of our lives that disrupt and fracture the fellowship of faith?

There are no easy answers, of course. But Jesus' teaching here demands that we wrestle with the issues. We cannot claim fidelity with God and at the same time play cavalierly in our daily relations with those around us. Each person and each congregation will have to be part of the process of determining how the community and its leadership will invest in reconciliation and restoration.

Thomas Merton, when writing about the religious community with which he spent many years, noted that every prospective participant was initially brought in and made to stand in the center of a circle formed by current members. There he was asked by the abbot, "What do you come seeking?"

The answers varied, of course, in line with the individual's recent experiences. Some said, "I come seeking a deeper relationship with God." Others were more pragmatic: "I desire to become more disciplined in my practices of life." And there were always a few who were simply running away: "I hope to find solace from the world and refuge from the problems that have plagued me."

But Merton said that there was really only one answer which all needed to voice before they could take up residence. "I need mercy!" was the true cry of the heart. "I need mercy!"

Merton said that any other answer betrayed our prideful assertion of self-determination. We wanted, we planned, we were running away from, we desired ... But the person who knew his need of mercy had stepped out of the myopic circle of self-interest long enough to begin to see the fragile interdependence of all who were taken into the larger fellowship of faith. We cannot create community, for it does not revolve around us. We can only enter community or receive it as a gift. Hence, we need mercy in order to walk through its door.

If we know this, then when we experience tension and broken bonds with someone else in the community, it is not ours or theirs to resolve in isolation. The community itself has a stake in all lives and their interactions. Therefore, says Jesus, it is absolutely imperative that we engage the power of the community in addressing the hurts that affect any of its members. Failing to do so does not so much destroy community as it does isolate us from it. We become impoverished when we think we have all the resources to force others into obedience to our way of thinking or living.

362

Keep It Focused

One more thing that becomes apparent in Jesus' teaching is that the entire emotional content of our relational difficulties needs to be reframed. Jesus says that our goal is to have a brother restored. Moreover, if that does not happen through our own initiatives and those of the community, the outcome must be that we treat the other person in the broken relationship as if he were a "pagan or a tax collector."

These designations sound ominous to us. They are off-putting to our sensibilities of associating with "nice" people. But we need to recall that Jesus was accused of spending too much time with tax collectors and sinners. To treat people in this manner is not to throw stones at them or to turn away in disgust. Rather it is a call to re-engage with them as those whom God is seeking and saving.

When Bill Hybels was a college student in Iowa, he had a roommate who trained his pet dog to growl whenever the town mayor's name was mentioned. No matter what might be happening at any time, if someone happened to say the mayor's name in passing, the little mutt would bristle and growl.

So it is with each of us, when relationships have become strained or undone by someone's carelessness, craft, or calumny. We bristle and growl. In the middle of other conversations, the name might be mentioned and we can feel our stomachs tighten and our breath catch. There is an autonomic response that drives us to pain and frustration.

Only if we can somehow reframe the other person's image in our senses as a "pagan or tax collector" — that is, someone who needs to experience the grace of God — can we still the inner growls and get the beast of our hatred to stop bristling. It is not easy. I have two names in particular that set me off every time I hear them. I wish it were otherwise, but it is not. These people have genuinely hurt me badly in the past, and I carry angst about them into my eternal present.

Yet, I have also learned, over the years, to imagine Jesus standing next to each of them. I have pictured Jesus sitting at table with them, and carrying on conversations of earnest intensity or goodhearted laughter. When I have seen Jesus eating and drinking and sharing the kingdom of God with these two people, the growling of my heart stops, and the menace of bristling disgust or bitterness is tamed.

It is only then that I can hear Jesus saying to me, "You have gained again your sister. You have found again your brother." And something in the world smells sweeter because of it. Amen.

Political Pardon

My parents were married in the wave of weddings that followed World War II. Dad came home from military operations in Europe to start a new life on the farm, and Mom became his partner in the enterprise. There was only one problem — Dad had an older brother who was destined to take over the family agricultural enterprise, and there was not enough work or income to support two families.

So Dad began to look for other opportunities. For a while he drove a cattle truck, bringing fattened animals to the sales stockyards in south Saint Paul. But then a farming assistant job became available in the neighborhood. There was an older couple with a large farm, and none of their children had decided to stay on to work it. Dad and Mom became the hired help, looking after the animals and the fields, and beginning a family of their own.

In time they became indispensable to the older couple. When senior years caught up with them and they decided to move to a small house in town, Dad and Mom were asked to take up residence in the "big house," and manage the farm as if it was their own. For many years, our family grew up on an agricultural expanse known as "The Evergreen Lane Farm" because of the trees that lined its drive and the sign posted over its entry at the rural gravel road that ran past.

On that farm we learned to play and work and live. We pulled weeds, raised pigs, hauled water, built tree houses, and slathered gallons of red paint on barns and sheds. We settled in there as if we owned the place. But we didn't. Dad and Mom knew all too well that we were sharecroppers. Three-fifths of each harvest belonged to us, but two-fifths went every year to the family that still owned the place. We were never to forget that we only stayed there by their good graces.

By the time I had graduated from high school, changes abounded. Dad had purchased other land, so he now had farming investments of his own. Moreover, my grandparents had retired, and Dad and Mom bought their land as well. And when they moved to the old Brouwer homestead, the land that they had sharecropped for so many years remained under their care as rental property. After all, no one could be trusted more with its well-being than Dad and Mom, who had invested their toil and sweat and family into it for decades. The old sharecropper arrangement was turned into a self-renewing rental contract. If neither the landlord nor my parents said anything by August 1 each summer, the rental arrangement continued for another year.

Even in rural areas, however, things can sometimes change rapidly. Sugar beets as a cash crop were aggressively spreading in the neighborhood, and land prices shot up astronomically. On August 6, one year, the landlord came by to demand more rent. Others would pay it, he said. But Dad rightly pointed out that the rental contract was legally renewed for another year. Perhaps the next spring they should talk about it.

That was the start of six weeks from hell. The landlord demanded more money, but my father remained adamant. Then the landlord started calling at all hours of the day or night, saying nasty things and making strange demands. Since the man was a friend and a neighbor and even an elder in the same rural church of which both families were members, Dad relented and agreed to split the difference with him. It wasn't necessary on Dad's part, since he had a legally binding agreement that would stand up in any court. But good relations were more important to my parents than money, so they thought they would make a concession.

It didn't work. The landlord refused the offer. He had an even higher price in mind, and nothing short of that would be acceptable. He became more and more obnoxious in his demands and dealings. Sometimes he would wait until Dad had gone out into the fields before he would come in his pickup truck and park on the middle of the yard, blowing his horn until Mom went out to talk. Then he would berate her until she was in tears.

That was the limit for Dad. Although he had every right to keep farming that land for another year, and at the rental price prescribed by the contract, he gave it all up. "Go rent your land to someone else," he told the landlord. And the man did.

My parents said very little about it all after the deed was done. They never spoke harshly of the family that had so crassly abused and misused them. It was almost by chance that I later found out that months after the final incident my father went to the landlord's place and asked to talk with him. Dad made the trip to ask forgiveness. Dad told the man that he (my father) had been harboring vengeful thoughts and ill-wishes in his heart, and he requested that the landlord forgive him for wronging him in that way.

Playing the Game

I don't know the outcome of their conversations. All I know is that something inside of me changed when I heard what my father had done. It wasn't even about him or about the deeply emotional respect I had for him. It was more about what life is supposed to be like and how it had glimmered more brightly in that moment. To wrestle anger and bitterness and revenge to the ground and defuse it with grace and mercy and an all-encompassing desire for restored relationships was as strange as it was redemptive.

I thought, of course, of Peter's words to Jesus, "Lord, how many times shall I forgive my brother when he sins against me?"

Peter must have felt pretty good about his request. After all, he went on to suggest extravagant limits: "Up to seven times?"

The wisdom of the day said that forgiveness was a three-times matter. If someone did you a misdeed, it was your obligation before God to forgive him or her. If they were so stupid as to repeat their wrongdoing, you should forgive them again, said the rabbis. After all, it was the God-like thing to do. Even a third expression of magnanimous graciousness was encouraged, because it increased your public esteem and your religious long-suffering character. But there had to be limits on mercy, for justice required its day.

Therefore three times forgiving was the general rule for the truly devout.

So Peter must have felt very good about his inquisitive request, and quite confident that Jesus would commend him for it. Along with the other disciples Peter was well aware of Jesus' less-than-complimentary views about the practices of the religious leaders of the day. If they thought three times of forgiving were enough, Peter doubled it and added one for good measure. This, surely, will resonate with Jesus' high hopes for his followers. A word of praise was certainly about to come.

Needless to say, Peter and those with him were more than taken aback by Jesus' response. "I tell you not seven times, but seventy times seven."

Beyond Numbers

Jesus steps outside of the numbers game and creates a new playing field which is so large that no scores can be kept. In effect, the message Jesus sends is not "You must try harder to learn the discipline of forgiving!" but rather "You must continually remember who you are!" This is what Jesus affirms in the powerful story he next tells.

A man owes an insurmountable debt, says Jesus. His creditor decides to close the books on the account and prosecutes him for failure to pay. At the court hearing the man begs for mercy. Moved by the tragedy of it all, the creditor cancels the debt and gives up his legal actions.

Hardly out of court (and jail) this same man bumps into another fellow who owes him a minor sum. In great belligerence the forgiven man pummels the other into submission. This debtor speaks the same words that his own creditor used a short while before to plead his case in the larger debt settlement: "Be patient with me and I will pay back everything!"

But the newly released debtor feels power surge through his veins. "Not a chance, fellow! You are going to prison until your family can come up with the dough!" And so it happens.

But people are watching. And those who saw what had occurred earlier, when this little bully was treated kindly by his own

368

creditor, report the matter to the one who showed great mercy. He, of course, becomes mightily angry and resumes his legal (and now vindictive) action against the one who refused to show mercy.

Jesus ends his parable with a moral of great force: "This is how my heavenly Father will treat each of you unless you forgive your brother from the heart."

Personal Pain

① Several themes emerge from Jesus' story. First, it becomes obvious that forgiveness is always personal because pain is personal. Peter asks about what he should do when his "brother" sins against him. That makes sense to us, even if we don't want to admit it. It is far easier to pretend to deal with people and matters that are at a distance. We can choose to hate terrorists and then choose to talk with politically correct understanding about them because few of us have ever actually been terrorized firsthand. But if a murder has happened in our family, or if a drunk driver has destroyed our property or our health or the life of a loved one, things become highly personal and our glib forgiving spirit runs away.

When Eric Lomax was posted to Singapore in 1941, he knew nothing of the horror that lay ahead of him. With hundreds of other soldiers he was taken captive, and then declared a spy by the Japanese victors. They broke both his arms, smashed several ribs, and left him barely alive. Yet, somehow he survived the death camps and returned home, albeit a damaged man. For fifty years, his seething bitterness poisoned his relationships, first with his father and then with his wife. The former died and the latter divorced him.

In 1985, Lomax received a letter from a former Army chaplain who had made contact with Nagase Takashi, the man who had served as interpreter at Lomax's cruel interrogation. Nagase was deeply offended by his nation's treatment of war prisoners and had devoted the rest of his life to whatever restitution or recompense could be made. He even built a Buddhist temple near the place where Lomax and others had been severely beaten or killed.

Lomax felt the anger of boiling vengeance swell through him. He shared his frustrations with Patti, his second wife. She was indignant that Nagase could write about feeling forgiven and at peace, when she knew the troubles that had dogged her husband for decades. In irritation, she wrote to Nagase about Eric's ongoing emotional pain.

To her surprise, she received a letter of response from Nagase. At first she was almost afraid to open it, but with trembling curiosity she finally relented. What spilled into her lap was "an extraordinarily beautiful letter," as she put it. Even Lomax found himself moved deeply by its compassion and desire for reconciliation.

A year later, Eric and Patti Lomax met Nagase at the location of the famous River Kwai Bridge. In halting English, Nagase repeated, over and over, "I am very, very sorry."

Lomax, in tears, took him by the arm and said, "That's very kind of you to say so."

They met for hours, and Lomax gave Nagase a short letter. In it he said that he could not forget what happened in 1943, but that he had chosen to offer Nagase "total forgiveness." Nagase wept with emotion.

When interviewed later, Lomax said simply, "Sometime the hating has to stop."

There is no end to the hostilities that can erupt between good friends or neighbors or relatives when a slight is incurred or a tragedy can be laid to someone's blame. No end, that is, until someone chooses to say, "Sometime the hating has to stop." That is the very personal moment of forgiveness. It does not come easy. But if we live under the umbrella of God's mercy, it can come.

One-Way Street

②A second thing Jesus teaches us in his parable is that forgiveness is essentially one-sided. While we hope for reconciliation — a two-sided outcome — in matters of hurt and broken relationships, forgiveness is not the same thing. Forgiveness is initiated by one party, and is often rebuffed or rejected by the other. That does not undo forgiveness, but it does remind us that forgiveness is essentially one-sided. Forgiveness is what I do or he does or she does. If it leads to mutual restoration, only then does the one-sided forgiveness become two-sided reconciliation.

370

Jesus emphasizes this in his teaching by showing that when the rich creditor chose to cancel the initial debt, it was neither required nor expected. It happened only because of the choice made by the king. The outcome of the debt cancellation was two-sided, to be sure, but it was initiated as a one-sided movement on the part of the king.

This is a very important point to remember. If we can't have our way in some matter, we often want to make sure that at least the other person can't have her way either. If I hurt, he has to hurt. If I have been wronged, at minimum the other person should be required to make a public show of sorrow. Tit for tat. We want the scales to be balanced somehow, even if it is by way of some kind of mutual expressions that hurt has been caused.

But Jesus is not asking us to be fair people. He is asking that we become excessively unfair in mercy, in the same way that our Father in heaven is merciful with us. It begins as a one-sided initiative.

In February of 1982, Max Lindeman and Harold Wells were sentenced to modest prison terms by a New York judge. Police had booked the pair on rape and assault charges in a highly publicized case. Four months earlier, they had entered a convent in New York City and had brutally victimized a thirty-year-old nun. Not only had they repeatedly raped her, they had also beaten her and then used a nail file to carve 27 crosses into her body. It was a crime which brought even the insensitive to tears.

But when it came time to press charges, the nun refused. She was fully aware that these were the men who attacked her. She did not deny that something evil had happened to her at their hands. Yet, when it came time to overtly accuse the men of their crimes, she chose instead to tell the police and the reporters that, after the model of Jesus, she forgave them. She hoped, she said, that they would learn something from this act of one-sided forgiveness and change their ways.

The police were almost livid. Here were two rotten scoundrels who needed to be punished, yet the nun had tied their hands. Social outrage mounted as the two were tried on lesser charges and jailed for significantly shorter sentences than their basest crimes really demanded.

371

Did it work? Did the nun's forgiving spirit soften the hearts of Lindeman and Wells? Did they change?

The nun believes that is the wrong question to ask. In her heart, forgiveness works. She is more like Christ, and lives in greater harmony with the Spirit of God than if she had followed through on the requests to press charges.

We cannot know, of course, whether the nun's actions are better or worse for the men or for society generally. We probably could not endure a world where no justice was meted, and where the fabric of social responsibility became a mockery through expectations of convenient, unilateral forgiveness.

Nevertheless, the wisdom of Jesus' words is found precisely in their unusual instruction. Jesus himself would die upon a cross that he did not deserve, and while hanging there would breathe words of divine forgiveness. It is the very contrary nature of forgiveness that requires of us respect. To forgive is an unusual way of life that cuts across our otherwise jaded senses and renegotiates the character of power in our world.

Michael Christopher probed it well in his play *The Black Angel*. He told of Hermann Engel, a German general who was sentenced to thirty years in prison by the Nuremberg court for war crimes. Nearly forgotten by the time he was released, Engel escaped from society and built a small mountain cabin near Alsace to live out his final years in obscurity.

But a journalist named Morrieaux would not let the story die so easily. After all, it had been his village and his family that were destroyed by Engel's brutality. Working carefully by spreading rumors and stirring up old feelings of bitterness, Morrieaux fomented a plot to burn the man's house down around him, and sear him painfully to death.

Even this, though, was not enough. Morrieaux had a thirst for revenge. He wanted to hear a confession from Engel. Then he wanted Engel to understand what was about to happen to him. Morrieaux desired to watch the horror invade Engel's eyes at the moment when his destruction was assured.

So Morrieaux sneaked ahead of the mob he had stirred up, and connived to enter the general's cottage on pretense. But the person he met there was not at all what he expected. There was no gruesomeness about him; he held no monster-like qualities. This was just a feeble old man. In fact, as Morrieaux tried to draw out from him the awful details of his war experiences and crimes, Engel was halting and confused. He could not fully remember all that took place. Dates had blurred and incidents were lost or rewoven. Morrieaux began to realize that his vengeance would not be sweet, and that the plot he had instigated against the old man was a terrible act of murder. In desperation, he revealed himself and his intentions to Engel, begging that the general escape quickly with him. Even as they spoke there were distant sounds of the mob climbing to do the nasty deed.

Engel finally understood what was going on. But before he would leave with Morrieaux, he required one condition. "What is it?" asked Morrieaux.

"Forgive me," replied Engel.

The journalist was frozen. What should he do?

As the lights come down Morrieaux slipped out of the cottage alone. The mob did its work and the horrible war criminal died. But the journalist remained forever locked in his own prison of unforgiveness.

Forgiveness is a choice, and a unilateral one at that. It cannot go on the bargaining block or it becomes something other than its essential character. Forgiveness is not fair. It is mercy offered, and that act alone sets aside certain demands of justice. It does not negate justice, but it says that a higher power will be entered to trump the ordinary scheme of things for extraordinary purposes.

Growing In Grace

(3) There is a third element of meaning to note in Jesus' teaching parable, and that is that forgiveness is not merely a one-time event, but rather a growing disposition of graciousness. Matthew makes this clear by placing the parable in the middle section of his gospel. Those events leading up to the Transfiguration in chapter 17 show Jesus focusing most of his attention on the crowds who gather around, and emphasizing the character of the kingdom of heaven. Later, following the entry into Jerusalem on Palm Sunday (ch. 21),

most of Jesus' teachings will anticipate his death and resurrection and the Messianic Age that these usher in. But here, in between, Jesus spends most of his time with his disciples and tries to help them understand the character of a committed spiritual lifestyle. We call it discipleship.

Jesus makes it clear in his story to Peter that there are others looking on as they practice their piety. It is a group of otherwise undescribed folks who notice how the forgiven debtor treats the man who owes him a little. These people also report the man's actions to the king who had originally laid aside the huge obligation that could never have been paid.

In telling this part of the story, Jesus reminds his disciples and us that the goal of any spiritual formation in our lives is not merely to make us feel good, or to give us a sense of accomplishment. This is quite important, since it was Peter's question that sparked the teaching in the first place. Peter had come asking what it would take for him to know that he had done enough, that he was good enough, that he had arrived as some new level of spiritual graduation.

But accomplishments that become self-serving and occasions for self-congratulations are not the goal of discipleship. Jesus, in fact, had said earlier, in the Sermon on the Mount, that those who pray in public and make a big show of giving to the poor have their immediate gratification, but it holds no heavenly value. The goal of spiritual growth is transformation, not arrival. We are to be engaged in a process whereby we become different people, and through which our world begins to look more and more like the kingdom God intended it to be.

So forgiveness is not merely an act that is repeated on occasion to make us feel good in our accomplishments. Rather, it is a growing disposition of graciousness that is an unfolding process of discipleship identity and lifestyle. Peter ought not to think about how many times he forgives one person or a hundred. Instead, the question is whether his character is continually evolving to become more reflective of God.

Lewis Smedes imported a powerful parable from the Netherlands to illustrate that point. Fouke was the baker in a small Frisian

374

town named Faken. He was a very righteous man. In fact, it seemed often that when he spat out his few words, they sprayed righteousness from his thin lips. He walked with upright dignity, and no one could find a fault in him. Except, maybe, that few found him warm or tender. But then, one does not become as righteous at Fouke by blurring the edges of rigorous spirituality through relational compromises.

Fouke was married to Hilda, and they lived a rigid life of regular hours and faithful church attendance. Fouke carried his Bible prominently in his arm as they strolled with purpose to and from worship services each Sunday, and all could see that this book was well used in between. Fouke was a righteous man, and expected others to be as well.

So it was shatteringly shocking when he came home from the bakery one day to find Hilda in bed with another man. How could she do such a thing? How could she violate their bed? More importantly, how could she tarnish the righteousness of their home, or Fouke's reputation in the community?

Word spread quickly in the small town of Faken, and soon everyone knew that Fouke was about to send away his wife in disgrace. So all were surprised when that didn't happen. Fouke chose, instead, to forgive Hilda and to keep her on as his wife. Fouke made it very clear that he was choosing to forgive Hilda, like the good book said. Everyone knew it, and they commended the baker for his fine show of spiritual depth and mercy.

But Fouke's forgiveness was something he wore like a badge of prideful humility, and never did it actually penetrate his heart of hearts. Not a day went by, but Fouke reminded Hilda of his gracious mercy toward her and how undeserving she was of it. She was a tramp, a hussy, a damaged woman with a weak and willful conscience, and she should be glad that a man of his righteous stature did not get rid of her or hold her to public ridicule.

Every day, Fouke's righteousness and forgiveness sparkled like a cheap bauble that weighed them down like costume jewelry. But in heaven, Fouke's fakery didn't sit well. Every night an angel was sent down to Faken to drop a small pebble into Fouke's heart. In the morning, when he exercised again his righteous vindictiveness, a sharp pain slashed through his body.

Day after day the tiny pebbles accumulated, and the hurting in his chest increased. Before long, tall and upright Fouke began to walk with a bit of a bend, and stoop more when he was working. And his boundless energy seemed sapped by the changes taking place in his body. Within several months Fouke trudged down the street nearly doubled over, and his face wore a constant grimace of pain. In desperation he cried out to God. Surely he did not deserve this! What was happening to him? How could he find relief and release from the awful torment?

That night, an angel was sent to Fouke in Faken. Very patiently the angel told Fouke of the observations that had been made, and the decision to drop a pebble into his heart at every expression of righteous bitterness toward Hilda. By this time, Fouke was in too much pain to protest, or to sputter a declaration of his righteousness over against Hilda's gross waywardness in this sordid matter. All he could do is plead for some way to be healed.

The pebbles could be stopped, he was told, and the pain lessened, if he gained the miracle of Magic Eyes. What might these be, he asked, these Magic Eyes?

The Magic Eyes would allow him to see Hilda as she was before the adultery, Fouke was told. "But you can't change what happened," he protested.

That is true, came the angel's reply. No one, not even God, can change the past. But sometimes the future can be changed. Sometimes hurts can be healed. This is why Fouke needed the Magic Eyes.

"Where do I get them?" he pleaded.

You only need to ask with genuine desire, he was told.

But Fouke was too proud to ask for the Magic Eyes. After all, he was righteous. And besides, Hilda was a guilty woman; why should he look at her in any other way? She was the one who nearly destroyed their marriage. If it were not for righteous Fouke, it could never have been saved.

Yet, day-by-day Fouke's debilitating pain increased, as angels continued to drop pebbles into his heart. By the time he finally relented, he was almost walking on his head, and there was no longer any way to hold himself high and rigid with pride. So, in the dark of night, as a lightening bolt of agony ripped through him, he cried out, "O God, save me!"

The relief didn't happen at once. At least Fouke could not notice any difference for several days. But then life became nuance in little ways. First, through sideways glances from near the floor, Fouke thought that Hilda was looking more pretty. She seemed to have a new glow of beauty emerging from within at times. He couldn't believe it, of course, for the adultery had made her very ugly to him. Yet there it was, and he found himself looking at her more and more often.

Then the critical edge of his chest pains began to subside. After several weeks, he found he could walk with less bend and stand with less stoop. His work at the bakery was easier, of course, but so was his time at home with Hilda. Another month or two went by, and Fouke was walking the streets upright, with a lighthearted step. More importantly, the citizens of Faken noticed that Fouke often took Hilda by the arm, and that there was a genuine warmth between them. Some thought, too, that Fouke's lips were less thin than they used to be, and all were certain that the spray of righteousness had subsided.

No one thought Fouke had become less godly in the process, though. In fact, there was a new aura about him that made people sidle up to him in a way they had never desired before.

Hilda was never sure what had happened to her husband. He never told her about the Magic Eyes. But the way things were turning for them, she didn't need to know.

It makes me wonder though, whether I need those Magic Eyes. How about you? Amen.

Why Is God Unfair?

One of my favorite courses to teach is "Introduction to Biblical Literature." It is a 200-level course, and therefore only open to upperclassmen. These are college students who have already been around the block once or twice, and they know the rules of the game for getting good grades.

Because the course is a biblical survey, there is a lot of material to cover, and little that can be pursued in depth. Yet, I want my students to think theologically, so I place before the group every year one question that I tell them will be on the final exam. I will ask them to give me some comprehensive ideas for why these writings are collected into the single book we call the Bible, and how this idea weds them together in some form of literary or theological or structural unity.

I tell them that they need to do well on this question above all, and that if they don't give a reasonably appropriate answer, they will not be able to get a high grade for the course. Furthermore, I assure them that I want everyone to pass, and that I would love for all to get an A. To that end, I will help each of them as much as I am able to. They may see me at my office, or correspond with me by way of email. But they must do the work. If they don't do the work, they cannot get the grade.

Sounds reasonable, doesn't it? "You get what you deserve," we say. "He had it coming." "She made her own bed; now she has to lie in it." These are proverbs we use to highlight the fact that ours is a moral universe, and there are causes and effects within the system. More than that, we believe that God made the world in this way, and holds it to certain measures of justice that are not arbitrary.

This Isn't The Way We Like Our Religion

So Jesus' parable at the beginning of Matthew 20 catches us by surprise. The kingdom of heaven is like people working in a vineyard. Some are hired at the crack of dawn, others mid-morning or noon or sometime in the afternoon, and some are even brought to the field just as dusk is setting in. All get paid. But to the chagrin of those who toiled all day, the wage is the same for everybody. No one gets compensated more for greater effort or longer hours. In fact, the inequity of the situation is publicly displayed, for the paymaster deliberately makes a show of giving the late-comers their big bonus in front of all the rest, and then very obviously ignores the extra toil of the strong ones who accomplished more than a dozen times the work of the new guys.

Someone ought to report Jesus to the labor relations board. He either needs to learn a lesson or two in economics, or we would like him to move to another town so he doesn't destroy our lives and livelihoods here.

We have to admit it: According to Jesus' parable, God is unfair. He gives all the same reward regardless of the hours of labor. I remember the stir caused by reports that Jeffrey Dahmer, convicted of so many murders, had become a devout Christian in his short time before execution. There was even a push by some to get his sentence commuted, since he now espoused a faith that changed his behavior and caused him to be sorry for his sins of the past.

That news was greeted with incredulity, of course. Many were suspect of a last-hour conversion. They thought Dahmer was probably trying to manipulate the system in order to save his life. Who wouldn't confess to a little religion if it kept one away from the execution chamber?

But there were others who were indignant on more confessional grounds. Dahmer was a murderer, a deliberate killer who stalked his victims, played with their bodies and their psyches, tortured many of them, and took their lives with cold-blooded calculation before going on to do it all over again. Here is a man (if

380

we can call him that) who showed no remorse and who violated ever humane and moral principle. He does not deserve favor from us or mercy from God. If God grants Jeffrey Dahmer mercy, would we want to be covered under the same umbrella?

For most of us this discussion feels edgy and raw, but it doesn't grab us entirely. We can sit on the sidelines and watch other people debate and wrestle. But I know a family whose daughter lived three blocks from where Jeffrey Dahmer was during much of the time that he was murdering others her age. And I know one family who lost their daughter to a murderer like Dahmer. For them the mercy of God is a matter of serious mishandling if it reaches too far into these lives who brushed up against their own daughters at such a tragic price.

So if we run Jesus' scenario backward, from the point of view of deathbed conversions of criminals and the like, we find the values he espouses even more maddening. More than that, Jesus seems to reward laziness. Some of the folks in his story came early, eager for work and looking for a job. Why should so much attention be paid to the latecomers who couldn't even get up on time in the morning?

But if God is going to reward bad behavior, what is the point of trying hard? Why live as if morals and good behavior are worth anything? What is the point of teaching public piety or instilling values in the younger members of our community? Nobody benefits in the end anyway. All get the same outcome, according to Jesus.

There are some who try to mitigate the differences in lengths of times worked by saying that the latecomers labored with greater diligence than those who were brought to the vineyard early. In the Jerusalem Talmud, there is a very similar story told through the mouth of Rabbi Zeira. He was giving the funeral oration at the premature death of young Rabbi Bun who died when he was 28. This would have been around 300 BC, for Rabbi Bun's father Rabbi Hiyya can be dated to those years.

Rabbi Zeira told a parable about workers on a king's estate who were hired at different times but received the same pay. This was his way of trying to explain the young man's seemingly untimely death. He said that when the workers were presented to the king for payment at the end of the day, all were given the same wage. "We have been working hard all the day, and this one who only labored two hours receives as much salary as we do," the full-day workers complained to the king.

"It is because he has done more in two hours than you in the entire day," came the response.

This, then, fueled Rabbi Zeira's eulogistic homily. "In the same manner [Rabbi Bun], although he had only studied the law up to the age of 28, knew it better than a learned man or a pious man who would have studied it up to the age of 100 years." According to his telling of the parable, the wages are earned appropriately, for the last who were hired worked harder than the first, and accomplished more.

Yet, Jesus won't give us that room for interpretation. He clearly says that the last to be hired have been "idle" all day (Matthew 20:6-7), not just preparing for harder work. No, there is no way that we can make Jesus come out resonating with justice in the telling of this tale.

Even the way in which the pay is handed out at the end of the day is infuriating. Since those who came to work most recently are told to get their reward first, everyone gets to see what it is they earned. And it far exceeds their expectations, since it is the going rate for a full day's work. Talk among the earlier hires is mixed. Some are excited, thinking that this master is incredibly generous, and that they should be making three or six or even ten times as much as these slackers, if their reckoning is correct. Others grow quickly suspicious that the owner of the vineyard is out to lunch at best, or an insensitive fool at worst, as they watch others moving ahead to take exactly what the first were paid. If the guy in charge wanted to deal in several pay scales at least he should be more discreet about it. Because of his open partiality he now has a mad mob forming. The earliest to be hired and last to be paid are ready to revolt and take by force what they believe is coming to them.

382

This is not a good story, Jesus. It violates our senses and sensibilities!

But maybe we need to read it again. Let's give Jesus the benefit of the doubt and assume that this parable, like his others, is on track with divine wisdom, and that there is another, better interpretation that we miss at first glance.

What Time Of The Day Were You Hired?

Indeed, if you think about it, there is a strangeness about the way that we tend to jump into Jesus' story. We assume quickly that we are part of the group of workers hired early in the day. Maybe that has to do with our years as faithful church members. Maybe we get that from the historic strength of the church in our communities or nation. Maybe we see those who have been objects of our denominational mission efforts as the newbies on the block.

But why should we view it that way? Why do we have this secret suspicion that someone else is getting a better deal than we are? Perhaps Jesus is trying to point that out to us, along with his first listeners. Maybe we need to reposition ourselves in the parable in order to appreciate the character of grace. It may well be that we are the last to arrive, that the Israelites of the Old Testament are the early workers, and that we are getting the good deal called grace.

Are You Getting What You Bargained For?

There is a second thing that is bothersome in the story, if you think about it for a while. Those who were first hired actually bargained for what they received at the end of the day. They do not agree to work for the master of the vineyard until they have put their demands on the table and have sufficiently assured themselves that they will get what they earn, what they think they deserve.

While we may have problems with the lavish graciousness of the master toward those who begin the work day late, we ought also to be a bit queasy about those who make these kinds of deals. In the work places of our lives it is a healthy thing to bargain well for fair wages. But there is something insidious and bordering on evil when other forms of relationship take on measured tones of such justice. Think, for instance, of a child who argues that she or he deserves a bigger allowance because of work done around the house. If all the expenses of that household were assigned in proportion to all the income generated by members of that family, what would a truly fair allowance for a nine-year-old be? In reality, she or he should be working 1,000 lemonade stands just to get food into the kitchen and have a place to sleep.

Once a relationship of trust and love and care is reduced to monetary value, it destroys the fiber of the bond itself. That is why divorce settlements are often so acrimonious. What was begun as a sharing of lives has suddenly devolved into the apportionment of assets. It has to be done, of course, but it violates everything that was taking place when the wedding vows were spoken.

Helmut Thielicke remembered an occasion when that came home to him. He was serving as a hospital chaplain for a time, and noticed the extraordinary care of one particular nurse. She was usually working the night shift, but never used the slower time as a means to slack or loaf. Instead, she was constantly busy, checking every patient on a very regular schedule, and often holding hands with those who were fearful of surgery, praying with the dying, and reading to those who could not sleep for pain or worry.

Thielicke stopped to thank her for her marvelous nursing care. It seemed to make such a difference for those whom he came to visit as a pastor. He asked her if she ever tired of her exhausting hours and often thankless job.

"Not at all," she told him. "In fact, every night I am adding jewels to my crown."

That took him aback, so he asked her what she meant. "Our Lord has promised to reward our good deeds," she replied. "If my tally is correct, I now have 1,374 jewels in my crown in heaven."

Suddenly, wrote Thielicke, he saw her through new eyes. The person he had admired for her inner beauty, tender care, and sacrificial service became in an instant a greedy religious ogre, choosing to locate herself in spots where more heavenly goods could be looted from her unsuspecting prey. It made him sick.

So it should. We only have to remember another story of Jesus, the one we call the prodigal son, to see this crassness reflected back to us in a similar way. There, if you recall, the older brother to the young man who left and squandered his inheritance was irate at the party given when the shiftless fellow returned home. He brazenly reminded their father that he, the more responsible son, had stayed home all these years and had slaved in the fields. Surely he deserved a bigger party and a better piece of the pie than he appeared to be getting.

But his self-centeredness and mercenary spirit were clearly at odds with the character of the Father and the values of the kingdom. So, too, the bargaining that takes place at the beginning of the day in this parable, and then again at the end. "Didn't you bargain for what you got?" the early hires are asked. "Why do you think that is unfair? You are only getting what you thought you were worth." And maybe that is the problem. When we try to mark a service with some value, invariably the price tags never fit.

Who Are You Working For?

There is one other almost deceptively hidden odd point about the story as Jesus tells it. Where is the landowner throughout the tale? It is his estate, his vineyard, and his work that is being done. Yet, he seems to spend most of his time out in the marketplace looking for people. There is a strangeness about his priorities that is at odds with the values driving at least some of the workers. The owner is interested in people and their well-being to a degree not found among the rest. They are good workers, or they are mercenary hires, but they do not have the same care for one another as the master of the estate exhibits.

It is a sobering thought in our consumerist age. Christians are often willing to be classified merely as "church goers," and congregational life in our world is caught up with worship wars and herd-like rushes to the newest and latest and most experiential fads in the next "prevailing" ministry on the block. Church attendance follows value of presentation, so that there is often a direct link between what is given and what is received.

385

But where is the master of the house in all of this bargaining for better church conditions and greater rewards for service? According to Jesus' tale, he is out in the marketplace looking for those who don't have what it takes to be fully human or fully alive. Maybe it is not so important to God whether we get much out of worship services; maybe we ought to be renegotiating the values of our hearts to see whether our "needs" are tracking with that of the master.

There is something terribly shocking about this parable that alerts us again to the radical meaning of grace. After the initial wonder of our salvation wears off we quickly become merely religious. And in that devolution there is great danger.

No Longer Surprised By Grace?

One college professor presented his class syllabus on the first day of the new semester. He pointed out that there were three papers to be written during the term, and he showed on which days those assignments had to be handed in. He said that these dates were firmly fixed, and that no student should presume that the deadline did not apply to her or him. He asked if the students were clear about this, and all heads nodded.

When the first deadline arrived, all but one student turned in their papers. The one student went to the professor's office and pleaded for more time — just a single day! The student spoke of illness and hardships that had prevented him from completing the assignment, but all the research was finished, and a few more hours would allow the paper to be ready. The professor relented, and granted a one-day extension without penalty. The student was extremely grateful, and sent a note thanking the professor profusely.

When the second deadline arrived, three papers were missing from the pile of student productions. The student who had previously asked for an extension was back, and so were two others with him. As before, all the reasons expressed for failure to complete the assignment were touching and moving and tear-jerking, and the professor again allowed some latitude. The deadline was set aside, and the papers were required by the end of the week. A veritable chorus of praise filled the professor's small office, and blessings were heaped upon him.

When the third due date arrived, the professor was inundated with requests for extensions. Nearly a quarter of the class begged for more time — so many other assignments and tests were due, so many books still needed to be read, so much work was required this late in the semester. But this time the professor held firm. No extensions were to be given. Grades would be marked lower for tardiness. Stunned silence filled the classroom.

The large delegation that met the professor in the hallway near his office was very vocal in their anger. "You can't do this to us! It isn't fair!"

"What isn't fair?" asked the professor. "At the beginning of the term you knew the due date of each paper and you agreed to turn in your work at those times."

"But you let so-and-so have extensions. You can't tell us now that we can't have a few extra days."

"Maybe you are right," said the professor. He opened his grade book and made a rather public subtraction from the grades given to the four former late papers. Each of those students, now also in this group, protested loudly. "You can't do that, Professor! That's not fair!"

"What's not fair?" asked the professor. "Justice or mercy?" The question blanketed them heavily as each student silently slipped away. And the professor? When he reported the incident to others, he simply concluded (paraphrasing Henry Higgins from *My Fair Lady*), "They'd grown accustomed to my grace!"

We grow easily accustomed to God's grace. We need to become "Wow!"ed again by the amazing thing that happens when God chooses to start over in love toward us, even after the "Great Syllabus" demands a divine reckoning.

In her wonderful collection of poetry called, *The Awful Rowing Toward God*, Anne Sexton examines her life like someone in a canoe rowing against the stream of life, encountering hazards along the way, and finally docking at the island of God's home. The concluding poem in the book is called "The Rowing Endeth." In it she sees herself called by God's great laughter to join him for a game of poker. When the cards are dealt, she is surprised and thrilled. She has a royal straight flush. She will trounce God and win for herself whatever prizes God has brought to the table. In great excitement she slaps down her cards, claiming her winnings. Nothing can beat this hand!

But God only laughs, a great, rolling, joyful exuberance that energizes everything around. In rich good humor, with no malice at all, God throws down his cards. Five aces! That's impossible! But there it is. And when Anne loses to God, she knows that really she wins. For God is not stingy with his wealth or his earnings. There are never any losers when they sit at table with God. God's laughter is always without malice or one-upmanship.

This is the gospel according to Jesus' parable. In spite of our good fortunes or savvy playing skills or sheer hard work, we never really win at the game of life when we play it by our own rules. But if God is bending them in the direction of grace, something wonderful always happens. Amen.

A Career In The Kingdom

When Sadie and Bessie, the famed "Delany Sisters," were in the early years of their second centuries (103 and 105, respectively) they told interviewers, "God only gave you one body, so you better be nice to it. Exercise, because if you don't, by the time you're our age, you'll be pushing up daisies." Fitness gymnasiums ought to put the Delany Sisters on their billboards and quote them into larger profit margins.

Some people get into exercise in a very big way. When Teddy Roosevelt was president of the United States, his exploits at physical endurance were legendary. French diplomat, Jean Jusserand, stationed in Washington DC at the time, developed a good friendship with the president. Teddy often used this friendship to coerce Jusserand into sharing his morning exercise rituals. One day, according to Roosevelt in his autobiography, *Theodore Roosevelt: An Autobiography*, the two of them played several sets of tennis, jogged a number of miles, and then worked out with the medicine ball for an hour. After all of that the president was just getting warmed up, and he asked Jusserand, "What would you like to do now?"

Gasping for breath, Jean replied, "If it's all the same to you, lie down and die!"

Where Did That Come From?

Some people know when enough is enough. Others never seem to quit. For them, tortures like the Hawaiian "Ironman Triathlon" are a happy day — a 2.4 mile swim in the ocean as appetizer, a main course of bicycling for 112 miles, and then a dessert marathon run of 26 miles to finish things off.

Joni Dunn entered the Ironman Triathlon in 1985 at the age of 43, and managed to come in first in her division. Not only that — she set a new record time.

Two things made Joni Dunn's win a real surprise. First, Joni nearly died in a skiing accident a dozen years earlier. She plunged over a cliff and fell more than 100 feet into a deep ravine. Her spine was fractured in seven places and her neck was broken. Joni also suffered several fractures to her head.

At first, doctors held little hope for Joni's survival. She would later remember lying on her hospital bed catching whispers of concerned professional conversation through a blanket of morphine haze. "I heard them say, 'She won't live through the night.' I knew that if I stopped concentrating on living, I would die."

But live she did. It took countless operations to put Joni back together. She emerged from the hospital two inches shorter, and so hunch-backed that when she first saw herself in a mirror she didn't recognize the image.

It was during her long years of therapy that the idea of competing in the Ironman Triathlon began. Still, it took Joni a decade to work up the courage and stamina to enter.

That is the first thing that makes Joni's win in 1985 so surprising — moving from near death to sports endurance triumph. Here is the second — Joni Dunn says that there is only one thing that pulled her through the torture of the grueling race: her religion. "Just moving caused me incredible pain," Joni told her interviewers. "But I knew I had to do this. I come from a very disciplined Dutch Reformed family in Illinois. That discipline has always been with me, and it makes me strong."

That is a surprising testimony, isn't it? Joni Dunn says her religious identity gave her the determination necessary to see her through a life-threatening accident, and then pushed her down the road to win the grueling Ironman Triathlon.

Cafeteria Christianity

Most North American Christians lack such discipline and focus, according to social researcher, Reginald Bibby. His book, *Fragmented Gods* (Ontario, Canada: Irwin, 1987), declared that historic Christianity was all but dead. People today are consumers, he reminded his readers. They go shopping for this and that, a new toy here, a new emotion there, a new sensation each time around. When one pastime doesn't excite them anymore they move on to a new one.

Those same people have become religious consumers in the vast array of church supermarkets, said Bibby. A ritual here, a prayer there, a cause in the next parish, an entertaining preacher on the other side of town, and the Christian population grazes through the cafeteria of weekly specials. Bibby said that most Christians treat religion like a wardrobe — they take different garments out of the closet each Sunday, depending on their spiritual moods, and then they put them all back in the closet on Monday when they take out their "secular" clothes and get on with the real business of life.

Eugene Peterson put it this way in his book, *A Long Obedience* (Westmong, Illinois: InterVarsity, 1980, p. 12): "Religion in our time has been captured by the tourist mindset. Religion is understood as a visit to an attractive site to be made when we have adequate leisure. For some it is a weekly jaunt to church. For others, occasional visits to special services. Some, with a bent for religious entertainment and sacred diversion, plan their lives around special events like retreats, rallies, and conferences.

"We go to see a new personality, to hear a new truth, to get a new experience, and so, somehow, expand our otherwise humdrum lives. The religious life is defined as the latest and the newest: We'll try anything — until something else comes along."

Reviewing Terminology

That is a tragic indictment of our spiritual expressions — particularly so, since the Bible uses two words to describe the character of religion in its truest form, shaped far differently than by either the consumer mindset or the tourist mentality.

The first word is "disciple." This is the term by which the followers of Jesus are known. A disciple is someone who is apprenticed to a master. A disciple is someone who will stick close to him, someone who will follow him through thick and thin, and someone who will not lose energy too quickly, or seek to go his or her own way too soon.

A disciple is a learner, but not in the classroom or a schoolhouse. A disciple is one who follows the master craftsman as he shapes his world. Such an education is not something completed in five hours on an afternoon, or even during a term at college or university. It is something that involves a whole-life commitment, surrounding every motive of our hearts and every choice of our minds. This is what Jesus expected of his relationship with the twelve when he called them to himself as "disciples."

The other word in the Bible for those who take religion seriously is "pilgrim." A pilgrim is someone who is on a journey in life. A pilgrim is someone who has a past in which she is not wallowing, someone who has a present to which he is not tied, and someone who has a future which is not certain, but which is very specific and very real; a future that belongs to God.

When Jesus was questioned by the religious leaders of his day to give credentials for his growing public prominence, he would not comply. It was not because Jesus had no credentials to offer, but because those who were asking for such documents were themselves in no mood to become either disciples or pilgrims. They did not want to submit to religious authorities other than those they believed were already theirs to manipulate. This had become obvious in their interaction with John the Baptist, as Jesus reminded them.

Although this silenced Jesus' would-be accusers, Jesus himself took the matter one step further. He told them a story and then demanded that they explain it for him. Two sons were asked by their father to work the fields. One quickly said, "Yes," but didn't make a move and never stepped out to do the labor. The other was belligerent and immediately refused to be part of his father's livelihood; yet later he realized who he truly was and what he had become, and he then went out to the field to do the work.

What was the point? Jesus' detractors understood quickly that he was speaking about them. It is one thing to parade religious values as high-minded ideals, but quite another thing to put them into practice. No one who refuses to be a disciple can ever become a pilgrim. The disciple gives up his will for the sake of the master's teachings and good graces. The pilgrim sets out on the road of the kingdom in a journey of obedience.

Therein lies the rub, of course, because the wandering steps of pilgrims only reach hallowed ground by first experiencing the bruising of walking too long on the jagged stones of unholy territory. To become a pilgrim means first to become a disciple. Moreover, it requires that one gets to work.

Language Of The Lie
To become this follower of Jesus starts with the sob of a soul that no longer believes the lie of society. We hear the lie every day in its subtle forms: "Things are really getting better and better all the time." "Everyone has an equal opportunity in life." "Education will conquer all our ills." "If you just try hard enough, you can make it on your own."

The advertisements tell us that people are really pretty good, and that the world itself is a rather pleasant and harmless place when we dress right, smell right, eat right, exercise right, and drive the right cars or invest in the right companies. Everything will work out well for the nice people.

Cornelius Plantinga Jr. documented the leaching power of evil well in *Not the Way It's Supposed to Be* (Grand Rapids: Eerdmans, 1995). He called his "breviary of sin" a reflection on life. Like a stranded motorist in the wrong part of town being hustled by ominous turf lords brandishing Saturday night specials, we feel the creeping cancer of a world coming undone.

But the way of the disciple takes its first step with prayer. She cries for help. He confesses that he cannot make it on his own. This was the call and invitation of John the Baptist which too many had refused to heed. From Jesus' perspective, John was the first hint of dawn calling to minds newly awakening from the twisted darkness of the world in which we are trapped: the advertiser who claims to know what I need and what I want and who can make everything better with just a single credit card; the entertainer who promises me a quick fix, a cheap trick, a sensuous fling that really *is* love; the politician who has my best interests at stake, and who will make me ruler with him if I just give him my vote; the psychiatrist who will help me achieve gain without pain by lowering my standards to the mud around me.

Religious Displacement

A disciple sees the world through different eyes and begins the journey of the pilgrim with a cry of repentance. It is the kind of thing one of the psalmists wrote about when confessing that he "dwells in Meshech" (Psalm 120), a place thousands of miles northwest of Jerusalem, somewhere in what we know today as southern Russia.

There was nothing inherently wrong with Meshech as a land. Nor were its people uncontrollably cruel. Instead, within the economy of ancient boundaries, God had placed his people in Palestine for a particular reason. The bridge territory between Africa and Asia, between the deserts of Arabia and the Mediterranean Sea, formed a natural stage on which the drama of divine revelation and redemption could be played. Jerusalem was only a city of the Jebusites until David and God together made it "Zion," the house of the Yahweh. The history of Israel was only a catalogue of tribal squabblings until God chose David and Solomon to create a world-class empire that brought the nations to seek its unusual character.

For the psalmist to decry that he "dwells in Meshech" meant that somewhere along the line he sold out, that he left home, that he boarded the wrong ship and followed a faulty flag. He was the original prodigal son, living in a land where the slur of his dialect brought only stares of alienation. Whether for wealth or adventure, he had stepped down the wrong path long ago, trading his homeland and its covenant with God for a puppet show hitched to deceptive fingers.

Such people have been caught up in the fashions of their day, majoring in minors and having no direction or purpose or real meaning for what they are doing. They find themselves like alcoholics who have been warned by every friend and challenged by every enemy, but remain blind to the dangers of their drinking habits until one morning they struggle awake in an unknown bed, family gone, reputation destroyed, with all their begged and stolen income bargained insanely away for another hangover. "Woe is me!" they cry, in the first note of repentance.

It is then, and then alone, that a ray of hope dawns. The journey begins in that moment, just as Bill W. testified in *The Big Book* of Alcoholics Anonymous. It starts at the bottom.

Cry For Help

The Bible is full of calls for repentance, precisely because none of us will take the journey to God on our own. It is not until we come to our senses, down in the hog wallows of our lives, that we begin to cry in agony for the grace of deliverance. That is the meaning of Jesus' harsh words to those who challenge his authority. They will never know who they are until they first begin with confessions like these:

- Woe is me!
- Too long I have wasted my time in building an empire I cannot keep!
- Too long I have spent my hours in the cult of self-worship, dressing to kill and twisting the lives of others to do my bidding!
- Too long I have wandered in search of myself, only to find that I don't really exist!
- Too long I have lived in a world that will never be home for me!
- Woe is me!

When repentance comes, it can be a devastating thing. I will never forget the torment in my own soul the afternoon that my life collapsed around me and I lay face down on the carpet of a dark room, pounding the floor with my fist, painting my cheeks with my tears, and crying out in the anguish of my soul, "I need you, God! I need you, God! I need you, God!"

It is not the same for everybody, of course. But this I know — I have yet to meet the person in life with true spiritual depth who has not come through some agonizing moment of inner turning: turning from this to that; turning from one set of values to another; turning from lesser gods to Someone far more profound. This, in the Bible, is the meaning of repentance. *Metanoia* is the Greek term. It means the turning of our inner selves from one direction to another.

It is like the old Shaker song:

> *When true simplicity is gained,*
> *To bow and to bend we shan't be ashamed.*
> *To turn, turn will be our delight*
> *Till by turning, turning. we come round right.*

Rattlesnake Blessing

This, obviously, goes against the consumer mentality that has gripped our society. We have been drugged into believing that we are okay on our own, that we have all the means and resources necessary to see us through any jam in life's river. That is why, in a culture guided by consumption, we are not really on the way to anywhere. We do not need to repent, according to pop psychology, but only to obtain. We do not need to change our ways, only our strategies. We do not need some outside power to help us, only to encourage us. We can do just fine on our own, thank you! So Jesus' call to discipleship and pilgrimage often dies before it gets a good response from our lips or a faithful commitment in our actions.

Still, "the longest journey begins with the first step," as the Chinese philosopher, Lao Tzu, put it. And repentance is the first step on the road to healing. Grace has no place in the self-satisfaction of a do-it-yourself religion. Jesus himself said earlier in Matthew's gospel that he did not come to gather the so-called righteous (such as the ones who are satisfied with where they are), but *sinners* to repentance (Matthew 9:12-13).

Some years ago, I heard Madeline L'Engle speaking at a conference. She explained to us how she came, one day, to understand the meaning of her life. At the time she was the "Writer in Residence" at the Cathedral of St. John the Divine on Fifth Avenue in New York City. She met regularly with the rest of the staff at the church, and developed a fast friendship with the Cathedral bishop.

One day, the two of them were talking about the times in their lives when they felt they had grown the most in terms of inner graces and spiritual depth. It did not take long for each to realize that the most creative energies had come to life only at the end of periods of great struggle, often filled with agonizing mental and emotional torment. In fact, said Madeline L'Engle, the best of her books were written just after the worst times of her life!

As they talked, each experienced the growing realization of what poet and hymn-writer, Margaret Clarkson, identified when she penned *Grace Grows Best in Winter* (Grand Rapids: Eerdmans, 1984). More than that, they also found that the turning point leading out of the dark night of the soul was, for each of them, always a moment of repentance.

After some tender moments of further sharing, the bishop got up to leave. At the door, said L'Engle, he stopped for a moment and then turned round to face her. "Madeline," he said to her, "I don't know how to say this, but have a *bad* day!"

He was the best kind of friend, Madeline told us, for he truly cared about her. He did not wish for her to experience the nastiness of life. Yet, he did wish for her to find the grace of God that only emerges with power out of the repentance that comes to those who realize the insufficient, incomplete, inept, and inconsistent state of their hearts. Only a very kind and truly great friend could see that sometimes what we need most is a bad day that will help us turn our hearts toward home.

It reminds me of the story of a cattle rancher who despised religion as something only for wimps. The local pastor had visited him a number of time but got nowhere against the grizzled one's spiritual intransigence. In fact, the last time the preacher had dared approach the ranch house, he had been run off with a shotgun.

The rancher had always taken care of himself. He didn't need any namby-pamby religion stuff to make a go of his life. That is what he taught his three sons, as well.

So the pastor was mighty surprised one day to get an urgent call from the ranch. Could he come out right away and have prayer with Tom, one of the rancher's sons?

Rushing out to the ranch house he found the doctor leaving. "Snakebite," said the doctor. "There's nothing more I can do."

The rancher welcomed the pastor with uncharacteristic warmth and pulled him quickly through the house to a room where Tom was writhing on the bed. "Could you say a prayer for him?" asked the worried father.

He took off his hat, revealing a balding spot the pastor had never seen. Not only that, but he knocked the hats off Dick and Harry, too, standing on the other side of their agonizing brother. And there, in the dimness of that bedroom, the preacher began to pray over Tom: "We thank you, Lord, for sending this rattlesnake to bite Tom, for this is the first time in his life that he has admitted that he needs you. And Lord, we pray for two more rattlesnakes to come along and bite Dick and Harry, so that they, too, might receive this blessing. And then, Lord, we pray for an especially big and ornery cuss of a snake to come along and bite the old man, so that he, too, will know what it means to need you!"

Now, that is probably a prayer we would never dream of praying. Still, the idea is clear. Life begins at death: dying to the trappings of the life around us; dying to the little things that keep us self-absorbed; dying to ourselves in order to find the things that really make us alive. As Jesus put it just a few chapters before this, "What will it profit a man if he gains the whole world, but loses his own soul?" (Matthew 16:26 cf).

Gospel Truth

There is a familiar gospel song that breathes with both the pain and the urgency of Jesus' pleading challenge in these verses. Thomas Dorsey was born in 1899 with music in his soul. He was known as "Georgia Tom," entertainer and blues singer. When he became a Christian, his music took on more depth as Dorsey explored the profound spiritual blues of scripture.

In 1938, Dorsey was scheduled to be the lead singer at a series of revival meetings in St. Louis, Missouri. His wife was pregnant, and Dorsey grew more hesitant to leave her as the due date approached. But she knew the impact of his ministry, and urged her husband to keep his musical commitments for the sake of those who were seeking God. So he traveled the long road from Chicago to St. Louis.

On the first night of the revival, while Dorsey was already on the platform and the service was in progress, a telegram came. Dorsey's wife had died in a sudden and serious childbirth. Dorsey left for Chicago immediately, and found his infant son barely hanging onto life. The child died a few hours later. In a moving funeral service, Thomas Dorsey buried his beloved wife and tiny son in the same casket.

Despondency set in. The great blues singer wandered in a depression that seemed to know no limits. A friend took him in for a while, just to care for his physical needs. One evening, Dorsey wandered over to a piano and began to improvise on the keyboard. A melody gradually emerged, and the words soon followed. It sings in the heart of every person who has started the steps of faith that begin at the point where the resources of self prove insufficient:

Precious Lord, take my hand,
Lead me on, help me stand,
I am tired, I am weak, I am worn.
Through the storm, through the night,
Lead me on to the light.
Take my hand, precious Lord; lead me home.

When my way grows drear,
Precious Lord, linger near —
When my life is almost gone.
Hear my cry, hear my call,
Hold my hand lest I fall —
Take my hand, precious Lord; lead me home.

When the darkness appears,
And the night draws near,
And the day is past and gone,
At the river I stand,
Guide my feet, hold my hand,
Take my hand, precious Lord; lead me home.[1]

Amen.

---

1. "Precious Lord, Take My Hand," words and music by Thomas A. Dorsey, 1932.

Kingdoms In Conflict

When Vince Lombardi was hired as head coach of the Green Bay Packers in 1958, the team was in dismal shape. A single win in season play the year before had socked the club solidly into the basement of the NFL, and sportscasters everywhere used it as the butt of loser jokes. But Lombardi picked and pulled and prodded and trained and discipled the players into become a winning team. They were NFL champions in three consecutive seasons, and took the game honors for the first two Super Bowls.

Lombardi was a drill sergeant and a strategist, finding and developing the best in each of his players individually and then crafting a team community that could visualize the prize. "Winning isn't everything," he was often quoted as saying, "It's the only thing!" His Packers proved him true, time and again.

Where's The Team?

Coaching is nothing without a team that responds. Leaders are merely overblown egos if there is no one who will follow. During the tumultuous French Revolution of 1789, mobs and madmen rushed through Paris streets. One journalist reported a wide-eyed, wild-haired wastrel lumbering along one day, feverishly demanding from all he saw, "Where is the crowd? I must find them! I am their leader!"

This is the problem Jesus pointedly identifies in his parable. God is the greatest coach, but the team is unwilling to follow. Because of that, people mill about or wander aimlessly. England prior to Churchill was a patchwork of competing ideologies stymied at the crossroads of the twentieth century's critical international events. India before Gandhi lacked cohesive identity and played a game of competitive kowtowing to expatriate authorities, and it was only turned around when he helped inspire a national common cause. Even more tragic is the situation in the kingdom of heaven.

The problem, as Jesus' story puts it, is that the great leader has come — twice over, in fact — but those who are sub-coaches think they can play the game without a head coach. They use a different play book and try to win minor trophies that will gather dust on their mantles, rather than looking for the winning season that would honor the owner.

Quick History Lesson

Jesus' short story mirrors the vast sweep of biblical theology, and frames it in the strong political language that opens the Pentateuch. In the world of the Bible, Genesis functions as the prologue to the covenant God makes with Israel at Mount Sinai (Exodus 20-24). Modeled after the Suzerain-Vassal covenants widely used in that day to organize affairs between kings and subjects, these covenants had standardized parts. The prologue rehearsed the background to the making of the covenant, and gave reasons why it was necessary. Thus Genesis was built, literarily, in four major sections that each helped ancient Israel understand a portion of the historical necessity that brought about this treaty ratification. Chapters 1-11 told of the good world God created and also the nasty civil war that threatened to destroy it. Chapters 12-25 spoke of Abraham and the way that God selected him to head the team which would become the advance troops in taking back God's world from the evil intruders. Chapters 26-36 are a character study of how Jacob became "Israel" (one who struggles with God) and thus bequeathed the nation with a name and an identity. Finally, Genesis 37-50 focused on Joseph, and described how the nation eventually wound up in Egypt, from which it had so recently emerged. The result was a new and winning team that would form God's estate among the rest of the nations of the world. This is the picture Jesus presents in summary form in his parable.

402

In Israel's world there were three kinds of covenants regularly made. The first was a "Parity Agreement" which shaped relations between individuals of similar social rank in the ancient world (think of Jacob and Laban forming their parity treaty at the end of Genesis 31). In addition there were two varieties of king-subject covenants. One was a "Royal Grant." This was essentially a gift bestowed by a person of power and political privilege upon someone down-caste a rung or more. Usually the king noticed an act of bravery in battle, or striking beauty in the ballroom, or uncommon beneficence in bearing, and gave a gift in public recognition. One obvious example is that of Persian king, Xerxes, honoring Mordecai in the story of Esther (chs. 3-6). The Royal Grant was always a one-way act, with no specific reciprocal deed required.

The second type of king-subject covenant was known as the "Suzerain-Vassal Treaty." It was quite different from the Royal Grant. It moved on a two-way street, with both parties giving and expecting much. When a Suzerain-Vassal Treaty was ratified, kings would provide safety and food and shelter and relief and community building grants, while the people were obligated to pay taxes, offer troops for the regiments, send food supplies, and enlist in government work projects. Rather than merely a bequest awarded by one to the other as was true with the Royal Grant, the Suzerain-Vassal treaty ensured that both parties invest in the relationship.

Interestingly, in the series of covenants developed between God and Abram in Genesis 12-17, the first three (Genesis 12, 13, 15) appear to be "Royal Grants." Each time a gift is proffered — land (twice) and a biological heir who will help establish a great Abram-family nation. Strikingly, after each Royal Grant is spoken, Abram seems to lose confidence in the gift. Rather than stay in the land of promise, he runs to Egypt to find better grazing for his crops and food sources for his crew. Similarly, instead of mating again with wife Sarai to realize a biological heir, Abram and the younger Hagar bond to produce Ishmael. Three times God makes Royal Grants with Abram, and each time Abram takes matters into his own hands.

In the fourth covenant ceremony in Genesis 17, however, God changed tactics, and Abram came out of the deal with a transformed heart. There God established a Suzerain-Vassal covenant.

403

In it God promised land and blessings and descendents, but God also called Abram to respond with faith and fealty. Abram was not merely the target of a nice gift; he was now called to share the mind and the mission of the Maker. God declared name changes for Abram and Sarai, and also required the act of circumcision which would publicly mark all the males of the family as "owned" by God.

The outcome to this fourth covenant-making event was strikingly different than that following the previous three. Most notably, when pushed to the limit of trust in Genesis 22, the new Abraham gave evidence that his covenant relationship with God superseded all other loyalties and commitments. Because of the Suzerain-Vassal covenant established in Genesis 17, faith stuck deeply in Abraham's life.

Of course, for the Israelites at Mount Sinai who reviewed this history, the lesson was clear. God's gifts alone do not bind us into God's redemptive enterprises. A faith response and loyal service round out the picture. Without investment on our part, no great blessing of God lingers for our enjoyment. Abraham and his descendents form a great team because they have a great coach who gives the right incentives and demands the right stuff in return.

This is the plot underlying Jesus' words in the parable of the tenants. Israel was blessed by God to share in the divine enterprise of making the garden come alive on planet earth. Unfortunately, too many of the leaders among the people had other ideas, and set themselves up as alternative kings, thinking they could divert the treasures of the kingdom into their own bank accounts. The result was the religious confusion that plagued Israel throughout its later history. Even the prophets could not steer the nation back to obedience and trust for the original great coach and leader.

Whose Fault Is It?

Abbott and Costello entranced an earlier generation with their side-splitting routine "Who's on First." Pretending to discuss the players of a baseball team, names were confused with positions until tracking the game became an exercise in futility.

404

Among the religious discussions of Jesus' day, there was a similar confusion of identities. For some, evil was inherent in the system like yin's twin yang. For others, humans had incurred the wrath of the gods and were punished through the spread of vices that flowed out of Pandora's mythical box. Others still believed divine perfection was trapped by a mean-spirited creator into the corrupt and forgetful stuff of human flesh, waiting magical gnostic liberation.

Jesus' design in his sweeping tale is to give a different view of the origins of evil. God is good; creation is good; and human alienation from the good is a late introduction brought about by our sinful choices. For Jesus' audience of religious leaders, the message communicated was that all of humanity had the same opportunities to remain in fellowship with the creator, and all are equally responsible for their distance from God.

But Jesus also couched the story in swaddling folds of never-ending grace. Time after time God initiated a restoration of relationships with humanity. All are welcome to be part of the team. As part of our latter days, in fact, God sent in Jesus to spur the team to new spiritual victories. Jesus is the expression of God's righteousness inserted recently into our world, and the means by which we are attached to the righteous endeavors of God. He is the glue that binds the team together and keeps them connected both to the owner and the game.

By this time, according to Matthew, Jesus has clearly expressed his divine power and wisdom. Enough so, in fact, that he can begin to speak about the sacrificial death toward which he is heading. In these verses he almost shouts out what is about to happen, hoping to shock us into spiritual recovery in a kind of critical intervention. Winning, for Jesus, means playing by a set of rules that has not been used for a long time on planet earth. It is like the "deep magic" of Aslan in C. S. Lewis' great tale, *The Lion, the Witch, and the Wardrobe*. Most don't understand it, but without it the game becomes a never-ending cycle of violence in which there are only losers.

Forging A New Team

For that reason Jesus gives a brief exhortation about the characteristics that mark those on his team. It is not self-preservation but service that counts. It is not superiority but selflessness that wins points. It is not stridency but sacrifice that finds recognition from the owner of the club. Jesus is building a team that will change the world. Unfortunately, on that day, too few people seemed willing to show up at the try-outs.

There is a scene in Tolkien's *The Fellowship of the Ring*, where a partnership is forged among those who would accompany Frodo on his journey to destroy the ring of power. The movie version makes for a very gripping visual illustration, and the original literary text is equally as moving. What comes through is a sense of selflessness as the bond that unites these creatures. Furthermore, each subsumes his will to the greater cause, and trusts an unseen and transcendent good for an outcome that will bless all of Middle Earth, even if the trek itself causes the demise of any or all of the compatriots.

So it is in Jesus' small glimpse of the mission of God. In a world turned cold to its creator, in an age riddled by Delphic oracles and temple prostitutes and emperors claiming divinity, in a little corner of geography where messianic hopes ran high, God called together a strange team to make its mark by playing a different game.

Walter Wangerin Jr., in his great allegory, *The Book of the Dun Cow* (along with its wonderful sequel, *The Book of Sorrows*), captures both the scope of the divine mission as well as the underrated character of the team. If the focus remains on the team apart from the mission, the point is lost. God is reclaiming God's creation, but does so through human agency. The game is fierce and the playing field is rough. Only those who can tear up their personal score sheets in order get into God's game will make the team. Only they are truly called. Only they are equipped to serve and follow and play on the greatest winning team of all time.

Jesus is on the road to the cross, and he calls others to join him in that pilgrimage. The cost of dscipleship, as Dietrich Bonhoeffer noted in his book, *The Cost of Discipleship*, is self-denial, and Jesus' words are a strong call to that vocation, not as an end in itself or as a means to a self-help goal (like dieting), but rather as a counter-cultural missional testimony. Those who travel this road do not get to Easter without first enduring Good Friday; they do not presume a glorious outcome that gathers the media like paparazzi vultures, but sense that the journey of service brings light in darkness, hope in despair, healing for pain, and faith where power corrupts and destroys.

Have you entered the cause? Amen.

Sermons On The Gospel Readings

For Sundays
After Pentecost
(Last Third)

Ready For God's Reign

Chris Ewing

Dressed For The Banquet

This is an ugly story — and the better you understand it, the uglier it gets.

Both Matthew and Luke record versions of this parable that Jesus told (Luke 14:16-24), and it is not a comfortable story no matter who tells it; but Matthew's version is downright harsh and, as we'll see, extremely inflammatory. Because, no matter what Jesus may have originally meant in telling it, Matthew has worked it into his gospel as a very fierce piece of anti-Jewish polemic. To understand why, we have to understand what was going on at the time.

Matthew's gospel was written fairly late in the first century, after a couple of major developments. The first was that, although Jesus' first followers were all, like Jesus himself, observant Jews, who had come to believe that he was the Messiah, that opinion did not come to be shared by Judaism as a whole; and eventually the Christians, who were also being joined by many non-Jews, were forced to break away from the synagogue. As is often the case with family feuds, it was a very bitter breakup. So in many communities, there was tension between the Christian church and the Jewish synagogue; and that certainly appears to have been the case in Matthew's community, which was probably Antioch in Syria.

This tension was exacerbated by the second major development of this period: in response to a Jewish patriotic uprising, the occupying Romans had marched in full force to put down the rebellion, and while they were at it, they had razed Jerusalem and destroyed the temple. Need I say that Jews and Christians had differing interpretations of this event? For the Jewish community, of course, this was a national tragedy on a par with the Exile six centuries earlier. For many in the emerging Christian church, however, it looked like a vindication of their claim that Jesus was the Messiah, and they held that the destruction was God's judgment on those who chose not to believe, a judgment in particular on the temple, which Christians believed that Jesus had replaced with his own body and sacrificial death.

These events, and the Christian reading of them, are clearly visible behind the parable as Matthew tells it. "The king was enraged. He sent his troops, destroyed those murderers, and burned their city. Then he said to his slaves, 'The wedding is ready, but those invited were not worthy' " (Matthew 22:7-8). In other words, God has rejected the Jews.

Whether Jesus intended the parable to be read this way we can never know for certain; but it is altogether too clear that Matthew read it that way, and he made sure the point was not lost on the readers of his gospel. If you had been part of Matthew's church in Antioch, you'd have had to be sound asleep in the back row not to get it.

Matthew begins by putting the parable very late in Jesus' ministry, during the highly charged final week of Jesus' life, when he had entered Jerusalem to messianic acclaim, and when all the gospels show him in mounting conflict with the religious authorities, culminating in his execution at the time of the Passover. Luke, in his gospel, has Jesus tell the story of the wedding banquet at an earlier stage of his ministry, as one of a series of sayings and stories about the nature of the kingdom of God. Not Matthew. Matthew has Jesus telling it — or perhaps retelling it, we don't know — as one of a series of increasingly pointed parables told in response to the questioning of his authority by the religious leaders. And there is no missing the hostile tone. Jesus is aware that the time of crisis is approaching. He seems to be drawing lines in the sand and insisting that people choose sides, even as he uses his stories to lay out his own interpretation of history — or perhaps his followers' interpretation. We are unfortunately not always sure in the gospels whether it's Jesus himself speaking or the community that grew up after his departure — faithful, Spirit-filled people, to be sure, yet fallible humans nonetheless, who may have been swayed by the passions of the moment as well as by the wind of the Spirit.

So here's the story as we have it in Matthew. Unlike most of Jesus' stories, this is not actually a parable, it's an allegory. A parable is a realistic story, often one with a surprising twist, which makes one main point. An allegory, on the other hand, is a story where every piece stands for something: each character in the story is a mask for someone in the real world, and the events of the story are thinly disguised references to events known to the audience. Because of this "coded" character, allegories often end up not being very realistic on their own. For instance, in this story, you have a wedding feast put on hold while the king sends his troops out to destroy his enemies and burn down their city. Hardly the kind of realistic story that Jesus usually told!

But everyone listening to this story would have known what he was driving at. "The kingdom of heaven may be compared to a king who gave a wedding banquet for his son" (Matthew 22:2). He makes it clear right off the bat that he's picking up a very common Jewish image for the reign of God: the Messiah's banquet where the redeemed will feast with their God. Remember how many times the prophets spoke of Israel as God's bride? And that place in Isaiah where it talks about God spreading a feast for all peoples on the holy mountain? (Isaiah 25:6 ff).

Here we have the Messiah bringing Israel to the altar, and the great celebration afterward. Oh, but there's a problem! The people who were invited — Israel, the chosen — decided not to come. They'd been expecting this wedding for a while, but when the servants went out to tell them the feast was ready, "... they made light of it and went away, one to his farm, another to his business" (Matthew 22:5), just as people had often shrugged off the words of the prophets in times past. But where Luke just has people ignoring the messengers, and the king therefore sending the messengers out to round up other guests, Matthew digs the knife in a little deeper: He has the king send out other slaves to summon the original invitees again — "other slaves" probably meaning the Christian church. And these messengers, he says, have been mistreated and even killed (Matthew 22:6).

Now, it is true enough that, in the ugly divorce between synagogue and church, there were some nasty moments, and it was not unusual for people to be shunned by neighbors and even family members, sometimes actively persecuted, rarely perhaps killed, just as Jesus had been. And Matthew wants his listeners to know that this makes God angry. So angry that God sent his troops — and I'm sure Matthew's hearers would have understood him to mean the Romans stamping out the Jewish state — to destroy "those murderers" who had killed Jesus, and burn their city, Jerusalem. Only after this act of punishment did the invitation go out to others who would be willing to come in — Samaritans, Gentiles, people from the ends of the earth.

With 2,000 years of distance on the events of that time and place, and 2,000 years of maturing under the ongoing tutelage of God's Spirit, *we* may be more dismayed by Matthew's glaring anti-Semitism than by the synagogue's rejection of Jesus. Or not. Much depends on the presuppositions with which we come to this story. But it may serve as a cautionary tale to us to remember our human sinfulness and fallibility at the same time as we take seriously our claim to guidance by the Spirit of the God who works in human history.

We do not in fact know what God is going to do about the reality that substantial numbers of Jews did not and do not recognize Jesus as the Messiah. Neither do we know what God is going to do about the fact that many Christians did not and do not respect Jews as their elder siblings in the household of faith — as Paul put it, the cultivated olive tree onto which we wild olives were belatedly grafted (Romans 11:17 ff). We all certainly have our theories; but in the end we would be wise to admit that, no matter how honestly we try to listen to God, we are not in fact God, and there remains always some room for doubt concerning opinions we hold in God's name. Just because we're in the door does not always mean we're in the right.

414

This is approximately the point of the end of Jesus' story, that odd little trailer about the guy who got in without a wedding robe. This is unique to Matthew, and there has of course been no end of discussion about what it means. It appears that guests were expected to wear some kind of festive garment,[1] or perhaps just ordinary clean clothes; in any case, it seems that this fellow came as he was without bothering to clean up. The allegorical implications become clear when we understand that the parable is about the last judgment, and when we remember that within Judaism good deeds were seen as the passport to the Messiah's great feast. Indeed, the Mishnah said that "he who fulfils a command gains for himself an intercessor" before God.[2] Our actions speak for us, the rabbis recognized, announcing in a voice louder than words whether we are children of God. And in this story, someone who had been welcomed into the feast had no actions to speak for him, and so, Matthew tells us, "he was speechless" (Matthew 22:12).

In Matthew's story, this probably means that the Christians, and perhaps particularly the non-Jewish Christians, who had had the good sense to respond to the invitation and follow Jesus into God's kingdom, should not get up on their high horses too quickly and look down their nose at those who had rejected the Messiah. Just because you're in the door, warns Matthew, doesn't mean you'll get to stay there. As Jesus had warned in other parables, the kingdom can and will be taken away from those who fail to bear its fruit.

And that perhaps is the most fruitful place for us to engage this prickly story. Whether we believe that Jesus is the only way, and those who reject him reject God, or whether we believe that God has many ways to bring us home, we would be wise to take seriously this final warning against presumption. Whatever may or may not be true for other people, we trust that through Jesus we have been brought into God's banquet, and that is cause for celebration. It is also cause for attention to our own wardrobe: what do our deeds say about us? While it is surely important to seek to discern what God is up to in history, it is perhaps even more important to show up wearing the garments that Jesus told us were

415

most important: to love God with everything in us, and our neighbors as we love ourselves (Matthew 22:37-39 and parallels, paraphrased). Or, as one of God's earlier servants put it, "act justly, love mercy and walk humbly with your God" (Micah 6:8 cf NIV). Amen.

---

1. For instance, see J. C. Fenton, *Saint Matthew*, Pelican New Testament Commentaries, D. E. Nineham, ed. (New York: Penguin Books, 1963), p. 350.

2. *Ibid.*

**Proper 24
Pentecost 22
Ordinary Time 29
Matthew 22:15-22**

In Whose Likeness?

Okay, teacher, you think you're so smart — is it lawful to pay taxes to the emperor?

Talk about your loaded question!

If we're talking about the law of Rome, the law of the imperial government, the law of this part of the world, of course it's legal to pay taxes to the emperor — it's illegal not to! And just in case Jesus was hoping to fudge a bit on the answer, there are among his questioners members of the Herodian party, supporters of the puppet king, toadies to the Roman government, here listening to his answer. If Jesus so much as hints that the taxes paid to Rome are out of order, the full force of the law will be down upon him.

However, he can't just say, "Of course, pay your taxes!" Because here *with* the Herodians — odd bedfellows if ever there were — are some Pharisees, the guardians of Jewish purity, of Jewish law and piety, sticklers for religious correctness. And there are serious religious objections to paying taxes to the pagan Roman occupiers; why, the very coin used to pay the tax bears a graven image, strictly against Jewish law, a graven image of the emperor. And the inscription upon the coin identifies that emperor as a divinity, son of the divine Augustus Caesar. How can any self-respecting monotheist pay tribute to someone who claims to be God? And how can a healthy Jewish patriot stomach paying taxes to occupiers anyway? If Jesus gives an un-Jewish answer, lacking in either theological correctness or patriotism, he will be completely discredited as a teacher of his people; he will probably also lose

417

most of his popular support. It seems that no matter how he answers, he's in trouble. Which, of course, is exactly what his questioners want. Coming from these people, the question about taxes is not a faith or conscience query; it is a hostile question designed to make Jesus discredit himself. And it looks as if they have him over a barrel.

Is it right for the chosen people of God, citizens of Israel, who have no king but God and God's anointed, to pay tribute to an occupying pagan power whose emperor demands to be worshiped as a god?

Or again, is it right for citizens of a conquered nation to withhold taxes from their established government — taxes from which come benefits like roads and aqueducts and a justice system renowned for its even-handedness?

Is it right to pay taxes to Caesar?

The particular issues may be different for us, but the problem of thorny questions of allegiance is a familiar one. There are times when deeply held values and nonnegotiable realities seem to pull us in opposite directions: times when we feel as if, no matter what we decide, we will be wrong, and/or in deep trouble. Who among us hasn't struggled with how to respond to some situation in the wider world, or to a personal moral quandary?

For instance, a central question that all of us face in this society — *our* central question of allegiance as Christians living in a consumer society, and especially in a consumer society existing in a poor and hungry world — a central question for *us* is: do I live for my personal standard of living, or do I live for God's realm of integrity, justice, and peace? To whom, metaphorically speaking, do I pay *my* taxes — and to whom should I? If you haven't pondered that one lately, you may be overdue. As citizens of a democratic nation, we bear a special responsibility not only for our personal choices but also for the life of our nation and the priorities of our government. So where, both literally and metaphorically, should our taxes go?

In response to the question, Jesus says, show me a coin. "Show me the coin used for [paying] the tax" (Matthew 22:19). Show me what it takes to get by in this world as it is.

418

The coin used for paying the tax is not a Jewish coin. It is not the historic currency of Israel, it is not the symbol of loyalty to God and God's values. *Those* coins are no longer in use, except for making offerings in the temple. With Roman rule came Roman money — except in the temple. Roman coins were not suitable there, because of their idolatrous image and inscription. So there were moneychangers in the temple, to keep the Roman coins outside and to provide holy Jewish coinage for the treasury. But we're not in the temple right now. We're on the street. And out here, for day-to-day use, and certainly for paying the tax, what you need is Roman coins.

So somebody produces one. And I imagine they all stood around for a moment looking at the coin as it lay glinting in the questioner's palm: the symbol of so much tension among neighbors; a symbol of pain and shame for a conquered people, yet also a symbol of a mighty civilization and a cosmopolitan existence. A symbol of failure, a symbol of success. A symbol of resentment, a symbol of allegiance. So many conflicting feelings, so many issues, centred around this little piece of metal winking in someone's palm.

And Jesus breaks in on their reflections: "Whose portrait is on the coin? And whose title?" (Matthew 22:20 cf).

The emperor's. Call him a divinity, call him a demon, this coin belongs to the emperor. For better or for worse, we're under Rome.

Just as *we* may be inclined to say that, like it or not, we live in a consumer society. We have to abide by its values.

And Jesus says, yes, the coin belongs to Caesar. Let him have it. Give to God what belongs to God.

Now that may sound like a concession to the realities of this world, an acknowledgment that when in Rome you have to do as the Romans do. It may sound like a justification for living as unabashed consumers all week long, so long as we come to church and say our prayers on Sunday. Put the holy coins in the treasury, but live by the pagan stuff all week long.

Think again.

If the coin belongs to Caesar, if the likeness it bears is that of the emperor, to whom it should be given, then what should be given to God? What belongs to God? What is stamped with *God's* likeness in this world?

We all, if we think about it, know the answer to that, just as surely as Jesus' hearers did. Way back in the first chapter of Genesis it tells us, "God said, 'Let us make humankind in our image, according to our likeness ...' " and so "God created humankind in [God's] image, in the image of God he created them, male and female [God] created them." And God then set the human beings *as God's agents* in the world, to exercise stewardship over the creation on God's behalf (Genesis 1:26a, 27, 26a, 28).

We are the coin of *God's* realm. God's likeness stamped on us declares that we belong wholly and entirely to God.

Next to that, who cares who owns the penny? All the power of human love and thought and action belong to God — and if these are properly rendered, if we actually *give* to God what belongs to God (all the love of our heart and soul and mind and strength, issuing in a love of neighbor as strong as our love of self) — if *these* powers of human love and thought and action are properly rendered, the coin is a non-issue. Human beings who are wholly given to God will not fail to use their money in a God-honoring, Kingdom-building manner, no matter whose picture is on it.

To live as Christians in a consumer society is no easier and no harder than to be faithful Jews in a Roman-ruled one. God knows we have to play by the rules of the occupier, and Jesus' answer acknowledges that. But playing by the rules is completely different from buying into the game. Yes, we need to go to work and earn money so we, and our families, have a decent standard of living. But we will not think only of our families in the way we spend our money, we will also care for the needs of others less fortunate, and we will support those who work for justice. Yes, of course we will dress the way the people with whom we associate dress — but we will be sure that we purchase our clothing as much as possible from employers that provide fair wages and healthy working conditions. Yes, we will drive similar cars to our neighbors — when we cannot walk, that is, out of deference to the fragility of God's creation. We will participate in the normal life of our society — but not uncritically or without thought to its impact on others both here and abroad, for we are citizens of God's realm, and we share God's concern for all of humanity and the whole of creation. We will not be overly concerned to keep up with the Joneses, because we have someone much greater to keep up with: Jesus Christ, who counseled would-be followers to cut off whatever might come between them and God, be it their wealth or their arms and legs, so that they could be wholeheartedly dedicated to embodying God's reconciling love in the world (Philippians 3:14; Luke 18:22; Matthew 18:8; Matthew 5:38-48; 2 Corinthians 5:18).

Jesus reminds us, by his answer to the question about taxes, and by his own life and death in full obedience to God, that we are, body and soul, the people of God, created in God's likeness, living here as stewards of earth and ambassadors of God's reign.

We are the coin of God's realm. May we each remember, each day, in whose likeness and for whose purposes we are created. Amen.

Test ... Test ...

Sometimes things happen that push us back to our deepest questions and force us to answer. A marriage breakdown, loss of a job, kids leaving home, or simply the midlife re-evaluation that all of us go through — any of these can push us back to asking what it's all about, what we really want in our lives, what matters and what doesn't ... what we want our life to count for.

Sometimes the question gets asked more directly. An Islamic family moves in down the street, and their children ask your children what they believe. You become friends with a Buddhist co-worker, and find yourself deeply impressed with the quality of his or her life, and wondering if that is available in your own tradition. The local Jehovah's Witness buttonholes you and you wish you could put into words what it is *you* believe.

Moments like that *test* us — not so much in the sense of knowing the answers, passing or failing, but more in the sense of what we mean when we're setting up the mikes for a concert, and we go around to each one and tap on it to see if it makes a noise; and then we lean in close and we say, "Test ... test...."

We're trying to find out if it works, what kind of sound quality and range we get with it, how wide a field of pickup it has — in other words, how is it going to serve us in the concert, and do we need to adjust the mike stand's height, or move things around a bit, or change the balance back at the mixing board? That kind of a test — a test to see what's working and what needs adjustment, and to figure out how we can step in and run with it.

That's the kind of test that the Pharisees brought to Jesus. Here's this guy who's giving amazingly penetrating responses to challenging questions, who faces hostility with courageous integrity, and who makes people really think about where their life is going. We want to know more about what he thinks. We want to try him on for size: is he leading somewhere I'm trying to go myself? Has he got something to say that I should be listening to? What would it mean for me to start paying attention to him?

And so they come up and tap him and say, "Test ... Test.... Of the 613 commandments given in the Torah, and the hundreds more elaborated by our rabbis[1] — out of all these hundreds of precepts guiding our lives — which is the most important? Or *can* we rank them? *Is* there one that is most important, or must they all equally be remembered and obeyed?" Test ... test....

Haven't you ever felt life tugging at you with similar questions? Is it more important to be truthful or to be kind? To fully develop the capacities God gave me to use in this world, or to sacrifice my desires to the needs of others? As a Christian am I primarily supposed to care for and be kind to others, or am I primarily supposed to stand up for my beliefs and the Lordship of Jesus Christ? How does this religion I've inherited work? Test ... test....

And you know what? Jesus doesn't condemn the Pharisees for asking the question. In fact, he seems to welcome the debate, because after he answers this question he turns around and asks them one, a challenge to them to think about the implications of one of their favorite messianic texts, to probe what it is they hope for and whether their ideas are big enough. Can your ideas carry the weight of the day? Test ... test....

To paraphrase an important dictum of the pioneering psychiatrist Milton Erickson, "Until you are willing to question what you already know, what you know will never grow bigger, better or more useful."[2] Just as testing allows us to perfect the setup of the sound system, so these kinds of probing test questions allow our faith to become stronger and more useful.

So what did Jesus have to say to that perennially nagging test question about what it is in our religion that matters most? Since we already "know" what answer he gave — love the Lord your God with all your heart and soul and mind, and your neighbor as yourself — it may be hard for us to hear this really ring in the auditorium, and to appreciate what incredible equipment it is. In fact, when Luke tells about this question, he has Jesus go on to tell a startling, stand-up-and-bite-you story to help unpack the implications of it. You can go home and read it beginning at Luke 10:25. But today we're sticking to Matthew's telling of it, and Matthew just drops it in like a time bomb and waits for it to explode in the middle of some situation in our own lives.

So pick one. Pick something in your life that's pushing you, asking you, whether you've quite realized it or not, what your priorities are, what matters most, what's most important. Pick something that's tapping you and saying, "Test ... test...." *(pause)*

Okay. Got the scene? Now, as you feel the tug in two directions, *now* hear Jesus say, "The greatest and first commandment is this: love the Lord your God with all your heart, and with all your soul, and with all your mind" (Matthew 22:38-37 cf). *(pause)*

What do you suppose it might mean to love God with total commitment in this situation? *(pause)* What else might it mean? *(pause)* And would somebody else have another way to look at it? *(pause)* Love the Lord your God with all your heart, and with all your soul, and with all your mind.

Oh, but there's more. There's another top-ranker, one that accompanies and perhaps interprets the first. "You shall love your neighbor as yourself" (Matthew 22:39b). What might *that* mean in the situation you're considering? *(pause)* What could it mean to be as concerned for the well being of the other people involved as you are for yourself? To seek their highest good as well as yours? *(pause)* What about the people who aren't directly involved, but who are ultimately affected? *(pause)* What does it mean to hold everyone's needs as equally important in this? *(pause)* Does this help you to see your way more clearly? Does it feel like something you can do? Test ... test....

Sometimes it's hard to know what it means to "love" someone, whether God or our neighbor or even ourself. We may think it means to have warm and cozy feelings about them, which we all know simply isn't going to happen all the time — even for people we deeply and truly love, like our life partner or our kids. I don't believe God commands us to have warm fuzzy feelings. Love is *action* on behalf of the loved one's greatest good; and while the regular practice of such action *is* likely to be accompanied sooner or later by warm emotional concern, it's not the emotion that matters. It's the action.

But what does that action mean? It surely can't mean the same thing toward God, who strictly speaking needs nothing from us, as toward, say, our children; and what is loving toward our children may be something quite different from what is loving toward our spouse, or our boss, or the homeless person we pass on the way to the bus each day.

Ah! Another "Test ... test...." question! What does it mean to love?

Well, if you want part of Jesus' answer on that, you can turn to Luke 10:25 and read the story he told there, about the guy who got beat up on the way to Jericho, and the folks who cared about him, or not.

But I don't think that's going to be enough to unpack the meaning this has for Matthew. Because Matthew tells of this testing encounter at a different time — during the last week of Jesus' life — and in a different context. For Matthew, this episode is part of a whole series of discussions about what it means to love *God*. We've already heard a whole string of parables about the kingdom of God and the last judgment; we've had Jesus answer a sticky question about how a faithful Jew can live under a pagan empire; and Jesus is about to go on from here to lambaste the current religious leadership for totally twisting the meaning of religious observance and turning it into a petty and burdensome matter of six thousand picky regulations, while totally missing the really important matters of justice and mercy and honesty. From there, Jesus will go on to bewail the way his people consistently resist and reject God's messengers, and to warn about the disaster descending on the nation. In all of this he is talking at least as much about what it means to love and obey God as he is about the neighbor ... not that these can ultimately be separated. But we obviously need guidelines that go beyond the Good Samaritan and stopping to help those in need. What does love mean when it comes to God?

Peter Michaelson, a minister in Rhode Island, noted several years ago in an online discussion, "Love is lots of things, but one main one is a commitment to pay attention."[3] It's fairly easy to see how that plays out with human beings: "It's no good to give a homeless person [an electronic game,] and it's no good to give a rich kid a pair of socks."[4] *Paying attention* to the situation and needs of each one would lead us to give appropriate gifts.

It's the same way with God. To *pay attention* to God is much more than scrupulously observing the minutiae of the laws. Very often we use laws and rules to *excuse* ourselves from paying attention — we substitute a law for the hard work of being present. God demands of us something more. To fulfill the law and the prophets, to rightly love God and our neighbor, we must pay attention. We must spend time getting to know who this is that we worship, steep ourselves in the scriptures and in prayer and in the cares of the world around us, until our hearts beat to God's pulse ... until, as the prophet Mohammed said, *we* become "the hearing by which [God] hears, the sight by which he sees and the hand with which he grasps and the foot with which he walks."[5] Until we become the love that God is.

As you *pay attention* to the testing situations in which you find yourself, as you *pay attention* to God and to others and to your own being and needs, as you hold all of these in honest and attentive compassion, you will find something amazing happening. You will find yourself growing and deepening and resonating with a much wiser and more loving voice than your own as it whispers, "Test ... test ..." out into your world. Amen.

---

1. Rabbi Wayne Dosick, *Living Judaism* (New York: Harper Collins, 1995), pp. 31, 33.

2. Quoted in Dawna Markova's, *No Enemies Within* (Berkeley, California: Conari Press, 1994), p. 118. Erickson said "be confused about" rather than "question."

3. Peter Michaelson, note #45 to sermonshop_1996_10_27.topic@ecunet.org.

4. *Ibid.*

5. From *Introduction to Sufism* (author and publisher not given), p. 79, as quoted by John Lohr in note #7 to sermonshop_1996_10_27.topic@ecunet.org.

Unwanted Freedom

The trouble with words is that they can mean so many different things, depending on who is using them. And the bigger and more important the word, the more this tends to be true. Take, for instance, the word "freedom," or "free." That is a very important word to North Americans — to most of the world, in fact — and it appears to have been a very important word to Jesus. But I really wonder if we're all talking about the same thing?

Jesus stated in John 8:32 that the *truth* would make us free. In a runaway consumer culture, it often seems as if nearly the opposite is intended. We often define freedom as *escape* from everyday reality and normal constraints. Take, for instance, the article I recently read about the launch of the world's biggest (so far!) cruise ship. "In the maritime machismo battle to be biggest and the best," states an online journal, Royal Caribbean International "has bulked up a normal-sized vessel to create an ocean-bound behemoth unlike any seen before."[1] The massive ship, which is wider than the White House is long, is not only larger than any previous cruise ship, it also takes the idea of a floating fantasyland to new extremes. It was not enough to have rock-climbing walls and ice-skating rinks at sea, nor merely a promenade lined with shops, restaurants and bars. Those now-familiar staples of Royal Caribbean ships had to be made "bigger and better." The new ship's "Royal" promenade is a 445-foot-long boulevard with nightly street parades; and the climbing wall is now a 43-foot-tall by 44-foot-wide structure with no less than eleven routes of varying degrees

429

of difficulty. There are no fewer than twenty restaurants, oodles of fitness options, and the lap-of-luxury list goes on and on.

And what is this over-the-top adventure in extravagance called? "Freedom of the Seas," what else? For it just about epitomizes the American Dream of having the time and the means — the *freedom* — to do whatever you blessed well want, especially if that means kicking back and enjoying life. As the author explains at the conclusion of the article, after describing the ship's cantilevered solarium whirlpools with their breathtaking ocean view, "The thing you should be thinking about as tiny, warm bubbles surround you is, well, freedom on the seas."[2]

I somehow don't think this is quite exactly what Jesus had in mind when he promised his followers that they would be "free indeed" (John 8:36). Indeed, he might have some pointed words to say to us about our slavery to self-indulgence.

So if by freedom we are not intended to hear "unlimited indulgence," then what *does* Jesus mean? What *is* a freedom worthy of the name? On Reformation Sunday, when we recall and pledge to continue the liberation of our faith from error and abuse, that is a particularly pointed question, one whose full answer we may not always want to hear.

The *Oxford Reference Dictionary* fills most of a densely-printed column with definitions of the word "free" and of expressions incorporating it, from "free and easy" to "free world," via "free enterprise," "free-for-all," the soccer "free kick," "free loader," "free love," and "free trade," to name just a few — and at that, they missed "freedom fries"! The column makes for very interesting reading. However, the most basic definition of the word "free," according to Oxford, is, "not a slave or under the control of another; having personal rights and social and political liberty...; subject neither to foreign domination nor to despotic government." Expanding a bit on this concept, "free" can also mean, "not fixed or held down; able to move without hindrance; permitted *to* do; unrestricted, not controlled by rules."[3] Or, as the *Friberg Greek Lexicon* says of the Greek word translated as "free" in today's gospel, it means "allowing for self-determination."[4]

Now, on the surface that would appear to play right into our common cultural definition of "able to do whatever I darn well want." Not held down. Unrestricted. Not controlled by rules. Having self-determination. *Turn me loose, man! I am free!*

Well. Hmm, now. Really? Is that what Jesus was offering? Is that what he was hoping people would accept? If you read the gospel conversation more closely, it would seem not. This conversation is unfolding on another level entirely.

First-century Palestine was a world very different from twenty-first-century North America, and the kind of freedom we know now was virtually unheard of. Democracy did not exist — well, maybe across the Mediterranean in Athens, but not in Palestine where a local monarch answered to Imperial Rome. So there was no political freedom of the kind to which you and I are accustomed. Freedom of speech has severe limits, as does freedom of religion. And most people are chained to the grind of daily circumstance to a degree few of us today can imagine: although there is a wealthy class, the majority of the population will never take a vacation — at best they'll manage a pilgrimage to Jerusalem for one of the major festivals — and they lead a hand-to-mouth existence that allows for few dreams. So in discussing "freedom," the kind of political voice and consumer "good life" that we take for granted are not even on the table; they would not have entered Jesus' hearers' imaginations. A much more gritty kind of reality is in view.

In Jesus' day, slavery was commonplace. Some slaves were captured in military raids, and of course some were born into slavery, but it was much more common for people to be enslaved as restitution for debt, or to enter slavery voluntarily as an escape from poverty. While the degree of slavery varied — some slaves actually had quite a bit of autonomy and even respect[5] — there was always a certain insecurity to being a slave, because if push came to shove, the slave's life was not his own. He could be reassigned, sold, married, or deprived of a partner, all without his consent. And while he might well find a degree of economic and social security in the household of a good master, he was never fully a part of that household, but a kind of onlooker to the lives of those who had choices. So when Jesus spoke of freedom as opposed to

431

slavery, his audience understood viscerally what he meant, and keenly appreciated the distinction between the slave and the son of the household. The latter had choices. The former did not.

And many of those who heard Jesus compare them to slaves were offended. "We are descendants of Abraham and have never been slaves to anyone," they protested. "What do you mean by saying, 'You will be made free'?" (John 8:33).

Now that actually is a very interesting protest, because on the surface it wasn't true. The Israelites *had* been slaves in Egypt, nearly a thousand years before; more recently they had been, if not exactly slaves, certainly not free, during the long exile in Babylon. And finally, the very people now arguing with Jesus were in a very un-free state, subject to Rome and ruled by a puppet king. To say, "We have never been slaves to anyone" is an affront to historical reality.

But in another sense, they were absolutely right. Remember the book of Esther, where Esther's courage to speak up foiled Haman's wicked plot? Haman had wanted to massacre all the Jews in the Persian Empire — and why? Because Mordecai the Jew had refused to bow down to the powerful noble when he passed by. Never mind that bowing to nobles was what everyone in Persia did; Jews didn't. They acknowledged the sovereignty of no one but God. They might be exiles over a thousand kilometers from home, subject to a foreign power — whose laws, by the way, they obeyed — but they would not give anything that could be construed as worship or absolute loyalty to any earthly sovereign. It just wasn't going to happen. In spirit they were slaves to no one; and their tenacious fidelity to their nation and their God earned the grudging respect of many of their conquerors.

But if Jesus' interlocutors were talking about a spiritual autonomy and resilience[6] that gave the lie to political subjugation, Jesus was talking about something deeper yet, something that challenged their confident identity as people of God ... something that challenges us, too. He was talking about slavery to sin, subjugation to anything that is less than God and apart from God — and it is a slavery we all fall into. As an example let's consider a woman Carter Shelley told about, a woman named Agnes.[7]

432

Agnes had a knack for church work. Had she been 25 instead of 72, she would have been a natural for the professional ministry. The Sunday school classes she taught were excellent. Her energies were limitless. She'd served on the church session, had been to General Assembly and was currently Presbyterial president. Agnes' church commitment was frequently used as an illustration to other church officers, young adults, and teens as a fine example of Christian charity and commitment. She was always the first in the house of grieving. Ever ready to bolster the weak or say a corrective word to a noisy child.

Neither the minister nor any of her friends could ever remember having seen Agnes angry. If she didn't like the new inclusive language "Alternate Lifestyles," Agnes didn't pout or get angry. She would merely discuss these unnecessary changes with others, do a little telephoning, and in no time at all things would be back the way they were supposed to be.

You see, Agnes was a good communicator and a good source of information. If something good, bad, or interesting happened to anyone in the community Agnes would know all the details. She could tell you which recent widower was rumored to be entertaining which recent widow, or how much the MacAlileys' new house had cost, and whether Mr. Jones would soon be going out of business or not.

People were shocked when a new member complained that Agnes Hayes was a gossip. No one would think of criticizing Agnes! And sure enough, not long after this, it was discovered that this new member had had reason to be concerned. Did you know that she had recently left a husband who had abused her for years and had come to town to start a new life? Agnes knew and soon everyone knew.

If Jesus had met Agnes on the street and demanded that she "repent, turn away from your sins," Agnes would have readily agreed to forsake the second lump of sugar in her morning coffee, would acknowledge her tendency to eat too many sweets and that she wasted too much time watching television. Beyond that, Agnes would be hard put to know what she could do differently. With her many years of church service, committee work, and faithful participation she was a full member of the household of God.

The hard part for Agnes, and perhaps for us, is in recognizing our own subjugation to sin. After all, we're not cocaine users, child molesters, or streetwalkers. Jesus' words aren't as necessary for us as they are for Agnes or the Pharisees or Osama bin Laden. But we are wrong.

We are as much enslaved to sin as any of these others; if we are to be free, then we must let Jesus tell us the truth about the lies *we* live, not just the easy-to-spot sins of somebody else. And we must let him tell us the truth about the lies that our present-day church lives — often very difficult to tease out from things we need to hold onto. We dare not presume to say to ourselves, "We have John Calvin as our father," and let that excuse us from facing our own slavery today. For, as the Reformers wisely recognized, the church must always be reforming, always breaking away from its slavery to all that is less than God and apart from God.

This is not freedom as the luxury to do what we please, but freedom as the often costly and difficult move away from the besetting sins of our own life, our own church, our own society, in order to realize more fully God's intention for us. And like any departure from slavery, it often brings a very intense insecurity, as we learn to live without certain familiar structures, and to make our own decisions and take responsibility for our own choices.

It is not easy to live with freedom. As poet Irving Layton once observed, "Only the tiniest fraction of mankind *want* freedom. All the rest want someone to tell them they are free."[8] Genuine freedom — freedom rooted, as Jesus described it, in knowing the truth — is tremendously demanding. It is much easier to sell our freedom to whoever will most advantageously relieve us of it: a family, a church, a nation, an opinionated newspaper editor, anyone who will tell us what to think and what to do, so that we don't have to figure it out for ourselves.

Knowing Jesus, in the kind of depth that gives us a foundation for genuine freedom, is as demanding as knowing — and continuing to know, continuing to break new ground with — your spouse. It's not easy. God does not change, but the world in which we meet God does, and so there is a constant need to question yesterday's truths and revise yesterday's practices. It is frankly much easier to find a good rut and stay there. And in church we often do just that, mistaking our rut for a viable relationship.

"If you continue in my word," Jesus said to those who had been nodding agreement to his teaching, "you are truly my disciples; and you will know the truth, and the truth will make you free" (John 8:31-32). Continuing in Jesus' word is like continuing in any other relationship: to do it well requires constant effort, not assuming you already know everything you need to know, or are already doing everything you need to do.

In our present moment, when people are abandoning the church in droves, we would do well to look at which of our ruts have become sins — things that are keeping us apart from God and what God is doing in the world.

Have we become indistinguishable from a bankrupt culture?

Have we so deeply overwrapped the Christian message with worn-out patterns of communication that no one realizes there's anything worth hearing in there?

Have we gotten so caught up in internal institutional concerns that we have nothing to say to the crying needs of the world?

Come break new ground with me, says Jesus. Continue in my word; deepen the relationship; be truly my disciples, so that I can break you free of stagnation and futility, and make you full partners in both the work and the reward of the household of God. Now *that* would be freedom! Amen.

---

1. "Lots of fun, luxury on *Freedom of the Seas*, world's largest cruiser," by Aaron Sagers of *The Morning Call*, August 27, 2006 (http://www.mcall.com/travel/all-freedomcruiseaug27,0,1579907.story).

2. *Ibid.*

3. Joyce M. Hawkins, Editor, *Oxford Reference Dictionary* (Oxford: Oxford University Press, 1986), p. 319. Punctuation slightly altered for pulpit use. Italic in original.

4. *Friberg Greek Lexicon*, electronic edition included with BibleWorks 6.0.012d, defining ελευθερος.

5. E. A. Judge and K. A. Kitchen, "Slave, Slavery," in Douglas et al, editors, *New Bible Dictionary*, 2nd edition (Wheaton, Illinois: Tyndale House Publishers,1982), pp. 1121-1125.

6. John Marsh, *Saint John*, Pelican New Testament Commentaries (New York: Penguin Books, 1968) p. 363.

7. From Carter Shelley's response to my "Marketing the Messiah" piece for December 11, 2005, *The Immediate Word*, online publication of CSS Publishing Company. I have altered Carter's wording slightly. www.sermonsuite.com.

8. Irving Layton in *The Whole Bloody Bird* (1969), as quoted in *Colombo's Concise Canadian Quotations*, edited by John Robert Colombo (Edmonton: Hurtig Publishers, 1976), p. 88. Emphasis mine.

All Who Share This Hope

There's nothing like a week with two funerals, a wedding, Halloween celebrations, a community farewell party, a church tea, and several pastoral crises to make a body realize that none of us is an island. Mind you, just now, I'd kind of like to be an island for about three days! But only for three days. For the truth is, we are profoundly connected with and dependent upon each other ... and on the whole, that is good.

Did you ever think about the implications of the fact that as human beings the God in whose image we are created is known to us as a Trinity? Relationship is at the very heart of the nature of God, and that also says something very important about us. None of us is an island. We are not made to live only to ourselves. We are made for relationship, both with God and with each other and God's world; and so we live out our lives in a complicated and ever-changing web of associations.

We turn toward each other almost instinctively as we celebrate our joys, mourn our losses, and need support through tough times and transitions. We work together to accomplish our goals; we look to each other for reassurance that we're on the right track or for guidance if we're not; and we scarcely ever in adulthood make a decision that does not take somebody else into consideration. We look to our parents, grandparents, and mentors for wisdom; we look to our children for zest and inspiration; we look to our friends for help in sorting through the muddle of our daily lives. None of us is an island, and thank God for that!

On the first of November every year, we in the Christian church remember that we are not islands, and give thanks for that, in the celebration called All Saints. As the name of the day suggests, it is a time for recalling all the "saints," known and unknown, who have preceded us, marking our way.

And what is a saint?

Well, of course, there are those who have been especially recognized by the church — Roman Catholic church, anyway — for their exemplary lives. Since we Protestants do not officially recognize saints in that sense, we have a more generalized — and perhaps more idealized — vision of a saint as someone absolutely loving and Christlike, who not only knows what God wants them to do, but who always does it. A saint in this definition is an exemplary (and probably unreal) model of faith, whose example may make the rest of us feel like failures, or at least may tempt us to think that, since we're never going to be in *their* league, it really doesn't matter how we live.[1]

There are other ways of describing saints. Paul's letters to his churches often begin with greetings to "those called to be saints," and those greetings were addressed to the entire congregation — in other words, to any and all Christians.[2]

The word "saint," in fact, simply means "holy": one like, or one set apart for, God. Says Frederick Buechner, "A saint is a life-giver ... A saint is a human being with the same sorts of hang-ups and abysses as the rest of us, but if a saint touches your life, you become alive in a new way."[3]

This is kind of like the definition you may have heard, given by a child who had been told that the figures in stained-glass windows were saints: "A saint is someone the light shines through."

Lydia Gruchy[4] was that kind of saint. She was not "perfect" (whatever that means), but she was wonderfully human. She was a Christian, a respected model of faith, a person through whom others saw the light of God's presence and grace shining into the world, and she was a life-giver. It was a gift to have her around.[5]

It's people like her whom we remember, and people like her whom we need to give us the courage to face our lives. We all have such saints in our lives — perhaps a much-loved grandparent, or admired mentor, or the friend who wouldn't let us be less than God called us to be. Such everyday saints help us to remember that it matters that we are faithful today; and they show us how to be faithful. We need them. We need to know that we are not alone, that we are not little islands, that we are not the first to feel the pounding of the sea, and that it is possible to stand firm against the waves. We need to know that we are part of a great community of saints who have kept the faith throughout history and who even now are doing so around the world. We need to know that, in order to keep on being the saints *we* are called to be, where *we* are.

I'm reminded of what one of our young men said to me some months ago, when he was preparing to join the church. He's living and working in Winnipeg, but he commented that he finds it important to come back to Myrtle and Roland periodically, for reinforcement. In the city, where most people remain anonymous, it's too easy to slip into a kind of indifference; coming back to his home community, to the saints he grew up with and to whom he still feels accountable, reminds him of the kind of life he wants to live, the kind of person he wants to be. Coming here, he gets a fresh glimpse of his Christian values in action; he is reminded that what he does and the way he treats others matters; and so he is encouraged to keep putting one foot in front of the other back in the city.

That's what the communion of saints does for all of us. It reminds us of who we are, it gives us pictures of faith in action, and it encourages us to keep living out our calling in Christ Jesus.

We need that, because when we are baptized into Christ, although we remain part of the human family in the same way as everybody else, we are inducted into the Christian family, which has a unique way of looking at and living in the world. We don't always get encouragement for the Christ-life from the world at large, so we need to keep looking to each other and to our predecessors in the faith — to the communion, or community of saints — to keep from getting worn down and eroded in our Christian living.

I think it was Flannery O'Connor, the American novelist, who paraphrased Jesus to say, "You shall know the truth, and the truth shall make you ... odd."[6]

Nowhere is the oddness of the Christian outlook more clearly displayed than in the Beatitudes, which we read today from Matthew. Blessed are you, says Jesus — or, according to some translations, happy — when you are poor, mournful, persecuted, hungry for a justice you don't see. That's hardly our society's usual definition of happiness. Who will help us discover the blessing, and who will help us to keep living by kingdom values, if not the communion of saints, the family of faith?

Blessed are you, says Jesus, who go ahead being meek, merciful, and peacemakers in a world where such efforts are doomed to failure and their doers to mistreatment. None of us is such a saint that we can keep doing that without support. We need the communion of saints to remind us that we are blessed when we live as if the love of God were the most important and the most reliable reality in life. We need the community, and the community needs us. With each other's help, we can live the life to which Jesus calls us, the life of God's kingdom on earth, "tomorrow's life today."[7]

None of us ever does that perfectly. But enough of us do it enough of the time that, over the centuries, the church has — through the daily life of its members as much as through its preaching and teaching — been able to nurture a distinctive vision, a unique outlook on the world that results in a different kind of living in it. That's a pretty remarkable achievement.

Our heritage is summed up in the words of the first letter of John, "We are even now children of God; and what we shall be has not yet been made known. But we know that when it is, we shall be like him, for we shall see him as he is. All who have this hope purify themselves — they get rid of whatever does not belong to that hope — just as Christ is pure" (1 John 3:2-3 cf).

What we shall be does not yet appear. But we know that we are already God's children, and when Christ appears we shall be like him, for we shall see him as he is. Keeping that hope alive is what the communion of saints is all about, and it's why we take time each year to reaffirm our connection with the family of faith, because we want to be recognizable as children of God. We want to keep clear before our own eyes what that's all about. And we need both to receive and to contribute to the resources of the gathered community — the example of others, the reflecting together on scripture, the prayers with and for each other, the sacraments of baptism and communion, the giving of spiritual counsel, and all the rest — we need both to give and to receive these things if we are to live ever more fully into the nature of Christ. For, as Christians, we were never intended to go it alone. We are not islands; we are part of the body of Christ. Thanks be to God. Amen.

---

1. Jeff Cook, "Sermon Resources: Lydia Gruchy," in "Suggested Worship Resources, November 3, 1996," sheets provided by St. Andrew's College, Saskatoon.

2. *Ibid.*

3. Frederick Buechner, "Faith and Fiction" in *The Clown in the Belfry* (San Francisco: HarperSanFrancisco, 1992), p. 19, quoted by Jeff Cook.

4. Lydia Gruchy was the first woman ordained in the United Church of Canada, in 1936.

5. *Op cit*, Jeff Cook.

6. Quoted by Richard Bolin, note #9 of sermonshop_1996_11_01.topic@ecunet.org. Exact source not indicated.

7. Brian Wren, "There's A Spirit In The Air," in *Voices United* (Carol Stream: Illinois: Hope Publishing Company, 1979).

Masks

There are going to be a lot of people running around out there with masks on this week. People pretending to be something they're not — or maybe trying on something that in part they are, or want to be. *(put on mask)*[1]

Masks are interesting things. We all wear them, you know, and not just on Halloween. We put on the brave smiling mask when our hearts are breaking. We put on a gruff mask to keep people at a distance. We put on a wild and crazy mask to get attention or to avoid responsibility. We put on an "expert" mask to gain respect or to earn a living. Most of us have many masks.

Masks can be a means of survival for us, a way of hiding, perhaps, in a world that seems hostile. I have heard gay people talk about having to put on a mask, or perhaps a whole lion suit, to disguise their real identity so that they can be accepted enough to function in their daily work. Most of us do not have to hide in such an extreme way, but all of us hide at least occasionally. Sometimes that is a positive thing. Counselors and pastors must set aside, or mask off, their own problems while they are supporting someone else through a crisis.

Sometimes masks are not so benign. The wolf in sheep's clothing is a menace to all who fail to see through the disguise, and we have all had our fill of corrupt business and political leaders who hide behind a filibuster or the letter of the law.

Most often, however, masks are just part of living in society. They keep us from overwhelming each other with our undigested lives. As we all know, "How are you?" is not always an invitation to tell the whole truth! Masks allow us and others some privacy; they hide or screen off things that should not momentarily be on view.

Masks can hide, but they can also display. A mask can be a way of exploring another side of ourselves, or of bringing something deep within to light.[2] Sometimes when we're on vacation we try on a different side of ourselves — the cautious accountant goes skydiving, the shy child goes to camp and starts enthralling cabin mates with tall tales, and the white-collar worker tries life at a dude ranch, while the busy life-of-the-party person takes a silent retreat. For some people, getting drunk may be a kind of party mask, giving them the freedom to try on a different approach to social relations. In that case, the alcoholic mask tries both to hide shyness and to bring out a more daring and connected personality. Masks can conceal, or they can reveal; often they do a bit of both at once.

What masks do *you* wear day to day? *(pause)* What masks do you wear here at church? *(pause)* Are there sides of yourself that you feel you can't show here? *(pause)* Are there sides of yourself that you feel you can't show anyone? *(pause)* What do you hide behind, and when, and why? *(pause)* What facets of yourself are you masking off from view? *(pause)* What masks do *you* have, and why do you wear them?

When Jesus watched some of the Pharisees in action, they reminded him of the masked actors at the Roman theaters in the big town of Caesarea. So that's what he called them — *hupokritai* — hypocrites, as we say in English. The word actually means masked actors. Jesus says the Pharisees are like actors wearing their masks: they're playing a role, they're hiding as much as they show. They're not the real thing.

Now, *what* they are acting out, the things they represent, are valuable and important, and Jesus is the first to acknowledge that. These religious leaders, he says, are the heirs of Moses, fulfilling that great teacher's role of interpreting God to the people. Listen to them. What they are teaching is correct. But it should go more than mask-deep. If it's *just* a mask, something's wrong. *(remove mask)* Boy, it's good to get that off!

You know, if we just *put on* our religion — or any other aspect of our personality — if we are just a "mask" of piety or propriety or vitality or anything else, it soon becomes evident — to others if not to ourselves. People will eventually see that we are actors — portraying a wonderful and valuable thing, perhaps, but if at root we are unchanged by it, then we become hypocrites who hide as much as we reveal. When the face we present to life is just a mask, it narrows our vision and stifles our breathing, and it keeps others from seeing and knowing us as we are. So it's a relief to us and to others when we take it off.

Did you ever think that people might like you better without the mask? Now that's a scary thought. We're often afraid to put our real selves on display, because if people reject a mask that we wear, they're not really rejecting us, but if we *don't* wear a mask and we get rejected, then that hurts. So often we put the mask on in advance, and we don't give people a chance to reject the real thing. But people can see that mask for what it is, they sense it's not quite the real thing, and then they suspect that you can't really be trusted. The tragedy is that by then, we often don't know how to get the mask off.

It's not that our masks are necessarily bad. They may show and tell valuable things, and help us to fill important roles, as Jesus remarked about the Pharisees. But if what we present is *only* a mask, it's completely inadequate, and in some ways it's a lie, for it does not define us in our deepest and truest selves. And it is so easy to start out just by putting on a mask to cover up a bit of momentary untidiness, but then as we get busy, or as we get to liking the ways people respond to the mask, we begin to let more and more distance creep in between the mask and the reality, until we don't know how to pull them back together — maybe we even lose track of the fact that we're wearing a mask — and the day comes when the face looks great but the reality behind it is full of holes, and we're nothing more than a hypocrite, an actor, an emptiness behind a mask.

That so often happens in the church. We see what wonderful things God calls us to, and we try to live up to them, but we don't always manage it; and it becomes tempting to whitewash a little.

You know, fake it 'til you make it, dress the part until you grow into it, put on the mask to help you get into the act. It is, after all, how we grow into things — by trying them on, by acting "as if." There can be such a fine line between a mask that draws something out in us and a mask that conceals what we're ashamed to own. Sometimes we put that mask on because of the intolerance of others: if we can't *be* good, we'll at least try to *look* good, because it saves a lot of friction. I think that for leaders this has a special edge. We want to believe in those high ideals, and so we preach them, and we do what we can to model them outwardly at least. Sometimes it just gets too painful to ask about what's going on inwardly, and we mask it off, maybe even from ourselves, until we're nothing more than a hypocrite, an actor, an emptiness behind a mask.

Paul, in his letter to the church at Thessalonika, demonstrates that it doesn't have to be that way. The face he presented there, to the Thessalonian congregation, was bone-deep. The whole of his life and relationships reflected what was in his heart (1 Thessalonians 2:9-10). He dared to live in the kind of intimacy and transparency with his congregation that allowed them to see who he really was all the way through.

The thing is, though, that is what eventually happens whether we intend it or not. Sooner or later, our real character becomes apparent, mask or no mask — just as we can recognize our close friends even in costume, or our children in hockey gear. We recognize the whole build and manner of moving, and are not fooled by the mask.

Jesus was not fooled by the Pharisees; and Paul knew that the congregation in Thessalonika would sooner or later see to the core of him. I wasn't wearing any mask, he says; rather, in a way, I *became* a mask: a mask for God, a face for the invisible God to present visibly to the world. Paul's life became a way of showing not only the truth of what was in Paul, but the deeper truth of what was beyond Paul, beneath and sustaining Paul, the reality of Paul's God.

The apostle says, "I was like a father with his children, urging and encouraging you [into the life of God's realm]" (1

446

Thessalonians 2:11-12 cf). God's own fatherly care of him shone through into Paul's fatherly care of this new congregation, enabling them, as he says, to receive the message he brought as God's own word, and not merely as human posturing. So the Thessalonians saw, not a masked actor evangelist, but the very light of God shining through the whole of Paul's speech and living.

We are all called and invited into such a transformation. Not a transformation to cover ourselves up with this or that or the other mask, but to dare to remove our masks, to expose our deepest selves to the presence of God and the needs of our neighbors. And so, to *become* whole-person masks of God in this world, showing and telling, through the nuances of our daily living, what God is about in the world.

We are the one gospel our neighbors are guaranteed to read. Amen.

_____

1. Wear a Halloween mask for the first part of the message. The nature of the mask is unimportant: any mask that allows reasonably clear vision and speech, and does not portray anything upsetting or offensive, is suitable. The idea of wearing the mask, and some of the development of the mask theme, is from Dawne Taylor's meditation on this subject in *Aha!!!* volume 9 #1 (October to December 1999), p. 27.

2. From Jan Bush in *Marks of the Maker*, quoted in *Aha!!!* (*Ibid*, p. 28): "Masks are not meant to hide behind, but to reveal a sacred part of you."

Ready For God's Reign

This parable has to be one of the least liked in the whole Bible. It speaks stern words to those who are not ready for the moment of truth — and it leaves uncomfortably vague just what "being ready" might entail.

To understand what Matthew interprets Jesus to mean by readiness for the final judgment, we have to read his whole gospel, and in particular the final third of this chapter, that famous scene of the sheep and the goats, which we'll be reading in another two weeks. But already today there is an important clue to how we can be ready for judgment, in the centrality to this parable of the symbol of a supply of oil.

Oil was an essential commodity to the people of Jesus' day. The beautiful silver-grey leaves and gnarled trunks of olive trees were visible everywhere in Palestine, because everyone needed lots of olive oil for daily life. You needed oil to cook, and to make your food filling and tasty. Olive oil was the base for such essential things as medicines, as well as for such luxuries as cosmetics and perfume. Oil and grain were among the mandated sacrifices to be offered in the temple. And oil was used in the most sacred rituals of the nation, the anointing of kings and priests, where it became a rich symbol of God's favor.

And, of course, oil was used as fuel. In those days before electric lights, the usual means of illumination was the humble clay lamp, whose wick drank precious oil to burn brightly so all could see. And so, not surprisingly, the oil that fueled those lamps became a symbol of human obedience to God, a way of talking about the kind of life that God can shine through to brighten the dark places of the world.

Centuries before Jesus, the prophet Micah picked up on this symbolism when he asked, "With what shall I come before the Lord, and bow myself before God on high? ... Will the Lord be pleased with thousands of rams, with ten thousands of rivers of oil?" And then he went on to answer his question, to describe what was as delicious, as precious, as useful, as necessary and as holy as oil — in fact, even more precious and necessary and holy, for he maintained that oil was not enough, not even endless rivers of it. No, what is really a worthy offering to God, he said, is a life that draws its fuel from God's own heart. "[God] has told you, O mortal, what is good; and what does the Lord require of you but to do justice, and to love kindness, and to walk humbly with your God?" (Micah 6:6-8). This life of piety outweighs the richest sacrifice; loving justice and humility are better far than oil.

So when we get to Jesus' parable, the mention of oil is a kind of clue to the alert listener that what we need to have in good supply to face the judgment is a life of obedience to the commandments of God. It is a life in which justice and kindness can be seen to flow freely and to fuel all one's actions — a life that makes you, as Isaiah said, a light to the nations (Isaiah 42:6; 49:6; 60:3); or, as Jesus said earlier in Matthew, a lamp on a stand, giving light to all in the house — the light, in fact, of the world (Matthew 5:15, 14). To have oil is to burn bright in this world with the nature of God. That's how we welcome God's kingdom.

When Matthew recorded this parable, he did so for the sake of a church that was getting off-track in its anxiety about the future. The first Christians thought Jesus was returning for them *soon*; and when he didn't, when years dragged into decades and the end still hadn't come, many began to get caught up in trying to read the "signs of the times" and figure out when Christ would come — in spite of Jesus' warnings that no one could know, that even Jesus himself did not know, only the Father (Matthew 24:36). That didn't stop people from speculating, and arguing, and creating much more heat than light.

450

Others, on the other hand, when Jesus did not return, simply gave up hoping in him, and returned to their former, non-Christian, lives and commitments.

Some things never change. The turn of the year 2000, for instance, saw all kinds of bizarre speculation and panic over the possibility that our computer-dependent society would come unglued when the numbers turned over. When that didn't happen, a lot of backyard bunkers began looking pretty silly and a lot of generators got returned as people resumed ordinary life.

But their mistake was not confined to the year 2000. There is, and for about the last century has been, a whole wing of the church — and for the last thirty years or so, a very lucrative movie and publishing industry as well — that is forever cranking up anxiety by means of apocalyptic speculation. "The end is near. Don't be left behind!" Meanwhile, we see many other people drifting away from the church as it seems less and less relevant to daily life; and many others for whom religion is not so much a matter of genuine commitment to the reign of God as it is a matter of buying fire insurance. Pay the minimum possible — say, a theologically correct confession of Jesus as Savior — and you'll be bailed out when you need it.

In fact, many people who bring their babies to me for baptism are at least a little afraid that if not baptized their babies will go to hell! Don't even get me started on what awful theology that is — that's another day's sermon. Yet, these same people who fear that God would condemn someone to hell on the basis of a technicality of water seem also to think that God is concerned about nothing more than that technicality of water, since once the ceremony is completed we rarely see them again. Once saved from hell, whether real or imagined, it doesn't seem to occur to them that God might have anything more of importance to say to their lives or to ask of them as God's people.

That is an appalling distortion of the Christian promise of salvation, which we have allowed to become current, and it is one that today's parable speaks to sternly. Just showing up, Matthew warns, is not enough — even if you hang around the bridegroom's gate for much longer than some of the people we baptize. Being

451

there is not all it takes — as the saying goes, coming to church doesn't make you a Christian any more than sitting in the garage makes you a car (although it's a not bad place to start!).

Jesus never intended to offer himself as fire insurance. The promise he holds out is both infinitely more wonderful and infinitely more demanding than "get out of hell free," or even "pie in the sky when you die." It's about being whole — "salvation" means "wholeness" or "health" — and that involves life here and now, not just after we die.

Throughout his ministry Jesus spoke of a new creation, a reality that, if it will be fully realized only at his return, nonetheless begins to take visible shape here and now in the lives of those who follow him: the already-present yet still-to-be-realized kingdom of heaven or reign of God.

It is *this* that Jesus calls us to be part of, even though the world around us hasn't caught on. "Live tomorrow's life today." Fuel yourselves with all that you know and have experienced of the love and the nature of God and of God's concern for the world; let that oil, drawn into the fibers of your daily existence, flame brightly, bringing God's light to your world. Get some oil in your lamp, keep on burning!

A fire-insurance baptism isn't going to do that — a hurried dash to the bridegroom's house with your lamp half-full and no thought to bring more for the long hours ahead. Far too many of us, even those who do show up for church and Sunday school, are like the dozing bridesmaids, nodding off when we should be paying attention, drifting off into purely personal priorities and commitments instead of actively living into the coming reign of Christ. Far too many of us are falling asleep and letting our oil run out. We may show up here Sunday after Sunday, or at least often enough that the minister knows us — we may even *be* ministers — but there's little to distinguish us from any other well-behaved North American. Is that all the kingdom of God is about — being nice people? I don't think so!

When Jesus calls us the light of the world, he's assuming that the world is in darkness. And I don't believe he means just the world outside our national borders, or even only the world outside our church doors. Remember back in the Sermon on the Mount when he spoke of how the eye is the lamp of the body? "If your eye is healthy," he said, "your whole body will be full of light; but if your eye is unhealthy, your whole body will be full of darkness. If then the light in you is darkness, how great is the darkness!" (Matthew 6:22-23).

The light we take in, the light we live by, is another way of talking about what we're ultimately committed to, often without realizing it. It's the lens we see through. As North Americans, we naturally see things in light of consumerism, in light of individualism, in light of certain political and economic and social realities that just seem to us to be given. To a point, there's nothing wrong with that: we are, after all, called to live life where we are and not where we aren't. But when we start to imagine that these conditions are "The Way It Is" and "The Way It Should Be" — or, perhaps more accurately, when we *fail* to imagine that there could be any other way of viewing the world — then the light in us is darkness, and great is our darkness indeed.

The length and breadth of scripture, and the living Spirit of Jesus, soak us in a whole different light, a rich-as-oil vision that we're invited to draw up into the fibers of our being, and which will then burst into brilliance showing up all the dark corners of our lives and of the world. And that vision, that light, is God's profound love for all of humanity, all of creation, and God's insistence on justice and compassion in all human dealings. An individualistic consumer society certainly isn't going to deliver that! To imagine that it can is deep darkness indeed.

If our eye is going to be healthy, if we're going to live as people with light to share, we need to buy into another vision — beginning with our imagination, and flowing then into every aspect of our lives. We need to stock up on oil, on dedication to the reign of God in the middle of here-and-now.

If I believe, for instance, that God created the earth, whether directly or through evolution, then I will be concerned with respecting the earth and its ecosystems, and with reducing the size of my ecological footprint: by leaving the car at home when possible, by turning down my thermostat a few degrees, by minimizing my

453

use of harmful chemicals, and so on. My belief in God as creator has some practical implications!

Similarly, if I believe that God demands justice in all human dealings, then I will not be content to seek bargains on my clothes or demand the cheapest possible food, because to do so is to demand that the people who grow my food and make my clothing not be justly compensated for their work. I will instead patronize stores that source their products in socially and environmentally responsible ways, and employers who pay a living wage and who give back to their communities. This is living by the light of God's love. It is what Jesus calls me to do. It's a matter of oil in the lamp. And it is the only way to have a future worth having, here *or* hereafter. Jesus is quite unequivocal about what happens if we choose not to have oil.

We do not like to think that our actions or inactions can have such dire consequences, but they do. Jesus warns us to brighten our vision with the whole of what we know about God's nature and will, and to take seriously what God says about the world to come. He urges us not to wait passively for it, or to think that there's a cheap ticket into it, but instead to stock up on the oil of anticipation: to live tomorrow's life today, so that when God's future arrives we are ready to welcome it, and to be welcomed into it. Amen.

**Proper 28
Pentecost 26
Ordinary Time 33
Matthew 25:14-30**

Investing In God's Future

(Note: At the time of reading this passage to the congregation, explain that a single talent was worth more than fifteen years' wages of a laborer [per NRSV footnote to Matthew 25:14] — in other words, easily a cool quarter of a million dollars in today's terms!)

"I was afraid," quavered the third servant, "because I knew that you were a ruthless businessman, expecting profit even when it is impossible. I was so afraid of losing your money that I put it in a box and buried it. Here is your money, exactly what you gave me."[1]

I was so afraid of losing your money — or maybe I was so afraid of *having* your money.

Marianne Williamson wrote:

> *Our deepest fear is not that we are inadequate. Our deepest fear is that we are powerful beyond measure. It is our light, not our darkness, that most frightens us. We ask ourselves, who am I to be brilliant, gorgeous, talented and fabulous? Actually, who are you not to be? You are a child of God. Your playing small doesn't serve the world. There's nothing enlightened about shrinking so that other people won't feel insecure around you. We were born to make manifest the glory of God that is within us. It's not just in some of us, it's in everyone. And as we let our light shine, we unconsciously give other people permission to do the same. As we are liberated from our own fear, our presence automatically liberates others.*[2]

455

Our deepest fear is not that we are inadequate but that we are powerful — that we *have* a quarter million dollars worth of impact — or maybe more.

And it is true.

You can see it at funerals. Why do people attend a funeral? It's because the deceased person has had some impact on their lives. Every person I have ever buried — even the mentally handicapped person who had been in an institution for fifty years — is remembered by dozens, and perhaps hundreds, of people whose lives have been affected by that life. There are people around that grave who have deeply loved and been loved by the person who has died. There are those who have been caregivers through the declining years, who have given up a part of their lives to sustain the life of this one. There are those that this person has cared for — raised, perhaps, or guided, mentored — people this person has laughed with, played with, worked with ... changed. And, though you don't usually find them at the funeral, there are the people this person has hurt, the lives that have been injured or bent out of shape by the failings, sins, and errors of this person in their life. Every human being who ever lived has the kind of impact a quarter of a million dollars has. And some of us have much more.

That's a frightening thought.

Many of us spend much of our lives trying to pretend it isn't so. We refuse to think about the true impact of what we're doing, about the depth of our effect on others. Or we try to avoid having an impact — we hide away the deepest springs of our lives, trying not to touch or be touched; we resist taking the risk of living and loving and getting involved. We try to bury the money.

And God says to us, in this parable, "Oh no you don't! I gave you all you are for a reason." As theologian Walter Brueggeman says, "What God does first and best and most is to trust people with their moment in history."[3] God trusts us with our moment in history. It's ours to do something with.

Does that mean that the investment will always work out? If you read only this parable, you would think so. The two servants who did invest their master's money made handsome returns. But does it always work like that in life?

Has it always worked that way in yours?

Someone once wrote in to an online discussion about this passage: "The only real risk is to risk not taking the perceived risk."[4] There's nothing to fear in investing for God; in God's economy it will all come out right.

And someone else wrote in to disagree.

> *Life is not [always] as cooperative as the parable. I [once] risked taking a leadership I believed needed taking, and came out alive but burned to the bone, with much of what should have been good work seriously screwed up. [It's] still unresolved several years later. I personally have grown a great deal through this, but the "investment" is still in bad shape! Praying God isn't finished with this yet, I nonetheless have to say that the risk is quite real, and that, for reasons both controllable and uncontrollable, some investments do sour quite badly, and people do lose their master's shirts!*[5]

Maybe you know the truth of that all too well.

There are reasons why we are afraid. There are reasons why we try to "bury the money."

But do we have the right?

Jonathan Kozol once interviewed a young man living in the South Bronx, and the topic of evil came up.

> *"Evil exists," [said the young man,] not flinching at the word. "I believe that what the rich have done to the poor people in this city is something that a preacher could call evil. Somebody has power. Pretending that they don't so they don't need to use it to help people — that is my idea of evil."*[6]

Somebody has power.

We all have power. We all have impact — the kind of impact a quarter of a million dollars has over our lifetime, and maybe more. Pretending we *don't* have that power, pretending we don't have

457

that impact, avoiding our responsibility to *use* that power to help people, to build God's kingdom, *that* is evil — *not,* trying and failing and screwing up hopelessly. That is tragic, but it is not evil. Evil is having the means to do something, and choosing not to.

Clarence Jordan, a famous activist in the southern States, and author of the *Cotton Patch Version of the New Testament*, wrote:

> *I've heard so many sermons preached on this idea: "Give your talents to the Lord." They got that thing backward. The Lord gives the talents to us ... What are these talents? Are they money? No, Jesus had no money to give. What did he have? What is the stock-in-trade of a great teacher? It's his ideas, his concepts, his teaching. He leaves them to his followers. All these three years he has been talenting them. Now he's saying, "You want me to come in here and pull some angels out of the sky and set up a revolution? Oh, no. I've been giving you, over all these months together, the currency of the kingdom, and if it comes, it's gonna come by your doin' business with what I've turned over to you."*[7]

It's going to come by your doing business with what I've turned over to you.

Jordan continues:

> *To us he says, "I've turned over to you the idea of brotherhood."*
>
> *And some of us can say, "Yes, Lord, I got out and dealt with that idea and multiplied it."*
>
> *But others of us turn in an accounting like this: "Yes, Lord, I remember you talkin' about brotherhood but, You know, I was scared. I started to preach a sermon on race relations one Sunday, but Deacon Jones said, 'Hmmm.' You know I didn't want to upset the deacon. No point breakin' up your church. Besides, Deacon Jones, he's one of our major tithers, and he got something to tithe. So, Lord, I was scared, I was scared of the whole proposition and I buried this idea of brotherhood."*

458

[And Jesus says,] "I gave to you the idea of peace."
[And some of us say,] "Yes, Lord. But you don't
understand the civilization we live in. You gotta talk
force. Force is the only language most folks understand
today. Really, it's the only language people know how
to talk. So, Lord, I had a chance to witness for peace,
but I was kind of scared somebody might identify me
with those flower children, and I jes' buried the whole
thought."[8]

I jes' buried the whole thought.
I had the power and wouldn't use it.
That's the evil. That's what God condemns.

If the kingdom comes, it's going to come by our doing business with what God has turned over to us. The resources of our own individual character and gifts that God has created in us and that experience has shaped; the resources of faith and love and Christian virtues, given us by the Spirit of Christ; the central resource of the vision of God's kingdom, and the power of the indwelling Holy Spirit to fulfill it: These are our treasures, to multiply or to bury — our spiritual capital, to do business with or to reject.

When the offering plate comes around today, I want you to take something out as well as put something in. You will see in each plate a stack of "gold ingots" — little pieces of gold paper. I invite you to take one, and on it prayerfully to write down one thing God has given you — a talent, an attribute, a material resource, a deeply held value, you name it — some part of God's capital in you. Write down one thing that is part of this quarter-million dowry that you are. Take that "ingot" home, place it on your refrigerator or your mirror or your dashboard, someplace where you'll see it in the course of daily life. For the next six weeks I want you to do business with that gift of God. I want you to see how you can strengthen and expand it, how you can use it to make a difference in the lives around you, how you can give some of it to those who need it. I want you to invest what God has given you.

And then on the Sunday before Christmas, or at whichever of the Christmas services you will be attending, I want you to bring that ingot back, with an accounting. Staple it to a 3x5 card on which you've written a brief account of how you've invested that gift, and what has come of it. You don't have to write your name — God already knows that. Just bring your gift and your accounting, and make that part of your offering on Christmas Sunday.[9]

Let us not be afraid. God has trusted us, and God will empower us. So let us go out and do business for the kingdom. Amen.

---

1. From a recast in business terms by Reverend Allen Hulslander of Towanda, Pennsylvania. Posted (note #26) to sermonshop_1996_11_17.topic@ecunet.org by Bob Stump.

2. Marianne Williamson in *A Return to Love: Reflections on the Principles of A Course in Miracles* (New York: Harper Collins, 1992), pp. 190-191. Posted to sermonshop_1996_11_17.topic@ecunet.org (note #19) by Robert Stuart, mistakenly attributed to Nelson Mandela. Correct attribution supplied by Charles F. Brumbagh in note #95 of same meeting.

3. Walter Brueggeman, source not indicated. Quoted in *The Whole People of God* adult study for Nov. 14, 1999, p. 2A-33.

4. Jeffrey Jackson in note #12 of sermonshop_1996_11_17.topic@ecunet.org.

5. My note #25 to sermonshop_1996_11_17.topic@ecunet.org.

6. Jonathan Kozol, *Amazing Grace*, p. 23. Quoted by Rob Stuart in note #19 to sermonshop_1996_11_17.topic@ecunet.org.

7. Clarence Jordan, source not indicated. Quoted by Richard Bolin in note #78 of sermonshop_1996_11_17.topic@ecunet.org.

8. *Ibid.*

9. Idea from Nancy Jo Kemper, described in notes #112 and 132 of sermonshop_1996_11_17.topic@ecunet.org.

Nations On Trial

A Readers' Theater for Five Voices

A few suggestions for staging this....

It probably makes sense for the minister to be Voice 1, and an "ordinary layperson" to be Voice 2. Voice 3 (Christ) is probably best read by a respected adult male, in order to avoid confusion or dissonance. When Voices 4 and 5 bring in quotes from news stories, other parts of scripture, and prominent contemporary thinkers, it may be helpful (or then again merely distracting!) to have these sources identified, either on cards that the speakers hold up, or on a projection screen if the congregation is so equipped. Source acknowledgments such as "News flash," "Theologians Gustavo Gutierrez and Ernesto Cardenal," "Economist Barbara Ward," "Ezekiel 34," "Luke 10" and so on should be sufficient. Voice 4, bringing contemporary stories as well as the witness of scripture, would be embodied especially effectively by a local broadcaster or news reporter. Because Voice 5 brings in the "outside expert" voice, it can be effective, if feasible, to assign this part to a college professor or other community authority, particularly if that person is not part of the immediate congregation (but is known to them). And do, of course, rehearse!

If you have a projection screen, and the time and technical expertise, this message could be greatly enhanced by the use of complementary visuals. For instance, in the opening reading from Matthew 25, project a world map; at the mention of the nations, bold the boundaries; and when it speaks of separating them, "burst" them apart from each other slightly. (Do *not* separate them into two groups — that's God's job, not ours! Just spread them out a little from each other in their usual configuration.) This image can be brought back to the screen at appropriate intervals throughout the message, and at the conclusion.

Additionally, projecting images, particularly from current news, of human need and/or headline collages illustrating the topics under discussion (immigration, hunger, sickness, and the like) can powerfully enforce what the different voices are saying.

If the screen is used for images, it may be confusing to have Voice 4 and 5 attributions on the screen, unless the quoted words are also posted (or excerpted, in the case of longer accounts). If the screen is not used for attributions, the readers could hold up cards, or key lines could be printed in the service bulletin, with proper attribution, or the words could be allowed to stand on their own merit.

———————————

1: When the Son of Man comes in his glory, and all the angels with him, then he will sit on the throne of his glory. All the nations will be gathered before him, and he will separate them one from another as a shepherd separates the sheep from the goats.[1]

2: The *nations* will be gathered?

1: The nations.

2: Not individuals?

1: Not individuals.

2: He will separate the nations? That's what it says?

1: That's what it says. The nations.

2: All the nations will be gathered before him, and he will separate them one from another as a shepherd separates the sheep from the goats.

1: Yes. The nations will be separated as a shepherd separates the sheep from the goats.

2: Oh. The nations.

1: He will separate them one from another as a shepherd separates the sheep from the goats, and he will put the sheep at his right hand and the goats at the left. Then the king will say to those at his right hand,

3: Come, you that are blessed by my Father, inherit the kingdom prepared for you from the foundation of the world; for I was hungry and you gave me food, I was thirsty and you gave me something to drink, I was a stranger and you welcomed me, I was naked and you gave me clothing, I was sick and you took care of me, I was in prison and you visited me.

1: Then the righteous will answer him, "Lord, when was it that we saw you hungry and gave you food, or thirsty and gave you something to drink? And when was it that we saw you a stranger and welcomed you, or naked and gave you clothing? And when was it that we saw you sick or in prison and visited you?" And the king will answer them,

3: Truly I tell you, just as you did it to one of the least of these who are members of my family, you did it to me.

2: How can a nation do that?

1: Then he will say to those at his left hand,

3: You that are accursed, depart from me into the eternal fire prepared for the devil and his angels; for I was hungry and you gave me no food, I was thirsty and you gave me nothing to drink, I was a stranger and you did not welcome me, naked and you did not give me clothing, sick and in prison and you did not visit me.

1: Then they also will answer, "Lord, when was it that we saw you hungry or thirsty or a stranger or naked or sick or in prison, and did not take care of you?" Then he will answer them.[2]

4: In the spring of 2002, we spent two weeks in France. While in Paris, we dedicated a day to Notre Dame. We were awed by the grandeur of the cathedral. We spent the day snapping pictures, trudging up and down its steps, and listening in on the insights of tour guides. We were awed by the feats of engineering, physical design, and artisan skill that had gone into its creation ... but we were also awed by the number of Eastern European and Middle-Eastern beggars who roamed the cathedral's square competing with the pigeons for tourist handouts.

2: The strangers?

1: The strangers.

4: In fact, it wasn't possible to eat our picnic lunch in peace, because so many young women with nursing babies and toddlers approached us begging for money. Furthermore, it wasn't possible for me to make my way to the public toilets without being accosted by young boys and girls between the ages of five and twelve seeking money and food. They should have been in school, enjoying free lunches and educational opportunities, not spending their days in the dark, smelly washrooms. But of course, they weren't in France legally, and they needed all the help they could get.

2: Help from the nation?

1: From the nations.

4: Hungry, thirsty, a stranger, close to naked, and one petty crime away from incarceration, these children and young women working the crowd outside the hallowed halls of Notre Dame could not have embodied Jesus' mandate any better if they'd tried.[3]

2: They should have been in school. There should have been food and work. They shouldn't have had to leave their homelands for hope.

1: They needed all the help they could get.

2: So is France a goat? Are the countries they came from goats?

4: On the face of it, Elvira Arellano seems an unlikely fugitive from justice. A study in pink, the 31-year-old Mexican mom appears relaxed, if preoccupied, chatting on her cell phone in a shabby storefront church. For the past twelve days, the some-time cleaning worker has been at the center of a firestorm that has made headlines across the United States.

2: Hey, I think I've heard of her!

4: It began on August 15 [2006], when Arellano sought sanctuary in this community church rather than surrender to US immigration authorities to be deported back to her native Mexico. "It's been pretty difficult. I draw comfort from the people who drop in to pray for me and reassure me," said a wan and weary Arellano. "But I don't know how it will end. The immigration system is broken. Even President Bush recognizes that. If I could have come here legally, I would have, but I didn't have that option."[4]

3: I was a stranger and you did not welcome me (Matthew 25:43).

2: Does that make the US a goat?

4: The immigration system is broken. Even the president recognizes that. We need new options.

2: New options?

5: Different choices, which we'll only have with different structures.

2: Different structures?

5: We must avoid the pitfall of individual charity.[5] That will never solve the injustices of this world. It may sometimes be all that is possible, but we need to start thinking about "collectivized charity: [about] a whole system where injustice no longer exists."[6]

2: A whole system?

1: All the nations will be gathered before him (Matthew 25:32a).

2: Including my nation.

1: Including your nation.

2: So I need to think about whether my nation feeds the hungry and cares for the thirsty.

5: And about why there are hungry and thirsty people in your nation.

2: Hm. Maybe because they're lazy?

5: Some of them. Laziness is often a name onlookers give to despair.

2: Why would anyone in this country be in despair? It's the land of opportunity!

5: *If* you start with some social, educational, or financial capital, yes. *If* there are doors of opportunity that you can see, that you can reach, and that you're equipped to go through. That's a lot of ifs.

2: So we're back to structures?

5: Charity alone can't create justice.

4: This message came to me from the Lord: "Son of man, prophesy against the shepherds, the leaders of the nation. Give them this message from the sovereign Lord: What sorrow awaits you shepherds who feed yourselves instead of your flocks. Shouldn't shepherds feed their sheep? As surely as I live, says the sovereign Lord, you abandoned my flock and left them to be attacked by every wild animal. And though you were my shepherds, you didn't search for my sheep when they were lost. You took care of yourselves and left the sheep to starve. Therefore this is what the sovereign Lord says to his people: I will judge between one animal of the flock and another, separating the sheep from the goats. Isn't it enough for you to keep the best of the pastures for yourselves? Must you also trample down the rest? Isn't it enough for you to drink clear water for yourselves? Must you also muddy the rest with your feet? Therefore, this is what the sovereign Lord says: I will surely judge between the fat sheep and the scrawny sheep. For you fat sheep pushed and butted and crowded my sick and hungry flock until you scattered them to distant lands. So I will rescue my flock, and they will no longer be abused. I will judge between one animal of the flock and another" (Ezekiel 34:1-2, 8, 17-18, 20-22 NLT cf).

2: God will judge our country, our citizens, and our leaders because of inequality?

1: God will judge our country, our citizens, and our leaders because of inequality.

2: And as a member of my society and a citizen of a democracy I have some responsibility for this?

5: Christians are in a unique position. "Christians alone straddle the whole spectrum of rich nations, and therefore Christians are a lobby or can be a lobby of incomprehensible importance."[7]

2: That doesn't sound like the kind of Christian lobbying that's getting press right now.

3: I was hungry and you gave me no food, I was thirsty and you gave me nothing to drink, I was a stranger and you did not welcome me, naked and you did not give me clothing, sick and in prison and you did not visit me (Matthew 25:42-43).

1: Is that the kind of record you want for your country?

2: Well, that's hardly the whole story!

1: True. Are you asking what is the least we can do and still be sheep, not goats?

4: A lawyer stood up to test Jesus. "Teacher," he said, "what must I do to inherit eternal life?" He said to him,

3: What is written in the law? What do you read there?

4: He answered, "You shall love the Lord your God with all your heart, and with all your soul, and with all your strength, and with all your mind; and your neighbor as yourself." And he said to him,

3: You have given the right answer; do this, and you will live.

4: But wanting to justify himself, he asked Jesus, "And who is my neighbor?" Jesus replied,

3: A man was going down from Jerusalem to Jericho, and fell into the hands of robbers, who stripped him, beat him, and went away, leaving him half dead ... Who, do you think, was a neighbor to the man who fell into the hands of the robbers? (Luke 10:25-30, 36b cf).

2: The one who helped him.

5: "If we ... come ultimately before our heavenly Father, and he says, 'Did you feed them, and did you give them to drink, did you clothe them, did you shelter them?' and we say, 'Sorry, Lord, but we did give 0.3% of our gross national product,' I don't think it will be enough."[8]

4: Love the Lord your God with all your heart, and with all your soul, and with all your strength, and with all your mind; and your neighbor as yourself (Luke 10:27).

3: Do this, and you will live.

4: But the king will say to the nations on his left,

3: You that are accursed, depart from me into the eternal fire prepared for the devil and his angels; for truly I tell you, just as you did not do it to one of the least of these, you did not do it to me (Matthew 25:41, 45b).

Amen.

---

1. Matthew 25:31-32 slightly altered to more accurately reflect the Greek. "He will separate *people* one from another" has been changed to "He will separate *them* (i.e. nations) one from another" because the Greek is αυτους, which refers back to ταεθνη; a different entity, such as τους ανθρωπους (people) is not introduced.

2. Matthew 25:32-45 altered only as noted in note 1.

3. Carter Shelley, response to Steve McCutchan's "Signs of Judgment on a Nation" in *The Immediate Word* online lectionary resource (CSS Publishing Company, Inc.) for November 20, 2005. Slightly altered and condensed. www.sermonsuite.com.

4. "Mexican Mom Defies Deportation in Bold US Immigration Standoff," *South Asian Women's Forum News* online article posted on August 27, 2006 to http://news.sawf.org/Lifestyle/19346.aspx. © AFP/File Tasos Katopodis. Slightly condensed.

5. Gustavo Gutiérrez, "A Theology of Liberation," cited in Robert McAfee Brown, *Unexpected News: Reading the Bible with Third World Eyes* (Philadelphia: The Westminster Press, 1984), p. 134.

6. Ernesto Cardenal, "The Gospel in Solentiname," cited in Brown, *Unexpected News*, p. 135.

7. British economist Barbara Ward, in a speech to the World Council of Churches World Conference on Church and Society in 1966, quoted in Brown, *Unexpected News*, p. 141.

8. *Ibid.*

Kiss The Chef!

Years ago, during summer vacation, I took a whole pile of books out of the library and spent days and days just reading. Today I'd have trouble telling you what most of those books were, never mind what they were about. But there's one little snatch of dialogue from one of the books that has stuck with me all these years — the bit of dialogue, in fact, that gave the book, and later the movie, its name: a snippet of conversation about the color purple. Actually, it's a bit of conversation about appreciation. Shug Avery is talking to her friend Celie, and she says, "More than anything God loves admiration."

"You saying God is vain?" demands Celie.

"No, not vain," replies Shug, "just wanting to share a good thing. I think it [ticks] God off when you walk by the color purple in a field and don't notice it."

Celie considers this. "You saying it just wanna be loved like it say in the Bible?"

"Yeah, Celie," says Shug. "Everything wanna be loved. Us sing and dance and holla just wanting to be loved. Look at them trees. Notice how the trees do everything people do to get attention ... except walk?" The two of them laugh ... and then Shug looks around and exclaims, "Oh, yeah, this field feels like singing!"[1]

When was the last time you took a good enough look around to recognize that, "Oh, yeah, this field feels like singing!"?

I love that bit of dialogue, because it so effectively captures the essence of gratitude, which is *noticing*. How *could* you walk past a field in glorious bloom and fail to notice? But we do it all the time. I'll never forget the day I came home from work and noticed that the manse committee had fixed the hole in the fence that I'd mentioned to them. I walked into the house, set my things down, and happily announced, "The fence got fixed!"

The children looked up and said, "Mom ... it's been like that for two weeks!"

How did I manage to walk past that fence every day for two weeks and not notice that the hole had been fixed? Easy. I had other things on my mind. We do it all the time. And even when we do notice, we don't always remember to appreciate.

Imagine you've come home from a long day at work, and you find that your spouse has gotten home ahead of you and cooked a wonderful tasty dinner so that all you have to do is sit down and enjoy it. Now, there are several things you can do. One — and I'm sure we've all done it — is to sit down with your briefcase still in your head, shovel the food down mechanically, hardly tasting it, while you continue to mull over the problems at work. Or perhaps you turn the television on to distract you from your thoughts, but it's also distracting you from the food. Either way, you've got a full belly but not much else.

Or, you can leave the briefcase and all it represents at the door, and sit down and really pay attention to the meal. It is *good* — the steak is just so, the baked potato is hot and fluffy, the salad crisp and delicious with your favorite dressing on top. Now, isn't that a much more satisfying meal than the one wolfed down with your mind elsewhere?

But it can get better yet. Early in my relationship with Tom, I learned one of the best life lessons there is: he inducted me into his family's expectation that "you always kiss the chef." When the plate lands on the table, before you dig in, you stop and you turn to the person who took the trouble to do this for you, and you thank them with a big hug and a kiss. You make a point, in other words, of noticing and of appreciating both the dinner and the person. And that does wonderful things for the meal ... and for the marriage, and for the soul.

Kissing the chef is what today's gospel lesson is about. Ten lepers recognize Jesus as someone who may be able to give them their lives back, and so they hail him from a distance and ask for his help. He agrees. "Go to the priests," he says, "and show them that you are ready to re-enter society." And as they go, lo and behold, they *are* ready to re-enter society: Their leprosy is cleansed. Wow! I bet they ran the rest of the way there, pell-mell — quick, before it turns out to be an illusion, quick, so we can get on with our lives, quick, so we can dance the night away! Oh, I'm sure they were all thrilled. But only one came back to kiss the chef. And he received the best benefit of all.

All ten of the lepers were healed, they were "cleansed," as the people of that time said when speaking of leprosy. But only the one who came back was said to be made *well*, or as the underlying Greek can also be translated, "saved." Something deeper, more encompassing came into his life than just the end of an isolating illness. Something to do with faith and gratitude toward God. Something that opened life up in a new way.

Like the difference between scarfing down a meal with your mind still on the job, or even eating and enjoying the meal without thinking beyond it — the difference between that, and kissing the chef: when you notice, and appreciate, the effort that has been made on your behalf, and the love that this person has for you, and you enter into that loving relationship with your participation: you reach out, and you smile, and your eyes soften, your heart lights, and your lips touch and you do so much more than kiss the chef. You renew the relationship, and you refresh your own soul. *That*'s the kind of difference there is between being "cleansed" and being "made *well*," being saved, being whole. That's the difference gratitude can make.

When we talk about the importance of giving thanks to God — and the Jewish and Christian scriptures alike are full of this — we are not talking about a God who is a megalomaniac, who must be praised or his vanity is injured. Oh, no. We're talking about our own need to recognize the gift in order to fully receive it. As Shug said to Celie, it's not that God is vain, but rather is "wanting to share a good thing."

The Bible makes over 200 references to thanksgiving, and more than twice that many to praise.[2] This is such a core Judeo-Christian value: We *need* to remember and to recognize the abundance that surrounds us, the love that enfolds us, the providence that guides us. In a very real sense, gratitude is the key to a functioning faith.

"I did not make the air I breathe," says Rabbi Ben Zion Bokser, "nor the sun that warms me ... I did not endow the muscles of hand and brain with the strength to plough and plant and harvest ... I know I am not a self-made man."[3] I know that I have received benefits I could not have provided for myself. I also know that I do not have to carry the world upon my shoulders, or to struggle alone through the trials of life. I know that I can trust in one who is greater than I to provide what is needed; and I know that most days I am surrounded by so much more than I could ask or imagine, such an embarrassment of riches, that if I only notice I will realize that my times are safe and well in God's great hand. I am not a self-made man.

What a gift it is to realize that! What a relief to have the weight of the world rolled off of one's shoulders, to recognize that not everything depends on you; and what a wonder it is to soak in the awareness of blessings already received! Not just once a year, but once a week, once a day, once in every painful hour, we need to stop and recognize just how much we have to be thankful for.

One family I know of has built this right into their weekly routine. Once each week, at the beginning of the meal, the mother asks family members and guests to share something good or memorable that happened to them during the week. "Usually everyone," says the father, "even those who have had difficult weeks, can think of at least one pleasurable moment that occurred during the preceding week. In the rare instance when someone cannot summon up even one positive recollection, family members or friends generally remember something good that the other person has forgotten."[4] And what a gift that practice is, especially when life is difficult! It shines a light into daily life, it warms and encourages the heart, and it gives us an opportunity to kiss the chef, as it were, to recognize that God is still there and "wanting to share a good thing."

When you go home today, when you gather with those you love around the Thanksgiving table, take a few minutes to kiss the chef. Look at each of those precious people who has gathered with you around the table, and thank each one for being there. Admire the food that has been laid out, and thank each person who helped to get it there. Invite each person present to share one thing in the past week for which they are thankful. And then join hands and together offer thanks to God for all these good things that have been shared, for all you have received. On Thanksgiving Day and every day, never pass up an opportunity to kiss the chef. Amen.

---

1. From *The Color Purple* by Alice Walker (movie 1985), as quoted at http://www.imdb.com/title/tt0088939/quotes. Language slightly altered for pulpit use.

2. The New Revised Standard Version counts 213 uses of "thank" and its derivatives (64 in the New Testament of which 35 are in the letters of Paul, and 149 in the Old Testament), and 436 of "praise" and derived terms (402 of these in the Old Testament), according to BibleWorks for Windows 6.0.012d (2003).

3. Cited in *The Book of Jewish Values* by Rabbi Joseph Telushkin (New York: Bell Tower, 2000), p. 303 f.

4. *Ibid*, p. 99.

Lectionary Preaching After Pentecost

The following index will aid the user of this book in matching the correct Sunday with the appropriate text during Pentecost. All texts in this book are from the series for the Gospel Readings, Revised Common Lectionary. (Note that the ELCA division of Lutheranism is now following the Revised Common Lectionary.) The Lutheran designations indicate days comparable to Sundays on which Revised Common Lectionary Propers or Ordinary Time designations are used.

(Fixed dates do not pertain to Lutheran Lectionary)

Fixed Date Lectionaries *Revised Common (including ELCA)* *and Roman Catholic*	Lutheran Lectionary *Lutheran*
The Day Of Pentecost	The Day Of Pentecost
The Holy Trinity	The Holy Trinity
May 29-June 4 — Proper 4, Ordinary Time 9	Pentecost 2
June 5-11 — Proper 5, Ordinary Time 10	Pentecost 3
June 12-18 — Proper 6, Ordinary Time 11	Pentecost 4
June 19-25 — Proper 7, Ordinary Time 12	Pentecost 5
June 26-July 2 — Proper 8, Ordinary Time 13	Pentecost 6
July 3-9 — Proper 9, Ordinary Time 14	Pentecost 7
July 10-16 — Proper 10, Ordinary Time 15	Pentecost 8
July 17-23 — Proper 11, Ordinary Time 16	Pentecost 9
July 24-30 — Proper 12, Ordinary Time 17	Pentecost 10
July 31-Aug. 6 — Proper 13, Ordinary Time 18	Pentecost 11
Aug. 7-13 — Proper 14, Ordinary Time 19	Pentecost 12
Aug. 14-20 — Proper 15, Ordinary Time 20	Pentecost 13
Aug. 21-27 — Proper 16, Ordinary Time 21	Pentecost 14
Aug. 28-Sept. 3 — Proper 17, Ordinary Time 22	Pentecost 15
Sept. 4-10 — Proper 18, Ordinary Time 23	Pentecost 16
Sept. 11-17 — Proper 19, Ordinary Time 24	Pentecost 17
Sept. 18-24 — Proper 20, Ordinary Time 25	Pentecost 18

Sept. 25-Oct. 1 — Proper 21, Ordinary Time 26	Pentecost 19
Oct. 2-8 — Proper 22, Ordinary Time 27	Pentecost 20
Oct. 9-15 — Proper 23, Ordinary Time 28	Pentecost 21
Oct. 16-22 — Proper 24, Ordinary Time 29	Pentecost 22
Oct. 23-29 — Proper 25, Ordinary Time 30	Pentecost 23
Oct. 30-Nov. 5 — Proper 26, Ordinary Time 31	Pentecost 24
Nov. 6-12 — Proper 27, Ordinary Time 32	Pentecost 25
Nov. 13-19 — Proper 28, Ordinary Time 33	Pentecost 26
	Pentecost 27
Nov. 20-26 — Christ The King	Christ The King

Reformation Day (or last Sunday in October) is October 31 (Revised Common, Lutheran)

All Saints (or first Sunday in November) is November 1 (Revised Common, Lutheran, Roman Catholic)

US/Canadian Lectionary Comparison

The following index shows the correlation between the Sundays and special days of the church year as they are titled or labeled in the Revised Common Lectionary published by the Consultation On Common Texts and used in the United States (the reference used for this book) and the Sundays and special days of the church year as they are titled or labeled in the Revised Common Lectionary used in Canada.

Revised Common Lectionary	Canadian Revised Common Lectionary
Advent 1	Advent 1
Advent 2	Advent 2
Advent 3	Advent 3
Advent 4	Advent 4
Christmas Eve	Christmas Eve
The Nativity Of Our Lord/ Christmas Day	The Nativity Of Our Lord
Christmas 1	Christmas 1
January 1/New Year's Day	January 1/The Name Of Jesus
Christmas 2	Christmas 2
The Epiphany Of Our Lord	The Epiphany Of Our Lord
The Baptism Of Our Lord/ Epiphany 1	The Baptism Of Our Lord/ Proper 1
Epiphany 2/Ordinary Time 2	Epiphany 2/Proper 2
Epiphany 3/Ordinary Time 3	Epiphany 3/Proper 3
Epiphany 4/Ordinary Time 4	Epiphany 4/Proper 4
Epiphany 5/Ordinary Time 5	Epiphany 5/Proper 5
Epiphany 6/Ordinary Time 6	Epiphany 6/Proper 6
Epiphany 7/Ordinary Time 7	Epiphany 7/Proper 7
Epiphany 8/Ordinary Time 8	Epiphany 8/Proper 8
The Transfiguration Of Our Lord/ Last Sunday After Epiphany	The Transfiguration Of Our Lord/ Last Sunday After Epiphany
Ash Wednesday	Ash Wednesday
Lent 1	Lent 1
Lent 2	Lent 2
Lent 3	Lent 3
Lent 4	Lent 4
Lent 5	Lent 5
Passion/Palm Sunday	Passion/Palm Sunday
Maundy Thursday	Holy/Maundy Thursday
Good Friday	Good Friday

Easter Day	The Resurrection Of Our Lord
Easter 2	Easter 2
Easter 3	Easter 3
Easter 4	Easter 4
Easter 5	Easter 5
Easter 6	Easter 6
The Ascension Of Our Lord	The Ascension Of Our Lord
Easter 7	Easter 7
The Day Of Pentecost	The Day Of Pentecost
The Holy Trinity	The Holy Trinity
Proper 4/Pentecost 2/O T 9*	Proper 9
Proper 5/Pent 3/O T 10	Proper 10
Proper 6/Pent 4/O T 11	Proper 11
Proper 7/Pent 5/O T 12	Proper 12
Proper 8/Pent 6/O T 13	Proper 13
Proper 9/Pent 7/O T 14	Proper 14
Proper 10/Pent 8/O T 15	Proper 15
Proper 11/Pent 9/O T 16	Proper 16
Proper 12/Pent 10/O T 17	Proper 17
Proper 13/Pent 11/O T 18	Proper 18
Proper 14/Pent 12/O T 19	Proper 19
Proper 15/Pent 13/O T 20	Proper 20
Proper 16/Pent 14/O T 21	Proper 21
Proper 17/Pent 15/O T 22	Proper 22
Proper 18/Pent 16/O T 23	Proper 23
Proper 19/Pent 17/O T 24	Proper 24
Proper 20/Pent 18/O T 25	Proper 25
Proper 21/Pent 19/O T 26	Proper 26
Proper 22/Pent 20/O T 27	Proper 27
Proper 23/Pent 21/O T 28	Proper 28
Proper 24/Pent 22/O T 29	Proper 29
Proper 25/Pent 23/O T 30	Proper 30
Proper 26/Pent 24/O T 31	Proper 31
Proper 27/Pent 25/O T 32	Proper 32
Proper 28/Pent 26/O T 33	Proper 33
Christ The King (Proper 29/O T 34)	Proper 34/Christ The King/ Reign Of Christ
Reformation Day (October 31)	Reformation Day (October 31)
All Saints (November 1 or 1st Sunday in November)	All Saints' Day (November 1)
Thanksgiving Day (4th Thursday of November)	Thanksgiving Day (2nd Monday of October)

*O T = Ordinary Time

480

About The Authors

Charles L. Aaron Jr. is the pastor of Cornerstone United Methodist Church in Garland, Texas. In addition to serving in the parish ministry, Aaron has also taught at Perkins School of Theology, Austin Presbyterian Theological Seminary, and Duke University Divinity School. Aaron is a prolific writer whose articles, sermons, and book reviews have appeared in many publications, including *Lectionary Homiletics*, *Preaching Great Texts*, *Catholic Biblical Quarterly*, and *Word and Witness*. He is the author of *Preaching Hosea, Amos, and Micah* (Chalice Press) and *Your Faith Has Made You Well* (CSS). Aaron is a graduate of Lambuth College (B.A.), Memphis State University (M.S.), Perkins School of Theology at Southern Methodist University (M.Div.), and Union Theological Seminary in Virginia (Ph.D. in Old Testament).

Lee Griess is the Assistant to the Bishop for Mission and Outreach in the Evangelical Lutheran Church in America's Nebraska Synod. Prior to that he served for fifteen years as the senior pastor of Luther Memorial Church in Omaha, Nebraska. Griess has also been the director of ministry resources for Stephen Ministries and a missionary to Japan. While serving as a pioneer evangelist in Tokyo and Sapporo, he helped establish Shin-Sapporo Lutheran Church. Griess is the author of *Taking the Risk Out of Dying* (CSS).

Mark Ellingsen has had a rich and varied career as both a parish pastor and a seminary professor. In addition to serving several Lutheran congregations in Pennsylvania and North Carolina, he has held teaching positions at Luther-Northwestern Seminary and the Institute for Ecumenical Research in Strasbourg, France.

Ellingsen is now on the faculty of the Interdenominational Theological Center in Atlanta, the largest historic African-American seminary in the United States. The prolific author of fourteen books and hundreds of articles, Ellingsen currently writes the "Political Pulpit" column for the preaching journal *Emphasis* (www.sermonsuite.com). His most recent books include *The Integrity of Biblical Narrative: Story in Theology and Proclamation*; *The Richness of Augustine*; *Reclaiming Our Roots*, a two-volume introduction to church history; a political commentary titled *When Did Jesus Become Republican?: Rescuing Our Country and Our Values from the Right*; and the sermon collection, *A Word That Sets Free* (CSS).

Wayne Brouwer has been a pastor in the Christian Reformed denomination for nearly three decades, serving congregations in both Canada and the United States (most recently Harderwyk Ministries in Holland, Michigan). He has also taught at several colleges and seminaries, and is currently a member of the religion department faculty at Hope College. Brouwer is the author of more than a dozen books, including *Humming Till the Music Returns* (CSS), and more than 600 articles for various publications including *Emphasis* (www.sermonsuite.com). He holds degrees from Dordt College (B.A.), Calvin Theological Seminary (M.Div., Th.M.), and McMaster University (M.A., Ph.D.).

Chris Ewing has ministered to both French- and English-speaking congregations of the Presbyterian and United Churches of Canada, serving most recently at St. Paul's United Church in Kindersley, Saskatchewan. She is a former contributing writer for the online preaching resource *The Immediate Word* (www.sermonsuite.com) and her work has also appeared in *La Vie Chrétienne*, *Gathering*, and *Celebrate God's Presence*. Ewing is a graduate of Wilfrid Laurier University, McGill University, and Presbyterian College (Montreal).

WARNING
Removing or tampering with the card on the back side of this page renders this book non-returnable.

Title: Sermons On The Gospel Readings, Series II, Cycle A

ISBN: 0-7880-2453-1

INSTRUCTIONS TO ACCESS PASSWORD FOR ELECTRONIC COPY OF THIS TITLE:

The password appears on the reverse side of this page. Carefully cut the card from the page to retrieve the password.

Once you have the password, go to

http:/www.csspub.com/passwords/

and locate this title on that web page. By clicking on the title, you will be guided to a page to enter your password, name, and email address. From there you will be sent to a page to download your electronic version of this book.

For further information, or if you don't have access to the internet, please contact CSS Publishing Company at 1-800-241-4056 in the United States (or 419-227-1818 from outside the United States) between 8 a.m. and 5 p.m., Eastern Standard Time, Monday through Friday.